MONASTIC WISDOM SER… …EN

# The *Rul…* …enedict

*Initiation int… …ne Monastic Tradition 4*

## MONASTIC WISDOM SERIES

Patrick Hart, OCSO, General Editor



MW1 Cassian and the Fathers: Initiation into the Monastic Tradition
*Thomas Merton, OCSO*

MW2 Secret of the Heart: Spiritual Being
*Jean-Marie Howe, OCSO*

MW3 Inside the Psalms: Reflections for Novices
*Maureen F. McCabe, OCSO*

MW4 Thomas Merton: Prophet of Renewal
*John Eudes Bamberger, OCSO*

MW5 Centered on Christ: A Guide to Monastic Profession
*Augustine Roberts, OCSO*

MW6 Passing from Self to God: A Cistercian Retreat
*Robert Thomas, OCSO*

MW7 Dom Gabriel Sortais: An Amazing Abbot in Turbulent Times
*Guy Oury, OSB*

MW8 A Monastic Vision for the 21st Century:
Where Do We Go from Here?
*Patrick Hart, OCSO, editor*

MW9 Pre-Benedictine Monasticism:
Initiation into the Monastic Tradition 2
*Thomas Merton, OCSO*

MW10 Charles Dumont Monk-Poet: A Spiritual Biography
*Elizabeth Connor, OCSO*

MW11 The Way of Humility
*André Louf, OCSO*

MW12 Four Ways of Holiness for the Universal Church:
Drawn from the Monastic Tradition
*Francis Kline, OCSO*

MW13 An Introduction to Christian Mysticism:
Initiation into the Monastic Tradition 3
*Thomas Merton, OCSO*

MW14 God Alone: A Spiritual Biography of Blessed Rafael Arnáiz Barón
*Gonzalo Maria Fernández, OCSO*

MW15 Singing for the Kingdom: The Last of the Homilies
*Matthew Kelty, OCSO*

MW16 Partnership with Christ: A Cistercian Retreat
*Eugene Boylan, OCSO*

MW17 Survival or Prophecy?
The Correspondence of Jean Leclercq and Thomas Merton
*Patrick Hart, OCSO, editor*

MW18 Light for My Path: Spiritual Accompaniment
*Bernardo Olivera, OCSO*

MONASTIC WISDOM SERIES: NUMBER NINETEEN

# The *Rule* of Saint Benedict

*Initiation into the Monastic Tradition 4*

by

Thomas Merton

Edited with an Introduction by

Patrick F. O'Connell

Preface by

Joan Chittister, OSB

Cistercian Publications
www.cistercianpublications.org

LITURGICAL PRESS
Collegeville, Minnesota
www.litpress.org

A Cistercian Publications title published by Liturgical Press

**Cistercian Publications**
Editorial Offices
Abbey of Gethsemani
3642 Monks Road
Trappist, Kentucky 40051
www.cistercianpublications.org



1 2 3 4 5 6 7 8 9

**Library of Congress Cataloging-in-Publication Data**

Merton, Thomas, 1915–1968.
The rule of Saint Benedict : initiation into the monastic tradition 4 / by Thomas Merton ; edited with an introduction by Patrick F. O'Connell ; preface by Joan Chittister.
p. cm. — (Monastic wisdom series ; 19)
Includes bibliographical references and index.
ISBN 978-0-87907-019-9 (pbk.)
1. Benedict, Saint, Abbot of Monte Cassino. Regula. 2. Benedictines—Rules. I. O'Connell, Patrick F. II. Title. III. Series.

BX3004.Z5M47 2009
255'.106—dc22 2008053270

# TABLE OF CONTENTS

Preface vii

Introduction xi

The *Rule* of Saint Benedict 1

Appendix A: Textual Notes 246

Appendix B: Table of Correspondences 261

Appendix C: For Further Reading 263

Index 266

# PREFACE

"Change is inevitable . . . change is constant," Disraeli wrote. Well, yes and yes and no. Change is inevitable because time, life, and growth do not stand still. Change is constant because it is of the essence of living things to grow from one stage into another. But change does not necessarily require that we obliterate what has gone before. "Change" and "destroy" are not synonyms. What is valuable can be maintained—even though only differently.

The fact is that the courage to change may be exactly what enables us to remain the same. When we discover that what once spoke to an entire culture—like carrying popes through the piazza of Vatican City on a *sedia gestatoria*, a sedan chair, or failing to recognize "mixed marriages"—now ceases to speak to a people, to energize them spiritually, to make sense to the present, it's time to change the practices in order to save the faith.

Change is what makes a thing different—but, at the same time, it is also, often, what is needed to make it authentic, realistic, consonant with the changing times. There are, in fact, instances in every dimension of this ever-dynamic world that do change and change again, but which never go out of style, never really lose the essence of themselves. Those things are the "classic" elements of life, the prototypes of the categories they embody, the paradigms of the best in art and architecture, in painting and statuary, in literature and drama, in culture and religious sensibilities, in government and civilization.

These are the models to which the world looks again and again to gauge the quality of what, in their names, has come after them. They set the standard. They define the principles, the elements, that make what follows them clearly one thing and not another: great rather than simply good, "a superior example" of the category rather than just one more of its kind. The classics in every arena last from age to age, always true, always universal in their appeal and their meaning, always attuned to the best in the human soul.

The *Rule* of Benedict, a spiritual document written over 1500 years ago, is one of them. It is still the basic spiritual guide for more than 1,400 autonomous Benedictine/Cistercian monasteries of 30,500 monks and nuns, and of 25,000 lay oblates around the world. Every continent on the globe has been touched by the Benedictine tradition and by this same Rule of Life for centuries. North America, for instance, has 155 monasteries of monks, nuns, or sisters; Canada, 8; Central America, 15; South America, 104; Africa, 109; Europe, 656; Asia 153, Oceania, 8—as well as 350 Cistercian monasteries worldwide. That is what is called "outreach." That is what is called "impact." Most of all, that is what is called "classic."

The *Rule* of Benedict is still the basis of life in each of these separate monasteries, though no one would maintain that life as it is lived in a Benedictine monastery now is exactly the way it was lived in Monte Cassino in 520 C.E. Nevertheless, in every instance, this one document stands as the chief arbiter of the lifestyle, definer of the values fundamental to each whatever the culture in which they live, and the common spiritual vision of all of them.

Someone should ask, why? How is it that so ancient a document can go on era after era shaping different generations and vastly different cultures. How does any one spirituality go on living in the mind and soul of generations so distant from its own? This book is a clear answer to that question. In this text we have the rare opportunity to see a conversation between the ancient text itself, written in the sixth century, and Thomas Merton, one of its most prolific exemplars of the life in the United States of our time.

Merton, a Cistercian monk of the Abbey of Gethsemani in Kentucky from 1941 to 1968, gave a series of conferences on the *Rule* of Benedict to the novices of that abbey. This book brings those lectures into print for the first time so that the rest of the world can study not only the text of the *Rule* itself but Merton's exegesis on its meaning and implications for our time. They are a landmark example of the way the *Rule* continues to stay the same—and change at the same time.

Merton teaches the *Rule,* not the document. His intention is not to maintain its letter but to capture its spirit. And by that very process he does honor to the essential character of the *Rule* itself. He demonstrates how it is that a document written for Roman men in the sixth century can still have meaning for both women and men of our own day. He preserves the three essential dimensions of the *Rule*: it is moderate; it is flexible; it is a spiritual document, not a legal one. It is, in other words, dedicated to the maintenance of a set of values, not to the preservation of a set of arcane behaviors.

The *Rule* of Benedict, unlike many religious documents that followed it, is not an exercise in spiritual athleticism. It requires no arduous fasts. It promotes no unusual behavior for the sake of religious eccentricity. It sets out to teach seekers how to live the ordinary life extraordinarily well. It does not pretend to turn humans into angels; it sets out to help average human beings become fully human by helping them to become fully spiritual as well. It teaches the spirituality of the presence of God and that changes everything in life.

The *Rule* of Benedict is a flexible way of life. Perhaps the most telling line in the *Rule,* after having laid out an order of prayer for twelve straight chapters, is the last one. "If anyone knows a better way," Benedict writes, "let them arrange things differently."

Merton is quick in his commentary to impress on the novices of a modern monastery the fact that some of the examples Benedict uses in the *Rule* were simply common practices of the time, not sacred acts to be continued into the twenty-first century as they were in the sixth. Any rule that can last for fifteen centuries is surely one that has been able to live well in all centuries—and to be true to itself, Merton implies, must continue to do the same.

Finally, the *Rule* is a spiritual document, not a legal one. It implies no overarching institutional connections, no body of constitutions, no clerical regalia or hierarchies. It is a document written by a lay man for a lay community—which may be why it works for women monastics, as well. There is nothing in this *Rule* designed to categorize people or to diminish anyone. Rank is not built on either social status or clerical standing. It is a *Rule* for modern-day mystics of all times meant to fly the soul of the seeker on the backs of the scriptures to the heart of God.

Most of all, Merton stresses to the novices the number of commentaries already written to preserve the character and autonomy of the myriad communities throughout time who have decided to take the *Rule* of Benedict as their spiritual guide. He points out that not even the various streams of the Benedictine family—Black Benedictines, White Cistercians, Camaldolese, men and women—all live the *Rule* the same way. Why? Because the *Rule* is about the values it preserves, not about the ways communities seek to preserve them as time and life go by in all their flavors and places and colors and centuries. It is, indeed, then, a classic document whose purpose is universal, whose aim is unending, whose human insight is great, and whose values of community, obedience, humility, conversion of life, hospitality, and stewardship are perennials.

No doubt about it: "Change is inevitable . . . change is constant," and change is very Benedictine—which is obviously why we manage to stay the same.

This is a fine book, a real contribution to Benedictine literature, a monument to fine scholarship, both Merton's and editor Patrick O'Connell's. It may well stand as a study in moderation, flexibility, and spirituality itself. It is a gift to us all.

Joan Chittister, OSB
Benetvision, Erie, PA

# INTRODUCTION

As Thomas Merton wrote in *The Waters of Siloe*, his 1949 history of the Cistercian Order, the "new monastery" of Cîteaux was founded in 1098 to enable monks to live out the *Rule* of St. Benedict with a degree of fidelity that was no longer possible in the Benedictine monasteries of the time, including the Abbey of Molesme from which the founders of Cîteaux had come: "The ideal of the founders was a return to the perfect integral observance of the Rule of St. Benedict: which meant a return to the cenobitic life in all its simplicity."[1] During the decade in which

1. Thomas Merton, *The Waters of Siloe* (New York: Harcourt, Brace, 1949), xxii. See also Thomas Merton, *Cistercian Contemplatives: A Guide to Trappist Life* (Trappist, KY: Gethsemani Abbey, 1948), 16–17: "Anyone who has read the *Exordium Parvum*, which was the manifesto left by the founders of the Order to their posterity, will be able to tell us at once that the ideal which led our first Fathers into solitude in the woods of Cîteaux was simply to keep the Rule of St Benedict to the letter." He goes on to say that "it is not enough merely to say" that literal application of the *Rule* was the purpose of the order; rather, as St. Bernard taught, "the true end of the Cistercian vocation came to be considered as nothing less than the mystical marriage of the soul to the Word of God in a union of perfect love" (18), through the practice of the common life, and concludes, "To anyone who has read the Rule of St Benedict it is evident that this is simply the application of that Rule to the exigencies of the contemplative life in all its purity" (19). A decade later, in *The Silent Life* (New York: Farrar, Straus & Cudahy, 1957), Merton returns to the question of Cistercian observance of the *Rule* with somewhat greater textual precision: "In seeking to restore the primitive Benedictine life, St Stephen Harding was therefore not merely striving to pacify his conscience by bringing his life into perfect conformity with the written code by which he had vowed to live. He was going much deeper into the reality of things: and here we might as well remark that nowhere in the *Exordium Parvum* does St Stephen use the phrase the 'letter of the Rule.' On the contrary, what he speaks of is *rectitudo*

he served as novice master at the Abbey of Gethsemani (1955–1965), it was thus essential for Merton to introduce the young men embarking on monastic life to the guiding document of that life. In fact, as Merton notes early on in this set of conferences (5, 6), he explored different aspects of the *Rule* in three distinct novitiate courses. The most basic introductory conferences, entitled "Our Monastic Observances,"[2] were largely taken up with explaining the *opus Dei*, the pattern of the liturgy of the hours, described in great detail in the *Rule*,[3] that occupied a substantial part of the monk's daily life. "An Introduction to the Life of the Vows"[4] presented an extensive discussion of the three vows of stability, obedience, and conversion of manners, derived from the *Rule*,[5] that the novices would take when they made monastic profession at the conclusion of their two years of preparation. The third set of conferences, the content of the present volume, provided an overview of the *Rule* itself and of the life of its author as traditionally presented in the *Dialogues* of St. Gregory the

---

*regulae* and the *puritas regulae*, the 'integrity of the rule,' the 'purity of the rule.' These words embrace not only the letter but also the spirit, and indicate that St Stephen realized the rule was not merely an external standard to which one's actions had to conform, but a *life* which, if it was lived would transform the monk from within. And so, as a matter of fact, instead of violently forcing the monks of Cîteaux into a servile acceptance of the letter of the Rule, precisely as it was written, nothing more and nothing less, St Stephen actually brought about an adaptation of the Rule to twelfth century conditions which was the work of religious genius" (102–103).

2. Thomas Merton, "Our Monastic Observances," a set of conference notes for a course given by Merton as master of novices and found in volume 15 of "Collected Essays," the 24-volume bound set of published and unpublished materials assembled at the Abbey of Gethsemani and available both there and at the Thomas Merton Center, Bellarmine University, Louisville, KY.

3. Chapters 8–20 of the *Rule* are concerned with the recitation of the divine office.

4. Thomas Merton, "An Introduction to the Life of the Vows," in "Collected Essays," vol. 14.

5. Chapter 58 of the *Rule* specifies the promises made at profession (not yet called vows), though the topics of obedience, stability and *conversatio morum* are discussed repeatedly throughout the *Rule*.

Great. These conferences on the *Rule*, then, form a kind of bridge between the more directly praxis-oriented instructions of the "Observances" and "Vows" courses and the historically and textually focused conferences on the development of monastic tradition such as *Pre-Benedictine Monasticism*[6] and particularly *Cassian and the Fathers*,[7] to which the *Rule* conferences form a kind of sequel, both in terms of chronological sequence and the actual order of presentation at Gethsemani.

In comparison with those two sets of conferences, *The Rule of St. Benedict* is of course more narrowly focused, and also possesses a greater degree of internal organization and coherence. Unlike the *Cassian* conferences, which add an extensive "Prologue" in its revised version,[8] the text of the *Rule* conferences remains relatively the same in successive presentations, and unlike the *Pre-Benedictine* conferences it does not veer off in a decidedly different direction from that which Merton had originally intended.[9] If it is much less wide ranging and less path-breaking than either of these courses, it has the virtues of providing a lucid, unrushed overview of the guide, both person and work, that his charges would be following for the rest of their lives if they chose to remain at Gethsemani. As with all the novitiate conferences, Merton's major intent is not to provide an objective academic treatment of his subject, though here as elsewhere his text shows evidence of his own assiduous reading and digesting of primary and secondary sources, but to engage in monastic formation, to encourage the students to appreciate the wisdom of the texts and

6. Thomas Merton, *Pre-Benedictine Monasticism: Initiation into the Monastic Tradition 2*, Monastic Wisdom [MW], vol. 9, ed. Patrick F. O'Connell (Kalamazoo, MI: Cistercian Publications, 2006).

7. Thomas Merton, *Cassian and the Fathers: Initiation into the Monastic Tradition*, ed. Patrick F. O'Connell, MW 1 (Kalamazoo, MI: Cistercian Publications, 2005).

8. For the revisions to this set of conferences, see *Cassian and the Fathers*, xxii–xxiii, xxvii, liv–lxii.

9. For the change in focus of these conferences, see *Pre-Benedictine Monasticism*, xvii–xx, xxxv–xxxvii.

to apply the material to their own lives. In order to do this he tries to contextualize the material in its own historical and cultural setting and also to "translate" it into a contemporary idiom, with pertinent connections made to the lives and times of his audience, himself, and the world, monastic and non-monastic, in which they were now living.

* * * * * * *

*The Rule of St. Benedict* conferences are divided into three unequal parts. The short introductory section on "Study of the Rule" (7–16) is preceded by a brief prefatory overview of the contents of the text (5–7), probably written last, that emphasizes the importance of considering the *Rule* from a perspective that is neither narrowly legalistic nor overly intellectualized, but marked rather by commitment to the goal of Benedictine monastic life, which is not simply to obey the *Rule* but to love and serve God. Approaching the *Rule* in the proper context is essential for appreciating its perennial power and value.

> The important thing is for monks to love the *Rule*, not as a document printed on paper but as a life that should take possession of their inmost hearts. St. Benedict did not call us to the monastery to serve him, but to serve God. We are not here to carry out the prescriptions of men, but to love God. The purpose of the *Rule* is to furnish a framework within which to build the structure of a simple and pure spiritual life, pleasing to God by its perfection of faith, humility and love. The *Rule* is not an end in itself, but a means to an end, and it is always to be seen in relation to its end. This end is union with God in love, and every line of the *Rule* indicates that its various prescriptions are given us to show us how to get rid of self-love and replace it by love of God. (6)

This same point is made in the Introduction proper, where Merton first emphasizes that the entire tradition of Christian spiritual teaching, both the developments of the Christian and specifically the monastic life preceding Benedict and subsequent forms of spirituality, such as those of the great Carmelites, can and should be studied and practiced,[10] but always viewed through a Benedictine lens (8). He stresses the need for monks to love the *Rule*, to love the person of Benedict himself, and to love the tradition that Benedict brought into focus and transmitted to future generations, ultimately including the first Cistercians and their successors. "To love St. Benedict means to *love our monastic tradition* that goes back to him and beyond him to St. Basil and St. Anthony—and to Jesus. Hence, our study of the *Rule* will be relatively sterile and useless if we only study the *Rule* itself, without any background, without any roots, in monastic tradition. . . . [W]e go to him as *to the authoritative and inspired guide* who will open to us all the rest of monastic tradition and show us how to understand it and apply it to our own monastic lives" (9–10). Merton warns his charges against any sort of narrow, "partisan" reading of the *Rule* that would pit Cistercian "purity" and "authenticity" against supposedly "lax" practices among the Black Benedictines, a tendency not unknown in previous eras:

> we would not be faithful to our own monastic tradition if we confined ourselves narrowly within purely "Cistercian" or "Trappist" limits in our study of the *Rule*. On the contrary, to be true Cistercians we must, like our fathers, seek with all spiritual thirst the *pure springs of the monastic tradition*. And here again, everything that is living and authentic, especially in all forms of monastic reform and return to primitive sources, is not alien to us. We must be acquainted with all that is genuine and vital in the monastic tradition. (10)

This brief section concludes by acquainting the novices with the respect and veneration in which St. Benedict has been held throughout the centuries, by the Cistercian Fathers such as

10. See Merton's 1961 conferences for newly ordained monks, *An Introduction to Christian Mysticism: Initiation into the Monastic Tradition 3*, ed. Patrick F. O'Connell, MW 13 (Kalamazoo, MI: Cistercian Publications, 2008), which provides an overview of the Christian contemplative tradition from its origin through Teresa of Avila and John of the Cross.

St. Bernard, who considered "*St. Benedict* himself as a quasi-'sacrament' of God's will and God's love for monks" (10), by the liturgy and by Church councils, and most recently by the pope, Pius XII, who had commemorated the fourteenth centenary of Benedict's death in 547 with an encyclical that Merton summarizes as an authoritative presentation of Benedict's historical and contemporary significance.

Part II, on "The Life and Character of St. Benedict" (16–38), takes a close look at highlights of Gregory the Great's *Life of Benedict* as found in the second book of his *Dialogues*.[11] Merton considers the *Vita* reliable in the main, though written for the purpose of edification and spiritual nourishment rather than according to modern canons of scientific biography (16–17). He shows his appreciation of the picturesque or even amusing details in the *Vita*, such as the fact that at the outset of his ascetic journey Benedict is still accompanied by his old nurse (21), the appearance of the friendly crow who carries away the poisoned bread sent by Florentius (29), and the warning Benedict gives to the slave Exhilaratus that the bottle of wine he had concealed for himself should be checked before drinking (for the serpent now hidden in it) (31). He retells the vivid stories of Benedict's reclaiming of the ruined pagan shrine on Monte Cassino (30), hurling the flask of oil denied to a poor supplicant over a cliff (33), confronting the Goth tyrant Zalla (34), being "bested" by his sister

11. Merton would of course have been unaware of the recent questioning of the Gregorian authorship of the *Dialogues* and consequently of the historicity of the *Vita*, as proposed by Francis Clark (and opposed most notably by Adalbert de Vogüé); for a summary of the controversy (which finds Clark's thesis persuasive), see Terrence G. Kardong, OSB, "Who Wrote the *Dialogues of Saint Gregory*? A Report on a Controversy," *Cistercian Studies Quarterly*, 39.1 (2004), 31–39. In a June 6, 1961 journal entry, Merton does however mention a "good talk on Monastic Tradi*tions* and tradi*tion*, both necessary," given to the community by Dom Jean Leclercq during a visit to Gethsemani, that included "Recent theories about St. Benedict and the Rule," and adds, "What seems to have stirred people most is the hypothesis that St. B. never existed. By this Dom L.'s visit will be most remembered" (Thomas Merton, *Turning Toward the World: The Pivotal Years. Journals, vol. 4: 1960–1963*, ed. Victor A. Kramer [San Francisco: HarperCollins, 1996], 124).

Scholastica when he wished to part early during their final meeting (33), and receiving his culminating vision of the "whole world gathered together as though in one ray of the sun" (37–38). Merton provides his own meditative reflections on the highlights of the *Vita* and their pertinence to contemporary monastic life. He observes that Gregory's presentation shows Benedict passing through "all the stages of monastic life known in his time—ascete, hermit, Pachomian cenobite. Having tried all these, he has reached his own conclusions and it is at Monte Cassino that he puts his own formula into effect" (18). Commenting on the key phrase from Gregory's prologue, "*soli Deo placere desiderans*," he notes, "it is not said that Benedict desired to possess, or to enjoy God alone, but to *please* God alone. {The} emphasis {is} on the fact that God is not for him a commodity to be 'had' but a Person to be loved and honored with one's whole heart. (It is only in that way that He can be possessed!)" (20). In discussing Benedict's taking the monastic habit, he points out both the undeveloped state of monasticism in Italy at the time, where the act of clothing itself, unaccompanied by vows, was regarded as monastic consecration, and the lesson for his own particular audience: "Let us remember however that the mere wearing of a religious habit, although the novice does not yet take vows, implies a desire to consecrate one's life to God, and the intention to live a holy life entirely pleasing to God" (23). In the next episode, when Benedict combats fleshly temptation by throwing himself naked into a briar patch, Merton is careful to warn his charges: "All must be generous and uncompromising in renunciation of self, but all are not called to take an equally dramatic or drastic exterior way of fighting temptation. . . . This is a good example of a case in which we should imitate the *spirit* with which a saint overcomes himself, and reproduce his generosity, while not at the same time taking the exact same exterior means that he used" (24). He proposes the ideal of *custodia cordis*, guarding the heart, as one to be imitated by sons of Benedict, but warns against too narrow and rigid an interpretation of this virtue, a comment that is certainly reflective of Merton's own ever more catholic breadth of interests: "A person can have Benedictine *custodia cordis* and yet retain a variety of interests and occupations. It is not so much a matter of what you do and what you know, as how you do it and how you know it. Here too the motive is all-important. Cultivate self-custody not by strained and rigid introspection which leads to an unhealthy state, but by seeking God in all things and embracing His will with simplicity wherever it is made known to us" (27). Benedict's contests with the devil, which occupy a considerable part of the *Vita*, are considered as exemplifying the vocation of the monk as "the chosen instrument, the soldier of Christ who, by his prayers and self-denial, continues the work of the Incarnation which is a reconquest, by God, of His creation." This "work of spiritualizing and divinizing the world" is shared by all Christians, Merton says, but he goes on to note that "the principal part is played by the great saints, those with special charismatic gifts, special purity of heart" (29–30). Gregory's portrait of Benedict is seen as one that balances austerity and moderation, severity when needed with mercy and compassion, "a great tenderness and understanding of human frailty" (34). The key monastic themes of obedience, poverty, good works, penance, and fidelity to the common life are all found in the *Vita* as essential elements of Benedict's teaching (32–33). It is above all Benedict as a model of prayer that Merton proposes to his novices: "If we truly have the spirit of St. Benedict we will seek the face of God always in prayer, and will prefer nothing not only to the work of God but also, as did Benedict, to those hours of silent and solitary union with God in interior prayer" (35). The life of Benedict, and consequently the Benedictine life, is according to Merton "simply living the Gospel without fanfare." Benedict "*lived* the Gospel without talking about it. The mainspring of everything in St. Benedict is the *love of Christ*—in Himself, in the poor, in the monastic community, in the individual brethren. . . . This is the key to the monastic life and spirit" (37).

Part III, which constitutes more than three-quarters of the entire text (39–216), focuses on the *Rule* proper. Following brief comments on dating and sources (particularly scripture), Merton looks at some of the textual problems associated with the *Rule*, the largely successful scholarly efforts to untangle the confusion, and a few examples of instances in which the seemingly dry, even pedantic efforts to restore correct readings to the text can be shown to have a significant impact on the actual way in which the *Rule* is lived out, concluding that "the findings of scholarship regarding the ancient text of the *Rule* . . . have a great importance for our true understanding of the mind of St. Benedict," and that the "mentality which would prefer the rigidity and oversimplification of the *textus receptus* is also very likely to be the mentality which hates and distrusts scholarship. We must try not to cultivate such a mentality—it leads to ossification and stupor in the spiritual life" (46). Here as throughout the notes the focus invariably is directed eventually to the impact of the particular topic on the concrete practice of monastic living.

Merton then provides a rapid historical overview of the reception of the text by mentioning the major commentators through the centuries and their particular perspectives (borrowed largely from the *Benedictine Monachism* of Dom Cuthbert Butler, whom he praises as "one of our best students of St. Benedict and . . . a great modern representative of the black Benedictine tradition" [50], thus exemplifying the "ecumenical" openness toward non-Cistercian authors he had earlier recommended). He will make relatively sparse use of this commentary tradition in what is to follow, but on occasion he does provide a few citations, particularly from Dom Edmond Martène, the scholarly seventeenth-century Benedictine whose massive commentary, which summarizes and quotes from most of his predecessors, is printed with the *Rule* itself in the edition found in the *Patrologia Latina*; most, though not all, of Merton's references to commentators other than Martène himself are actually borrowed from this source as well.

The main body of the text is subtitled "A Spiritual Commentary on the *Rule* of St. Benedict," and Merton immediately explains that his "main purpose is to look at the *Rule* in so far as it *forms us* as spiritual sons of St. Benedict" (50). The two major aims of his commentary are therefore to find the major spiritual ideas of the *Rule* and to discover how the principles based on these ideas are to be lived out in the day-to-day experience of the monastery. The *Rule* is to be regarded as "not merely a body of external regulations to direct the outward actions we perform all day long; it is more than just a legal code, intended to establish good order in the monastery. It is a *discipline* which forms the monk in his entirety, reaches into every department of his life and brings it under the direct action of divine love, of the Holy Spirit" (51). The commentary has three principal areas of concentration: first the Prologue, in which Merton finds "the theological foundation of the whole spiritual doctrine of St. Benedict" (51), to which is appended a discussion of the various types of monks as presented in the opening chapter of the *Rule*; second, examination of key chapters on the abbot and the monastic community, which includes consideration of monastic work, spiritual reading, and poverty; finally, occupying more than a quarter of the entire text, a thorough explication of chapter 7, on the degrees of humility, which Merton like most commentators considers the spiritual heart of the entire *Rule*.

Merton's discussion of the Prologue (51–71) provides both a synthetic overview of the key theological and spiritual themes that undergird the entire *Rule*, and a detailed textual analysis of certain key passages. His starting point is the recognition that the *Rule* is properly to be understood as "a *way of salvation*"—or rather as *the* way of salvation, for there is only a single way—as "adapted and applied" to a specific group, cenobitic monks (51). Thus the theological principles he finds governing the Prologue are the basic truths of the Christian proclamation, the good news of salvation in Christ. The starting point is God as loving and patient Father urgently calling His children to respond to His invitation "to seek union with Him, to dwell with Him in 'his tabernacle'" (53). The second dimension is of course human sinfulness and the need for ascetic discipline to overcome what Benedict calls "the sloth of disobedience"—*inobedientiae desidia*: Merton finds in this phrase "the connotations of boredom, futility, aimlessness, inertia, pointlessness of an existence given over to the cult of our own whims and impulsions" (54–55). Such an attitude leads to a kind of paralyzing fear and hopelessness from which one can be freed only by the Word of God, Benedict's third key theological theme. The call to conversion, and the power for transformation, come through the Scriptures, which the *Rule* echoes and channels to its monastic audience. Here Merton unfolds phrase by phrase the teaching of Benedict on the "voice of God" which "awakens in us *desire and zeal*—and confidence," which "calls us with equal *tenderness* and *urgency*" (60). Ultimately of course the Word teaches "that without Christ we can do nothing, but that if we have trust in Him He can and does work in us miracles of grace—and we extend this thought to embrace the entire human race" (63). Here is Benedict's fourth great theme, the working of divine grace, the "light of love that works in our souls, transforming them into the likeness of our divine Exemplar, Jesus Christ" (65). This grace "must bear fruit in good works, without which we cannot be sons of God and cannot reach the end of our journey," and to bring forth fruit "we must abide in Jesus, the true vine" (66). This theology of grace, Merton sums up, "is sufficient to give us the full theology of the Prologue. It contains implicitly all St. Benedict's teaching on humility and obedience, the principal good works by which we correspond with grace and allow it to bear fruit in our lives" (69). But "for grace to work effectively in our souls, we must establish ourselves *in a favorable milieu*, where everything is ordered to promote correspondence with grace"—this, for those called to it, is the monastery, the school of the Lord's service, "a place where there is *leisure for thought, study and prayer*" marked by "a certain strictness and ascetic labor" (69), and above all by the obedience that will reverse the sloth (*desidea*) of disobedience, the life of unreality. Such a life, Merton concludes, is profoundly paschal: "we taste the joy of being *united with Jesus Christ* on the Cross, and realize that therefore we are destined, by His mercy, for a share in the joy of his Kingdom," and also oriented toward union with God, "a truly contemplative life, alone with God in silence and love" (71).

Having considered principles, Merton, with Benedict, then turns to practice in the first chapter's examination of the types of monks, cenobites and anchorites, sarabaites and gyrovagues (71–79). While affirming and developing Benedict's basic insights here, Merton provides some helpful context that puts Benedict's critique in perspective. Noting the "spontaneous development" of early oriental monasticism when "many original and unusual forms of monastic life sprung up of themselves," as well as the outward similarities of the later mendicant orders to the pattern of life "of the *wandering monk* which St. Benedict seems to reprove in its very nature," Merton warns that "These qualifications should teach us to read St. Benedict's chapter with care and with understanding, and not with a rigid and absolutistic mentality" (72). He then applies this caveat to the question of whether Benedict allows for anchorites within the context of the *Rule*, a question of course that was of fundamental personal importance for Merton throughout his monastic life, including the period during which he was giving these conferences. He maintains that Benedict allows for a life of monastic solitude "no longer live[d] according to the fixed rule of the cenobium" after "*long training* . . . in the cenobium, under a rule and an abbot. In other words, {there is} no sanctity without discipline, and discipline in practice is not learned without obedience and regularity" (73). What unites cenobite and anchorite and distinguishes them from undisciplined types of monks is their participation in the common battle against evil, as members of a common body, the Church, in responding to grace whether mediated by the community or received directly from God or His angels. Sarabaites, in contrast, are untrained, guided by their own will and therefore controlled by their own subjective "fancies and illusions," including even the illusion of sanctity (75). What is missing above all is the initiation into the specifically Christ-centered dimension of authentic spiritual experience: "Hence the sarabaites and gyrovagues *really know nothing of Christ*; they have not learned, by subjection, to share in the monk's interior, spiritual knowledge of union with Christ in the mystery of His passion and His humility and His obedience to the Father" (76). There is no stability, no perseverance, no obedience to rule and superior: "The gyrovagues quite obviously are not only running away from the regular life but are in full flight from all responsibility whatever. They are in a lamentable condition, escapists who cannot bear to face themselves or to face other men for any length of time, always hoping for something better just around the corner. It is clear that they are simply the *logical consequence* of sarabaitism pushed to its extreme" (78). While Merton points out that "*Today*—obviously the sarabaite and the gyrovague exist only in spirit" (78) rather than as distinct monastic types, that does not mean the attitudes and state of mind they represent cannot and do not assume contemporary forms.

The section on "The Abbot and His Monks" (79–152) that follows is the most wide-ranging, apparently somewhat heterogeneous in content, but in fact providing a broad and quite thorough picture of how life in the monastery actually operates. The fundamental role of the abbot for Benedict is evident from the fact that he turns his attention to him, addressing him directly, immediately after the introductory chapter on the kinds of monks. Merton stresses that for Benedict the abbot's role is not merely to oversee the monastery, or to enforce obedience to the *Rule*, but to act in the place of Christ, "to lead the monastic community as Christ led and formed and instructed the band of the Apostles. . . . He takes the place of Christ in the monastery. His leadership is the leadership not of a human organizer, but of Christ. His doctrine and formation are those of Christ" (81). This happens not automatically but through the faith of both abbot and community, who trust that the Holy Spirit will act through the abbot despite inevitable human weaknesses. The abbot has a responsibility both to the monks under his care and to God, to make the will of God for the community known and lived by both teaching and example, using discretion and discernment to deal with different types of monks in ways most appropriate to each. Merton points out that the complementary qualities of firmness and kindness in Benedict's portrait of the abbot receive different emphasis in the two chapters allotted to him: "Firmness is stressed more in chapter 2; kindness is more in the foreground in chapter 64, the fruit of later years and of his most mature reflection" (90). The latter chapter, with its succinct phrases "*prodesse magis quam praeesse*" ("to benefit more than to rule") (93), "*oderit vitia; diligat fratres*" ("Let him hate the vices; let him love the brothers") (94), and "*ne quid nimis*" ("nothing in excess") (95), is seen as Benedict's seasoned wisdom on the principles of abbatial governance, though to conclude his discussion Merton returns to Benedict's reminder in chapter 2 that legitimate concerns for the material well-being of the monastery must never take precedence over "the true office of the superior, to see that love is sought above all else in the monastery" (97).

Just as the abbot represents Christ to and for the community, so the community itself is called to represent Christ. Therefore the community is not merely passive and inert in carrying out the abbot's commands, but participates in the life of Christ in freely and dynamically loving God and one another. The community is responsible not only for choosing the abbot, but for advising him about important matters, though decisions finally rest with him. Merton points out that such decisions are never made arbitrarily, in a vacuum, but according to the principles set down in the *Rule*. "He must judge according to the virtues of *prudence* and *justice*. In so doing, he will above all *follow the Rule* himself. The abbot does not just interpret the *Rule* to suit his own pleasure and interest—he is guided by the *Rule* like the others; he *applies* the *Rule* with freedom and prudence. But his government follows the lines laid down by the *Rule*" (101–102). Community members, on their part, are called to be frank yet detached and respectful in giving their ideas and opinions, and above all willing to surrender their own will and let go of their own desires whatever a decision and directive may be: "detachment and humility crown the work of the disciple. He follows the decision of the superior with a truly supernatural spirit, and gives up the will of his own heart. This, again, is one of the tests of the true monk" (103).

Relations among community members should likewise be marked by "mutual respect and affection," especially toward the "seniors," those who are "elder" in the monastic life, whatever their relative age, who in turn should be "a *channel of grace*" (104) for those junior to them. Merton stresses the realism of the *Rule,* which doesn't naively presume that everything is perpetually "lovely and spiritual"; monastic life requires "much patience, self-denial, prudence, discretion, mortification, and above all *humility. . . . It is simply a question of taking things as they are, but with patience, humility and a spirit of faith,* and thus overcoming evil with good" (107). Benedict's repeated warnings against "murmuring," discontent whether expressed or suppressed, are "really fundamental to the whole Benedictine spirit, so that a monk who allows himself to complain and criticize, even if only interiorly, no matter how regular he may be in everything else, is not really a monk according to the mind of St. Benedict" (112). Merton lets his novices know that such detachment and equanimity are far from easy, even for "souls who have progressed a great deal" (113). He points out that "in so far as it leads to a recognition of our own poverty and weakness, and prompts us to pray for help and forgiveness, the inner bitterness may be turned to good account" (113). Ultimately, the foundation on which relations within the community are to be based is to regard others as Christ, a phrase explicitly used to refer to the sick and to guests, but implicitly extending to all within (and outside) the monastery (115).

In turning to the other offices mentioned in the *Rule,* Merton emphasizes that qualifications for leadership include first of all bearing witness to "Christ living in the monastery" (118), then a sense of maturity and responsibility and a certain amount of initiative, being "someone who can be left on his own to carry out an assignment—not one who has to be constantly watched and told what to do next" (118). In St. Benedict's portrait of the cellarer, the monk most responsible for the efficient operations of the monastery, Merton finds not just a list of job requirements but "a picture of *a completely mature monk,* according to the mind of St. Benedict" (119). He is marked by wisdom, "a *wholesome blend of faith and common sense*" (120), reflectiveness, sobriety, fear of the Lord, humility, kindness toward others, "treat[ing] those in their care *as persons and not as objects*" (122). Merton points out that "The officers in a Benedictine monastery are *not mere functionaries or bureaucrats*" (122): the relations between officials and subordinates are not institutional and impersonal, the mentality of the secular world, but marked by care, affection and understanding. The same sense of responsibility, of being of service to others, should be evident in all assigned tasks—manual labor, cooking, reading in the refectory, etc.

These reflections lead naturally to consideration of the role of work in the monastic life, and from there to the balance of work and prayer, with consideration of the importance of *lectio divina*, spiritual reading. Merton questions the standard view that "the monk has three main obligations: choir, *lectio divina*, and manual labor—their importance graduated in this order" and suggests that it is "more truly the mind of St. Benedict to put it this way: the monk leads an overall life of prayer, in which two things are important . . . : (a) formal prayer whether public (divine office) or private; (b) useful activity" (130). Merton lays heavy emphasis on the principle of balance and integration: "A contemplative life that is all words and ideas and never takes effect in any kind of work is utterly useless. Work (intellectual or physical) integrates thought and life into a single unity. Without this integration, 'contemplation' leads only to illusion and ruin. On the other hand, *busy and solicitous activity* or 'activism' is equally ruinous for the monastic spirit. The monk must learn to strike the happy medium, in humble, peaceful and productive activity of mind and body" (131–32). He also notes that Benedict speaks not simply of labor but of manual labor, from a Cistercian perspective, at least, "an *integral part in the life of a monk*, and this cannot be passed over without harm and loss" (132), both as a way of earning one's living and as "a true safeguard of a genuine interior life" (133). This is balanced not only by the public prayer of the *opus Dei* but by *lectio*, "listening to God, hearing His word, and preparing to respond to His word with our whole being" (134). Returning to the dimension of work, Merton notes the way the *Rule* fosters respect for genuine craftsmanship "because even humble skills are gifts of God and enable man to participate in some measure in the creative activity of God. In the exercise of his skills and arts, as well as in all other work, man acts as a child of His Father, the Creator" (136). Such an attitude toward skillful work counters an over-dependence on time-saving technology as a supposed way of increasing opportunities for prayer: "{It is} good to use machines {but we should} avoid using them merely to 'get through work and get to prayer,' avoid using machines to highlight {a} false opposition between work and prayer" (136).

Neither individual members nor the community as a whole should regard the products of such work primarily from the perspective of material gain. The community should be self-supporting to the extent possible, "But the *desire of gain* and especially *the desire to hoard up and accumulate money or goods* is absolutely alien to the monastic spirit and is disastrous to it—so much so that in a monastery where the love of money and possessions prevails, it is extremely difficult even for a detached monk individually to become a saint" (140). In this context, the central importance of poverty for the monastic life is considered as the culmination of this lengthy discussion of the community. "The spirit of the *Rule* is to renounce all proprietorship, even spiritual—including attachment to everything that is distinctly 'mine,' even 'my' spiritual life, 'my' way of doing and seeing things, 'my' contemplation" (144). Poverty is seen first of all as a means of being joined with Christ, "dying with Christ—the bare Cross," then as a way to "reproduce the *charity of the apostolic community gathered around Christ*" (145). In the Jerusalem community, the first Christians gave up private ownership of property and shared all they had with the community as a whole.

> These two elements are essential to the idea of monastic poverty. It is a poverty in which proprietorship is renounced *in favor of the community* (or of the whole Church). The monk

> becomes poor in order to share whatever earthly goods he may have had with the poor and with the community. He labors to share the poverty and labors of the poor. He shares the fruits of his labors with the poor. The fruits of the monastic labor are then distributed by the abbot to the brethren *not according to their merit but according to their need.* (148–49)

Such detachment, then, is both integral to the material well-being of the community and at the heart of the monk's own commitment to center his life on Christ present in "the least of these," among his monastic brothers and among those who look to the monastery for sustenance, material and spiritual.

The final portion of Merton's "Spiritual Commentary" turns to "the longest" and "most important" chapter of the *Rule*, chapter 7 on humility (152–216), both the culmination of Benedictine asceticism and the foundation for genuine contemplation: "*here we have for St. Benedict the real interior life of the monk*. Hence this section of the *Rule* is of the greatest importance. Nothing is equal to it in the whole teaching of St. Benedict. This is, in a nutshell, the *whole* of the monastic life . . . . [T]he degrees of humility are a summary of the whole *praxis* (active life) which prepares us for *theoria* (contemplation) which is hinted at as the chapter ends" (152–53). Merton begins by encouraging the novices to learn the chief points of the chapter by heart, not only to memorize them but through meditative reflection to allow them to penetrate beneath the surface, to "go down into the depths of the heart, and reach the real roots of our nature" (154). This reflection must be complemented by action: "No amount of commentaries can help us to understand St. Benedict's humility better if we do not *practice* it" (154). The monastic vow of conversion of manners, of commitment to deep inner transformation, is dependent upon a progressive appropriation of the successive stages of growth in humility, drawing the monk to embrace truth, the truth about himself but also Christ the Truth, who is also the Way and the Life: "It is by union with the humble Christ that we travel to union with Christ Who is Truth and Light. The way of humility is simply the way of the imitation of Christ" (157). Chapter 7 is even more rooted in the scriptures than the rest of the *Rule* "because St. Benedict believed that the way of humility was essentially the way of the Gospel, and that it summed up in practice the whole ascesis of the Gospel" (158–59). In this conviction St. Benedict is in conformity with the patristic and monastic tradition that preceded him, as Merton illustrates by his examination of St. Basil's *Homily* 20, *On Humility*, which shows how the authentic glory of being created in the image of God was distorted by the fall into the false glory of human vanity, and can be restored only by the way of humility in union with the humble Christ.

Reflecting on the introductory lines of this chapter, Merton uses language that corresponds closely to that found in some of his most familiar and influential writing. He notes that for St. Benedict, "the essence of pride lies in *exalting ourselves above others*, giving ourselves an exaggerated preference, imagining we are vastly greater than we actually are, or than others are. This means in effect placing ourselves practically in the position that belongs rightly to God alone. *Pride then is making of oneself one's own god*. Humility is only restoring the right order and truth" (168). Because it is built on illusion, pride inevitably breeds insecurity, a constant desire to be affirmed in our own falsehood, whether that desire is expressed in an aggressive desire to control others, in constant criticism and jealousy of others, or in "the virulent form of pride that is hidden under the apparently sweet and humble, apparently self-deprecating exterior of so many of us in this country" who want to be liked, accepted, affirmed by everyone (169). Such efforts, whatever form they may take, involve an "immense waste of energy" in one struggling "to manipulate reality and make things come out in accord with his illusions about himself" (169). In contrast, facing and accepting reality, above all the reality of one's own common humanity, "brings relief and rest. . . . In this sense, he who humbles himself is exalted: he is relieved from the tyranny of his illusions about himself. He no longer has to struggle for vain feelings of security —he can have *real security* in acceptance of the truth. And he becomes *able to love*" (170). Here Merton makes the teaching of this sixth-century document come alive for his mid-twentieth-century audience by finding a tone and terminology that powerfully convey the essential meaning and perennial significance of a life of humility. "The degrees of humility properly understood," he sums up, "do not by any means imply an artificial and strained *perfectionism,* but rather a complete and integral adaptation to reality" (173).

The same perspective marks the discussion of the individual degrees of humility that occupies the rest of the text. The first degree, "*the avoidance of all deliberate sin*" (173), is motivated above all by a sense of the continual presence of God. More explicitly than Benedict, Merton notes that God looks upon human actions not just to judge and to punish but to show love and mercy, and that this can be a powerful motive to overcome temptation: "The thought that *Love* sees me is a deterrent from sin. Shall I hurt Him Who loves me infinitely? . . . At the same time, the thought that God sees me is a source of hope. He will give me grace." Consistent with his contemplative outlook, Merton also points out that God is watching not only in His transcendence, "from heaven," but "in a mysterious way God sees us from the depths of our own soul" (177). Ultimately what is fundamental to this degree is to surrender one's own will, which is also to surrender one's own limited and distorted perspective: "Thus to preserve ourselves from illusion and blindness and to retain our spiritual vision, we must *deny ourselves* and turn aside from our desires and try *to see things as God Himself sees them in us*" (181). The second degree moves from avoiding deliberate sin to making "what is good in itself or good for others," rather than one's own desires and preferences, the criterion for one's actions (182). In the third degree, "the motive of love comes in to color the whole concept of humility," not just fear or prudence or a sense of duty (184). One is obedient to God in union with the love of Christ who "humbled himself, becoming obedient unto death" (Phil. 2:8): "ours is a life of *imitation of Christ,* and not just of imitation of His virtues and life in general but above all imitation of *His Passion.* . . . In imitation of Christ, the monk *empties himself of his worldly self* and renounces worldly liberty in order to become obedient even to the point of laying down his life if necessary" (185). Humility is seen by Benedict, and by Merton, not just in a moral but more deeply in a soteriological context, as a participation in the kenosis of Christ. The fourth degree puts this in concrete, practical terms—putting up with unpleasant and even unjust demands of the life of monastic obedience patiently and without resentment. Merton sees this degree as the real test of growth in humility, because it entails the surrender of what he calls elsewhere the empirical ego. "We are not willing to give up our superficial and outward self, and live in the depths where insults do not penetrate. But it is this superficial and worldly identity that must be renounced" (186). To realize the fourth degree of humility is to become sharply aware of the distinction between the illusory "persona" created by one's own desires and fears and "the true person of a man, his inner spiritual self, [which] is not affected by insults and lack of consideration" (186). The fifth degree moves to a willingness to be perfectly honest with one's spiritual director in "putting aside *all fear* of being known for what we are, of being known by another as we know ourselves, the good points and the bad points, without glossing things over, without ambiguities" (191), in order to receive appropriate guidance; Benedict explicitly mentions evil thoughts, but Merton points out that true humility also involves openness about positive aspirations without giving way to pride or self-satisfaction. The experienced novice master also cautions that this manifestation of conscience is not to be equated with scrupulosity, or with placing on display a complicated personality. "*Beware of trying to gain attention by being too interesting or important in the eyes of the director*. Just be yourself, *and desire to be known as you are, not as you would like to be*" (192). The sixth degree, contentment with poor and insignificant goods and circumstances, is not only a way of being detached from one's own will but a way of sharing the lot of those on the margins of society: "The poor don't get what they want" (197). It is not merely a matter of putting up with discomfort or deprivation:

"it means *contentment and peace* in the sacrifice of the ordinary natural goods, or even in some way spiritual goods, of the monastic state. . . . A monk who has reached this degree of humility will not complain or even be surprised or distressed interiorly: if the community is not perfect, if there are many things lacking in it, if even the atmosphere of peace and regularity is somewhat lacking, provided it is not his own fault" (199–200). To practice the sixth degree of humility is to let go of the desire to be recognized and appreciated, to be held in high respect by others: "*it is the humility of a man of virtue who has altogether ceased to attach any importance to his virtue*, and does not give himself any airs before God, knowing that his virtues are as nothing in God's sight" (201). It is even the surrender of the desire for consolations in prayer, or of "progress" in the spiritual life: "So many monks are disconcerted because they have 'made so many efforts' and still 'don't get anywhere.' Why do they think it so important to 'get somewhere'? The important thing is to do the will of God, not to be rewarded for it in this life. . . . It is a form of pride to be surprised and to get upset because we do not feel ourselves to be like saints. Who do we think we are?" (201). The seventh, the last of the "interior" degrees of humility, the acceptance of one's own nothingness, must not be equated, Merton cautions, with "morbid self-depreciation" (201). It is not a matter of putting oneself down, but of "complete self-forgetfulness in order to have one's eyes wide open to the wonderful qualities of others and to rejoice in these with childlike simplicity. . . . *The humble man does not regard himself as the last in a collection of criminals but the last in a community of saints*. This is the real key" (202–203). Moreover it has its real effect in binding one more closely to the humble Christ.

> It implies also *union with Christ on the Cross*—and communion in His self-emptying. . . . [T]o try to practice this seventh degree without reference to the Cross of Christ and union with Him would be silly and morbid. Merely to consider oneself a worm and no man, as an isolated human individual lost in his own nothingness, without any access

> to God, would be almost hellish. One must be prepared to *feel* this extreme isolation, perhaps. But faith always shows us that the value of such a moral trial consists in our secret union with Christ, *and in the fact that He suffers in us*—that consequently it is good to be humbled thus in the sight of men in order to be united to the sufferings of Christ, the key to all true glory. (204–205)

Merton spends less time on the last five, exterior, degrees of humility, noting first of all that they "have no meaning, or very little meaning, when they are not founded on interior humility" (205). Outward actions need to be an expression of, not a substitute for, inner transformation. Apart from interior humility, the eighth degree, faithful practice of the common rule of the monastery, "would be *mere conformism* which would be a plague in the monastic life" (206) instead of a Christ-like willingness to share fully the ordinary lives of one's brothers. The ninth, tenth, and eleventh degrees, all of which "refer to the monk's manner of speaking and his outward expression of what is in his soul," should be "an eloquent expression of the interior peace and tranquility of a soul united to God" (207). Love of silence, refraining from laughter, practice of sensible speech are the hallmarks of a humble monk who does not need to be constantly calling attention to himself. At the same time, while warning against a kind of artificial and self-conscious piety that has no depth, Merton notes that "it cannot be said either that one should wait until he has acquired the seventh degree before he even attempts to practice the exterior degrees of humility. Some would never begin at that rate" (208). The development of a humble spirit will naturally show corresponding effects in one's outward deportment, but the important thing is for humility to grow from the inside out, which explains why the exterior degrees are placed after the interior. This applies to the twelfth and final degree as well, which is not merely walking around with eyes lowered: "The true essence of this degree is that the monk's whole body and all his actions should be penetrated by humility and manifest it, just as his soul is penetrated and saturated with it. . . . The twelfth degree implies that a man is everywhere just as quiet and collected as he is at prayer" (212–13).

Merton concludes his discussion of the degrees of humility, and thus of the *Rule* as a whole, by noting that the ladder of humility leads the monk from a salutary fear of the Lord "to a charity *which casts out fear altogether*" (215). The humble person is freely and joyfully drawn toward the good, in "*union with the Incarnate Word*, implying the realization that all our works are His works and that all our faults have been assumed by Him," and in response to the interior leading of the Holy Spirit (215). The spiritual guidance of the *Rule*, and therefore of this "spiritual commentary" on the *Rule*, leads "not to absolute perfection, nor even to the highest perfection possible in this present life, but only to the summit of the *bios praktikos* or active (ascetic) life. Here a new life begins, the life of charity and contemplation, the life of purity of heart" (214). As Merton points out in his concluding words, the *Rule* directs those who follow it to drink more deeply from the sources of its own inspiration: "UNDER THE GUIDANCE OF THE DIVINE SPIRIT THE HUMBLE MONK IS NOW READY FOR THE CONTEMPLATIVE LIFE for which St. Benedict refers us to other books, especially Cassian and the Fathers" (216)—which is, not by coincidence, the title of another set of conferences, one that introduces the novices to contemplation in the monastic tradition.

* * * * * * *

The handwritten title page of Merton's own typescript of the *Rule* conferences, now at the Thomas Merton Center in Louisville, includes the date "1957"; the same date is also found on the typed title page of the multigraphed version of the notes retyped from Merton's typescript and distributed to the novices. On some copies of these notes, however, reproduced from the same masters, the date "1957" is crossed out and "1960" is added by hand. It is evident, then, that these conferences were given at least twice during Merton's tenure as novice master. Other documentation, while fragmentary, can provide somewhat greater precision as to the time period during which the conferences were given. Not surprisingly, perhaps, there is very little mention of these conferences in Merton's private journals, since their preparation required considerably less wide-ranging reading than for other courses with more historical breadth. Since Merton's talks to the novices only began to be taped in April, 1962, they are unavailable for most, though not all, of the period when Merton was presenting these conferences. There is, however, documentary material that can assist in the dating of the presentation of the *Rule* conferences. On the verso pages of Merton's typescript he frequently jotted brief notes for introductory comments before beginning the conference proper. Some of these notes concerned practical details of communal life (e.g. "Leaving books around // Laughing + talking" [2v]; "clean feet / save water—shaves" [74v]) or instructions for performing certain monastic functions (e.g. "Agnus Dei—beat breast" [21v]; "Chapter Faults—short objective . . . not humorous" [32v]) or work details ("work. power line. Martin / Basil / Yvo / Alberic" [9v]; "Work—woods—big trees—Fence" [70v]); but frequently there was mention of feast days, or of particular persons or events, whether pertaining to the monastery or to the world at large. While the writing is tiny, the references often cryptic, and the notations usually cancelled after use, enough information can be gathered from these notes to provide a fairly clear idea of the sequence of the conferences.

The 1957 conferences were evidently begun sometime during the summer, as a work schedule for "oblates" extending over six days of the week is presented, which would seem to suggest people staying at the monastery for a fairly extended period; in the same note, "Fr [i.e. "Frater"—"Brother"] Lawrence" is mentioned; this is Ernesto Cardenal, who was still a postulant in July 1957.[12] Page

12. See Merton's letter of July 5, 1957 to Dom Gabriel Sortais, the Abbot General, in which he mentions "a postulant who as a poet is fairly well known in Nicaragua" (Thomas Merton, *The School of Charity: Letters on Religious Renewal and Spiritual Direction*, ed. Patrick Hart [New York: Farrar, Straus, Giroux, 1990], 103).

15v of the typescript[13] mentions "L'ville Dickey etc." which is likely a reference to a trip to Louisville that Merton made on September 6, 1957 to consult Terrell Dickey about layouts for a postulants' guide.[14] In the same note mention is made of "Bruno James" in connection with "St Bern[ard] statue" which may be a reference to a letter Merton had received from Fr. James "about his new book on St. Bernard."[15] No further useful information is found until typescript page 32v[16] where Merton mentions a Columbian postulant, Guillermo Jaramillo, who has apparently not yet arrived; he is first mentioned in a journal entry of January 24, 1958.[17] This reference is followed shortly (on page 34v[18]) by mention of Candlemas (the Feast of the Purification, February 2). Later references to "Our Father Athanasius," whose feast is May 2 (44v[19]) and to "Nativity BVM" (54v[20]) on September 8 apparently bring the conferences through the summer months. On typescript page 56v,[21] references to "Romanus", "bishop" and "war—pray peace" seem to refer to Merton's trip to Louisville on September 25, 1958, when he saw Fr. Romanus Ginn off to Rome for biblical studies and stopped at the Chancery to speak with Bp. Maloney; in the same journal entry, from the following day, Merton mentions the current crisis with China over the offshore island of Quemoy.[22] Further evidence for this dating is found in the left margin about midway

13. Page 42 of the present edition.

14. Thomas Merton, *A Search for Solitude: Pursuing the Monk's True Life. Journals, vol. 3: 1952–1960*, ed. Lawrence S. Cunningham (San Francisco: HarperCollins, 1996), 116 [9/10/57]; the typescript note also mentions "Carmel etc." but Merton's journal does not mention a visit to the Louisville Carmelite convent, so the identification is not certain.

15. *Search for Solitude*, 109-10 [8/10/57].

16. Page 82 of the present edition.

17. *Search for Solitude*, 159; he actually arrives, unexpectedly, on February 20 (see *Search for Solitude*, 173).

18. Page 86 of the present edition.

19. Page 108 of the present edition.

20. Page 132 of the present edition.

21. Page 139 of the present edition.

22. *Search for Solitude*, 218–19.

down page 57 of the typescript, where there is a notation that appears to be the date "9-1-58" with "p. 74" and an arrow pointing upward written above it, and a horizontal line extended between the lines of typed text; this marks the exact spot at which page 74 of the multigraphed copy of the text ends,[23] and suggests that the typist, probably one of the novices, marked the place where he had stopped typing for the day. Information becomes somewhat more abundant for the final section of the course. On typescript page 67v[24] there is a reference to "kerygma," which may refer to Merton's privately printed *Nativity Kerygma*, copies of which arrived on December 19, 1958;[25] reference to the antiphon "O admirabile" in the same note probably refers to the liturgy of the Feast of the Circumcision. Mention on the following page of "Hanekamp" (68v[26]) with the additional notation "loneliness" almost certainly refers to the death of neighbor and one-time monk Herman Hanekamp on December 30, 1958;[27] the same note mentions "F circumcision"—New Year's Day. Subsequent notes refer to "Epiph" (January 6) (70v[28]), "St Anthony" (January 17) and "Chair of Unity Octave" (January 18–25) (77v[29]), "St Agnes" (January 21) (81v[30]) and "St Alberic" (January 26) (86v[31]). On page 89 of the typescript[32] there is another marginal notation, presumably again by the typist, reading "1/31" with a horizontal arrow, pointing to the place where page 119 of the multigraphed copy begins.[33] Finally, on

23. Page 139 of the present edition (after ". . . tragedy.").
24. Page 162 of the present edition.
25. *Search for Solitude*, 240.
26. Page 166 of the present edition.
27. *Search for Solitude*, 242.
28. Page 171 of the present edition.
29. Page 187 of the present edition.
30. Page 194 of the present edition.
31. Page 203 of the present edition.
32. Page 209 of the present edition (at "b) Laughter").
33. There are two additional handwritten notations of dates: in the bottom left margin of typescript page 78 (page 187 of the present edition) is the date "1/17", and on typescript page 85 (page 201 of the present edition) is the date "Jan 29"; neither of these notations, however, corresponds precisely to page endings in the

typescript page 90v,[34] opposite the second last page of the notes, is a reference to "Foresters," who are also mentioned in a February 7, 1959 journal entry: "The foresters were here the other day looking at what we had done to the woods."[35] The evidence, then, indicates that the *Rule of St. Benedict* conferences began sometime during the summer of 1957, continued throughout the following year, how regularly it is impossible to determine, and concluded in early February, 1959.

The evidence for the 1960 conferences is more extensive and more varied than that for the earlier presentation of the course. Introductory notations for this second presentation can usually (but not always[36]) be distinguished by use of different ink or more generally by chronological sequence from those of the 1957–1959 conferences sometimes found on the same verso pages of the typescript. On page 5v of the typescript,[37] mention of the Bishop of Kandy (Ceylon) refers to his visit to Gethsemani in mid-June, 1960,[38] confirmed by mention of the Feast of Corpus Christi (June 16, 1960) on the same page. This dating indicates that the reference to Krushchev on page 4v[39] almost certainly pertains to the

---

multigraphed copy: page 103 of the copy ends 8 lines above the bottom of typescript page 78, and page 113 of the copy ends 8 lines beyond the end of typescript page 85.

34. Page 212 of the present edition.

35. *Search for Solitude*, 256.

36. References to the Feast of Corpus Christi and to an exam on July 4 (45v), and to the Feast of St. Camillus (July 18) (on a separate handwritten page following typescript page 47) could fit chronologically either the sequence from 1958 or that from 1961; other evidence suggests that Merton stopped giving exams in these courses in later years, so perhaps at least the first two references are more likely to refer to the first presentation; in either case the attribution does not affect determination of the overall chronological sequence for the course either time it was given.

37. This note is opposite the first page of Latin texts from Gregory's *Vita Benedicti*, inserted after the outline of Benedict's life in the text (page 18 of the present edition).

38. See *Turning Toward the World*, 14 [6/21/60].

39. Page 16 of the present edition.

U2 spy plane crisis referred to in Merton's journal for May 18, 1960,[40] and to Pasternak farther down on the same page (probably a note for the following class) to the author's death in late May.[41] Thus Merton began this second presentation of the *Rule* conferences sometime in mid- or late May 1960. Subsequent mention of the feasts of St. Innocent (July 17) (11v[42]), the Seven Sleepers of Ephesus[43] (July 27) (15v[44]), St. Bartholomew (August 24) (separate page after 19[45]), the Nativity of Mary (September 8) (21v[46]), Holy Cross (September 14) (separate page after 21[47]) and St. Jude (October 28) (separate page after 25[48]) bring the conferences through the summer and into the fall of 1960. The next traceable reference, on typescript page 42v,[49] reads "General in Bro Nov" and evidently refers to the visitation of Abbot General Dom Gabriel Sortais beginning on February 15, 1961.[50] There is no further definitely datable reference until mention of "Berlin Crisis etc." on typescript page 47v,[51] probably datable to September or October 1961.[52] A reference to "Pax bulletin—Pax Mvt" (55v[53]) corresponds to Merton's early acquaintance with this British peace

40. *Search for Solitude*, 391.

41. See *Turning Toward the World*, 6 [6/1/60].

42. Page 33 of the present edition.

43. Merton's interest in this legend was stimulated by his friendship with Louis Massignon, who encouraged its celebration as a bond of communion between Christians and Muslims, since it was also referred to in the Qurʾan; see *Search for Solitude*, 345 [11/18/59]; Thomas Merton, *Witness to Freedom: Letters in Times of Crisis*, ed. William H. Shannon (New York: Farrar, Straus, Giroux, 1994), 262 [8/24/59 letter to Herbert Mason]; 277 [5/12/60 and 7/20/60 letters to Louis Massignon].

44. Page 43 of the present edition.

45. Page 52 of the present edition.

46. Page 57 of the present edition.

47. Page 57 of the present edition.

48. Page 65 of the present edition.

49. Page 103 of the present edition.

50. See *Turning Toward the World*, 94–97.

51. Page 115 of the present edition.

52. See *Turning Toward the World*, 166 [9/30/61], 170 [10/15/61].

53. Page 135 of the present edition.

group, first mentioned in the journal on November 7, 1961.[54] "Xmas trees" are mentioned on the verso of the second inserted handwritten page after typescript page 56.[55] The only explicit reference in the journals to this set of conferences occurs on January 3, 1962, when Merton writes: "Talking to the novices about craftsmanship in the Rule, and [Eric] Gill, and 'Good Work' and Shaker furniture. All subjects that are dear to me. And the sunny quiet room. Their presence and their love."[56] Opposite the page of typescript text (56[57]) containing this reference is the note "Asbury" which probably is a reference to Merton's visit to Asbury Seminary on January 10, 1962.[58] This is the last clearly datable reference to this set of conferences in the typescript, but beginning on the Feast of the Translation of St. Benedict, July 11, 1962, sixteen conferences on chapter 7 of the *Rule*, running through December 19, were taped. As he mentions in the first of these conferences that it had been a while since the *Rule* had been discussed, Merton had evidently left off the *Rule* conferences shortly after his consideration of craftsmanship—probably after some discussion of poverty, the last topic before the long closing section on humility that he now takes up. It is evident from the tapes that these half-hour conferences were usually, but not always, given on Wednesdays,[59] generally on a weekly basis, though with a month-long gap between late July and late August. This schedule of approximately five months to discuss about a quarter of the text of the *Rule* notes is consistent with the time

54. See *Turning Toward the World*, 178.

55. Page 224 of the present edition.

56. *Turning Toward the World*, 193; see pages 135–36 of the present edition.

57. Page 136 of the present edition.

58. See *Turning Toward the World*, 194 [1/12/62].

59. Some of the tapes, now remastered on compact disc and part of the collection at the Bellarmine Thomas Merton Center, are dated; for some but not all others, dates can be determined from references made in the conferences themselves. A complete table of correspondences between the text and the tapes, including publication information for those tapes available commercially, is found in Appendix B of the present edition (261–62).

span of roughly a year and a half for each of the two presentations of the conferences. It is also clear both from the documentary evidence provided by the notations in Merton's typescript and from the absence of any further taped conferences on the *Rule* after 1962 that this series of conferences was only presented twice, in 1957–59 and 1960–62.

Merton did not teach from an identical text each time that he presented the course. Like any good teacher, he continued to add material for successive presentations. Over one hundred additional handwritten notes, most of them brief, are found in the typescript but not in the multigraphed version typed from the version of the notes in their original form. The references to Eric Gill and *Good Work* mentioned in Merton's January 3, 1962 journal entry, for example, are additions made after the typing of the first version. There are also ten longer handwritten notes made on separate sheets, not clearly integrated into the original text although generally on topics included there. Two of these notes, on the monk and study (222) and on *lectio divina* in the patristic tradition (224–25) draw on works published in 1961,[60] another, also on *lectio* (223–24), is based on a book he was reading in October of that year,[61] while that on faults and penalties (219–21) uses as a main source a work published in 1941[62] but only obtained in a photostatic version by the Gethsemani library in 1961, so these notes show Merton incorporating material he has recently discovered. His use of the new material in the conferences as delivered is evident in the recordings, as he draws on

60. A. J. Festugière, OP, *Les Moines d'Orient I: Culture ou Sainteté: Introduction au Monachisme Oriental* (Paris: Éditions du Cerf, 1961); Gerard Sitwell, OSB, *Spiritual Writers of the Middle Ages*, Twentieth Century Encyclopedia of Catholicism, vol. 40 (New York: Hawthorn Books, 1961).

61. See *Turning Toward the World*, 170–71 [10/19/61]: "Also have been reading more Biblical theology—esp. G. E. Wright, *God Who Acts* [Chicago, 1952], a book given to me by Eric Rust, the Baptist theologian. And a very fine book too."

62. Sr. M. Alfred Schroll, OSB, *Benedictine Monasticism as Reflected in the Warnefrid-Hildemar Commentaries on the Rule* (New York: Columbia University Press, 1941).

material from the last of the notes (229–32), on traditional images for spiritual ascent, to begin his July 11 opening conference on chapter 7 of the *Rule*, and continues to do so in the following conference of July 20. His conference of July 25 discusses in some detail a sermon of St. Bernard (158–59) that was not considered in the first version of the conferences. Even the minor addition of the word "*virtù*" to the revised text (178) is mentioned in the September 7 conference as pertaining to a current reading in the refectory. It is safe to assume that similar modifications based on added information would have been made during the earlier portions of the 1960–1962 course that were not yet being taped.

* * * * * * *

A comparison of the conferences as actually delivered with the written text reveals, as with previously published conferences,[63] that Merton made a considerable effort to present the material orally in as effective and engaging a manner as possible. Since the novices would eventually receive a multigraphed copy of the text (though in the case of the students of 1962, a somewhat outdated one), Merton did not have to concern himself that all his information was conveyed during his presentations. He could therefore concentrate on making the material as lively and pertinent as possible, and focus on the central spiritual message of, in this case, the degrees of humility as found in chapter 7 of the *Rule*.

One of Merton's standard tools in the classroom setting was humor, often directed at himself, as when during the July 11 conference, in the course of mentioning various patterns of spiritual ascent, he notes that a traditional number of stages is seven, and after a brief pause calls attention to books with "seven" in their titles. At the end of the same conference he mentions that as a novice he was tempted to pride by his skill at shoveling manure with a pitchfork. In the announcements at the beginning

63. See *Cassian and the Fathers*, xlvii–liv, and *Pre-Benedictine Monasticism*, li–lxi, for discussion of the oral presentation of these sets of conferences.

of the following class he asks who had been playing bebop at 5:30 in the morning, and remarks that it sounded like "somebody was trying to frame me" since it seemed to be coming from the direction of St. Mary of Carmel (the hermitage). Referring to the fourth degree of humility, to obey even in difficult circumstances, during a mid-July conference, he remarks that one of the greatest difficulties for humility and obedience comes when the superior has gone along with an idea of someone you profoundly disagree with, and adds, "It can be difficult—believe me" which draws a good deal of laughter from the novices.

He also makes continuous efforts to situate Benedict's teachings on humility in the context of other spiritual, social, and even political perspectives and events. In discussing the first degree of humility in the August 28 conference, Merton brings in the Bohemian reformer John Hus, who had appeared in the refectory reading of the previous day, in connection with the question of conscience, which he regards as basic for this first degree; he points out that Hus "got a dirty deal" from the Church, which was "a mess at the time," and that he was subjectively sincere, yet contrasts him with Joan of Arc, who remained loyal to the Church even in the face of institutional betrayal, and mentions the importance of the gift of counsel as the guidance of the Holy Spirit not to "go too far one way or the other." Later in the same conference he points out that consciousness of the last things, of death and judgement, is the basis of Buddhist meditation as well, and then goes on to relate a contemporary refusal to face death to the attitude of denial in the face of the massive destructive power of "the bomb." In the September 7 conference he contrasts Benedict's counsel of surrendering one's own will with the attitude of secular society, traced back to Adam Smith, that if everyone pursues his own will, "everything will work out for the best." On October 3, the Feast of St. Thérèse, he points out that her "little way" and the degrees of humility, particularly the fourth, have remarkable affinities; Benedictine humility and obedience exemplify "spiritual childhood" in the best sense. In discussing the fifth degree, on manifestation of conscience, in the following conference, he brings in a Zen saying about swallowing a ball of red-hot iron to illustrate the negative consequences of keeping interior struggles concealed from a spiritual director. In the October 24 conference, he connects the sixth degree of humility, the acceptance of poverty, with the Cuban Missile Crisis, commenting that the illusory idea that one can run the world on one's own "leads to the situation we're in now." By making connections such as these Merton is showing the novices that the degrees of humility, the *Rule*, and the monastic life in general are not to be studied, and more importantly not to be lived, in a vacuum, but must be situated in the wider life of the Church and of the world if they are to be truly fruitful.

Merton frequently shows his spiritual and psychological sensitivity in explaining the meaning and exercise of humility. In the July 20 conference, for example, he points out that humility cannot simply be equated with passivity, and that for some people who "prefer the back seat" genuine humility might involve putting oneself forward. He emphasizes that humility must be connected to love to be fruitful—putting the other before oneself is not necessarily the same as putting oneself below others, which can be a way of self-pity and so still centered on self. In the July 25 conference he follows St. Bernard in focusing on humility as going down to the root of truth, the truth of our own nothingness apart from God, and stresses that this cannot be simply a formula, an abstract idea, but must be an experiential reality in which one can "take refuge"—finding a source of consolation and strength in total dependence on and trust in God. Later in the same conference he points out that often there is no immediately clear indication what God wills or does not will in some particular situation, and humility entails a willingness to remain in "the provisional," without attempting to manipulate uncertainties to become certainties. In the September 26 conference, he observes that we are naturally inclined to defend the superficial ego-self, with which we too readily identify, yet it is this self that must be renounced in order that the deeper self, the real self, the person as image of God, can be recognized and accepted. Humility, he notes in the November 7 conference, is not just resignation, a fatalistic acceptance of the status quo: this is an unhealthy attitude, not a virtue. True contentment with one's situation, whatever it may be, is a matter of decision, of choice, a spiritual practice, an act of putting things in perspective: if I have God, the gain or loss of other things loses its significance. In considering the last of the interior degrees of humility, the seventh, Merton warns the novices that one can go wrong in two ways, by misunderstanding it or by simply disregarding it. To accept oneself as the worst of all must not be reduced to a pathological condition, a kind of self-denigration that is self-love turned inside out, a kind of perverse pride in one's inferiority that is still self-centered. It is rather to rejoice in a brother's goodness as if it were my own, to leave behind all self-concern. Likewise the exterior degrees (8-12) properly involve a renunciation of singularity, an outward tranquility that is a sign and expression of interior peace.

Throughout these conferences, Merton is above all concerned to highlight the ways in which the way of humility is the way of discipleship, of following Jesus to the cross and to the Father. The paradox of ascending by descending, he points out in the first of these conferences, finds its model in the self-emptying of Christ described by Paul in the Philippians hymn. In the following conference he notes that suffering is not an end in itself but a way of sharing in the passion of Christ, and that real suffering often results not from physical deprivation but from damage to our self-esteem, to our sense of our own identity, which if accepted humbly can lead to a salutary death to self. As members of Christ, he reiterates in the September 26 conference, we are never isolated, never alone in our problems, for Christ himself suffers what we are suffering. In considering the seventh degree, he considers the paradox that even my sinfulness, which separates me from Christ, can unite me with Christ, who has taken upon himself the burden of our sins; accepting without morbidness one's own sinfulness is an acceptance of the need for grace and salvation and therefore a point at which Christ breaks into our lives and brings about complete interior purification. The transformative power of the cross makes possible this completely supernatural dimension of humility.

* * * * * * *

It is no coincidence that *The Rule of St. Benedict* conferences were composed and delivered during the period when Merton's published writing focused largely on the monastic life, no doubt due in considerable part to his responsibilities as novice master for the formation of prospective monks. While there is no direct textual overlap between the conferences and the book and pamphlets written at this time, numerous thematic parallels help to situate the *Rule* conferences in the context of Merton's overall body of work in the latter part of the 1950s. *The Silent Life*, published in 1957 but written in 1955, around the time of first becoming novice master,[64] provides an overview of key aspects of monastic life in its opening section, entitled "The Monastic Peace," followed by discussions of "The Cenobitic Life" (Benedictines and Cistercians) and "The Hermit Life" (Carthusians and Camaldolese). Its early pages quickly focus attention on humility and obedience as the key virtues of monastic asceticism, described in terms that will characterize the conferences as well. Thus monastic humility is seen as "the victory of the real over the unreal—a victory in which false human ideals are discarded and the divine 'ideal' is attained, is experienced, is grasped and possessed, not in a mental image but in the present and concrete and existential reality of our life."[65] Such a victory is not attained through human effort but through the redemptive work of Christ and the invitation to share in the paschal mystery: "The monastic life is not only devoted to the study of Christ, or to the contemplation of Christ, or to the imitation of Christ. The monk seeks to *become* Christ by

64. See the February 7 and April 16, 1957 letters to Dom Gabriel Sortais for the circumstances in which this work was composed and the controversy that ensued (*School of Charity*, 99–102).

65. *Silent Life*, 5.

sharing in the passion of Christ."[66] The successive steps of humility as set out by the *Rule* are explicitly recognized as "participation in the mystery of the obedience of Christ" leading, as Benedict quotes from the First Letter of John at the end of chapter 7, to "that perfect charity which casts out fear."[67] In looking to St. Benedict, as presented by St. Gregory's *Life* and in the *Rule* itself, as the model of the monastic life, "the spirit, the 'form' without which no monk can truly call himself a Benedictine,"[68] Merton focuses on Gregory's key phrase "*soli Deo placere desiderans*"—"he sought to please God alone,"[69]—the same message that forms "the essence" of the *Rule*, where it is presented in a more Christocentric language: "the renunciation of self-will in imitation of Christ . . . the following of Christ in obedience, humility and charity."[70] While recognizing that the *Rule* is an adaptation of the monasticism of the Desert Fathers, Merton adamantly denies that "St Benedict was in any way repudiating the primitive monastic ideal,"[71] including a recognition and appreciation of the anchoritic life; he finds an "implicit orientation of the Rule of St Benedict towards eremitical solitude,"[72] which is realized most directly in the Camaldolese form of Benedictine life, but is not, Merton implies, limited to that branch, for "as a representative of the authentic tradition in this matter, [Benedict] takes it for granted that some monks, after long testing in the cenobium, will want to go off into solitude and will receive permission to do so."[73] The pertinence of this passage for Merton's own monastic aspirations, at the time and later, is of course quite evident.

66. *Silent Life*, 9.
67. *Silent Life*, 18–19.
68. *Silent Life*, 62.
69. *Silent Life*, 63.
70. *Silent Life*, 65.
71. *Silent Life*, 146.
72. *Silent Life*, 148.
73. *Silent Life*, 148.

The pamphlet *Basic Principles of Monastic Spirituality*,[74] also published in 1957, likewise predates the conferences.[75] This text too takes as its starting point a profoundly Christ-centered view of the monastic life as one that "like all Christian life, the life of the Church, prolongs the mystery of the Incarnation on earth . . . . We come to the monastery to live more fully, more perfectly and more completely *in Christ*."[76] Merton goes on to situate monastic life in the context of Christ's passion and resurrection: "we receive our Redemption by mystically dying together with Him and rising with Him from the dead."[77] Thus the whole purpose of the *Rule*, Merton writes in the central section of the pamphlet, of the disciplines "of silence, obedience, solitude, humility, manual labor, liturgical prayer," is "to unite us with the Mystical Christ, with one another in charity, . . . to form Christ in us, to enable the Spirit of Christ to carry out, in our lives, actions worthy of Christ. . . . Having ascended all the degrees of humility, our hearts are empty of self, and God Himself can produce the likeness of Christ in us by the action of His Spirit."[78] It is in this context that the liturgy, manual labor and *lectio divina* mandated by the *Rule* reveal their deepest value and purpose,[79] that the true meaning of the monastic vows is revealed,[80] and that monastic asceticism leads to a self-forgetfulness that makes possible both union with the Word, the Risen Christ—and also, Merton adds in the final section of the work, "The Monk in a Changing World," an "Epilogue" that actually follows the "Conclusion," "with those

74. Thomas Merton, *Basic Principles of Monastic Spirituality* (Trappist, KY: Abbey of Gethsemani, 1957); reprinted in Thomas Merton, *The Monastic Journey*, ed. Brother Patrick Hart (Kansas City: Sheed, Andrews & McMeel, 1977), 11–38.

75. See the August 26, 1957 letter to Thomas Aquinas Porter, ocso and the September 1, 1956 letter to Dom Gabriel Sortais for information on the circumstances of composition of this work (*School of Charity*, 96–98).

76. *Basic Principles*, 7; *Monastic Journey*, 15.

77. *Basic Principles*, 15; *Monastic Journey*, 22.

78. *Basic Principles*, 19; *Monastic Journey*, 26.

79. *Basic Principles*, 21-24; *Monastic Journey*, 27–30.

80. *Basic Principles*, 24; *Monastic Journey*, 30–31.

with whom he is actually or potentially united 'in Christ'—in the Mystery of our unity in the Risen Savior, the Son of God. . . . Their needs are his own, their interests are his interest, their joys and sorrows are his, for he has identified himself with them not only by a realization that they all share one human nature, but above all by the charity of Christ, poured forth in our hearts by the Holy Spirit Who is given to us in Christ."[81]

*Monastic Peace*,[82] another pamphlet published the following year but probably written around the time the *Rule* conferences began,[83] develops this "social" dimension of monasticism by presenting the monk as "before all else a peacemaker" insofar as he serves Christ the "*Rex Pacificus*, the king of peace"[84] as "a living member of a community which by its peace and unity fully represents Christ."[85] The whole purpose of the *Rule* is to form a community where this manifestation of the peace of Christ truly takes place. Merton points out that while the "monk is important more for what he *is* than for what he *does*,"[86] the *Rule* is primarily oriented toward what would have been considered the "active" life in St. Benedict's time, "the life of ascetic purification and the practice of virtue which leads to the pacification of our passions and brings them under the control of the spirit," in order to lead the monk to "a state of peace and interior purity (*apatheia*) which disposes his soul for contemplation." Thus "St Benedict legislates for beginners in terms of the 'active,' or ascetic life . . . with a view to contemplation later on."[87] But to be "transformed and

81. *Basic Principles*, 29; *Monastic Journey*, 35.

82. Thomas Merton, *Monastic Peace* (Trappist, KY: Abbey of Gethsemani, 1958); reprinted in *Monastic Journey*, 39–84.

83. This is probably the "pamphlet on the monastic life" written "this summer" that Merton mentions in his July 5, 1957 letter to Dom Gabriel Sortais (*School of Charity*, 103); it is definitely the "other booklet we are printing in St. Paul" mentioned in a journal entry of October 22, 1957 (*Search for Solitude*, 126).

84. *Monastic Peace*, 5; *Monastic Journey*, 41.

85. *Monastic Peace*, 11; *Monastic Journey*, 45.

86. *Monastic Peace*, 9; *Monastic Journey*, 44.

87. *Monastic Peace*, 12; *Monastic Journey*, 46.

elevated by community life"[88] requires not merely outward conformity to customs and observances but "surrender to God's action" of grace and love, "uniting us to Himself and to our brethren by His own Holy Spirit of love."[89] The vows are oriented to this great work of wholehearted self-surrender. Poverty is understood both as having the "prophetic" function of serving as "a silent and implicit condemnation of the misuse of ownership" marked by greed and injustice to the poor, and as expressing "a state of direct dependence on providence out of love for God, and for the poor."[90] Chastity, like poverty understood to be included in the Benedictine vow of conversion of manners, "does not merely stifle passion, but enlists the energies of our sensible nature in support of a higher love, the love of God."[91] Obedience is not "compulsive submission and abdication of responsibility" but rather a mature exercise of freedom, "a voluntary assumption of responsibility, a clear-sighted renunciation of private and limited interests in favor of the general good of the community,"[92] as a way of participating in the salvific obedience of Christ to the will of the Father: the monk "obeys above all out of love for Christ, in imitation of Christ, in union with the sufferings and the death of Christ, in order to share with Christ the great work of restoring liberty to mankind and of renewing all things in the power and sanctity of the Spirit of God."[93] Stability "is one of the foundation stones on which St. Benedict raised his edifice of monastic peace"[94] because it commits the monk to the ongoing work of making the Kingdom of God visibly present in a particular community, a specific place and time. Such a commitment is paradoxically a willingness to face inner conflicts and communal struggles with faith that genuine peace is "a gift of the

88. *Monastic Peace*, 22; *Monastic Journey*, 54.
89. *Monastic Peace*, 23; *Monastic Journey*, 55.
90. *Monastic Peace*, 31; *Monastic Journey*, 62–63.
91. *Monastic Peace*, 32; *Monastic Journey*, 63.
92. *Monastic Peace*, 34; *Monastic Journey*, 65.
93. *Monastic Peace*, 35; *Monastic Journey*, 66.
94. *Monastic Peace*, 36; *Monastic Journey*, 67.

divine mercy."[95] Therefore the monastery is not only a school of the Lord's service and a school of charity but a "school of freedom,"[96] where the monk is called not "to *renounce his freedom*, to remain inert and apathetic in the hands of others," but to make "a sacrifice of a lower and more material kind of autonomy in order to attain to a higher and more spiritual autonomy—the autonomy of one who is so closely united to the Holy Spirit that the Spirit of God moves him as his own spirit."[97] Such freedom is the fruit of long training, but it develops from the initial presence of "the four main signs" which "St. Benedict, with his usual simplicity, sets down in the Rule":[98] the desire to "*truly seek God*";[99] acceptance of obedience as the foundation of genuine community life; commitment to a life of communal and personal prayer; and finally, appreciation of "the value of humiliation and spiritual poverty" as the way to "love the cross which kills his self-love at the very roots and establishes him firmly and totally in the heart of Jesus Christ."[100]

The closest parallels to material in the *Rule* conferences are found in one of the more obscure items in the Merton canon, a multigraphed pamphlet, probably dating from Merton's early years as novice master, entitled "Monastic Courtesy,"[101] which is also the subtitle for a section of these conferences (104–16). While

95. *Monastic Peace*, 41; *Monastic Journey*, 71.

96. *Monastic Peace*, 48; *Monastic Journey*, 77.

97. *Monastic Peace*, 47; *Monastic Journey*, 76.

98. *Monastic Peace*, 54; *Monastic Journey*, 81.

99. *Monastic Peace*, 54; *Monastic Journey*, 81.

100. *Monastic Peace*, 56; *Monastic Journey*, 83.

101. Thomas Merton, "Monastic Courtesy," ed. Patrick Hart OCSO, *The Merton Annual*, 12 (1999), 13–21. Brother Patrick Hart speculates (13) that this pamphlet, which apparently survives only in a single copy in the Gethsemani archives, dates from Merton's time as master of students (1951–55), but the very basic nature of the directives, and in particular the mention of "Courtesy to postulants, when one is a guardian angel" (14)—i.e. an experienced novice assigned as guide to a new entrant to the monastery—suggests that novices were the more likely audience and that Merton wrote it after becoming novice master in October 1955.

the pamphlet goes into considerably more specific, and at times amusing and entertaining, detail,[102] both texts note the importance of bearing one another's burdens,[103] both cite the phrase "*honore se invicem praeveniant*" ("anticipate one another in showing honor") from chapter 72,[104] both focus on the idea of mutual obedience found in chapter 71,[105] both quote the phrase "*ut nemo perturbetur neque contristetur in domo Dei*" ("that no one may be troubled or saddened in the house of God") from chapter 31.[106] As the text of the conferences will also do (119–24), the pamphlet presents Benedict's portrait of the cellarer as a model for the mature monk.[107] While it is impossible to determine which text was written first, and while it seems clear that Merton did not have one text in front of him as he was writing the other, conference notes and pamphlet share a common perspective and spirit.

Perhaps the most remarkable piece of writing from this period that is related to the *Rule* conferences is a journal entry from October 27, 1957, a Day of Recollection at the monastery. It begins with a reflection clearly inspired by Merton's reading for the course: "There is nothing whatever of the ghetto spirit in the Rule of St. Benedict. That is the wonderful thing both about the Rule and the saint. The freshness, the liberty, the spontaneity, the broadness, the sanity and the healthiness of early Benedictine life. The same healthiness and sanity in the early commentaries—

102. See for example the instructions on "Courtesy in Choir": not "bowing in such a way that [one's brother] has no room left, pushing him out of the way in order to make a bow, bowing with your back in his face" etc. (17); "Avoid much head scratching, examining of nails, sighs, yawns, etc. Be discreet in keeping awake" (18); on "Courtesy When Serving Mass": "Nothing is more out of place than two ministers arguing in the sanctuary and refusing to give in on a point of rubrics" (18); on "Courtesy in the Refectory": "Avoid mouth noises—belching. Be restrained in coughing and nose-blowing. Don't pick teeth with your fingers. . . . Don't finger the bread to get a fresh piece" (19).

103. "Monastic Courtesy," 15; page 111 in the present text.

104. "Monastic Courtesy," 15; page 108 in the present text.

105. "Monastic Courtesy," 16; page 110 in the present text.

106. "Monastic Courtesy," 17; page 110 in the present text.

107. "Monastic Courtesy," 16.

Smaragdus, Hildemar (and therefore {Warnefrid })."[108] This warm praise for the *Rule* and its early interpreters then leads into a consideration of the meaning of authentic tradition and of the genuine principles of renewal that is one of the earliest expressions of Merton's mature vision of monastic life and its relationship with the world beyond the abbey walls:

> But closed in on itself, interpreting interpretations of interpretations, the monastery becomes a ghetto.
>
> Reforms that concentrate too excessively on a return to *strictness* do not in fact break the spell. They tend to increase the danger of spiritual suffocation. On the other hand, fresh air is not the air of the world . . .
>
> Just to break out of the ghetto and walk down the boulevard is no solution.
>
> The world has its own stink too—perfume and corruption.
>
> The fresh air we need is the air of the Holy Spirit "breathing where He pleases" which means that the windows must be open and we must expect Him to come from any direction.
>
> The error is to lock the windows and doors in order to keep the Holy Spirit in our house. The very action of locking doors and windows is fatal.
>
> What about enclosure? What about the world?
>
> St. Benedict never said that the monk must *never* go out, *never* receive guests, *never* talk to anyone, never hear *any* news—But that he should distinguish what is useless and harmful from what is useful and salutary, and in all things to glorify God.[109]

108. *Search for Solitude*, 130; text reads "Warnefaid"; see also the revised version of this passage in Thomas Merton, *Conjectures of a Guilty Bystander* (Garden City, NY: Doubleday, 1966), 6.

109. *Search for Solitude*, 130–31; the *Conjectures* passage ends with a brief additional paragraph that situates the issue more firmly in the context of the *Rule* itself, specifically chapter 53, on the reception of guests: "Rejection of the world? The monk must *see Christ* in the pilgrim and stranger who come from the world, especially if they are poor. Such is the spirit and letter of the Rule" (6).

The imagery of course anticipates that which Pope John XXIII would use a few years later[110] to describe the program of *aggiornamento* that led up to the Second Vatican Council (which would mandate both an openness to the contemporary world in *Gaudium et Spes*, the Pastoral Constitution on the Church in the Modern World,[111] and the recovery of the charism of the founder in *Perfectae Caritatis*, the Decree on the Renewal of Religious Life[112]). But it also prefigures Merton's own awakening from "the dream of my separateness, of the 'special' vocation to be different" at the corner of Fourth and Walnut Streets some five months after this passage was written,[113] and sounds a note that will recur in many of the powerful essays on monastic reform that will be written in the following decade. The passage provides an early indication that Merton's turn to the world was not only compatible with but even inspired by his commitment to authentic Benedictine monastic life. Much of his effort in his remaining years would be to "distinguish what is useless and harmful from what is useful and salutary, and in all things to glorify God."

110. The story, perhaps legendary, of the window and fresh air was popularized by Norman Cousins in "Pope John and His Open Window," *Saturday Review*, 46 (19 January 1963), 20–22; it is related to his call for "a new Pentecost" in his Apostolic Constitution "*Humanae Salutis*" of December 25, 1961, summoning the Council: see Walter Abbott, SJ, ed., *The Documents of Vatican II* (New York: Guild Press, America Press, Association Press, 1966), 709.

111. Abbott, *Documents*, 199–308.

112. Abbott, *Documents*, 466–82, especially n. 2 (468).

113. *Search for Solitude*, 181–82 [March 19, 1958, reflecting on the previous day's experience]; the more familiar revised version is in *Conjectures*, 140–42, with its memorable expansion of the quoted phrases that reject more explicitly the "ghetto" mentality of an inward-turning and rigid monasticism: "It was like waking from a dream of separateness, of spurious self-isolation in a special world, the world of renunciation and supposed holiness. The whole illusion of a separate holy existence is a dream. Not that I question the reality of my vocation, or of my monastic life: but the conception of 'separation from the world' that we have in the monastery too easily presents itself as a complete illusion: the illusion that by making vows we become a different species of being, pseudoangels, 'spiritual men,' men of interior life, what have you" (140–41).

Anyone familiar with Merton's life during these years knows of his restlessness and periodic dissatisfaction with life at Gethsemani. Little of this appears in the conferences, which generally present a view of life under the *Rule* as it should be lived, though not without a realistic recognition of individual and communal shortcomings. It is worth noting however, that Merton's efforts during these years are largely oriented toward finding an environment in which the *Rule* might be lived out more faithfully,[114] whether it be in the established milieu of Camaldoli[115] or in the putative Cistercian foundations in Ecuador or elsewhere in Latin America,[116] or in some connection with the primitive Benedictine foundation in Cuernavaca, Mexico of Dom Gregorio Lemercier,[117] or even in one of the quasi-eremitic locations in the American west, the island of Tortola, the Corn Islands etc.[118] How much of this was prompted by Merton's natural restlessness, both psychological and spiritual, and how much was due to a motivation similar to that which led to the original exodus from Molesme

114. Note his comment in a journal entry for July 5, 1959 that the problem is "Not because of the Rule of St. B but because of the hopeless way in which it is interpreted here" (*Search for Solitude*, 302), and his horarium for an experimental South American monastery in a July 25, 1958 journal entry considered as "A return to St. Benedict—or an application of St. B." (*Search for Solitude*, 209–10).

115. On Merton's efforts in 1955 to transfer to this eremitical branch of Benedictinism see Christine M. Bochen, "Camaldolese," in William H. Shannon, Christine M. Bochen and Patrick F. O'Connell, *The Thomas Merton Encyclopedia* (Maryknoll, NY: Orbis, 2002), 40–41.

116. See the journal entries for July 30, 1957 (*Search for Solitude*, 103–104), December 24, 1957 (*Search for Solitude*, 148–49), February 1, 1959 (*Search for Solitude*, 254), and the letters of July 5, 1957 to Dom Gabriel Sortais and July 15, 1957 to Dom James Fox (*School of Charity*, 102-106).

117. See journal entries for July 25, August 2, 17, 18, 30, September 9, October 6 and December 17, 1959 (*Search for Solitude*, 308–309, 314–15, 317–18, 324–25, 327–28, 335, 358–59) and for June 21 and August 19, 1960 (*Turning Toward the World*, 14, 32-33).

118. See the journal entries for June 30, July 2, 5, 12, 21, 1959 (*Search for Solitude*, 298–304, 307–308), and letters collected under the heading of "Vocation Crisis: 1959–1960" in *Witness to Freedom*, 200-30, which include correspondence with bishops of various mission territories and with Vatican officials, among others.

to Cîteaux is difficult to say, but his efforts are not intrinsically alien to or incompatible with his ruminations on the *Rule* in these conferences, however mainstream and uncontroversial they may be. In the event the building of the "retreat center" on Mount Olivet that would become his hermitage, occurring at the mid-point of the period spanned by these conferences in their double presentation, would provide a way for Merton to live out the *Rule* in a more unconventional but completely faithful (at least in intent if not always in execution) manner, and would provide the context for his more challenging and provocative insights on monastic life in later essays collected in *Contemplation in a World of Action* such as "Openness and Cloister,"[119] and "The Place of Obedience"[120] that would make him one of the most eloquent and influential voices for contemporary monastic renewal in the Benedictine tradition. *The Rule of St. Benedict* conferences need to be properly situated in this continuum and progression in order to appreciate their contribution to Merton's developing vision and revisioning of what it means to be a monk.

* * * * * * *

There are two versions of the Conferences on the *Rule* extant, the dittoed notes distributed to the novices toward the end of the course,[121] and Merton's own typed and heavily reworked notes that he had in front of him as he lectured. The first consists of a 123-page "spirit master" (purple) text run off on both sides, entitled "THE RULE / OF / ST. BENEDICT // GETHSEMANI / CHOIR NOVITIATE / 1957."[122] When the course was repeated

119. Thomas Merton, *Contemplation in a World of Action* (Garden City, NY: Doubleday, 1971), 129–42.

120. *Contemplation in a World of Action*, 117–28.

121. These notes are included in Volume 18 of the "Collected Essays"; while the Table of Contents to this volume reads "1960 reprint of '57 ed", the text, at least in the Bellarmine Merton Center copy, actually corresponds in its pagination to the 1957 version.

122. Pages 43-49 of this version are all mistyped "42" and altered on the ditto to: "43, 44, 45, 48, 46, 47, 49"; "48" is then changed in pencil to "46"; "46"

in 1960, the identical ditto masters were reused,[123] with only the date on the title page altered by hand.[124]

Merton's typescript begins with a handwritten title page: "THE RULE / OF ST BENEDICT. / Gethsemani / Choir Novitiate 1957."[125] The basic text consists of 92 numbered pages,[126] all but one typewritten,[127] preceded by a single typewritten introductory page.[128] Handwritten additions to the text are found both on the typed pages themselves and on the blank facing pages; some of these additions are included in the multigraphed version of the text and therefore date from the first presentation of the conferences, while others are not included in that version and therefore presumably date from the second presentation. Page 5

---

to "47"; and "47" to "48". In the process of reproduction page 24 was run off twice, and the verso of page 46 (misprinted "48") was left blank, so that for subsequent pages the recto pages were again odd-numbered.

123. Merton begins the fourth last conference by asking if anyone knows where the stencils for this course are; in the second last conference he mentions that they have shown up, and presumably they are run off and distributed by the end of the course, Merton's usual practice.

124. The mispagination of pages 46–48 was left uncorrected in this reproduction, page 34 was run off twice, and page 64 was also run off a second time instead of page 65, which is missing.

125. It is also marked with Merton's "Fr Louis" stamp, made for him from an eraser by fourteen-year-old Nelson Richardson, briefly a postulant at Gethsemani in the summer of 1960 at the time when Merton was beginning the *Rule* conferences for the second time (see *Turning Toward the World*, 14 [6/21/60], 25 [8/5/60]).

126. The first page is unnumbered; on pages 2–63 "St Benedict" generally precedes the page number (page 48 has "Rule of St Ben" and pages 52–53 have "Rule"); on pages 64–92 "Rule" generally precedes the page number (page 67 has "St Ben Rule"); on page 16, the original correct number is cancelled, "17" is interlined by hand above and cancelled and "16" is restored by hand on line; on the following page, "17" is added by hand on line following cancelled "16"; on page 69 "Rule 69" is added in pencil; on page 71 the correct number is added by hand after cancelled "70"; on page 84 "3" is altered by hand to "4".

127. Page 24 is handwritten.

128. This page, numbered "Rule a–" and headed "NOTES ON THE RULE OF ST BENEDICT." has the handwritten note "(to go in beginning of all the notes)" in the upper margin.

is followed by five separately numbered pages, typed on both sides of the page, of passages from St. Gregory the Great's *Vita Benedicti*.[129] A typed page numbered "55a" and headed "*Lectio Divina*" is inserted in the text after page 55; it is not found in the ditto. Ten handwritten pages on various topics relating to the course are inserted in the text; none of this material is included in the ditto, so it was added at the time of the second presentation. Four handwritten nontext pages, on various liturgical feasts, are also interleaved in the text.[130]

Merton's typescript, with its handwritten additions and alterations,[131] is the copy text for the present edition of *The Rule of St. Benedict*. Only the Table of Contents, not found in the typescript, a lengthy quotation added by the typist according to Merton's instructions, and a few minor changes, usually involving redundancy, are adopted from the ditto; these readings are recorded in the first section of Appendix A, Textual Notes. The second section of these notes lists all additions and alterations, including on-line corrections Merton made in the process of typing (i.e., crossing out one word or phrase and immediately substituting another) found in the ditto, and therefore dating from the first presentation of the conferences in 1957–1959; the third section lists all additions and alterations incorporated into the text of this edition that are not found in the ditto and therefore date from the second presentation in 1960–1962. The textual apparatus does not attempt to record every variation between the different versions of the text. Errors, whether of omission or of mistranscription, in the multigraph version of the text where

129. The note "Latin notes St Ben. Translate—" on the verso of the first page of text suggests that these excerpts were perhaps assigned to be translated by the novices.

130. Material on the Feast of St. Bartholomew is found after typescript page 19, of the Holy Cross after page 21, of St. Jude after page 25, and of St. Camillus after page 47. This material is not included in the present edition.

131. One handwritten addition, all the material of which is also found in a more extensive additional note, is not incorporated into the text of this edition; it can be found in Appendix A for page 134 of the text.

these are not being used as copy text, are not recorded since they have no independent authority vis-à-vis the copy text. Thus the textual notes allow the interested reader to distinguish between the preliminary draft of Merton's notes, the additions that he made before his initial presentation of the conference lectures, and those made for the subsequent presentation of the course.

Because the extra handwritten pages are not marked for insertion and cannot be easily integrated into the text, they have been separately transcribed and gathered as Appendix 1: Additional Notes on the *Rule* of St. Benedict (217–32). The passages from the *Vita Benedicti* have not been incorporated within the text proper,[132] where they would interrupt the flow of the material, but have been included, with translations by the editor, as Appendix 2 (233–45).

All substantive additions made to the text, in order to turn elliptical or fragmentary statements into complete sentences, are included in braces, as are the few emendations incorporated directly into the text, so that the reader can always determine exactly what Merton himself wrote. No effort is made to reproduce Merton's rather inconsistent punctuation, paragraphing, abbreviations and typographical features; a standardized format for these features is established that in the judgement of the editor best represents a synthesis of Merton's own practice and contemporary usage: e.g., all Latin passages are italicized unless specific parts of a longer passage are underlined by Merton, in which case the underlined section of the passage is in roman type; all other passages underlined by Merton are italicized; words in upper case in the text are printed in small caps; periods and commas are uniformly included within quotation marks; patterns of abbreviation and capitalization, very inconsistent in the copy text, are regularized. All references to primary and secondary sources are cited in the notes. Since Merton generally

132. A note in the typescript at the conclusion of the material on the *Life of Benedict* (38) reads "*Texts from St Gregory go here in the complete set of notes*" but in fact the Latin selections were not included in the ditto.

refers to Dom Justin McCann's edition of the *Rule*,[133] all citations of passages from the *Rule*, unless otherwise noted, are from this edition, although the text Merton quotes sometimes is not identical to McCann's. When Merton quotes only the Latin, or provides his own translation, page references are to McCann's Latin text only; when Merton quotes McCann's English translation, page references are to both the Latin and the facing English text. Untranslated Latin passages in the original text are left in Latin but translated by the editor in the notes. (McCann's rather archaic English translation of the *Rule* is thus not used, but page references to his Latin text are included with the translations from the *Rule* in the notes.) All identified errors in Merton's text are noted and if possible corrected. All instances where subsequent research and expanded knowledge affect Merton's accuracy are discussed in the notes.

A table of correspondences between the written text and the recorded conferences from July through December 1962 is included as Appendix B in order to facilitate comparison of Merton's version of the material as published in this edition with the conferences as actually delivered to the novices. A list of suggestions for further reading is included as Appendix C, consisting first of other sources in Merton's published works where the topic of this volume is discussed, followed by a list of important recent editions and studies on Benedict and the *Rule*, that will provide helpful updating on material discussed by Merton.

* * * * * * *

In conclusion I would like to express my gratitude to all those who have made this volume possible:

- to the Trustees of the Merton Legacy Trust, Peggy Fox, Anne McCormick and Tommie O'Callaghan, for permission to publish the *Rule of St. Benedict* conferences;

133. *The Rule of St. Benedict in Latin and English*, ed. and trans. Justin McCann, OSB (London: Burns, Oates, 1952).

- to the late Robert E. Daggy, former director of the Thomas Merton Center, Bellarmine College (now University), Louisville, KY, for first alerting me to the project of editing Merton's monastic conferences, and for his encouragement in this and other efforts in Merton studies;
- to Brother Patrick Hart, OCSO, for his friendship, for continued encouragement in the publication of the volumes of the conferences in the Monastic Wisdom series, for which he serves as editor, and for facilitating my research visits to the library at the Abbey of Gethsemani;
- to Sister Joan Chittister, OSB, for graciously accepting an invitation to provide the Preface for this volume;
- to Fr. Chrysogonus Waddell, OCSO of the Abbey of Gethsemani, and to Abbot John Eudes Bamberger, OCSO and Brother Augustine Jackson, OCSO of the Abbey of Our Lady of the Genesee, for assistance in locating materials in their respective libraries;
- to Paul M. Pearson, director and archivist of the Merton Center, and Mark C. Meade, assistant archivist, for their gracious hospitality and valued assistance during my research visits to the Center;
- to the Gannon University Research Committee, which provided a grant that allowed me to pursue research on this project at the Merton Center and at the Abbey of Gethsemani;
- to Mary Beth Earll of the interlibrary loan department of the Nash Library, Gannon University, for once again providing invaluable assistance by locating and procuring various obscure volumes;
- to library staff of the Hesburgh Library of the University of Notre Dame, the Latimer Family Library of St. Vincent College, and the Friedsam Memorial Library of St. Bonaventure University, for assistance in locating important materials in their collections;
- again and always to my wife Suzanne and our children for their continual love, support and encouragement in this and other projects.

# CONFERENCES ON

# THE *RULE*

# OF

# ST. BENEDICT

GETHSEMANI
CHOIR NOVITIATE

1960

# TABLE OF CONTENTS


Part I Introductory—Study of the *Rule* {7}

Part II The Life and Character of St. Benedict {16}

Part III The *Rule* of St. Benedict {39}

Date—Texts—Commentaries {39}

SPIRITUAL COMMENTARY ON THE *RULE* OF ST. BENEDICT {50}

The PROLOGUE: Theological Basis of the *Rule* {51}

*De Generibus Monachorum* (chapter 1) {71}

THE ABBOT AND HIS MONKS {79}

(covering chapters 2, 3, 21, 30, 31, 32, 53, 57, 59, 60, 62, 63, 64, 65, 66)

The Abbot—Representative of Christ {79}

The Monastic Community {97}

Monastic Courtesy and Unity {104}

Various Officers {116}

Manual Labor {130}

Craftsmen {135}

Poverty {142}

THE DEGREES OF HUMILITY (chapter 7) {152}

Introduction {152}

Pride and Humility {165}

First Degree {173}

Second Degree {182}

| | |
|---|---|
| Third Degree | {183} |
| Fourth Degree | {186} |
| Fifth Degree | {190} |
| Sixth Degree | {194} |
| Seventh Degree | {201} |
| Eighth Degree | {206} |
| Ninth, Tenth and Eleventh Degrees | {207} |
| Twelfth Degree | {212} |
| Conclusion | {214} |


As explained in the introductory note (pp. {5–6}) Benedictine obedience is discussed *everywhere* in these notes, and therefore no particular chapter is assigned to the subject.

# NOTES ON THE *RULE* OF ST. BENEDICT

These notes are not intended to cover thoroughly every aspect of the *Rule* or every chapter of it. They concentrate on some of the main features of the *Rule* in order to give a *detailed and concrete picture of what a real monk is like in the eyes of St. Benedict.* For this purpose we have started out with a discussion of St. Benedict's own life and character, for he is the model of his own monks, and his *Rule* must be seen in the light of his own practice. Then there is a detailed discussion of the Prologue, which contains the basic theological principles upon which the *Rule* is built. After that we go into the chapters on the abbot in order to show the responsibilities and tasks of the representative of Christ in the monastery and to indicate the correlative obligations of the monks who serve God under him. Chapters on the various officers in the monastery, on the work of the monks and on their poverty complete this picture of the monastic life in its externals and in the practice of obedience. The remaining pages of this commentary are devoted to a somewhat lengthy treatment of the Degrees of Humility which are the very heart of the *Rule* of St. Benedict and contain the marrow of his asceticism. We have not gone into St. Benedict's teaching on obedience *ex professo* since this is discussed elsewhere, in notes on the Vow of Obedience.[1] But everywhere in the chapters on the abbot, on humility, etc.,

1. See "An Introduction to the Life of the Vows," a set of conference notes for a course given by Merton as master of novices and found in volume 14 of "Collected Essays," the 24-volume bound set of published and unpublished materials assembled at the Abbey of Gethsemani and available both there and

not to mention the Prologue, the essential Benedictine doctrine of obedience is to be found on every page.

What we have *not* discussed here at any length includes the long sections on the *Opus Dei*[2] and the chapters on punishments and excommunication. The structure of the office is fully discussed in our notes on the Observances[3] and the chapters on excommunication, though important in their own right, cannot be fitted in due to lack of time.[4]

The important thing is for monks to love the *Rule*, not as a document printed on paper but as a life that should take possession of their inmost hearts. St. Benedict did not call us to the monastery to serve him, but to serve God. We are not here to carry out the prescriptions of men, but to love God. The purpose of the *Rule* is to furnish a framework within which to build the structure of a simple and pure spiritual life, pleasing to God by its perfection of faith, humility, and love. The *Rule* is not an end in itself, but a means to an end, and it is always to be seen in relation to its end. This end is union with God in love, and every line of the *Rule* indicates that its various prescriptions are given us to show us how to get rid of self-love and replace it by love of God.

It should be noted that the spirit of the *Rule* is a spirit of unaffected simplicity and deep piety. It is based above all on respect for *reality*. It accepts all the simple things of life and incorporates them into the work of serving God. St. Benedict wants his monks to avoid everything that savors of exaggeration and preoccupation with themselves. He does not encourage ascetic rivalries or spectacular feats of penance and prayer. His way of

---

at the Thomas Merton Center, Bellarmine University, Louisville, KY; the material on the vow of obedience is found on pages 137–60.

2. "the work of God"—i.e. the divine office (*Rule* of St. Benedict [*RB*], cc. 7, 22, 43, 44, 47, 50, 52, 58, 67) (*The Rule of St. Benedict in Latin and English*, ed. and trans. Justin McCann, OSB [London: Burns, Oates, 1952], 46, 70, 102, 104–106, 108, 116, 118, 130, 152–154).

3. See "Our Monastic Observances," in "Collected Essays," vol. 15; the material on the office is found on pages 16–63, 118–23.

4. But see Additional Note 3 below (219–21).

penance is a way of obedience and humility, a way of simplicity. He legislates not for outstanding individuals but for humble men living in community and loving one another in Christ. This atmosphere of simple and sincere charity pervades the whole *Rule*. Nowhere does St. Benedict incite the monk to "get ahead" of all his brethren in the "race" for sanctity. It is not a race. The community *is* holy and its members work together to make it more holy, by helping one another to grow in holiness. This can only be done by mutual love based on the faith which sees Christ in the community and Christ in every one of His members. *Faxit Deus.*[5] *Amen.*

## NOTES ON THE *RULE* OF ST. BENEDICT

### Part 1

The Study of the *Rule*—its importance; St. Benedict and the Cistercian Fathers; St. Benedict and the Popes

*The Study of the Rule*

We make vows to live until death according to the *Rule* of St. Benedict. This means not only carrying out the prescriptions of the *Rule*, and obeying those who command us according to the *Rule*. Much more, it means allowing ourselves to be *formed by the Rule*. {The} *Rule* {is to be understood} as *education*—{from} *educere*: what {is brought forth}? {the} image of God. Our whole life must be molded and shaped, it must develop, be nourished, by the *Rule*. Our life is a *discipline* in which God forms us through the instrumentality of the *Rule*, and through the fatherhood of St. Benedict, who exercises a very real formative influence upon

5. "May God bring it about" (a standard phrase in Medieval Latin); it is not found in the *Rule* of Saint Benedict itself but is used by Edmond Martène, OSB at the very end of his commentary on chapter 7 of the *Rule*: see J. P. Migne, ed., *Patrologiae Cursus Completus, Series Latina*, 221 vols. (Paris: Garnier, 1844–1865), vol. 66, col. 410A (subsequently referred to as *PL* in text and notes).

the souls of his sons. We are called to be sons of St. Benedict. The likeness of Christ must be formed in us as it was formed in St. Benedict. We must follow Benedict's *via vitae*.[6] We interpret the Gospel as he did, we live as he did, our sanctity is to be his sanctity. The Holy Spirit must work in us as He worked in him. In St. Benedict we see *the perfect form of our monastic sanctity*. The lessons of the desert fathers, of oriental monasticism, of other Western spiritual traditions before or after St. Benedict are good for us in so far as they accord with the spirit of St. Benedict, enable us to deepen that spirit, and understand it better. For this, they must come to us through St. Benedict.

Note: we must not be too absolute in excluding all other "spiritualities" and enclose ourselves in a rigid framework of what we consider to be "Benedictine," or even more rigid, "Cistercian," spirituality. One of the characteristic features of St. Benedict is the fact that he is *not exclusive* and that anything good for monks, in any spirituality, can be adapted to the monastic life according to the *Rule* of St. Benedict. Nothing is excluded except what is essentially opposed to the monastic life itself—for instance, {the} married state, or a completely active (apostolic) life, or a life without stability in the cloister, or without obedience, or without the office, or without silence. Anything opposed to these things would be opposed to the *Rule* and spirit of St. Benedict. But forms of spirituality that accord with the monastic life of prayer and penance can easily be adapted to the Benedictine life. Note, however, that the adaptation must be made. Carmelite spirituality must bring its values to us in a *Benedictine* context and with a Benedictine orientation. We cannot superimpose St. John of the Cross or St. Teresa upon St. Benedict. We must see the truths they saw as St. Benedict himself would have seen them, and apply them as he would have applied them.

We must first of all *love the Rule in a spirit of filial piety*. Our study of the *Rule* cannot and must not be merely an intellectual exercise. It is a meditation on which our life itself depends, for if

6. "way of life" (*RB*, Prol.) (McCann, 8).

we do not absorb the spiritual teaching of the *Rule,* we will not be monks. But we do not absorb that teaching merely by "knowing" what the *Rule* says. If we do not live the *Rule* we do not understand the *Rule* or know it. The spirit of filial piety with which we study the *Rule* should be based on faith in the mediation of St. Benedict in our lives. St. Benedict has a distinct mission for the sanctification of monks. He intervenes personally and directly in the lives of all his sons. He teaches them not only through the written word of the *Rule,* but through a charismatic intervention in the lives of his monks, which continues and will continue as long as Benedictine monasticism lasts. This is St. Benedict's great work as the Father of Western Monasticism.

But if we do not love St. Benedict, this supernatural action of his prayers and love cannot function in our lives. It is by love and filial trust and respect for him that we open our hearts to the graces that God has willed to bestow on us through his mediation. In order to love St. Benedict, we must have a personal knowledge of him. This personal knowledge is gained through a communion with the soul of our monastic Father and lawgiver, a union of will and understanding, and this union is brought about by obedience of faith, a faith which sees God speaking to us through St. Benedict and giving us St. Benedict as our guide in the ways of the Gospel.

*The spirit of St. Benedict lives on in the traditions of the Benedictine family.* Our tradition is a kind of corporate "memory" in which, guided by the Holy Spirit, we interpret and understand, as our fathers have interpreted and understood, the mind of St. Benedict, who himself understood the Gospel and monastic tradition as they had been understood by the monks before him. To love St. Benedict means to *love our monastic tradition* that goes back to him and beyond him to St. Basil and St. Anthony—and to Jesus. Hence, our study of the *Rule* will be relatively sterile and useless if we only study the *Rule* itself, without any background, without any roots, in monastic tradition. *Our love for St. Benedict includes a love for all things Benedictine and all things monastic.* To exclude other forms of monasticism from our view would in fact make us unable to understand St. Benedict completely. He is for us the *main organ of monastic tradition* and when we go to St. Benedict, we go not only to learn his doctrine as though it were opposed to other monastic teachings (for instance, of Cassian) but we go to him as *to the authoritative and inspired guide* who will open to us all the rest of monastic tradition and show us how to understand it and apply it to our own monastic lives.

*The Cistercian tradition*: from the beginning, the Cistercians sought to penetrate more perfectly and more deeply into the full teaching of St. Benedict, in all its completeness, and in all its purity. The first Cistercians were, to some extent, *exclusive* in matters of observance. They set aside observances which were good in themselves, but which seemed to them at the time to obstruct the real understanding of and fidelity to St. Benedict. In this matter we follow our fathers. We observe and interpret the *Rule* according to the tradition of Cîteaux. This tradition *is austere and simple*, and seeks to return to the pure sources of monastic tradition both in observance and in spirit—hence, {there is an} emphasis on poverty, manual labor, silence, enclosure, mortification, etc. But once again, we would not be faithful to our own monastic tradition if we confined ourselves narrowly within purely "Cistercian" or "Trappist" limits in our study of the *Rule*. On the contrary, to be true Cistercians we must, like our fathers, seek with all spiritual thirst the *pure springs of the monastic tradition*. And here again, everything that is living and authentic, especially in all forms of monastic reform and return to primitive sources, is not alien to us. We must be acquainted with all that is genuine and vital in the monastic tradition.

However it should be noted that the Cistercians and other branches of the monastic family are interested not primarily in an abstract tradition, but in the concrete persons in whom that tradition is embodied. Thus when St. Bernard goes to preach a sermon on St. Benedict, he preaches not on the monastic tradition, or the Benedictine ideal, but on *St. Benedict* himself as a quasi-"sacrament" of God's will and God's love for monks. Our monastic life, for St. Bernard, is built upon the life and miracles, the virtues and doctrine of St. Benedict. *Pascit vita, pascit doctrina, pascit et intercessione* (*PL* 183:379).[7] His *miracles* are important to us as the basis for our confidence in him, as the proof that he was the instrument of God, as the witness to his special divine mission. His *doctrine* is our way to heaven; it leads us in the way of peace. But his doctrine is embodied in his *life and example* which strengthen and nourish our faith. St. Ailred says that all the graces of prayer we receive as monks and the progress we make in virtue come to us through the intercession of St. Benedict our Father.[8] Bl. Guerric compares St. Benedict to Moses[9] (this comparison is made by the liturgy itself, which *says* St. Benedict was "filled with the spirit of all the just"[10]). Just as Moses led the chosen people out of Egypt, so St. Benedict by his charismatic action leads us out of the darkness of the world into the light of God. But St. Benedict is superior to Moses in the "law" which he gives us. Moses gave only the letter which killeth; St. Benedict gives the Spirit which bringeth life.[11] The whole *Rule* and teaching of St. Benedict is summed up by Guerric as: *Iste solam puritatem*

7. "He feeds by his life, he feeds by his teaching, and he feeds by his intercession": *In Natali Sancti Benedicti Abbatis Sermo* 8 (*PL* 183, col. 380A).

8. *In Natali Sancti Benedicti, Sermo* 5 (*PL* 195, col. 239A).

9. *In Festo S. Benedicti, Sermo* 4 (*PL* 185, cols. 111–16).

10. The phrase comes originally from the *Vita Sancti Benedicti*, c. 8: "*vir iste spiritu justorum omnium plenus fuit*" (*PL* 66, col. 150B; see below, n. 27). It is found in the vespers (eve) and lauds prayer for the Feast of St. Benedict (March 21): "*Vir Dei Benedictus omnium Justorum spiritu plenus fuit: ipse intercedat pro cunctis monasticae professionis*" ("Benedict the man of God was filled with the spirit of all the just; may he himself intercede for all who have made monastic profession") (*Breviarium Monasticum: Pauli V Jussu Editum Urbani VIII et Leonis XIII Cura Recognitum Pii X et Benedicti XV Auctoritate Reformatum* [*editio tertia*], 2 vols. [Bruges: Desclée, 1941], 1.851, 859); it is also found in the vespers (eve) and lauds prayer for the Feast of the Translation of St. Benedict (July 11), which begins: "*Deus, qui beatissimum Confessorem tuum Benedictum omnium justorum spiritu replere dignatus es* . . . ("God, who deigned to fill your most blessed confessor Benedict with the spirit of all the just . . .) (*Breviarium Monasticum*, 2.495, 510).

11. Col. 111D.

*evangelicam simplicemque morum tradidit disciplinam . . . rectissimam vitae {. . .} Regulam, sermone luculentam, discretione praecipuam . . .*[12] (*PL* 185:103-111).[13]

*The Church speaks*:

The Benedictine breviary: *O caelestis norma vitae, Doctor et Dux Benedicte, cujus cum Christo spiritus exultat in caelestibus: Gregem, Pastor alme, serva, sancta prece corrobora, via caelos clarescente fac, te duce, penetrare.*[14]

Council of Douzy (A.D. 874): "The Holy Spirit through St. Benedict wrote the *Rule* of the monks, in the same way as He speaks in the sacred Canons of the Church."[15] In other words, the *Rule* has the authority of the ordinary magisterium of the Church (*not* inspired in the same sense as Scripture).

Pope Pius XII {in} *Fulgens Radiatur*[16] stresses the following points about St. Benedict:

1. The *solidity* of his doctrine and spirituality. Strength of St. Benedict—his wisdom {is} a source of support and salvation for the whole Church in his time. {This} proves {the} perennial youth and vigor of {the} Church.

12. "He handed on only the purity of the gospel and clear instruction in how to live, . . . a most perfect Rule of life, rich in teaching, outstanding in discretion" (col. 112A, which reads ". . . *vitae scribit Regulam,* . . ." ["he wrote a most perfect Rule of life"]).

13. Though the references have been to *Sermo IV*, these columns contain the second (cols. 103B–107C) and third (cols. 107C–111C) of Guerric's four sermons on Benedict (the first is found in cols. 99A–103B).

14. "O Heavenly model of life, Benedict, teacher and leader, whose spirit rejoices with Christ in heaven, watch over your flock, kindly shepherd, strengthen it with your holy prayer, make clear the way so that led by you it may enter heaven" (Magnificat antiphon [vespers] for the Feast of the Translation of St. Benedict [July 11]) (*Breviarium Monasticum*, 2.495, 502; the first eight words are also found as the title for the portrait of Benedict used as the frontispiece of both volumes of the breviary).

15. *PL* 66, col. 214B.

16. *Acta Apostolica Sedis*, 39 (1947), 137–55 (March 21, 1947); an English translation is found in *St. Benedict: Encyclical Letter of Pope Pius XII on St. Benedict of Nursia* (Washington: National Catholic Welfare Conference, 1947).

2. The great work of his genius was *to adapt oriental monasticism to the West*. This he did by *a balanced cenobitic life* in which there was no undue austerity or severity, but in which all could become saints, especially by the royal way of *charity*. (*Read* #13, 14.[17]) His *Rule* is thus a "splendid monument of Roman and

17. "13. It was here that Benedict brought the monastic life to that degree of perfection to which he had long aspired by prayer, meditation and practice. The special and chief task that seemed to have been given to him in the designs of God's providence was not so much to impose on the West the manner of life of the monks of the East, as to adapt that life and accommodate it to the genius, needs and conditions of Italy and the rest of Europe. Thus to the placid asceticism which flowered so well in the monasteries of the East, he added laborious and tireless activity which allows the monks 'to give to others the fruit of contemplation', and not only to produce crops from uncultivated land, but also to cultivate spiritual fruit through their exhausting apostolate. The community life of a Benedictine house tempered and softened the severities of the solitary life, not suitable for all and even dangerous at times for some; through prayer, work, and application to sacred and profane sciences, a blessed peace knows not idleness nor sloth; activity and work, far from wearying the mind, distracting it and applying it to useless things, rather tranquillize it, strengthen it and lift it up to higher things. Indeed, an excessive rigor of discipline or severity of penance is not imposed, but before all else love of God and a fraternal charity that is universal and sincere. 'He so tempered the rule that the strong would desire to do more and the weak not be frightened by its severity; he tried to govern his disciples by love rather than dominate them by fear'. When one day he saw an anchorite, who had bound himself with chains and confined himself in a narrow cave, so that he could not return to his sins and to his worldly life, with gentle words Benedict admonished him: 'If you are a servant of God, let not the chains of iron bind you but the chains of Christ'. 14. Thus the special norms of eremitic life and their particular precepts, which were generally not very certain or fixed and often depended on the wish of the superior, gave way to Benedictine monastic law, outstanding monument of Roman and Christian prudence. In it the rights, duties and works of the monks are tempered by the benevolence and charity of the Gospel. It has proved and still proves a powerful means to encourage many to virtue and lead them to sanctity. For in the Benedictine law the highest prudence and simplicity are united; Christian humility is joined to virile virtue; mildness tempers severity; and a healthy freedom ennobles due submission. In it correction is given with firmness, but clemency and benignity hold sway; the ordinances are observed but obedience brings rest to mind and peace to soul; gravity is honored by silence but easy grace adds ornament to conversation; the power of authority is wielded

Christian wisdom."[18] N.B. {the} basis of {the} humanities here—what is Roman wisdom?

3. The Benedictine spirit is characterized by *the balance of prudence and simplicity* and *of humility with generous practice of virtue*. Obedience and silence bring peace, in an atmosphere of discipline and mercy and charity.

4. (#16) The monastic life is praised as *a Christian family life* in which sons live together under a loving and prudent Father, who represents God Himself, and whose decisions are seen by the eyes of faith as those of God. Note that it is *faith* and not natural feeling which is the basis of the monastic family spirit. It would be a mistake to seek this family spirit merely in the natural gregariousness of man, but our social instincts, offered and consecrated to God by our vows and by the spirit of faith, contribute much to this family spirit which is the nursery of all monastic virtues.

5. Monastic stability, manual labor, study {are} seen in this context of the "family." But the principal care of the monastic family is the common praise of God in the *Opus Dei*. In all his legislation, St. Benedict has produced a marvelous work of supernatural prudence which is nevertheless *most in accord with the good that is in man's nature*. History itself proves this, by the fact that the Benedictines kept alive arts, crafts, learning, etc. in the dark ages.

6. (#19) The principal thing about the Benedictine life (*hoc enim in Benedictinae vitae Instituto praecipuum est* . . .[19]—{the} English translation {of} *praecipuum* as "essential"[20] misses {the} point and changes {the} emphasis) *is constant prayer*—during work, reading, etc., by *raising our minds to Christ in perfect love*. The monk

---

but weakness is not without its support" (8–9; the quotations are from Thomas Aquinas, *Summa Theologiae*, 2a 2ae, q. 188, n. 6; Jean Mabillon, *Annales Ordinis Sancti Benedicti*, 1.107; Gregory the Great, *Dialogues*, 3.16, respectively).

18. This translation, which does not accord with that of the English version already quoted, is apparently Merton's own.

19. *Fulgens Radiatur*, 147.

20. "It is essential in the Benedictine way of life . . ." (11).

must know better than all others that earthly things are incapable of satisfying the heart, and he must base his life on St. Benedict's maxim *"nihil amori Christi praeponere."*[21] From this flows charity to our neighbor, which is equally essential. What neighbor? The poor, the sick, the guests who are received as Christ, and all one's brethren.

7. He praises the great *missionary work* of the Benedictines in the dark ages; their studies and learning; the sanctity of the monks; the great number of Benedictine popes and bishops.

8. Practical conclusions for sons of St. Benedict: to follow their Father and reproduce his virtues in our lives. *Addiscant imprimis . . . praeclaris ejus vestigiis auctiore cotidie studio insistere, eiusque virtutis sanctitatisque principia atque exempla in suum cuiusque vitae usum deducere.*[22] Thus they will taste sweet peace in their hearts and bear fruit in the Church of God.

9. All the Church must turn to St. Benedict to learn most valuable lessons, particularly his *sense of the majesty of God* and *respect for the divine will*; not only that, but supreme *love of God as our Father*; then *fraternal charity*; and the *dignity of labor*; *detachment* from material things. (Read #29-30.[23])

21. "to prefer nothing to the love of Christ" (*RB*, c. 4; McCann, 26).

22. *Fulgens Radiatur*, 151; "Let those first of all [who belong to his numerous family] learn . . . to follow daily ever more closely in his illustrious footsteps and let each reduce to the practice of ordinary life the principles and example of his virtue and sanctity" (14 [n. 24]).

23. "29. Besides, Venerable Brethren, the author and lawgiver of the Benedictine Order has another lesson for us, which is, indeed, freely and widely proclaimed today but far too often not properly reduced to practice as it should be. It is that human labor is not without dignity; is not a distasteful and burdensome thing, but rather something to be esteemed, an honor and a joy. A busy life, whether employed in the fields, in the profitable trades or in the liberal arts does not demean the mind but elevates it; does not reduce it to slavery but more truly gives it a certain mastery and power of direction over even the most difficult circumstances. Even Jesus, as a youth, still sheltered within the domestic walls, did not disdain to ply the carpenter's trade in his foster-father's workshop; He wished to consecrate human toil with divine sweat. Let those therefore who labor in trades as well as those who are busy in the pursuit of literature and learning

In the homily *Exsultent Hodie* (Sept. 18, 1947)[24] the Holy Father calls St. Benedict the "Father of Europe."[25] His "*ora et labora*"[26] sums up all that we need to know about man's true culture and life on earth.

## Part 2—*The Life and Character of St. Benedict*

1—St. Benedict's Life; 2—His Mission; 3—His Sanctity.

*1—St. Benedict's Life.*

All that we know of St. Benedict is drawn from St. Gregory the Great's life of Benedict in Book II of his *Dialogues* (written 593 or 594).[27] How credible is this "life"? St. Gregory was writing within fifty years of the saint's death. He was basing himself on

---

remember that they are performing a most noble task in winning their daily bread; they are not only providing for themselves and their best interests but can be of service to the entire community. Let them toil, as the Patriarch Benedict admonishes, with mind and soul elevated towards heaven, working not by force but through love; and a last word, even when they are defending their own legitimate rights, let them not be envious of the lot of others, labor not in disorder and tumult, but in tranquil and harmonious unity. Let them be mindful of those divine words 'in the sweat of thy face shalt thou eat bread'; this law of obedience and expiation holds good for all men. 30. Above all let this not be forgotten that looking beyond the fleeting things of earth we must daily and increasingly strive after heavenly and lasting goods, whether we be engaged in intellectual work or study or in a laborious trade; when we shall have gained that goal, then and then only will it be given to us to enjoy true peace, undisturbed repose, and everlasting happiness" (16–17).

24. *Acta Apostolica Sedis*, 39 (1947), 452–56.

25. *Exsultent Hodie*, 453.

26. "pray and work" (*Exsultent Hodie*, 453–54); this phrase, often considered the unofficial motto of Benedictine life, is not found in the *Rule*, but apparently was first used in the nineteenth century by Maurus Wolter, OSB, a German abbot: see M. D. Meeuws, "Ora et Labora: Devise Bénédictine?" *Collectanea Cisterciensia*, 54 (1992), 193–214.

27. The *Life* is found in *PL* 66, cols. 125A–294C, as an introduction to the *Rule*; the other three books of the *Dialogues* are in *PL* 77, cols. 149–430.

accounts given by those who had known the saint (see {the} names in *Dialogues* II: Prologue[28]). He knew many who had lived under Benedict, and Monte Cassino was not far from Rome. St. Gregory's intention was above all to edify, and not to write a scholarly history. It is possible that some of the details of the story are perhaps forced a little to fit this plan, without any insincerity on the writer's part. The biography is essentially simple and plain, {a} very straightforward narrative quite obviously clear of all frills and embellishments. The evident austerity of the style and the manner in which the story is told show that St. Gregory was striving to keep, with Benedictine simplicity, to the bare facts as he had received them. His only purpose as a writer was to interpret these facts in a spiritual way, and the spirituality that is assigned throughout to St. Benedict may well be colored by the personality and spirituality of St. Gregory himself, but one cannot help believing that it is essentially the true Benedict whom we see in this narrative. (The best modern life of St. Benedict is the beautiful book of Cardinal Schuster, OSB—a book full of true Benedictine spirit and monastic charm.[29])

*Outline of Benedict's Life*

{He was} born at *Nursia* or in the Province of Nursia about *480*. The people of Nursia are naturally austere, and Benedict had the character of his race. His family was not necessarily noble. *Liberiori genere ortus*[30]—a good family, but not necessarily of the high nobility. Perhaps about *495*—he goes to Rome to study, but immediately (496?) leaves for Enfide (near Tivoli). {He} lives with a colony of ascetes. About *500* {he} goes to Subiaco to live alone, after the manner of the Desert Fathers. {This is} a rocky valley, near the ruins of the country place of Nero. When disciples

28. Col. 126B: the names mentioned are Constantine, Valentinian, Simplicius and Honoratus.

29. Ildefonso Schuster, *St. Benedict and His Times*, trans. Gregory J. Roettger (St. Louis: B. Herder, 1951).

30. "born of a quite respectable family" (col. 126A, which reads "*exortus*").

come, he begins a cenobitic group like that of Pachomius—small "cells" of twelve monks each, scattered about the hillside. This {was} about 503.

St. Benedict at Subiaco gains the reputation of a great saint and miracle worker. He suffers from the jealousy of priests and other monks. The jealousy of Florentius gives Benedict an excuse to change his location and way of life. He goes to Monte Cassino around 529. This is about half-way between Rome and Naples —on a high mountain, {containing} ruins of an ancient acropolis with a temple of Jupiter (say the scholars, rather than Apollo as St. Gregory has it). Here at Monte Cassino Benedict has reached his full development, after the growth and evolution of his early years through all the stages of monastic life known in his time —ascete, hermit, Pachomian cenobite. Having tried all these, he has reached his own conclusions and it is at Monte Cassino that he puts his own formula into effect. Here also he writes the *Holy Rule*, the fruit of his maturity and experience and the inspiration of the Holy Spirit. The *Rule* was written probably *after 534* (since he quotes St. Cesarius,[31] whose rule for nuns was not written before this time). Benedict died on March 21, probably in 547. His feast is celebrated on that day. The Benedictines celebrate the solemnity of St. Benedict on July 11 ({which} commemorates the transfer of his relics to Fleury).

*The Youth and Conversion of St. Benedict*

Every word counts in St. Gregory's *Vita Benedicti*. It is by a close meditative study of the *Vita*, weighing the words in the light of monastic tradition, that we can begin to understand the sanctity and spirit of St. Benedict. This study is in a way essential to a true understanding of the *Rule*.

31. See *Sancti Benedicti Regula Monasteriorum*, ed. Cuthbert Butler, OSB (Freiburg: Herder, 1930), 8 [Prologue], 109 [c. 58], 190 [index]; the borrowed passages are actually taken from the first chapter of Cesarius' *Rule for Monks*, not that for nuns.

Texts have been gathered together (see below[32]). We refer to them only briefly here.

1. *Fuit vir vitae venerabilis*, etc.[33] The opening words of the *Dialogue* have made such a deep impression on all following generations that they have practically obsessed artists, and made them portray St. Benedict with a long white beard. St. Gregory, himself a great artist, here strikes the keynote of a theme that will recur throughout the *Vita*. A dominant characteristic of the saint is brought before us from the beginning:

*Gravity*, seriousness, maturity—this is not the seriousness of stupidity—the solemn vacuity of an empty and unimaginative mind—nor is it a sphinx-like pose—a front. (Too often the rather inept efforts of artists simply present Benedict with a gloomy and forbidding facade.) This seriousness and gravity of Benedict have a *charismatic* quality, which is therefore radiant and joyous. It is a seriousness that belongs to one filled from childhood with the Holy Ghost, radiating the power, wisdom, and mercy of God. It is a *gentle and prudent* seriousness, full of wisdom, recognizing the nothingness of the world and the greatness of God. It is not an aggressive and gloomy sulkiness of the irate Father who is always trying to find fault with his children and to prevent them from expressing themselves, trying to frown down all spontaneity.

*Detachment*—from the very beginning, Benedict, a wise child, prudently held himself aloof from the world and kept his heart untouched by its corruption and its illusions. The implication is especially that he recognized the transitory and fleeting character of worldly values, and that he made a *clear-sighted and deliberate choice*.

2. His withdrawal from Rome. Sent to Rome to study, Benedict observed how others rushed headlong into the life of vice as though

32. In his typescript Merton had written "*Texts from St Gregory go here in the complete set of notes*" at the end of his discussion of the *Vita Benedicti* as a note added on page 13v, but they were not included in the dittoed version. The Latin texts have been included in this edition with an English translation as Appendix 2 (233–45 below).

33. "He was a man whose life was worthy of deepest respect" (col. 126A).

plunging over a cliff into an abyss. St. Gregory portrays him marvelously as one who had just lifted his foot to put it into the world, and who prudently steps back. The whole picture is one of a quiet, alert, simple but prudent person who realizes what is going on while others are carried away by passion and imprudence.

3. His flight to solitude—his *experience* having taught him the vanity of worldly knowledge, he withdraws *scienter nescius*.[34] {The} implication {here is} of the higher knowledge of the spirit, which is beyond conceptual and discursive learning. St. Benedict was moved by divine counsel, and a very little human experience was sufficient to teach him more than volumes of ethical theory. Schuster points out that he was, however, *educated*.[35] Note, too, already here is implicit a character of *silence* about the wisdom of Benedict. He sees and acts. He does not make any speeches about it. But above all, it is not the negative side that is stressed, but his positive motive, which outweighs everything else: THE DESIRE TO PLEASE GOD ALONE—*soli Deo placere desiderans*.[36] He has seized intuitively upon the great value which is alone real: the will of God, the desire to please God. (For the will of God here is not a blind dictate of an inexorable Absolute; it is the love of a kind Father Whom His sons will seek to please and to gratify by a return of love.) But this love is *exclusive*: *soli Deo*. Note—it is not said that Benedict desired to possess, or to enjoy God alone, but to *please* God alone. {The} emphasis {is} on the fact that God is not for him a commodity to be "had" but a Person to be loved and honored with one's whole heart. (It is only in that way that He can be possessed!)

4. *Benedict embraces the life of an ascete*. He goes to Enfide, and joins a group of pious men (*multis honestioribus viris*[37]) living around the Church of St. Peter. The *ascetes* were the ancestors of the monks. They were not yet true monks, still less were they

34. "knowingly ignorant" (col. 126B).

35. See chapter 6, "Literary Progress" (41–42).

36. "desiring to please God alone" (col. 126A).

37. "many highly admirable men" (c. 1; col. 128A, which reads "*multisque*").

hermits. They had no organization; they just lived good lives, devoting themselves to prayer and penance and a certain degree of retirement, but without withdrawing completely from the towns or villages. St. Anthony had begun his monastic conversion in the same way. The amusing side of the story {is that} St. Benedict still has his "nurse" with him. She is in reality a faithful old servant, still acting as his housekeeper, and being somewhat of a mother to him. "Apparently she was one of those pious women from the mountains, full of faith and generosity. The young master regarded her as a second mother and she showed him a truly maternal affection" (Schuster, p. 43). Schuster compares her with the nurse of Aeneas, who followed him in his travels to Italy.[38] St. Benedict works a miracle when an earthenware sieve borrowed by Cyrilla (the nurse) is broken. The sieve was kept for about three centuries as a relic: *super fores ecclesiae*![39] St. Benedict decides to flee into complete solitude, to avoid the reputation and cult that rise up around him as a little thaumaturgus.

5. *Hermit at Subiaco*—St. Gregory gives the motives for the flight: here again {is} another *key theme* in the spirituality of St. Benedict. *Plus appetens mala mundi perpeti quam laudes*.[40] St. Benedict in the fear of the Lord remembered the warning of Christ: if you were of the world, the world would have loved its own. He realized the vanity of and deceptiveness of a reputation for holiness. Note these were good people, good Christian folk, and he had worked a genuine miracle. Why not settle down to a good fruitful apostolate. . . . ? That would have contained, in St. Benedict's case, a subtle worldly temptation. His ideal was *God alone*. He was not ready for the apostolate that God Himself would initiate later on. It is a *certain sign* of the Holy Spirit when one with true, sincere, interior purity of love for God seeks abjection

38. Schuster, 43; the reference is to *Aeneid*, 7:1-4, which refers to Aeneas burying his nurse Caieta upon reaching southern Italy.

39. "above the entrance of the church" (c. 1; col. 128C).

40. "preferring to endure the hostility of this world more than to receive its praises" (c. 1; col. 128C).

and hiddenness rather than to be in the limelight. {There is} no false humility here. {He is} not escaping in disgust from a world that shames him by his praises, but {is motivated by} a sincere desire for God, for intimacy with Him unobscured by the smoke-screen of human adulation, which blinds and perverts the clear vision of the soul.

*Plus pro Deo laboribus fatigari.* . . .[41] In addition to the sincere desire for a humble and hidden life, here is the desire for *labor and poverty*—not just labor as an amusement, a recreation: *laboribus fatigari,* labor as a salutary penance, labor in a spirit of compunction. Note how this key passage, on St. Benedict's vocation, is filled with the spirit of compunction, a spirit of salutary sorrow at the nothingness and dangers of the world, and at the thought that true values, the love and will of God, penance and prayer, are underestimated and neglected by the world which God so loved as to give His only-begotten Son to save it. So now he even flees from his faithful nurse, and leaves all friends, relatives, etc.

*Deserti loci secessum petiit.*[42] Here he is following the classical example of St. Anthony. For the early hermits—to seek the desert was to seek reality: that is to say, to evade the deceptive mirage of the world, and to face the fact that this life is an arid conflict and struggle. Benedict sought solitude in a spirit of *deep compunction*: not the "consolation" of being alone. To be alone in a place like Subiaco for three years would not, at first, be consoling: it would be a severe trial of strength and endurance. Undoubtedly there were very pure and spiritual consolations, but his solitude was first of all penitential, and led through suffering to a higher kind of joy. Subiaco—{note} the nature of the place—a rugged and stony gorge. But St. Gregory with his usual mastery paints an attractive and austere picture of it, with its streams and springs of fresh water. {It is} in the Apennines, forty miles or so from Rome. He speaks of the lake, then of the river which flows from

41. "rather to be exhausted by working for God" (c. 1; col. 128C).
42. "he sought the solitude of a deserted place" (c. 1; col. 128C).

it. *Frigidas atque perspicuas emanat aquas.*[43] He meets Romanus, monk of a nearby monastery {and} arranges with him for a secret supply of food. Romanus gives him the habit—"*Sanctae conversationis habitum tradidit.*"[44] He became a monk by this simple act. Why? The very wearing of the habit was the sign that he had consecrated his life to God by conversion of manners (*sancta conversatio*[45]) (*conversatio morum*[46]). It was assumed that this was sufficient. "Let your speech be 'Yea, yea' and 'Nay, nay'."[47] Benedict himself would realize later that it was not sufficient, in the case of most monks, just to put on a habit: there would have to be an explicit vow, which would imply certain very definite obligations. Let us remember however that the mere wearing of a religious habit, although the novice does not yet take vows, implies a desire to consecrate one's life to God, and the intention to live a holy life entirely pleasing to God. The incident of the bell {follows}[48]—{it is} typical of St. Gregory's manner as a writer: incisive, simple, clear. Note the presence of the devil in this story: this is the right place for the devil to make his appearance. Later (c. 2) the devil will make a more formidable assault, in the form of a carnal temptation, which St. Benedict overcomes in the most heroic manner.[49]

*St. Benedict overcomes temptation.* {Note the} delicacy and clarity of the story: the little bird fluttering around the saint—the suggestion that follows—his impetuous heroism, and the delicate

43. "it pours forth cold and clear waters" (c. 1; col. 128C).

44. "he provided the habit of a holy way of life" (c. 1; col. 128C).

45. "holy way of life" (*RB*, c. 21, which reads: "*sanctae conversationis*"; McCann, 68).

46. "conversion of manners" (*RB*, c. 58, which reads: "*conversatione morum suorum*"; McCann, 130); see below, n. 119, for the significance of this term.

47. Matt. 5:37.

48. Romanus lowered bread down to Benedict on a rope with a bell attached to let Benedict know when it was coming; the devil broke the bell by throwing a stone at it (c. 1; col. 130A).

49. He throws himself naked into a patch of briars and nettles (c. 2; cols. 132AD, 134AB).

psychology of the narration. He is at first obsessed, then returns to himself, called by grace, and throws himself into the nettles and briars nearby. It is, says St. Gregory, a question of fighting fire with fire—*bene poenaliter foris ardere . . . Vicit peccatum quia mutavit incendium.*[50] The problem of temptation is the problem of rechanneling the force of desire, and turning the energy of concupiscence into anger against oneself and holy desire for the justice of God—arming oneself against the flesh with a burning zeal for the will and law of God. True love cannot subsist without this foundation of burning zeal. If we do not hunger and thirst after justice and righteousness, the desires for our own selfish satisfaction and the gratification of the flesh will overcome us. The spirit of *generosity in penance and mortification* is therefore essential to the Benedictine life and *Rule*: but we must not overlook the fact that here we see Benedict in an early stage of his development, and reacting to temptation in a way that is, in its practical details, neither demanded nor recommended for all his disciples. All must be generous and uncompromising in renunciation of self, but all are not called to take an equally dramatic or drastic exterior way of fighting temptation. {The} reason {is that} in very many cases this would not work at all but would have the opposite effect. This is a good example of a case in which we should imitate the *spirit* with which a saint overcomes himself, and reproduce his generosity, while not at the same time taking the exact same exterior means that he used. We should take the means explicitly prescribed in the *Rule*—and use them with the *spirit* of ardent generosity here portrayed.

Having overcome the flesh in this heroic manner, St. Benedict has reached the end of the active life. He has attained to *apatheia* or complete control of the passions, and is now entitled to undertake the direction of souls. Observe carefully that in all this, St. Gregory is simply following the steps laid out by theo-

50. "he made himself burn exteriorly through this salutary pain . . . He overcame sin by exchanging fires" (c. 2; col. 132C, which reads ". . . *arderet* . . . *Vicit itaque* . . .").

logical tradition in his time—Cassian, the Greek Fathers, etc. *Praxis*—culminating in *apatheia*—leads to *theoria* and {a} capacity for charismatic spiritual fatherhood. As long as one is dominated by the eight capital vices, one is not able to see the light of God with an untroubled eye, and one does not have enough light to see into the souls of others and guide them. From this time on, it is explicitly said,[51] St. Benedict feels no more any movements of the flesh. Again, this is a very special charismatic grace, appropriate for one who had a particular mission, the spiritual fatherhood of all Western monasticism. Cf. St. Thomas received the same grace,[52] because it was necessary for his theological mission—but note at the same time the balance and sanity of St. Thomas' own teaching: we do not have to be free from all first movements of passion in order to lead virtuous and fruitful lives.[53] Even St. John of the Cross teaches this.[54] Avoid wrong and

51. Col. 132C.

52. See Jacques Maritain, *The Angelic Doctor: The Life and Thought of Saint Thomas Aquinas*, trans. J. F. Scanlon (New York: Sheed & Ward, 1931), 30–31: "The story is a familiar one, how 'the young and pretty damsel, attired in all the blandishments of love' was introduced into the bedroom where Thomas lay asleep; how he rose and, snatching a brand, drove the temptress out and burned the sign of the cross upon the door. And thenceforth, by an angelic grace, was never troubled by any impulse of the flesh."

53. See *Summa Theologiae*, 1a 2ae, q. 59, a. 2 ("Can There Be Moral Virtues Together with Passions"), in *Summa Theologiae*, ed. Thomas Gilby, OP, *et al.*, 61 vols. (New York: McGraw-Hill, 1964–80), 23.82/83–86/87.

54. See *The Ascent of Mount Carmel*, Bk. 1, c. 11: "it is true that all the desires are not equally hurtful, nor do they all equally embarrass the soul (we are speaking of those that are voluntary), for the natural desires hinder the soul little, or not at all, from attaining to union, when they are not consented to nor pass beyond the first movements (that is, all those wherein the rational will has had no part, whether at first or afterward); and to take away these—that is, to mortify them wholly in this life—is impossible. And these hinder not the soul in such a way as to prevent attainment to Divine union, even though they be not, as I say, wholly mortified; for the natural man may well have them, and yet the soul may be quite free from them according to the rational spirit" (*The Complete Works of Saint John of the Cross*, ed. and trans. E. Allison Peers, 3 vols. [Westminster, MD: Newman Press, 1946], 51–52).

exaggerated (essentially Stoic and pagan) ideas of *apatheia*.[55] At the same time, the negative work of asceticism being done, St. Benedict does not relapse into pure quiet and passive contemplation. He brings forth fruits of every virtue.

*St. Benedict becomes famous as a father of souls*. Discovered by a visiting priest (illumined by God Himself) and by shepherds, Benedict begins to attract disciples. He unwillingly accepts the abbotship of Vicovaro. They try to poison him, and he returns to solitude. He plunges into deeper and more perfect contemplation. *Solus in Superni Spectatoris oculis habitavit secum*.[56] The interesting commentary on this is entirely St. Gregory's spirituality, but one may assume that it is also quite proper to St. Benedict. St. Gregory's explanation {is that} it was better to retire without resistance than to waste his time and lose peace in a futile struggle —in which he would have lost his own soul without gaining theirs. The Prodigal Son in the "far country" does not "return" —not with his true self. "*Vagatione mentis et inverecunditia sub semetipso cecidit?*"[57] Gregory adds {that} Benedict might have stayed at Vicovaro if there were *some good ones* he could have helped. The idea of *cordis custodia*[58]—which is certainly found in the *Rule*[59]—is the basis of the degrees of humility and forms the

55. See "*The Question of Apatheia*" in Thomas Merton, *An Introduction to Christian Mysticism: Initiation into the Monastic Tradition 3*, ed. Patrick F. O'Connell, Monastic Wisdom [MW], vol. 13 (Kalamazoo, MI: Cistercian Publications, 2008), 102–106.

56. "He dwelt alone with himself before the eyes of the Heavenly Observer" (c. 3; col. 136B).

57. "He fell beneath himself through the unsteadiness of his mind and his shameless behavior" (c. 3; col. 138B, which reads ". . . *et immunditia sub semetipsum* . . .": Merton is evidently relying on a different version of the text here).

58. "guarding the heart".

59. The phrase itself is not found in the *Rule*, but cf. "*Qui malignum diabolum aliqua suadentem sibi cum ipsa suasione sua a conspectibus cordis sui respuens, deduxit ad nihilum*" ("Who has in some way brought to nothing the evil demon tempting him, driving him along with his temptation away from the sight of his heart") (Prol.; McCann, 8, 10) and "*Cogitationes malas cordi suo advenientes mox ad Christum allidere, et seniori spiritali patefacere. Os suum a malo vel pravo eloquio custodire*" ("To

substance of the first degree which is the foundation of the whole ascetic structure of the *Rule*. It is also prominent in all Benedictine mysticism: see especially Dom Augustine Baker, *Sancta Sophia*.[60] Attention to our own soul, purity of conscience, which permits us to see at once if anything is contrary to the will of God in us {is} *not* introversion in {the} psychological sense. The basis {is} not allowing ourselves to be carried away out of ourselves with trifles and superficial pursuits that lead nowhere. {See also} St. Bernard's *curiositas*[61]—concerning ourselves with things that have nothing to do with God's will for us and contribute nothing to our salvation. Note—this must not be taken in too absolute and rigid a sense. A person can have Benedictine *custodia cordis* and yet retain a variety of interests and occupations. It is not so much a matter of what you do and what you know, as how you do it and how you know it. Here too the motive is all-important. Cultivate self-custody not by strained and rigid introspection which leads to an unhealthy state, but by seeking God in all things and embracing His will with simplicity wherever it is made known to us. {The} emphasis {is} on sincerity—loyalty to truth.

---

dash immediately against Christ evil thoughts coming into one's heart, and to reveal them to one's spiritual father. To guard one's mouth from evil and depraved speech") (c. 4; McCann, 28).

60. Augustine Baker, *Sancta Sophia, or Directions for the Prayer of Contemplation*, ed. Serenus Cressy (Douay: John Patte and Thomas Fievet, 1657); *Holy Wisdom, or Directions for the Prayer of Contemplation, Extracted out of More than Forty Treatises . . . by Serenus Cressy*, ed. James Sweeney, 2.1.8.9 (New York: Harper, 1950), 238–39: "All the duties of mortification (and consequently the exercise of all virtues) may be reduced to *custodia cordis*, which is a wary guard of our heart, and it consists in not pouring forth our affections inordinately upon creatures, nor admitting into our souls any inordinate love: it is a chariness over our interior, to keep it in as much quietness as we can"; see Merton's article, "Self-Knowledge in Gertrude More and Augustine Baker," in *Mystics and Zen Masters* (New York: Farrar, Straus and Giroux, 1967), 154–77.

61. This is the first step of pride in St. Bernard's *De Gradibus Humilitatis et Superbiae* (X.28–38; *PL* 182, cols. 957B–963A); see also Appendix I, "Curiositas," in Étienne Gilson, *The Mystical Theology of St. Bernard*, trans. A. H. C. Downes (New York: Sheed & Ward, 1940), 155–57.

As Benedict was now famous, numerous disciples gathered around him at Subiaco. Here he divided them up into groups of twelve in separate houses, under minor superiors, according to the Pachomian tradition. It was at this time that he was joined by recruits from the Roman nobility, including St. Placid and St. Maur. At Subiaco, St. Benedict works several miracles and other stories are told of him which give indications as to his character:

1. (c. 4)—the monk who could not stay in choir during the "*oratio*"[62]—which all authorities take to be mental prayer. Hence there was mental prayer in common in the earliest Benedictine houses. Benedict does not hesitate to use corporal punishment to deliver a monk from the evil spirit of negligence and distraction. Benedict demands serious attention to prayer and the spiritual life, and knows *the danger of sloth and neglectfulness*. We must be persuaded, with him, that it is not enough just to "be in the monastery"; one must also constantly strive to live a life of prayer as a true monk, and to make the sacrifices that this demands. It means we cannot give in to whims and to desires for our own convenience all the time.

2. (c. 5)—because of the inconvenience given to the monks of three houses up on top of the cliff, Benedict works a miracle so that there will be a spring on top of the mountain and they will not have to come down to the lake every day. Some of the desert fathers would undoubtedly have disapproved—they made a virtue of walking miles to get a little water. Note: St. Benedict, far from receiving their complaint with a rebuke, consoles them (*blande consolans*[63]).

3. (c. 6)—the *Gothus pauper spiritu*[64]—who had received the task of cleaning away briars by the lakeside, a site for a new garden. He drops the sickle in the lake, and Benedict gets it back miraculously, but above all we note the gentleness and kindness

62. Col. 142A.

63. "gently consoling" (col. 144A).

64. "Goth who was poor in spirit" (col. 144B, which reads "*Gothus quidam* . . ." ["a certain Goth . . ."]).

with which he gives it back to the Goth—*Ecce labora et noli contristari.*[65] All these little indications are of great significance. St. Benedict *might* have said, "You careless numbskull, don't you know that all the tools are to be treated as the vessels of the altar?[66] Would you throw a chalice in the lake, you sacrilegious rascal?" etc. etc.

4. (c. 7)—the famous rescue of St. Placid by St. Maur. St. Benedict sees the accident in {a} vision. St. Maur asks a blessing—then *runs*, and keeps on running, even over the water. St. Benedict attributes everything to the merit of obedience. St. Placid says he saw the Abbot's *melotes* (cowl?) over him.

*The Transfer to Monte Cassino*: another attempt {is made} to poison St. Benedict {by} his enemy, the local priest Florentius (St. Gregory adds *hujus nostri subdiaconi Florentii avus* . . .[67]). Benedict gives the poisoned bread to a friendly crow that shows up every day at dinner time . . . etc. Then Florentius hatches a plot to harm the souls of St. Benedict's young disciples. Note that St. Benedict is not excited or scandalized. He looks out the window gravely and quietly decides to move to another place. This is the cause of the move to Monte Cassino. Note St. Benedict's refusal to rejoice at the punishment visited upon his enemy. Again, his sense of deeper realities {is paramount}. He laments his death and the possible loss of his soul. All through the narrative one gains a vivid impression of a *man who sees things differently, whose eyes penetrate into the values of a higher world*. This indeed is one of the outstanding characteristics of St. Benedict.

*St. Benedict vs. the Devil*: note—the devil pursues him to Monte Cassino. "*Loca non hostem mutavit.*"[68] {Note the} traditional idea that the monk is the enemy of the devil, the chosen instrument, the soldier of Christ who, by his prayers and self-denial, continues the work of the Incarnation which is a reconquest, by

65. "So then, go back to work and don't be upset" (col. 144D).
66. Cf. *RB*, c. 31 (McCann, 82).
67. "the grandfather of our own subdeacon Florentius" (c. 8; col. 148A).
68. "He has changed his place but not his enemy" (c. 8; col. 152A).

God, of His creation. Man plays a central part in this, the work of spiritualizing and divinizing the world. But note that the principal part is played by the great saints, those with special charismatic gifts, special purity of heart. It is clear that the other monks, more or less helpless, and not always aware of what is going on, depend almost entirely on St. Benedict to defend them, save them, open their eyes, undo the harmful work of the evil one, etc.

1. Benedict drives out the devil from Monte Cassino, in destroying the pagan shrines. Worship of the devil is united with worship of nature for its own sake; paganism and diabolism {are} intimately connected. (The devil curses Benedict—punning on his name—for "persecuting" him.)

2. {The} devil sits on a big stone so the monks cannot move it until St. Benedict gives his blessing. Then {follows} the *phantasticum incendium*[69] in the monastic kitchen. The devil overturns a wall and kills a young (child) monk. St. Benedict restores him to life.

*The severity of St. Benedict*: the discretion of St. Benedict must not be confused with softness. Realizing the seriousness of the struggle with sin and with the devil, St. Benedict is always firm and stern in regard to essential principles. He does not give in, where they are concerned (cf. the monk who kept leaving choir during mental prayer, above[70]). Several instances of sternness—in the matter of monks *disobeying* by eating outside the monastery —are supported by miraculous knowledge on the part of the saint. {It is} also {evident} in the matter of *poverty*.

1—Eating outside the monastery. Here it is a matter of a *custom of the house—mos cellae*.[71] (Later it became a point of rule not to eat outside without permission.) Two brethren are out late, and eat at the house of a pious lady. On returning, they do not make known the fact to St. Benedict and they deny having eaten when

69. "illusory blaze" (c. 10 [title]; col. 154B).

70. Page 28 (c. 4).

71. C. 12; col. 156B.

he reproaches them. He shows that he knew all about it; they fall at his feet and he forgives them because he knows they will not do it again, aware that he will be "present" wherever they are (c. 12).[72] Note—the issue whether or not it is serious in itself to eat outside {the} monastery does not arise. This is not considered. It is a point of *obedience*. Also the monks were in bad faith, because they tried to hide their action. Benedict therefore demanded *great fidelity in the smallest points of obedience*. "Let no one in the monastery follow the will of his own heart"[73]—this was to him a principle of primary importance, and one on which he did not compromise. Undoubtedly there is much that is light matter, and what is trivial must not be treated as a mortal sin. And here was slight matter, which St. Benedict easily overlooked, as long as the *principle of perfect obedience* was maintained. This is very important for a true understanding of the spirit of St. Benedict.

2—Note Benedict even rebuked the secular brother of one of the monks who had a resolution to come fasting to the monastery on his visits, and who broke this resolution once on the insistence of a fellow traveler.

3—The slave Exhilaratus—bringing two bottles of wine to the monastery—hides one for himself. St. Benedict knows of it, and knows that the wine has been changed into a serpent. Here we have two stories (this and the above) which legend may have embellished for the purpose of underlining St. Benedict's prophetic power.

4—Benedict is severe to a monk who tries to keep for himself some handkerchieves he had been given. {This is} a clear violation of poverty in which St. Benedict does not compromise. Note he is always gentle and kind with the offender, without relaxing on the point of principle.

5—He is equally severe with *proud thoughts*.

We conclude—that to be true sons of St. Benedict we must be extremely faithful even in the smallest points of obedience,

72. Col. 158B.

73. *RB*, c. 3 (McCann, 24/25).

poverty, humility of heart, avoiding {a} critical spirit, and all levity or sloth and carelessness. These are *essential* to St. Benedict's spirit. All these stories, though perhaps embellished in certain details, give us a very clear view of St. Benedict's spirit. It is definitely not a spirit of easy-going compromise. St. Benedict takes a very broad view of his principles, he considers the weakness of human nature, he is realistic and kind, but in the essentials thus laid down he is inflexibly firm. He does not demand heroic corporal macerations, or any of the ascetic feats of the desert fathers. But he does not dispense his monks from these in a spirit of relaxation. On the contrary, he realizes that these are all accidental, and that the true self-denial is in the denial of our will, our desires, and in the breaking off of all attachments.

*St. Benedict tolerates no inordinate attachments whatever.* This point must be made very clear, because so many take advantage of Benedict's discretion in order to favor the weakness of sinful nature in dangerous ways. This is by no means the spirit of the saint. He is realistic and kind toward nature, but he is never indulgent to self-love and to sin. Hence, though there is abundant food, sleep, etc. and the life is not too hard on the body, and the atmosphere of the life is luminous and joyful, filled with all the consolations of a supernatural family spirit, nevertheless there is a price which must be paid. The monk *must renounce himself.* To live without renunciation and penance is not to live as a monk.

St. Benedict is unyielding in his demand for:

a) perfect, uncompromising obedience, even in the smallest points, the slightest indications of the will of the superior;

b) perfect poverty—"*nihil omnino*"[74]—complete detachment from all material possessions, no exercise of ownership, no use of anything whatever without permission;

c) fidelity in good works, keeping good resolutions, perseverance in prayer, works of penance;

d) fidelity to the common life of the monastery is asked in a heroic degree—no one is to absent himself arbitrarily from com-

74. "nothing at all" (*RB*, c. 33; McCann, 84).

mon exercises, or from the common activities of the brethren (cf. the monk and mental prayer).

These are merely the points which we draw from the last few pages we have considered in the *Vita Benedicti*. There are of course many others. These are typical and suffice to make the desired point: ST. BENEDICT WILL COUNTENANCE NO COMPROMISE ON ESSENTIAL PRINCIPLES, ESPECIALLY OBEDIENCE AND POVERTY.

*Some other points on which St. Benedict showed himself severe*:

chapter 28—When someone asked for a little oil, St. Benedict was angry when the request was not granted. The one who refused to give the oil explained that then there would be none left for the monks. St. Benedict threw the bottle over the cliff, rather than retain anything that should have been given "as to Christ."[75] Here again, the matter is primarily obedience, but it also involves the *faith* by which the monk ought to see Christ in the needy, and ought to listen to the words of the Lord instructing to "give to all who ask of you."[76] On this St. Benedict could not see any possibility of compromise. Would that we shared some of his faith. However on one point the Lord Himself set aside the severity of St. Benedict in favor of the higher law of charity. The occasion was that of St. Scholastica's visit to him. He was with her all day in the guesthouse outside the gate and insisted on returning to the monastery at night according to his principles, but her prayers prevailed, a great storm arose, and St. Benedict was forced to spend the night in "holy conversation"[77] with his sister. Thus the Lord showed that He preferred charity to principle. However it was a special occasion—as St. Scholastica knew it was to be their last meeting on earth.

*The Interior Life and Prayer of St. Benedict*:

1. It is based above all on the solid foundation of Gospel virtues—unshakeable faith and confidence in God. St. Benedict

75. *RB*, c. 36: "*ut sicut revera Christo ita eis serviatur*" ("so that truly service may be given to them [i.e. the sick] as to Christ" (McCann, 90).

76. Lk. 6:30; cf. Matt. 5:42.

77. C. 33; col. 194B.

was one who firmly believed that having left all for God, he would always be taken care of by his heavenly Father. Cf. chapter 21—where he rebukes the lack of confidence of his monks when they see there is no more wheat, in time of famine. (Note he rebukes and comforts them at the same time.)

2. More than anything else, he is a *kind and compassionate* Father, with a great tenderness and understanding of human frailty. He is only severe when this is really necessary to deliver one from a fault—that is to say his severity is *medicinal* only, never merely punitive. He is a man of *longanimity and patience*. That is to say he has a great ability to *bear in silence* things which would rouse others to anger. He knows how to wait upon God's time, and is slow to get excited about anything. But this longanimity is closely connected with prayer. St. Benedict built the edifice of his interior life upon this longsuffering patience—meekness, gentleness. This is something we seem to have forgotten in modern times. A life of prayer that does not rest on meekness and patience, a life of prayer that cannot "take" many things in silence, has no solidity. The one who is impatient can *never really be a man of prayer*. He can pray sometimes, indeed, but sooner or later his own violence will disrupt his prayer, or he will find himself subject to strain. One of the most impressive features of St. Benedict is his monumental *calm*: cf. chapter 31—how he liberates the serf from the Goth Zalla. This chapter gains in effect from the vivid contrast between St. Benedict and Zalla—{the} violence of the latter, driving the bound slave up the road with whips—we have already learned that a priest or cleric could hardly escape from Zalla's hands alive. St. Benedict is found sitting outside the monastery gate, reading. Here we have not only a contrast with the violence of Zalla, but with the comparative violence of St. Benedict's own youth. The heroism of Subiaco is here transcended by Benedict's supreme simplicity. He does not even look up when Zalla approaches, shouting *magnis vocibus*.[78] The bonds of the serf fall off when St. Benedict looks at them—Zalla falls to the ground in fear.

78. "in a very loud voice" (col. 190B).

3. St. Benedict's life is full of *simplicity and love of order*. We must not think of Benedict as one who liked to organize for the sake of organizing—one for whom good order was a kind of fetish. In a word, he is by no means an obsessive character. The taste for order of itself is not enough to make a saint—more often it just makes a fanatic. In St. Benedict, order and simplicity are subordinated to prayer and the spiritual life. They are a simplification of life, to do away with obstacles to divine union. *Fidelity and constancy* in a very high degree accompany this simplification of life. To keep the spiritual life simple requires constant care. It is not a matter of following the line of least resistance. We have seen that St. Benedict, in his fidelity to principle, will have nothing to do with compromise.

4. His life of prayer is based on *deep humility of heart and a profound sense of the holiness of God*. Prayer, it must be remembered, is the great reality in the life of St. Benedict—or rather, God is the great reality. And because of this, Benedict remains always a man of prayer, a man who in all simplicity *applied himself* fervently to prayer—{who} would go out at night and pray on the mountain—{who} prayed before the night vigils in a tower room, etc. He is "accustomed to praying at night" alone (c. 35).[79] If we truly have the spirit of St. Benedict we will seek the face of God always in prayer, and will prefer nothing not only to the work of God but also, as did Benedict, to those hours of silent and solitary union with God in interior prayer. Note that the prayer of St. Benedict was frequently and perhaps normally accompanied by tears, when he was alone. Interior sorrow and compunction of heart {are} necessary for prayer.

5. Benedict continued to labor with his monks. Prayer and work were harmoniously united in his own life, as in the lives of the monks. He went out to work with them in the fields. He planned a new foundation (but only one—Terracina). He was zealous in *hospitality*, receiving Christ in guests. He did not look

79. Col. 198AB, which reads "*nocturnae orationis tempora praevenisset*" ("he used to precede the period of night prayer [i.e. with his own private prayer]").

upon the necessary contact with guests and pilgrims as a distraction. His genius, as Ryelandt points out,[80] is essentially *realistic*.

6. *Summary of his moral qualities*—read Ryelandt, *St. Benedict the Man*, p. 50–{52}:

> The physiognomy of St. Benedict, more than any other, is made of qualities apparently opposed, but balancing one another: he is contemplative, living from the divine, and yet he remains eminently a man, not only by his kindness, but also by a faithful attachment to his daily duties, by the humble simplicity with which he holds himself on the same level with all. His gift of organizing brings out the strength of his natural qualities.
>
> A final detail of character ought yet be noted. From the pages of St. Gregory comes the clear impression that the soul of the Patriarch, at the same time holy and human, lived as enveloped in a calm atmosphere of peace. In this soul, essentially well-balanced, where the tender and the strong, the simple and the grave, the love of work and of prayer are so excellently united, there reigned a profound peace, the peace of a man who knows that he is united to God and feels himself strong and mild through the inner power that he has from on high.
>
> The peace that St. Benedict loved was certainly that which results from removal from the noises of the world. He loved the quiet of the narrow and deep valley of Subiaco, the sovereign calm of the summit of the holy mountain: the peace of Monte Cassino. But there is another peace than that of the hermits: it depends only on God and the soul. St. Augustine defines it "the tranquility of order." It results from truth, from true goods, from justice, from all that which

80. "The Legislator of monks by his nature was of a positive character, a realist, concerned more with the practical than with theoretical speculation. His genius was indeed Roman and far from the more exclusive contemplative tendencies of the ascetics of the East" (Idesbald Ryelandt, OSB, *St. Benedict the Man: Authorized Translation of The Moral Physiognomy of St. Benedict*, trans. Patrick Shaughnessy, OSB [St. Meinrad, IN: Grail, 1950], 47–48).

> we have done and are—in ourselves and before God. This interior peace, gift of the Holy Ghost, ruled sovereignly in the soul of St. Benedict. It summarizes the supreme interior harmony of this profound and fertile existence.[81]

In a word, the whole life of St. Benedict is a life of simple and realistic love for God and for our neighbor. It is simply living the Gospel without fanfare. Note that St. Benedict, unlike so many others, did not make a great fuss about the fact that he was living the Gospel, and did not go around contrasting his practice with that of others and accusing them of laxity. He simply *lived* the Gospel without talking about it. The mainspring of everything in St. Benedict is the *love of Christ*—in Himself, in the poor, in the monastic community, in the individual brethren. *Amori Christi omnino nihil praeponere.*[82] This is the key to the monastic life and spirit. {The} monastic community *is Christ*. *All the other virtues are for St. Benedict merely exercises of love.* Obedience is the sign of one who loves Christ above all else. Silence {is} the mark of one who prefers interior union with God to exterior dissipation and self-seeking in amusement. Humility is impregnated with love. The divine praise in choir is a supreme exercise of love. Manual labor is an act of love, etc.

*What then was the degree of prayer which was the fruit of this interior life*? Towards the end of his life, Benedict is praying alone in a tower room before the others are awake. He prays how? standing at the window (*ad fenestram stans*[83]) looking out over the sleeping countryside. (Note: St. John of the Cross also liked to pray at a little window in a tower.[84]) *Omnipotentem Deum*

81. Copy text reads: 50–51; the quotation from St. Augustine is from *The City of God*, 19.13.

82. "to prefer nothing at all to the love of Christ": this is a conflation of *RB*, c. 4 ("*Nihil amori Christi praeponere*") (McCann, 26) and *RB*, c. 72 ("*Christo omnino nihil praeponant*") (McCann, 160).

83. C. 35; col. 198B.

84. While prior at Los Martires in Granada, beginning in January 1582, John of the Cross liked to pray at a window in a nook at "the corner of a staircase from which he could see a vast expanse of sky and countryside" (Bruno de Jésus-Marie,

*deprecans*[85]—this seems to indicate prayer of supplication, petition, but is not to be taken too strictly. In the midst of the darkness he suddenly sees a great light, brighter than the light of day. In this light, he sees the "whole world gathered together as though in one ray of the sun"[86]—a contemplative intuition of creatures in God, of creation itself in God—an intuition of the divine wisdom, the *Sophia* of God, containing all things. {This is} not a direct vision of the divine essence. St. Thomas explains (IIa IIae, Q. 180, a. 5 ad. 3)[87] it was a divine illumination in which all things are seen, not a vision of God Himself, but a vision of a divine light considered as somehow distinct from the divine essence—a light in which creatures are seen though not God Himself. What else {is it} but the wisdom of God? The vision is not enough in itself—he receives a prophetic vision of the soul of Germanus, bishop of Capua, ascending into heaven. Benedict was a soul of the highest contemplation, whose prayer was united with lofty charismatic gifts as well as attaining the heights of mysticism.

The beautiful death of St. Benedict is the climax of his life of prayer. Perhaps {it takes place on} Holy Thursday, 547. He dies in the midst of the brethren, "standing" in prayer,[88] supported by them after receiving the Holy Eucharist.

---

OCD, *St. John of the Cross*, trans. Benedict Zimmermann, OCD [New York: Sheed & Ward, 1936], 259).

85. "praying to almighty God" (c. 35; col. 198B).

86. C. 35; col. 198B.

87. St. Thomas Aquinas, *Summa Theologiae* (Gilby, 46.34/35): the whole article (30/31–34/35) deals with the question "Whether in this life the contemplative life can attain the vision of the divine essence."

88. C. 37; col. 202B.

## Part 3—*The Rule of St. Benedict*

*Date of the Rule—Texts—Commentaries*

*Date of the Rule*—Although the date of the *Rule* is not certain, all authors agree that:

a) It must have been written at Monte Cassino.

b) It is most likely that he wrote it after 534, as he apparently quotes the *Rule* of St. Cesarius, which was written before that time. It has been proved that St. Cesarius was not quoting St. Benedict—therefore—(cf. Schmitz, *Histoire de l'Ordre de Saint Benoît*, vol. I, p. 20, note 14[89]).

c) It is most likely that the *Rule* was not written all at once—it is evident that there were additions, corrections, etc. Especially see the obvious "conclusion" (?) to chapter 66; another, chapter 72.

d) It is very clear that the *Rule* was written not only for Monte Cassino but also for other monasteries. It envisages different climates, etc. On the date of the *Rule*—read McCann's Preface, p. viii–ix.[90] McCann believes that the section on punishments is the most ancient part of the *Rule*; that a first draft ended with chapter 66, etc.

89. Philibert Schmitz, *Histoire de l'Ordre de Saint-Benoît*, 7 vols. (Liège: Éditions de Maredsous, 1948–1956).

90. McCann suggests that the earliest parts of the *Rule*, providing a horarium for the office, study and work, duties of officials, and punishments for breaches of discipline, would date back to Benedict's time at Subiaco early in the sixth century, and that "St Benedict composed his Rule, so to say, 'as he went along', adding from year to year the conclusions suggested by experience and by his monastic reading, and in this gradual way constructing finally a complete code of monastic observance" (viii); he notes that "the sixty-sixth chapter . . . ends with a sentence that is plainly a terminal one, marking the final point of one draft of the Rule" (ix), followed by a second draft with seven additional chapters, probably completed in the decade 530–540.

*Sources of the Rule*

*Monastic sources*—the chief of these is CASSIAN.[91] There are clear verbal citations (Butler[92]—see his edition[93]) of the *Lives* of St. Anthony and St. Pachomius and from the *VERBA PATRUM* (*Apothegmata*). He also quotes from the following Monastic Rules—St. Pachomius, St. Basil, St. Macarius, St. Cesarius and St. Augustine.[94]

*Other Sources*—{there is} a notable quotation from St. Leo—rather a mosaic of quotations of three sermons of St. Leo[95] in the chapter on Lent (49) (cf. our Breviary[96]). "This implies a careful

91. See Cuthbert Butler, OSB, *Benedictine Monachism* (London: Longmans, Green, 1919), 62–64, which traces the terminology of Benedict's teaching on prayer to Cassian, and 165: "Among the monastic sources the first place is held by Cassian, to whom in matter of direct citation St Benedict is most beholden"; and Butler, ed., *Sancti Benedicti Regula Monasteriorum*, 188 [index].

92. "Of the *Vitae Patrum*, as contained in Rosweyd's great collection, he shows a knowledge of the Lives of Anthony and Pachomius, of Rufinus' translation of the *Historia Monachorum*, and of the collections of 'Apophthegmata' or Words of the Egyptian Fathers: of all these there are clear verbal citations" (Butler, *Benedictine Monachism* , 165).

93. Butler finds echoes of the *Vita Antonii* (*versio antiqua*), c. 13[14] in c. 4: "*Nihil amori Christi* . . ." (21), of the *Vita Pachomii*, c. 25, in c. 4: "*ad lucrandas animas*" (106), and of the *Verba Seniorum*, V.iv.31, in c. 40: "*vinum monachorum omnino non est*" (78); for the *Historia Monachorum*, see the Index (191).

94. "Of the earlier monastic rules, he uses with some frequency the translations of those of Pachomius, Basil, Macarius, and certain other Eastern Fathers; and of Western rules he uses those of Caesarius of Arles, and especially that contained in St Augustine's Letter CCXI, later called his Rule: this is definitely cited several times" (Butler, *Benedictine Monachism*, 165); in his edition, Butler lists numerous parallels but no direct quotations from the *Rule of Pachomius* (190), but specific citations from all the rest: see cc. 33 (68) and 48 (88) for Basil; cc. 43 (82) and 58 (109) for Macarius; Prol. (8) and c. 58 (104) for Caesarius; cc. 35 (72), 52 (95), 54 (100), 64 (119) for Augustine.

95. In his edition, Butler cites *Sermones de Quadragesimae*, 1.2, 4.1, 6 (92; 189 [index]).

96. The *Breviarium Cisterciense Reformatorum*, 4 vols., *Pars Vernalis* (Westmalle, Belgium: Typis Cisterciensibus, 1935) includes extended passages from St. Leo's Lenten Sermons during the night office for the Sundays of Lent: *Dominica Prima Quadragesimae*: second nocturne, *lectiones* 5–8 (*Sermo 4 de Quadragesimo*) (176–78);

reading and minute knowledge of St. Leo's Lenten sermons" (Butler[97]). It also especially recommends St. Leo to our study. Perhaps of all the Fathers he is the one whose spirit is most akin to that of St. Benedict—at least in his sobriety, strength, dignity, depth and profound sense of the liturgical mysteries. {There is also} evidence of familiarity with other Patristic writings.

*Scripture* is of course the principal source of the *Rule*. "His knowledge of Holy Writ is intimate and thorough" (Butler[98]). {He} quotes *mostly from the Psalms and Sapiential Books;* also from {the} prophets. That is in the Old Testament. In the New Testament he quotes freely from everywhere. {For an} example of his use of Scripture—see especially the Degrees of Humility, First Degree:

1. The introduction to Chapter 7—he lays down general principles from the Gospels, {in the} words of Jesus Himself: "Everyone that exalteth himself shall be humbled, everyone that humbleth himself shall be exalted" (Luke 14—READ context—guests at a banquet[99]). This is {the} foundation stone; then also Psalms, and the example of Jacob's Ladder from Genesis (cf. Ps. 130).

2. Beginning the first degree, he quotes several psalms to show the omnipresence and omniscience of God (7, 93, 138, 75). {He} concludes {the} first part of this degree with {a} quote from Ps. 17. Turning to the part of the will—he quotes from Ecclesiastes,

---

*Dominica Passionis*: second nocturne, *lectiones* 5–8 (*Sermo 9 de Quadragesimo*) (242–43); *Dominica Palmorum*: second nocturne, *lectiones* 5–8 (*Sermo 11 de Passione*) (262–64).

97. Butler, *Benedictine Monachism*, 165, which reads ". . . implies careful . . ."

98. Butler, *Benedictine Monachism*, 166, which reads ". . . Writ was . . ."

99. "But he also spoke a parable to those invited, observing how they were choosing the first places at table, and he said to them, 'When thou art invited to a wedding feast, do not recline in the first place, lest perhaps one more distinguished than thou have been invited by him, and he who invited thee and him come and say to thee, "Make room for this man"; and then thou begin with shame to take the last place. But when thou art invited, go and recline in the last place; that when he who invited thee comes in, he may say to thee, "Friend, go up higher!" Then thou wilt be honored in the presence of all who are at table with thee. For everyone who exalts himself shall be humbled, and he who humbles himself shall be exalted'" (14:7-11).

Proverbs, Psalms, goes on with the same and ends with powerful "*haec fecisti et tacui*"[100] from Psalm {50}.[101]

*Language and Texts of the Rule*

The *Rule* is written not in classical and literary Latin, but in colloquial or "vulgar" Latin[102]—or rather it is sometimes more classical, sometimes more colloquial. Some examples: "*Post expletionem trium psalmorum, recitetur lectio una, versus et Kyrie eleison, et* missae . . ."[103] The word "*missae,*" substituted for "*missio,*" had come to signify the concluding prayers of the office, and later was exclusively used in references to the Eucharistic Sacrifice (cf. c. 17). "*Sufficit monacho duas tunicas et duas cucullas habere propter noctes et propter lavare ipsas res*"[104] (c. 55). Because of the colloquial character of the *Rule it was revised* speedily, probably in France. There were many manuscripts made from new monasteries—the *Rule* was copied almost as much as the Scriptures.

The ancient manuscripts fall into *two main groups* (cf. {the} studies of Dom Edmund Schmidt of Wetten Abbey[105]). One group had more vulgarisms. Schmidt thought this was a second edition, and the vulgarisms came from the copyists. Another group was more "correct" in its Latinity. Ludwig Traube[106] completed the

100. "You did these things, and I remained silent" (McCann, 40).

101. Ps. 49[50]:21 (text reads 52).

102. Butler, *Benedictine Monachism*, 169.

103. "After the completion of three psalms, let there be recited one lesson, a verse, the Kyrie eleison, and the concluding prayers" (McCann, 60, which reads: ". . . *expletionem vero trium* . . . *versu* . . ." (*PL* 66, col. 459C reads "*versus*"); see also McCann, 178–79 [n. 40], where he discusses the usage of the term "*missa*" in the *Rule* and elsewhere).

104. "It is sufficient for a monk to have two tunics and two cowls, for nights and for washing these same items" (McCann, 124, which reads: "*Sufficit enim monacho* . . ."); "*propter*" followed by an infinitive ("*lavare*") is not standard classical Latin.

105. *Regula Sancti Patris Benedicti, iuxta Antiquissimos Codices Recognita*, ed. Edmund Schmidt, OSB (Ratisbon, New York, Cincinnati: Frederic Pustet, 1892).

106. Ludwig Traube, *Textgeschichte der Regula S. Benedicti*, 2nd ed. (Munich: Verlag der Königlich Bayerischen Akademei der Wissenschaften, 1910).

work of Schmidt and showed that the text with the vulgarisms was probably the original and the vulgarisms came from St. Benedict! Note the danger of seeing everything the way we ourselves are predisposed to see them. {Having been} taught in grade school by the sisters that slang is awful, we naturally tend to presuppose that St. Benedict would *not* use vulgarisms, etc., etc. The emphasis on gentility in speech with us is a relic of middle-class fretfulness about sliding down in the social scale. Do we have to impose this on St. Benedict *a priori*? Obviously, this does not mean that vulgarity and barbarism in speech is to become a monastic ideal. We do not have to offend our brethren who feel it necessary to be very genteel. The purpose of this remark is that we should remember not to give absolute and universal value to the prejudices of our own time, environment, and social class.

Returning to the two groups of Mss.:

1. Group I—Oxford Ms. etc. The one with fewer vulgarisms—was the most widely accepted text in the seventh, eighth, and ninth centuries.

2. Group II—came into vogue later—was a product of {the} Carolingian *revival*—but was copied *from a text at Monte Cassino which was believed to be St. Benedict's original*. A transcript of this original was sent to Charlemagne {and} became {the} exemplar for this whole group. *One ms. of this group still exists*: St. Gall Ms. 914. "St Gall 914 [if as is probable it is separated from codex of Monte Cassino by only a single link] is an authority for the text of the Rule probably unique in the case of any work of the first six or seven centuries; it may be doubted whether of any other work of such date we possess a copy separated from the original by only one intermediary" (Butler[107]). (But n.b. Butler himself is sceptical whether the Monte Cassino codex contained the actual autograph of St. Benedict.[108] No matter—it is close enough.)

107. Butler, *Benedictine Monachism*, 171.
108. Butler, *Benedictine Monachism*, 172.

3. Group III—a third text—{is a} combination of the above two—with certain glosses here and there. This is the *textus receptus*, the *one most commonly used since the Middle Ages.*

*Printed editions*: our official text, in the martyrology, is the *textus receptus* and differs greatly from the original. *There is an average of one variation per page.* Editions based on St. Gall 914 {include} McCann, Philibert Schmitz, Cuthbert Butler—all available in the novitiate.

*Interpretation of the Rule* according to textual variations—sometimes differences in the text can greatly affect the interpretation of the *Rule*. In chapter 3, l. 20—it is said that a monk must not argue with the abbot. *Textus receptus* says he must not argue *intus vel foris*[109]—in the monastery or outside it. The Monte Cassino text has only *foris monasterium*[110]—Butler concludes[111] that one may argue with the abbot inside the monastery but not outside it. He adds of course a qualification—and shows his interpretation is as follows: one may make polite and respectful representations to the abbot in the monastery, and no representations at all outside the monastery. This would seem to be a case where in fact the gloss makes the mind of St. Benedict *more clear for practical purposes* than the original text. It is more practical not to introduce a subtle and rather indefinite distinction, and simply to say: don't argue with the abbot. Nevertheless, the other reading is more realistic and objective. We should follow it.

Chapter 6—*Et ideo, si quae requirenda sunt a priore, etc. . . .*[112] *Textus receptus* adds: *ne videatur plus loqui quam expedit.*[113] {The}

109. *PL* 66, col. 288A reads "*proterve vel foris*" but notes "*proterve intus vel foris*" as an alternate reading (n. f; col. 288B); Martène notes that "*intus*" is missing in the best manuscripts (col. 295B).

110. "outside the monastery" (McCann, 24).

111. Butler, *Benedictine Monachism*, 176.

112. "And therefore, if anything be sought from the prior . . ." (McCann, 36, which reads: ". . . *si qua* . . .").

113. "lest one seem to speak more than is suitable" (*PL* 66, col. 356C; the note to this clause points out that it is missing in most mss. and rejected by Hildemar); see Butler, *Benedictine Monachism*, 176.

Monte Cassino text ends with {the} simple statement that we ask with humility and detachment or submission and respect. The addition of the gloss seems unnecessary.

Chapter 9 (beginning of {the} night office)—*Textus receptus* prescribes *Deus in adjutorium* etc.[114] Monte Cassino begins the office with no *Deus in adjutorium* but simply three times *Domine labia mea aperies* . . .[115] (Note: we now practice this in {the} office.)

Chapter 41—about the time of meals: the abbot should use his head and not impose {a} fast on Wednesdays and Fridays in summer if it is too hot and if there is a lot of work. He must arrange things so that souls are saved and that the brethren should do what they do . . . *Textus receptus* {reads} *absque* ULLA *murmuratione*;[116] Monte Cassino—*absque* IUSTA *murmuratione*.[117] There is a great difference in spirit between these two readings, and here the Monte Cassino text is more reasonable and more according to the mind of St. Benedict, who takes human beings as they are. Butler remarks that here the Monte Cassino "gives sound and valuable advice" and the other is "utterly paralyzing to all government."[118]

Interpretations of such texts are difficult. Different mentalities tend to read the *Rule* in the light of what they themselves hold and to assume *a priori* that St. Benedict's mind accords with their mind. It is also evident that there has existed a *tradition* all down through monastic history made by lesser men than Benedict, with less inspired discretion and less sense of realism, who have preferred rigid, cut and dried interpretations. But can we here prefer this tradition to the mind of the legislator himself—or to what really seems to be his mind? What is the good of trying to be more Benedictine than St. Benedict and trying to make him conform to our

114. "God, [come to my] assistance" (Ps. 69[70]:2) (*PL* 66, col. 421D).

115. "Lord, open my lips, . . ." (Ps. 50[51]:17) (McCann, 50; see also Butler, *Benedictine Monachism*, 176).

116. "without any complaint" (*PL* 66, col. 657A reads "*justa*" and while it notes that the Oxford Ms. is lacking this word, it makes no mention of "*ulla*").

117. "without justified complaint" (McCann, 98, which reads: ". . . *justa* . . .").

118. Butler, *Benedictine Monachism*, 177.

own rigid views, to save ourselves the trouble of conforming to his wholly supernatural outlook? This shows us some of the difficulties of interpretation of the *Rule*. The fact remains, that while the majority of commentators and abbots and monks for centuries would instinctively prefer that the brethren *never* murmur, St. Benedict would allow (and expect) just complaints. N.B. {the} two-edged interpretation of the "*ulla*" text. It can be read as aimed at the murmuring monks, which may well be what the gloss intended: "monks should *never* murmur!" Yet as it stands it really means (according to the structure of the sentence) the abbot should always, at any cost, arrange things so that the brethren will not complain at all—which would imply the ludicrous conclusion that he must make things utterly soft, rather than allow anyone to murmur at all. {This is a} total subversion of the mind of St. Benedict. Another fruit of textual criticism {is the} discovery of the phrase *CONVERSATIO morum*,[119] in {the} Monte Cassino text, and not *conversio morum*,[120] {as} in {the} *textus receptus*. This is important for the vow of conversion of manners, and will be discussed in that connection.[121] Conclusion: for our purposes, it is necessary to take into account the findings of scholarship regarding the ancient text of the *Rule*, as these findings have a great importance for our true understanding of the mind of St. Benedict. The mentality which would prefer the rigidity and oversimplification of the *textus receptus* is also very likely to be the mentality which hates and distrusts scholarship. We must try not to cultivate such a mentality—it leads to ossification and stupor in the spiritual life.

119. "conversion of manners" (c. 58; McCann, 130); see McCann's n. 91 (196) on the meaning of this term, and his summary note on the use of "*conversatio*" in the *Rule* (n. 107; 202–208), in which he maintains that it has sometimes the primary sense of "conversion" and sometimes the secondary sense of "monastic life and observance" (203); see also Merton's own essay "Conversion of Life," in Thomas Merton, *The Monastic Journey*, ed. Brother Patrick Hart (Kansas City: Sheed Andrews and McMeel, 1977), 107–20, for an extensive discussion of the meaning and usage of the term *conversatio morum* in the *Rule*.

120. *PL* 66, col. 805A.

121. "An Introduction to the Life of the Vows," 163–65.

*Commentaries on the Rule*[122]

1. *Paul the Deacon* (Paul Warnefrid) monk of Monte Cassino in the eighth century, wrote his commentary about 786 after having been in France.[123] {This is} the earliest commentary on the *Rule*—a unique commentary, written *before* the reform of St. Benedict of Aniane. {It is} not available here. (Note here—St. Benedict of Aniane—*Concordia Regularum*, in Migne.[124])

2. *Smaragdus*[125]—ninth century—Abbot of St. Mihiel near Verdun—"animated with the spirit of the Carolingian monastic movement" (Butler[126]). {This is} a very beautiful commentary, a fine book of meditation on the *Rule* and a wonderful source book for monastic spirituality—very simple, fundamental, solid. It takes us back to the spirit of the monks of a very great period, and yet is eminently practical for our own day. Everyone should read this when he gets the chance—in Migne *PL* (vol. 102) in professed common box.

3. *Hildemar*—{a} monk of Civate, near Milan, ninth century. {This is} really a series of lectures based on Paul the Deacon;[127] {it is} useful where Paul the Deacon is lacking. {It} is in fact available in {the} novitiate common box. {It is} a good commentary full of the ancient spirit. Martène calls it the "*optimum omnium.*"[128]

122. Here Merton follows closely Butler, *Benedictine Monachism*, 177–83.

123. *Pauli Warnefridi, Diaconi Casinensis, In Sanctam Regulam Commentarium* (Monte Cassino: Typis Abbatiae Montis Casini, 1880); according to Claude Peifer, OSB, however, "the work cannot be older than the mid-ninth century; hence the authorship of Paul, who died before 800, is out of the question"; he suggests it is probably by Hildemar: see "The Rule in History" in *RB 1980: The Rule of St. Benedict in Latin and English with Notes*, ed. Timothy Fry, OSB (Collegeville, MN: Liturgical Press, 1981), 125.

124. *PL* 103, cols. 701–1380; this was Benedict of Aniane's commentary on the Benedictine *Rule*, using materials from other pre-ninth-century rules he had collected in his *Codex Regularum* (*PL* 103, cols. 393–702) (see Butler, *Benedictine Monachism*, 181).

125. *Expositio Regulae Beati Benedicti Abbatis* (*PL* 102, cols. 689–952).

126. Butler, *Benedictine Monachism*, 179.

127. *Vita et Regula SS. P. Benedicti: Una cum Expositione Regulae a Hildemaro Tradita* (Ratisbon: F. Pustet, 1880).

128 "the best of all" (*PL* 66, col. 207A).

4. *Medieval Commentaries—Bernard of Monte Cassino*[129] (thirteenth century) {is} valuable for insights into life at Monte Cassino in those times, and for its spirituality. *Boherius*[130] (fourteenth-century monk)—"His main purpose was to illustrate the Rule from the writings of Cassian, St. Jerome, and others" (Butler[131]); {he} depends largely on Bernard of Monte Cassino, but does not equal him. {This is} available in {the} novitiate common box. *Trithemius* (d. 1516) {was} "one of the most remarkable abbots and monks of the early Renaissance, and an earnest reformer of things monastic in German lands" (Butler[132]). {This} commentary {goes} only up to chapter 7, but {is} valuable spiritually.[133] {It} is in the monastery (probably the vault). *Perez*[134] {was} general of a reformed Spanish congregation of {the} post-Tridentine period. After Trent one must admit that the monastic spirit is rather low; although there may be enough regularity in the monasteries, the spirit is no longer that of the early ages.

5. *Commentaries of {the} Seventeenth and Eighteenth Centuries*—{This is the period of} the return to sources. If the spirit of the Order right after Trent had almost run dry, a return to sources in the seventeenth and eighteenth centuries brought new life. *Haeften* {wrote} a theological treatise on the *Rule*—discussing all moot points with great learning but {with a} tendency to rigorism.[135]

129. *Bernardi I Abbatis Casinensis in Regulam S. Benedicti Expositio* (Monte Cassino: Ex Typographia Montis Casini, 1894).

130. *Petri Boherii in Regulam S. Benedicti Commentarium*, ed. L. Allodi (Subiaco: 1908).

131. Butler, *Benedictine Monachism*, 179–80.

132. Butler, *Benedictine Monachism*, 180, which reads: "among the most . . . monks and abbots . . . in the German lands."

133. *Regula S. Benedicti, cum doctiss[imis] et piiss[imis] Commentariis Ioannis de Turre Cremata, S.R.E. Cardinalis, et Smaragdi Abbatis. Item de viris illustribus ordinis S. Benedicti, Libri IIII. Ioannis Trithemij, Abbatis Spanheimen[sis]* (Coloniae Agrippinae: Geruinum Calenium & Hæredes Quentelios, 1575).

134. Antonio Perez, *Commentaria in Regulam S. Patris Benedicti, Monachorum Omnium Patriarchae* (Cologne: Bernardus Gualteri & Petrus Henningium, 1656).

135. Benedictus van Haeften, OSB, *Catechismus Monasticus, Sive, Regulae S. Benedicti Synopsis Analytica: In Gratiam Religiosorum Omni*, ed. Stanislai Sczygielski, OSB (Bamberg: Sumptibus Wolfgangi Mauritii Endteri, 1713–1715).

{This was written} before the work of the Maurist scholars. This work is in the monastery somewhere—probably {in the} vault. *Mège*—{a} Maurist. His commentary[136] was written as a direct reply to de Rancé on the Duties of the Monastic Life,[137] and attacks Rancé's rigorism. It was not popular in its time, and court pressure in {the} time of Louis XIV ({who} favored Jansenism) led to its suppression (in {the} vault). *De Rancé*—replies to Mège in his commentary,[138] insisting on strict and rigid interpretations everywhere; {it} is available in {the} library. *Martène*—{this is} probably the best seventeenth-century commentary;[139] {he} disagrees with both Rancé and Mège, and takes an intermediate stand. {It} is available in {the} novitiate common box, and in Migne *PL* 66 (with the *Rule*).[140] This commentary is *scholarly and well balanced,* with ample quotations from the Fathers and scholastics, one of the most useful and practical commentaries on the *Rule*. Martène was a Maurist. *Calmet*[141]—of the Congregation of St. Vannes—"His commentary is, in my judgement, the best of this group of learned commentaries" (Butler[142])—less archeological than Martène and

136. Antoine Joseph Mège, *Commentaire sur la Règle de S. Benoist* (Paris: Antoine Lambin, 1687).

137. Armand de Rancé, *De la Saintété et des Devoirs de la Vie Monastique* (Paris: François Muguet, 1683).

138. Armand de Rancé, *La Règle de Saint Benoît Expliquée selon Son Véritable Esprit* (Paris: 1689).

139. Edmond Martène, *Commentarius in Regulam Sancti Patris Benedicti Litteralis, Moralis, Historicus ex Variis Antiquorum SS. Commentationibus, Actis Sanctorum etc. Concinnatus* (Paris: Muguet, 1690).

140. Cols. 215–932.

141. Augustin Calmet, *Commentaire Litteral, Historique, et Moral sur la Règle de S. Benoît* (Paris: Emery, 1732); for Merton's plan, never carried out, to write an article on Calmet, see his December 24, 1960 letter to Jean Leclercq (Thomas Merton, *The School of Charity: Letters on Religious Renewal and Spiritual Direction*, ed. Patrick Hart [New York: Farrar, Straus, Giroux, 1990], 138; also found in Thomas Merton and Jean Leclercq, *Survival or Prophecy? The Letters of Thomas Merton and Jean Leclercq* , ed. Brother Patrick Hart [New York: Farrar, Straus and Giroux, 2002], 89).

142. Butler, *Benedictine Monachism*, 182.

perhaps "better brings out the spirit of the Rule" (*id.*[143]); {it is} available in {the} novitiate common box.

{6. *Modern Commentaries*}: *Dom Delatte*—{this is an} excellent modern commentary.[144] *Dom C. Butler: Benedictine Monachism*—all should be acquainted with this scholarly and solid study, one of the best in modern times. Some may not agree with many of Dom Butler's conclusions,[145] but the fact remains that he is one of our best students of St. Benedict and is a great modern representative of the black Benedictine tradition. *Dom Anselme Le Bail*—(mimeographed) Commentary on {the} *Rule*[146]—{this is} exhaustive—the most complete and useful modern Cistercian study of St. Benedict. *Dom Symphorien—La Règle Meditée*[147]—{this is} a work of edification by a Trappist definitor.

## A Spiritual Commentary on the *Rule* of St. Benedict

Having finished with the preliminaries, having gained a sufficient introduction to St. Benedict and seen something of the background of the *Rule*, let us now read the *Rule* itself. For historical and other background, the ordinary commentaries should be consulted. Our main purpose is to look at the *Rule* in so far as it *forms us* as spiritual sons of St. Benedict. Hence we are concerned above all *with the spiritual teaching* contained in the *Rule*. Our remarks will not attempt to exhaust the content of the *Rule*, but simply to:

a) Find the *main spiritual ideas* of the *Rule*, as they appear from page to page. Thus we will establish the *basic principles* on which

143. Butler, *Benedictine Monachism*, 182, which reads: ". . . spirit and meaning of . . ."

144. Paul Delatte, OSB, *The Rule of St. Benedict: A Commentary*, trans. Justin McCann, OSB (New York: Benziger, 1921).

145. Merton is perhaps thinking of Butler's assertion that Benedict is "expressly excluding hermits" from the monastic life he envisions in the *Rule* (*Benedictine Monachism*, 300).

146. Anselme Le Bail, OCSO, "The Spiritual Ideas Contained in the Rule of S. Benedict: A Synthesis of Doctrine" (translated at Gethsemani, Lent, 1955).

147. Symphorien Bernigaud, *La Règle de St-Benoît Méditée* (Nevers: Mazeron Frères, 1909).

our monastic life is to be built. In doing so, we hope the novice will learn to meditate on the *Rule* and study it for himself.

b) Then our main effort will be to *apply these principles* to our daily life in the monastery and study how to use the *Rule* as our guide in the spiritual life.

In this endeavor to apply the teaching of the *Rule* to our life we must remember above all that the *Rule* teaches a way of interior life, a way of the spirit; it forms our souls; it forms our entire lives. It is not merely a body of external regulations to direct the outward actions we perform all day long; it is more than just a legal code, intended to establish good order in the monastery. It is a *discipline* which forms the monk in his entirety, reaches into every department of his life and brings it under the direct action of divine love, of the Holy Spirit. We must first of all look at the *Rule* not merely as the work of a human legislator but as the teaching which God Himself wishes to give us, through the inspired medium of Benedict our lawgiver.

## The Prologue

This is the theological foundation of the whole spiritual doctrine of St. Benedict. The Prologue is packed with dogmatic truths. It is a theology of *Free will and Grace*: of "synergy"—man's cooperation with the divine action. St. Benedict makes clear from the very start that his *Rule* is a *way of salvation*—it is simply *the* one way of salvation (there is only one), the way of the Gospel, adapted and applied to a special class of men—to monks, more specifically to cenobites.

The theological content of the Prologue is made up of the following elements:

1) St. Benedict shows us *God*, Whose desire is that we be saved and united with Him—the end.

2) He shows us *fallen man*, the main characteristic of whom is "sloth of disobedience"[148] and lack of attention to God's will, lack of zeal, lack of *fear*.

148. McCann, 6/7.

3) He shows us the *Word of God,* in Scripture principally, by which God has revealed His plan of salvation to man. This is the word that man must hear, to which he must respond.

4) He shows us the *grace of God,* without which man cannot hear and obey. For this grace man must pray humbly and constantly; otherwise, he will never succeed.

5) He shows us the necessity of good works, which are all summed up in the one word of *obedience* to the divine call and to His will. By obedience we are saved.

6) He shows us that the monastery offers *particularly efficacious means* of carrying on this program. It is a school of divine service and of obedience.

7) The whole theology of the Prologue is a theology of FAITH AND GOOD WORKS—faith bearing fruit in zeal, charity, submission, thirst for God.

Let us take these elements in greater detail.

### 1. God Our Father and Savior

a) It is God Himself who addresses us in the very first lines of the *Rule,* asking us to listen to our Father—He speaks through St. Benedict, but Benedict himself constantly uses God's own word, and effaces himself that God may speak clearly and definitely through his instrumentality. However, the *Magister* and *Pater* of these opening lines is clearly St. Benedict, and the words are his, as instrument, and God's as principal cause.

b) God declares Himself to be a *loving Father* who with deep and tender concern seeks the salvation of His sons and shows them the right path to follow. As a loving Father He seeks above all the attention of our minds and the love of our hearts.

c) God declares through St. Benedict that He will be deeply grieved by our spiritual harm (*de malis actibus nostris contristari*[149]) and will rejoice in our spiritual good. But nevertheless if we reject the bounteous and abundant gifts with which He has showered

149. "saddened by our evil acts" (McCann, 6).

us, in order to save us, we will find ourselves rejected by Him. {He stresses} the sorrow and pain of separation from our loving Father!

d) Hence God is *constantly busy* with His love for us, seeking in every way to save our souls:

1. by an inner light he speaks to our hearts (*ad deificum lumen—divina cotidie clamans vox . . .*[150]);

2. He urges us to hasten, to wake up, to apply ourselves diligently (*currite dum lumen vitae habeatis*[151]);

3. He goes out into "the multitude of the people"[152] like the Householder in the Gospel parable, *quaerens . . . operarium suum;*[153] He seeks a response from anyone and everyone, and when we reply, He hastens to teach us and to show us the way of life; in this doctrine and discipline He sweetly teaches us of His own Fatherly love: *Ecce pietate sua demonstrat nobis Dominus viam vitae;*[154]

4. He invites us to seek union with Him, to dwell with Him in "his tabernacle";[155]

5. He gives us time; He extends our probation that we may have a better chance: *Nobis . . . hujus vitae dies ad indutias relaxantur;*[156] He is patient with us in the extreme because "He does not will the death of the sinner but that he be converted and live";[157]

6. He fills our heart with sweetness and joy in His service; when we respond to His grace, He makes us run fervently in the

150. "to the divinizing light—the divine voice crying out daily" (McCann, 6, where additional phrases separate "*lumen*" and "*divina*" and "*clamans*" and "*vox*").

151. "run while you have the light of life" (John 12:35) (McCann, 8).

152. McCann, 8.

153. "seeking his workman" (McCann, 8); the scriptural reference is to the Parable of the Vineyard (Matt. 20:1-16).

154. "Behold, by his lovingkindness the Lord shows to us the way of life" (McCann, 8).

155. McCann, 8.

156. "The days of this life are extended for us as a time of peace" (McCann, 10).

157. Ez. 33:11 (McCann, 10).

way of His commandments, and shows us how to be generous in sharing in the passion of Christ by patience, and finally He fills our hearts with hope of seeing Him in His Kingdom; this hope makes Him constantly present to the hearts of His sons, for it is His joy to dwell with them.

## 2. Fallen Man and His Way Back to God

(St. Benedict's asceticism: obedience is {the} center of his asceticism: (1) as opposed to {the} asceticism of {the} Desert Fathers; (2) {which emphasized the} father-son relationship of novice and "Abba"; {an} invitation {to live with the Abba prompted} unquestioning obedience: God speaks and acts through him; {eventually} one reaches his level and goes out on one's own. Cf. *bonum* obedientiae:[158]—for which *labor obedientiae*[159] is {the} means.)

a) St. Benedict sums up the whole problem of fallen man in two words: *INOBEDIENTIAE DESIDIAM*:[160] the sloth of disobedience. This is a complex and fairly subtle idea:

1. Refusal to obey—disobedience—{is} a *negation*, denying to God the attention, the respect, the submission, the homage, the love we owe Him as His creatures—a "no" given to God, a rejection of His love and of His care.

2. {It is} a turning away from God. St. Benedict's phrase here indicates not so much the active and malicious open opposition to God which we find in the modern atheist, but rather the sulky, confused, half-passive drifting away, {a} refusal to look, which is rather the attitude of a child who does not want to be bothered to obey, does not want to take the trouble to obey, and hence does not want to *see* and *hear* the expression of his Father's will.

3. *Desidia*: note all the meaning that this word adds to the phrase—the connotations of boredom, futility, aimlessness, inertia, pointlessness of an existence given over to the cult of our own

158. "the good of obedience" (c. 71; McCann, 158).

159. "the work of obedience" (Prol.; McCann, 6).

160. McCann, 6/7.

whims and impulsions. St. Benedict suggests all the emptiness of a life that has lost its point and lost its coherence by the fact that we have turned away from *reality* in neglecting the will of God.

b) The rest of the Prologue is positive rather than negative. St. Benedict shows us not so much what is wrong with us as what we must do to remedy the wrong. However, at the end of the Prologue, he gives another sharp insight into the condition of fallen man: his *weakness and fear*: NON ILLICO PAVORE PERTERRITUS.[161] We who have fallen into "sloth" are afraid of the effort required to return to God. More than that {is involved}, however. It is not just a question of fearing the effort, but St. Benedict in the context tells us implicitly that we also *fear that the effort itself will be useless*. It is a question not only of sloth, but much deeper than that, of a kind of implicit *hopelessness*. "What is the use of trying? I can't make it anyway. See how hard it is already!" Hence we are *irresolute and hesitant*, unable to seize upon a new venture, to make a strong and definite beginning. We are pusillanimous: {we} cannot embrace a great work. Note that for St. Benedict humility is by no means opposed to magnanimity. But our hope must not be based on our own efforts. This is clear from the context, where he tells us to rely entirely on prayer and on the grace of God. Hence implicitly, together with our other faults, is *lack of trust*, which means, basically, lack of faith. By our attachment to our own will and our own way, we are then blinded, weakened, fettered. We lack strength, zeal, courage, desire for good. All these must come to us from a realization of the goodness and love of God—a practical realization which cannot be had unless we take ourselves in hand and make a beginning of our conversion. Once we have begun, we will realize the power of God's grace without which we could not even have begun.

At this point it would be well to look at other passages in the *Rule* where St. Benedict completes for us his picture of fallen man. A composite picture will be most instructive:

161. "not instantly terrified with panic" (McCann, 12, which reads: ". . . *ilico* . . .").

1. We have begun with the picture of man's inertia, laziness, futility, passivity—his lack of hope, his cowardice, his immersion in darkness and confusion.

2. Chapter 1 gives a much more complete picture of fallen man, and his erring ways, *even in the monastic state*. In fact, all through the *Rule*, St. Benedict gives us a very matter-of-fact and realistic picture of monks who are far from perfect. It is for these that he legislates. Let us never forget it: a) Sarabaites—again, soft, irresolute, attached to {their} own will, hypocrites; b) Gyrovages, worse still, relinquish even the appearance of holiness and give themselves frankly to the desires of their own heart and to gluttony.

3. Other chapters: in chapter 2 ({on the} abbot) it is seen that the whole community may perhaps be "restless and disobedient."[162] They may condemn and despise the counsels and orders of the abbot, or argue with him heatedly. Some may be so tough and hard-hearted that the abbot will not be able to handle them except by corporal punishment. {In} chapter 5, St. Benedict foresees an almost universal danger of "murmuring"[163] and interior resistance to the will of the superior, on occasions. This is to be fought generously and without compromise. Everywhere St. Benedict assumes the great danger of PRIDE, attachment to self, refusal to yield to others, leading to rebellion and grave dissension in the community (v.g. c. 65, on the prior[164]). The brethren may try to go so far as to strike and excommunicate one another. They may be carried away by evil zeal, which leads even to hell (cc. 69, 70, 72). For all these very great evils, the *Rule* will prescribe many remedies, but above all humility and obedience in the spirit of charity.

## 3. The Word of God

a. *All through the Rule,* St. Benedict's teaching is simply a clarification of what God Himself has revealed to the Church in

162. McCann, 16.
163. McCann, 16/17.
164. McCann, 148, 150.

the Scriptures. To be more exact, St. Benedict, as a "doctor" and "Father" in a broad sense (he can rightly be numbered among the Fathers of the Church), interprets the Scriptures which God has given to His Church. In a word—St. Benedict is not just *a writer who quotes Scripture* to illustrate or to prove his points: he is a living witness of the Church's understanding of the Scriptures, an instrument of the Holy Spirit clarifying, for the Church, the revealed word of God and adding to the Church's living tradition. Thus through St. Benedict we hear the voice of the Church, the voice of Christ Himself—not the voice of a writer who quotes the words of God, but the voice of God speaking through the Church and to the Church, in a Father and a witness of tradition. St. Benedict, who has told the monk to *listen* (*ausculta*[165]) for every word of God, is himself an instrument well attuned to the voice of the Spirit speaking to the Church, and he is authorized to tell the rest of us what the Spirit says to us all. *CLAMAT NOBIS SCRIPTURA DIVINA, FRATRES, DICENS . . .*[166] (opening words of the chapter on humility, {the} foundation of St. Benedict's ascetic teaching). In the last chapter, when he says that "all perfection is not to be found in the *Rule*,"[167] he refers the monk who wants to go further to search the Scriptures: "what page or what utterance of the divinely-inspired books of the Old and New Testament is not a most unerring rule of human life?"[168] Then he also refers them to the Fathers and especially to Cassian and St. Basil.

b. *In the Prologue in particular*:

1. After the brief introduction, in which he says we are to return to God, and that the first thing to do is to *pray*, he then

165. McCann, 6—the opening word of the *Rule*.

166. "The divine Scripture cries out to us, brothers, saying . . ." (McCann, 36).

167. Not a direct quotation: Benedict writes, "*Ceterum ad perfectionem conversationis qui festinet, sunt doctrinae sanctorum Patrum, . . .*" ("For the one who would hasten toward the perfection of the monastic way of life, there are as well the teachings of the holy Fathers, . . .") (McCann, 160).

168. McCann, 160/161.

intimates that the answer to prayer will be the grace first of all, to *hear the word of God*—not only exteriorly, but interiorly with the ears of our spirit opened by divine grace. *Exurgamus tandem aliquando,* EXCITANTE NOS SCRIPTURA . . .[169] {The} implication {is} that perhaps if Scripture does not speak to the ears of our heart we will never awaken from our sloth. Hence the voice of God in Scripture is all-important, and the grace to hear and realize its urgency is one of the first, essential graces of the spiritual life—the first step in conversion (cf. St. Bernard: *De Conversione*[170]). This implies of course *constant familiarity with the Scriptures*, for how will the Scriptures open the ear of our heart if we do not listen to them?

2. What follows is a condensed outline of the doctrine of conversion, the call of God to souls as it echoes in the pages of Scripture:

*apertis oculis ad deificum lumen*[171]—when we *awaken* (through compunction and holy fear) we open our eyes to the light of grace, a *deifying light*. This light is not only *deifying*, but also *divine*. It comes from God and transforms us into the perfect likeness of God, by making us truly sons of God. A *light* appeals to the intelligence. Hence the ascent is not purely a matter of *blind* faith and doing violence to our will. We must first *see*. And the implication is that we must also be struck by the beauty of the divine light, and enamored of it. Yet if we see, it is only with the eyes of faith. Faith is darkness and light. It darkens the natural reason, but gives light to the spirit, and when we believe and love, then reason itself is enlightened and helps us to advance further into the darkness of faith.

169. "Let us finally arise at last, stirred up by scripture" (McCann, 6, which reads: "*Exsurgamus ergo* . . .").

170. See the opening chapter (*PL* 182, cols. 833B–835D), entitled "*Quod nemo converti ad Dominum, nisi Dei voluntate preventus et ejus voce interius clamante, possit*" ("That no one can be converted to the Lord unless the will of God and His voice calling within have prepared the way"); the divine voice continues to be the focus of the two following chapters (cols. 835D–837B).

171. "with eyes open to the deifying light" (McCann, 6, which reads: ". . . *oculis nostris* . . .").

*audiamus divina cotidie clamans quid nos admoneat vox . . .*[172] When he speaks of the divine voice crying out to us "every day," and then quotes a verse from the invitatory psalm, are we to think he is referring directly and especially to the liturgy? Is he saying that the divine voice cries out to us above all in the liturgy of each day? Doubtless he means that also, but more probably the principal meaning of this sentence is simply that every day, liturgy or no liturgy, God cries out to our hearts: *"hodie si vocem ejus audieritis."* [173] It is because of this fact, among others, that the invitatory psalm was chosen by St. Benedict to open the vigils of every day. In a word then, Benedict does not say that God cries out to us every day because the words occur in the office, but the words occur in the office because God cries out to us every day. It makes a difference which way you look at it. According to one interpretation, God speaks to us in the office. According to the other, He speaks to us in *everything*, and also, very especially in the office. The second is more satisfactory.

*Qui habet aures audiendi . . . quid Spiritus dicat Ecclesiae.*[174] It is by no means a subjective "listening" that St. Benedict preaches. We listen to the Scriptures, in a life in which, by obedience and charity, we enter more and more into *the common faith and the common spirit of the Church.* Hence what we hear in the Scriptures is not merely a special meaning reserved to us privately, but we understand what God has to say to us personally, only because we have the spirit of the Church and in so far as we have that spirit. God speaks to individuals not in so far precisely as they are individuals but in so far as they are members of His Church. (Membership in the Church makes them more truly persons than if they were isolated.)

172. "let us hear the warning that the divine voice, crying out daily, gives us" (McCann, 6, which reads: *"admonet"*).

173. "If today you hear his voice" (Ps. 94[95]:8) (McCann, 6).

174. "He who has ears to hear . . . what the Spirit is saying to the Church" (McCann, 6, 8, which reads: *"ecclesiis"*).

*Et quid dicit?*[175] The voice of God cries out to us in three imperatives: VENITE . . . AUDITE . . . CURRITE—*Come, listen* to me, *hasten*.[176] The voice of God awakens in us *desire and zeal*—and confidence. For if God calls us to Him, and calls us as His sons, then it is the voice of love and tenderness that calls us. Love calls us with equal *tenderness* and *urgency*. We need to be saved. The love of God in St. Benedict is no mere sentimentality. As our Father he wants to teach us and guide us and form us, and show us that the way of salvation is in the fear of the Lord, in filial fear which shrinks from offending His love, not servile fear. *Love* is the great transforming power in the *Rule* of St. Benedict. But he wants us to be men, not babies. We must "run" (again at the end of chapter seven it is the grace of the Holy Spirit and divine charity that makes us "run in the way of God's commandments"[177]). He asks of us a response not of sentimentality but of energetic and generous zeal. There is urgency in this, for the light of life will not always be with us. It is an echo of the Gospel phrase: *"venit nox quando nemo potest operari"*[178] (John 9:4). READ the context of St. Benedict's quote here—John 12:31-41.[179] Note that this

175. "And what does he say?" (McCann, 8).

176. McCann, 8.

177. McCann, 12/13 (n.b. this is part of the conclusion to the Prologue, not the conclusion to chapter 7, which does however stress the role of the love of Christ [*"amore Christi"*] and of the Holy Spirit [*"Spiritu Sancto"*] in drawing people away from vice and toward virtue [McCann, 48]).

178. "night is coming when no one can work" (McCann, 8).

179. "'Now is the judgment of the world; now will the prince of the world be cast out. And I, if I be lifted up from the earth, will draw all things to myself.' Now he said this signifying by what death he was to die. The crowd answered him, 'We have heard from the Law that the Christ abides forever. And how canst thou say, "The Son of Man must be lifted up"? Who is this Son of Man?' Jesus therefore said to them, 'Yet a little while the light is among you. Walk while you have the light, that darkness may not overtake you. He who walks in the darkness does not know where he goes. While you have the light, believe in the light, that you may become sons of light.' These things Jesus spoke, and he went away and hid himself from them. Now though he had worked so many signs in their presence, they did not believe in him; that the word which the prophet Isaias spoke might be fulfilled, 'Lord, who has believed our report, and to whom has

opening and basic section of the Prologue has a definite Johannine character, with this fundamental quote from St. John close to the other from the Apocalypse (2:7).[180] John {is} the Evangelist of light, {emphasizing} the struggle of light and darkness. *In the pericope of St. John,* Jesus is telling the Jews that he must be "lifted up" and they do not understand. They do not understand the meaning of life and death and the passage out of this world to the Father. As in St. John, so in St. Benedict, this text has *a paschal flavor*—Jesus is the light of the world. We must follow Him, or walk in darkness. The prophets were enlightened by Him, Isaias "saw His glory,"[181] but the light shone in darkness and men believed Him not. He leads us into the darkness of the Passion, but at the same time enlightens us with the light of the Resurrection, and His victory over death. The *lumen vitae*[182] is the Easter light, the light of Christ's Victory. But to "run in this light" means to accept the darkness and suffering of the Passion, that we may share in the glory of the Resurrection. Therefore it is above all the light of HOPE. This means that although we work generously we do not place our hope and trust in our works but in the grace of Christ, as St. Benedict will point out later on.

*Quis est homo qui vult vitam?*[183] God attracts us to good by showing us that obedience to His will is the way to life—*veram et perpetuam vitam.*[184] {It is} important in finding true life {to}:

a) Refrain from speaking evil—*prohibe linguam tuam a malo*[185]—avoid all unkind and untrue words, all that injures or

---

the arm of the Lord been revealed?' This is why they could not believe, because Isaias said again, 'He has blinded their eyes, and hardened their hearts; lest they see with their eyes, and understand with their mind, and be converted, and I heal them.' Isaias said these things when he saw his glory and spoke to him."

180. I.e. the reference to what the Spirit is saying to the churches (Rev. 2:7).

181. Jn. 12:41; cf. Jn. 1:14.

182. "light of life" (McCann, 8).

183. "Who is the man who desires life?" (Ps. 33[34]:13) (McCann, 8).

184. "true and everlasting life" (McCann, 8).

185. "keep your tongue from evil" (Ps. 33[34]:14) (McCann, 8).

deceives. The monk must be possessed of truth and meekness in the very depths of his being. Hence {the meaning of} monastic silence {is} not mutism; {it is} not merely for the sake of recollection—not mere absence of noise—but silence so that we can become saturated with goodness and truth, and speak accordingly, when God wills us to speak.

b) Refrain from hypocrisy and deceit: *labia tua ne loquantur dolum.*[186] {This means} not only {to} avoid "speaking" falsely, but every appearance of deception, to lead others into wrong interpretation of our true intentions.

c) *Diverte a malo et fac bonum:*[187] {this means} not only {to} avoid speaking and thinking evil; avoid all evil and *do good.*

d) *Inquire pacem et sequere eam:*[188] and seek true peace—not just an interior peace but peace with all our brethren is meant here.

The result of all this will be constant union with God: His eyes {are} upon us with Fatherly love, His ears ready to hear our prayers.

*Et antequam me invocetis, dicam vobis: Ecce adsum.*[189] We know He is guiding and loving us by the very fact that we seek to please Him. St. Benedict sums up most beautifully in an exclamation that reveals to us the depths of his heart: "What can be sweeter to us, dearest brethren, than this voice of the Lord inviting us? *Behold in His loving mercy the Lord showeth us the way of life.*"[190]

*Domine, quis habitabit in tabernaculo tuo?*[191] The words of Scripture are not only addressed by God to us—but they are also words of men to God—hence a *dialogue* with God in the words

186. "that your lips may speak no deceit" (Ps. 33[34]:14) (McCann, 8).

187. "Turn from evil and do good" (Ps. 33[34]:15) (McCann, 8, which reads: "*deverte*").

188. "See peace and pursue it" (Ps. 33[34]:15) (McCann, 8).

189. "And before you call upon me I will say to you: behold, here I am" (McCann, 8).

190. McCann, 8/9, which reads: ". . . of our Lord . . ."

191. "Lord, who will dwell in your tabernacle?" (Ps. 14[15]:1) (McCann, 8).

of Scripture. We "question Him with the Prophet,"[192] as we advance "following the guidance of the Gospel."[193] God Himself replies and shows us the way—an amplification of what has already been said above.

*Non nobis, Domine, non nobis.*[194] Finally Scripture itself teaches us that when we have done all that God asks of us, we will realize that all our merits are but gifts of His, praising the Lord who works in us. *It is to this summit that the word of God would lead us*—to lose ourselves in praise of His grace. It is easy to deduce from this last and most important quotation that our whole vocation is a life of praise and thanksgiving based on the growing experience of God's mercy and love in our lives. This is the foundation of our praise in the office, and our *lectio divina*[195] and labor teach us more and more this same fundamental truth: that of ourselves we are nothing, that without Christ we can do nothing, but that if we have trust in Him He can and does work in us miracles of grace—and we extend this thought to embrace the entire human race. The monk is never one who is merely selfishly enclosed in his own little interior life.

*Qui audit verba mea haec et facit ea. . . .*[196] The whole spiritual life is centered in this activity of *hearing and doing* the will of God (all the words that come from the mouth of God are by extension the "word of God"). This gives *solidity and stability* to the spiritual life. To build upon the word of God is to build upon rock. Faith gives our life this rock-like solidity. The winds and waves cannot beat down the house of the soul that is firmly established on the word of God and firmly believes in His promises.

*Nolo mortem peccatoris . . .*[197] Here Scripture teaches us two important things:

192. McCann, 8.

193. McCann, 8/9.

194. "Not to us, Lord, not to us" (Ps. 113:9[115:1]) (McCann, 10).

195. "spiritual reading" (c. 48; McCann, 110).

196. "He who hears these words of mine and does them . . ." (Mt. 7:24) (McCann, 10).

197. "I do not desire the death of a sinner . . ." (Ez. 33:11) (McCann, 10).

a) The value of time—it is a gift of God Who, in His patience, prolongs our probation to give us time to amend our lives.

b) The great mercy of God Who loves sinners and does not desire their death but that they should be converted and live. (But He does not want them to remain sinners!)

Such then is the teaching of Scripture about the monastic life as summed up and applied by St. Benedict in his Prologue.

4. The Grace of God ({we} need to meditate on this)

We have seen that the very heart of the Scriptural teaching outlined by St. Benedict above, is the *necessity of grace*. We have seen that our whole monastic life is a growing awareness of the effects of God's mercy in our lives, *culminating in a combination of perfect humility and perfect gratitude*—the sense that we are nothing and that God's mercy is all, and at the same time the perfect confidence that we can always count on His love:

1. Correlative to the *necessity of grace is the necessity of prayer*, for it is by prayer that we obtain grace. This is made clear at the beginning of the Prologue: *Imprimis—quidquid agendum inchoas bonum, ab eo perfici instantissima oratione deposcas*.[198] This is a practical solution to the apparent problems that arise, in connection with "faith and good works"! Grace is indeed all—whatever good we desire to do must be *carried out by the power of God—ab eo perfici*. But at the same time, we have our part—we have to pray and pray fervently with great ardor and greater faith: *instantissima oratione*. This implies *persevering* as well as *trusting* prayer. (N.B. the Canaanite woman: read Matt. 15:21-28[199]—{a} practical application.)

198. "First of all, whatever good work you begin to do, ask with an immediate prayer that it be brought to completion by him" (McCann, 6, which reads: "*Imprimis, ut quidquid . . .*").

199. "And leaving there, Jesus retired to the district of Tyre and Sidon. And behold, a Canaanite woman came out of that territory and cried out to him, saying, 'Have pity on me, O Lord, Son of David! My daughter is sorely beset by a devil.' He answered her not a word. And his disciples came up and besought

2. We realize from the very beginning that we have nothing with which to serve God except His gifts: *OMNI TEMPORE DE BONIS SUIS IN NOBIS PARENDUM EST*.[200] At every instant of our life we must serve Him not just with good things, but with the good things we have received from Him. We have indeed many gifts and they are all good. They are to be devoted to His service and glory and we must praise Him with them at every moment; we are not prohibited from taking joy in this use of His gifts, provided the joy is all referred to Him.

3. Grace also gives us, as it were, spiritual senses by which we perceive the "deifying light"[201] of God. Grace is in fact this light of love that works in our souls, transforming them into the likeness of our divine Exemplar, Jesus Christ.

4. If we respond to the action of grace we will be "astounded" by the discovery that God is always speaking to us, and by the message of love which He addresses to us. *Attonitis auribus audiamus*.[202] This implies that the life of grace is a mystery which interpenetrates our ordinary life and which we apprehend if we can penetrate the surface of things. Thus we discover a "new world" as it were, revealed to us by God, under the surface of everyday existence.

---

him, saying, 'Send her away, for she is crying after us.' But he answered and said, 'I was not sent except to the lost sheep of the house of Israel.' But she came and worshipped him, saying, 'Lord, help me!' He said in answer, 'It is not fair to take the children's bread and to cast it to the dogs.' But she said, 'Yes, Lord; for even the dogs eat of the crumbs that fall from their masters' table.' Then Jesus answered and said to her, 'O woman, great is thy faith! Let it be done to thee as thou wilt.' And her daughter was healed from that moment."

200. "at every moment he should be served by his own good gifts in us" (McCann, 6).

201. McCann, 6.

202. "Let us hear with astonished ears" (McCann, 6; see also 165 [n. 3], where McCann claims that in late Latin words such as "*attonitus*" and "*deificus*" have lost much of their force and should not be translated by strong English expressions like "astonished" and "deifying," which Merton nonetheless continues to do).

5. In this new world we discover a whole new set of values, all centered upon the fact that *God in His mercy is seeking us* (*quaerens Dominus in multitudine populi . . .*[203]), and that our life is really a dialogue with His Fatherly mercy (cf. what was said above[204] about the Word of God). The beauty and consolation of the new life of grace stems from the appreciation of God's "prevenient love." The fact that we can seek Him is due to the fact that we are already sought by Him. The fact that we can invoke Him means that by His grace He is already present in our hearts. *Antequam me invocetis dicam vobis: Ecce adsum.*[205] (Cf. St. Bernard: If you seek Him it is because you have found Him, or rather He has found you.[206])

6. But the fact that God surrounds us with mercy and anticipates our prayers with His grace, does not dispense us from *good works*. Grace must bear fruit in good works, without which we cannot be sons of God and cannot reach the end of our journey, and dwell in "His tabernacle"[207]—cf. the doctrine of John 15:1-8 (read[208]): we must abide in Jesus, the true vine, and abiding in Him we must bring forth much fruit (in this the Father will be

203. "the Lord, seeking amidst the multitude of the people . . ." (McCann, 8).

204. See above, pages 56–64.

205. See above, n. 189.

206. See *De Diligendo Deo*, VII.22 (*PL* 182, col. 987C): "*nemo te quaerere valet, nisi qui prius invenerit. Vis igitur inveniri ut quaeraris, quaeri ut inveniaris*" ("no one can seek you except the one who has already found you. You wish therefore to be found in order to be sought, to be sought in order to be found").

207. McCann, 8.

208. "I am the true vine, and my Father is the vine-dresser. Every branch in me that bears no fruit he will take away; and every branch that bears fruit he will cleanse, that it may bear more fruit. You are already clean because of the word that I have spoken to you. Abide in me and I in you. As the branch cannot bear fruit of itself unless it remain on the vine, so neither can you unless you abide in me. I am the vine, you are the branches. He who abides in me, and I in him, he bears much fruit; for without me you can do nothing. If anyone does not abide in me, he shall be cast outside as the branch and wither; and they shall gather them up and cast them into the fire, and they shall burn. If you abide in me, and if my words abide in you, ask whatever you will and it shall be done to

glorified). But in doing good works and bringing forth fruit, we are at every moment aided and guided and moved by grace. And furthermore we must *realize this* more and more: *Qui timentes Dominum de bona observantia sua non se reddunt elatos; sed ipsa in se bona non a se posse sed a Domino fieri existimantes* . . .[209] God Himself, by grace, does all the good that is done by us. Our free will cooperates, but our merits are only His gifts (St. Bernard[210]). ({This entails} detachment from results.)

7. The fruit of this cooperation between grace and our love is a *pure spirit of praise*. *Operantem in se Dominum magnificant*.[211] This is what the saints do forever in heaven—our heaven begins on earth if we have faith. We must recognize the work of God's mercy in our souls. We do not deny the good that is manifest in our lives, we do not try to pretend that it is not really good, or that it does not exist at all, but we praise God in all simplicity

---

you. In this is my Father glorified, that you may bear very much fruit, and become my disciples."

209. "Those who fear the Lord do not give themselves airs over their faithful observance; but realize that the good works in them cannot be done by themselves, but by the Lord" (McCann, 10).

210. See *De Gratia et Libero Arbitrio*, I.1-2 (*PL* 182, col. 1002A): "*Ubi, ergo, ais, sunt merita nostra; aut ubi est spes nostra? Audi, inquam: Non ex operibus justitiae quae fecimus nos, sed secundum suam misericordiam salvos nos fecit (I Tit. III:5* [*sic*]*). . . . Quid igitur agit, ais, liberum arbitrium? Breviter respondeo: Salvatur. Tolle liberum arbitrium, et non erit quod salvetur: tolle gratiam, non erit unde salvetur. Opus hoc sine duobus effeci non potest: uno a quo fit; altero cui, vel in quo fit. Deus auctor est salutis, liberum arbitrium tantum capax: nec dare illam, nisi Deus; nec capere valet, nisi liberum arbitrium. Quod ergo a solo Deo, et soli datur libero arbitrio*" ("Where then, you ask, are our merits; or where is our hope? Listen, I say: 'Not from works of righteousness which we have done, but according to his mercy has he saved us' (Tit. 3:5). . . . What then does free will do, you ask. I answer succinctly: it is saved. Take away free will, and there will be nothing to be saved; take away grace, and there will be nothing by which it will be saved. This work cannot be accomplished without these two: one by which it is done, the other to which, or in which, it is done. God is the author of salvation; free will is just what is able to receive it. Nothing can give it except God; nothing can receive it except free will. Thus it is given by God alone and to free will alone").

211. "They magnify the Lord working in them" (McCann, 10).

following the example of the Blessed Mother: *"fecit mihi magna qui potens est."*[212] St. Benedict here cites St. Paul: *gratia Dei sum id quod sum—qui gloriatur, in Domino glorietur.*[213] N.B. the *ecstatic* character of love (especially in St. Bernard[214]) enables us to understand this.

8. Again we come to the notion that "time" to amend our lives is also a grace of God and a great gift which we should use with all care and reverence (cf. above[215]).

9. *Practical conclusions*:

a) God is generous with His grace. In particular His vocation is a great grace, and so we must *prepare ourselves to correspond generously*: *praeparanda sunt corda et corpora nostra . . .*[216]

b) This correspondence consists *above all in obedience—sanctae praeceptorum obedientiae militanda.*[217]

c) We do not have in ourselves the power to correspond perfectly. Even this is—and indeed this above all is—the work of grace. Hence we must pray without ceasing for *grace to supply* all that is lacking in our natural powers so that we may serve God in spirit and in truth, with true supernatural love proper to His sons. *QUOD MINUS HABET IN NOBIS NATURA POSSIBILE, ROGEMUS DOMINUM UT GRATIAE SUAE JUBEAT NOBIS ADJUTORIUM MINISTRARE.*[218]

d) *Generosity* in facing obstacles, in entering upon the *narrow way* of penance and self-denial, is essential, especially at the beginning, for without this determination to bear the Cross we cannot

212. "He who is mighty has done great things for me" (Luke 1:49).

213. "By the grace of God I am what I am"; "He that boasts, let him boast in the Lord" (1 Cor. 15:10; 2 Cor. 10:17) (McCann, 10).

214. On ecstasy in St. Bernard, see Gilson, 18–20, 25–28, 106–13, 143–44, 237, n. 156.

215. See above, pages 53, 64.

216. "our hearts and our bodies must be made ready" (McCann, 10).

217. "to fight in holy obedience to his commandments" (McCann, 10).

218. "What is impossible for us by nature, let us ask the Lord to command the assistance of his grace to provide for us" (McCann, 10, 12).

"keep grace"—*restrictius . . . propter conservationem caritatis.*[219] Hence the life of grace will never be fruitful without *discipline* and energetic efforts, especially at the beginning. What has been said now about grace is sufficient to give us the full theology of the Prologue. It contains implicitly all St. Benedict's teaching on humility and obedience, the principal good works by which we correspond with grace and allow it to bear fruit in our lives. One thought only need be added: for grace to work effectively in our souls, we must establish ourselves *in a favorable milieu*, where everything is ordered to promote correspondence with grace. This milieu is the MONASTERY—*SCHOLA DOMINICI SERVITII.*[220]

What are the characteristics of the monastic milieu?

a) It is not a place where austerity is sought for its own sake. *Nihil asperum, nihil grave.*[221] St. Benedict explicitly excludes here a harsh, military authoritarianism. This is not his idea of monastic asceticism. It is clear from these words that though the monastic life demands discipline, it is not intended to be so hard that it will break the spirit of good souls, still less ruin them morally, mentally or physically. The monastic life must be indeed a little hard, but not so hard that the monk's whole effort is expended in surviving from day to day. But as Dom Delatte points out,[222] a *schola* is a place where there is *leisure for thought, study and prayer*. In the monastery, {it is} not leisure for {the sake of} an easy life, but the way is cleared so that we can meditate day and night on the law of the Lord. This requires liberty, peace, interior quiet, indeed a certain happiness. All this comes from freedom from sin and therefore depends on a certain strictness and ascetic labor.

219. "more strictly . . . for the preservation of love" (McCann, 12, which includes an additional phrase between "*propter*" and "*conservationem*"); the phrase "keep grace" is an allusion to ll. 9–10 of Hopkins' sonnet "As kingfishers catch fire": "I say more: the just man justices: / Keeps grace: that keeps all his goings graces" (Gerard Manley Hopkins, *Poems and Prose*, ed. W. H. Gardner [Baltimore: Penguin, 1953], 51).

220. "a school of the Lord's service" (McCann, 12).

221. "nothing harsh, nothing burdensome" (McCann, 12).

222. Delatte, 19.

b) However there must be discipline. The life must be "*paululum restrictius.*"[223] And one must face the fact that what may seem a "little strict" to a saint like Benedict might well appear *very* strict to an unmortified soul. Nevertheless it would be untrue to say that St. Benedict expected every novice to measure up to his own high level of sanctity and mortification. On the contrary, St. Benedict had deliberately come down himself to the ordinary level of other monks, and discarded all "heroic" practices, keeping only a few moderate extra observances of his own like praying at night when the others were sleeping. Every indication (cf. the *Vita*[224]) shows that St. Benedict lived the ordinary life common to the rest of his monks, a life that, proportioned to the standards of the time, was not really hard at all. It was a disciplined life but not a really arduous one. But he did require strict fidelity in little points of obedience, and interior mortification; see {the strictures} against murmuring.[225]

c) Reasons for strictness in the monastic life:

1. *Prudence*—right reason: *dictante* aequitatis *ratione.*[226] A life without difficulty and penance would not make sense in a monastery. It would be contrary to the very nature of things, a mockery.

2. The *reformation of life*: in the monastery, sinners strive to amend their lives and become saints. This is not possible without discipline, hardship, sacrifice and self-denial. One must give up bad habits and acquire good ones. *This cannot be done without generous efforts and constant sacrifice.*

3. Conservation of charity: it is not sufficient just to "relax"—{there is} more emphasis on individual decision, interior mortification.

d) *The reward of generosity in accepting the monastic discipline is consolation and fervor.* The monastery then is not a place of sad

223. "a little bit more strict" (McCann, 12).

224. See for example the opening of c. 32, where Benedict is coming in from working in the fields with his monks when he encounters the father of the dead child (*PL* 66, col. 192B).

225. cc. 4, 5, 23, 34, 35, 40, 41, 53 (McCann, 28, 34, 72, 86, 88, 96, 98, 120).

226. "as determined by reason of fairness" (McCann, 12).

faces and gloomy penitents, but a place where souls purified by grace and sacrifice run with joy in the way of God's commandments ({cf. the} meaning of generosity: in the will, in *love*, {in the} desire to give, to please).

e) The full joy of the monastic life is the flowering of the life of grace (cf. what has been said above on grace[227]). It is the realization that in the monastery we are in the house of God and God our Father is constantly teaching and forming us. Finally we taste the joy of being *united with Jesus Christ* on the Cross, and realize that therefore we are destined, by His mercy, for a share in the joy of his Kingdom. {This is} unspeakable sweetness—contrast mature {with immature joy}.

This then is the monastic "school of divine service," the antechamber of heaven, the *paradisus claustralis*.[228] On the foundation of this teaching about grace and love, we can easily see that St. Benedict intends the monk to build a truly contemplative life, alone with God in silence and love. In this school of God one thing remains—we must *persevere until the end—usque ad mortem*[229]—sharing by our patience in the passion of Christ. Let us not delude ourselves by seeking an end of suffering and trial before we have reached the end of the road!

### Chapter 1—*De Generibus Monachorum*[230]

First of all, we must remember that this chapter is in fact *a survey of the whole religious life* as it existed in St. Benedict's time. We tend perhaps to think at first that St. Benedict's "four kinds of monks" are character studies—"four monastic temperaments"—a classification of monastic types. No—he is making a clear division of the *different forms of monastic life* that were actually received and practiced. Notice that this chapter of St. Benedict gives us a

227. See above, pages 64–69.

228. "paradise of the cloister" (St. Bernard, *De Diversis*, 42 [*PL* 183, col. 663B]).

229. "right up until death" (McCann, 12).

230. "Concerning the Types of Monks" (McCann, 14).

historical picture of the point at which monasticism had arrived by a *spontaneous development*, as it were naturally and without special control, growing on its own. Compare the development of the "prophets" in the Old Testament. Where a movement like monasticism flourishes spontaneously and by itself, there will be, besides the central core of truly spiritual life, an efflorescence of much that is less spiritual. Note in the development of early sanctity—things like stylitism, and later the "fools for Christ" in the Christian Orient. Note also in oriental (pagan) monasticism a development much like that described by St. Benedict—still going on today. This spontaneous development is not in itself something harmful. It is true that extremes and abuses can only be blamed, and St. Benedict himself necessarily reacted against the great abuses existing in his own time. But it is not to be regretted that in the deserts of Egypt many original and unusual forms of monastic life sprung up of themselves; indeed many of these early forms were surely the work of the Holy Spirit. But they were not destined to have a lasting value. Note: all that was *good* in these rare forms of monasticism came from the *witness* they bore to the transcendence of God. Note also that the idea of the *wandering monk* which St. Benedict seems to reprove in its very nature, was in fact destined to revive providentially in the thirteenth century with the mendicant orders. It would obviously be wrong to encourage gluttonous and drunken gyrovagues such as St. Benedict depicted, but let us not forget the ideal and the concrete sanctity of the first Franciscans either! These qualifications should teach us to read St. Benedict's chapter with care and with understanding, and not with a rigid and absolutistic mentality. Some monks seem to think that St. Benedict is saying in effect: "there are no monks that are really any good except cenobites." And these often gratuitously insert into this chapter their own rather rigid and limited notion of what cenobitism is supposed to be. Let us not take chapter 1 of the *Rule* as a canonization of our personal prejudices about what *we* think a monk ought to be.

*What Is St. Benedict's Idea?*

a) Does St. Benedict hold that no one can be a true monk unless he lives at all times in a rigidly fixed mold, according to an unchangeable authoritarian norm? No. St. Benedict definitely does not say that all monastic perfection consists in following a rule and nothing else. He admits of a way of perfection that is outside the cadre of fixed norms: the life of the *anchorite*. But there are very *definite conditions* without which the life of the anchorite cannot be sanctifying:

1. The anchorite no longer lives according to the fixed rule of the cenobium. His "rule" of life (certainly an even stricter discipline than that of the cenobium) is *tailor-made*—to fit his own personal vocation. But he has been prepared for this by *long training* (*probatione diuturna*[231]) in the cenobium, under a rule and an abbot. In other words, {there is} no sanctity without discipline, and discipline in practice is not learned without obedience and regularity.

b) What does St. Benedict see in common in all the monks of whom he approves?

1. Whether they are hermits or cenobites, they *fight against the devil*, and this means in particular (according to the religious psychology and asceticism of Cassian[232]) they struggle to control the "spirits" or inner movements of thought and passion, in order to arrive at *purity of heart* (i.e., perfect love for God) *contra vitia carnis vel cogitationum . . . pugnare.*[233] This refers to the division of "spirits" which afflict a man—carnal spirits, like gluttony, sloth, impurity, and "spiritual" temptations like pride, vanity, avarice (in a certain sense). The *vitia cogitationum* are the pitfalls of the more perfect monks, and of course the hermit has to fight

231. "a long period of testing" (McCann, 14).

232. See *De Coenobiorum Institutis*, Books 5–12 (*PL* 49, cols. 201–476), on the eight principal vices, and the discussion of this material in Thomas Merton, *Cassian and the Fathers: Initiation into the Monastic Tradition*, ed. Patrick F. O'Connell, MW 1 (Kalamazoo, MI: Cistercian Publications, 2005), 156–202.

233. "to fight against the vices of the flesh and of the thoughts" (McCann, 14).

them more directly than anyone else. The anchorite is presumed to be free from serious temptations of the flesh.

2. Another thing they have in common is the fact that they fight and are trained as members of a unified body, the Church—*fraterna ex acie . . . multorum solatio.*[234] In saying that the hermit is able to get along without the consolation and support of his brethren, St. Benedict does not mean that he is spiritually cut off from them. He renounces their physical presence and help, but remains united to them in prayer, in the communion of saints. It is in this sense that the hermit fights alone *sine consolatione alterius.*[235] He is above all supported and consoled by the angels, for he is now living the "angelic life" and fighting the "angelic war."

3. Both are *helped by God* in their struggle. We are still following the theology of grace set forth in the Prologue. The hermit is helped by God directly or through the angels, and the cenobite receives the help of God not only interiorly but also exteriorly in the example and support of his community.

*In summary*—the hermits and cenobites, of whom St. Benedict approves, are both fighters, engaged in a common struggle. The cenobites fight in the serried ranks of the monastic community, and the hermit fights alone as a kind of commando, in the desert. In order to be a fighter, one must have *training*. And one must also have committed himself to the struggle, have "signed up" in the armed forces, without the possibility of withdrawing from the struggle at will. So the hermit and cenobite of whom St. Benedict approves are, implicitly, *trained fighters, committed to the battle*, knowing the Lord for whom they fight, and *totally loyal to Him*.

c) What does St. Benedict see in common in the other kinds of monks?

1. First of all, they are not "fighters." They are not really doing anything particular; they are not committed to anything; they are just vegetating. Note once again, he is condemning not so much

234. "from the fraternal rank . . . the consolation of many" (McCann, 14, which reads: "*solacio*"; the phrases are in inverse order in the text).

235. "without the consolation of another" (McCann, 14).

the "type" that vegetates as the "institution" which permits this type to exist. The sarabaites *have received no training*: they know *no rule*. Hence *they are soft*—like lead, not purified like gold, and hence while *appearing to fight for God against the world* their allegiance belongs entirely to the world. They are traitors. Their profession is a lie. What is the test? *Lack of discipline and lack of sacrifice*, lack of self-renunciation. It is not that their lives are necessarily less austere physically than that of the other monks, but THEY ARE GUIDED BY THEIR OWN WILL. The whole of St. Benedict's asceticism is implied in his condemnation of the sarabaites: *PRO LEGE EST EIS DESIDERIORUM VOLUNTAS*.[236] Here St. Benedict has put his finger on a very deep and important truth. What keeps a man from becoming a monk is his inability to "let go" of his own will, and to renounce *running his own life*. In practice, when we try to run our own life, we really waste much time and effort in trying to *manipulate* situations, persons, and events, to fit our own ideas. Too often, we seriously work to *twist* reality and make it conform *to our illusions*, which are based on our *subjective needs and compulsions*. Note how Communism does this *systematically*. One who lives by his own fancies and illusions will inevitably try to *distort reality*. This is all the more dangerous where there is some basis for an *illusion of sanctity*—the person thinks himself holier than others, and does in fact have certain virtues. Such men can do incalculable harm. Not strengthened and liberated by any rule, they are captives of another law, the "law in their members";[237] they are *slaves of their own desires*, and especially, slaves of the *pleasure* of following their own whims. This is for St. Benedict the true test of one who is *not a monk*, and who does not "fight for God."[238]

236. "they have for a law the will of their own desires" (McCann, 14, which reads: ". . . *eis est* . . ." and "*voluptas*" ["pleasure"]).

237. Rom. 7:23.

238. Cf. the Prologue: "*Domino Christo vero Regi militaturus*" ("to take up arms for Christ the Lord, the true King") (McCann, 6); c. 1: "*Deo auxiliante pugnare*" ("to fight with the aid of God") (McCann, 12); c. 61: "*uni Regi militatur*" ("he fights for the same King") (McCann, 138).

2. Secondly, they are not in the school of the Lord's service and hence they *have not learned* to serve the Lord. They talk about the spiritual life and appear to live a certain kind of spiritual life, but in fact they know nothing of the reality of the spiritual life. This information is drawn from the words: *nulla regula approbati experientia magistra*[239]—a phrase which throws much light on the concept of the "*schola Dominici servitii*"[240] which we met at the end of the Prologue. McCann translates this "not having been tested by any rule or by the lessons of experience."[241] We agree in his interpretation that *experientia magistra* is to be taken as an ablative absolute[242]—that it does not mean "as experience has shown," but refers to the teaching of the monk by experience. Pushing this interpretation even further along the lines suggested by McCann we {interpret} substantially as follows: (paraphrase) "not being tested by any rule they have not learned from experience." The idea is: the monk *subjects himself to the Rule* and in this state of subjection, as a necessary prerequisite, he is *taught by experience*. What experience? We shall see later, at the end of chapter 7, this is substantially a matter of spiritual experience imparted by grace. This is also indicated by the teaching of the Prologue on grace. It is in effect *an experience of sharing in the passion and obedience of Christ*. One who rejects a rule and a superior is not able to be taught by the Lord, not able to gain "that mind which was in Christ Jesus who was . . . obedient unto death."[243] Hence the sarabaites and gyrovagues *really know nothing of Christ*; they have not learned, by subjection, to share in the monk's interior, spiritual knowledge of union with Christ in the mystery of His passion and His humility and His obedience to the Father. (N.B. a wrong reading of the text is *experientia Magistri* . . .[244])

239. "tested by no rule nor by experience as a teacher" (McCann, 14).

240. "school of the Lord's service" (McCann, 12).

241. McCann, 15, which has an additional phrase between "tested" and "by."

242. This would seem to be an ablative with an appositive rather than an ablative absolute construction.

243. Phil. 2:5, 8.

244. "experience of the Master."

*Hildemar's* interpretation of this passage is that the true monk needs to be taught both by doctrine (*Regula*) and by practice (*experientia*).[245] He receives a theoretical formation, the principles of the spiritual life, in the *Rule* (which is therefore considered much more than just a legal document, but a kind of spiritual directory) and he receives practical training in carrying out the instructions and counsels of his spiritual Father.

3. Thirdly, they have *no stability in the good*. They are *weak*, through their own fault. Lead (says Hildemar[246]) is both heavy and malleable. The bad monks are "heavy" in their inclination to gravitate towards any evil, and "soft" or malleable in the way in which they are *ready to yield* to every new impulsion from the outside. They have no fixed form; they are constantly taking on now one form, now another, according to the *impressions of the moment*. Even though many of these impressions may in themselves be good rather than evil, yet this state is very bad, for it makes a true spiritual life impossible, and there is no real perseverance in good. Hildemar points out that they chiefly *lack patience*,[247] which is what makes the monk "solid as gold" and faithful and stable in good works and in suffering.[248] {For} a good illustration of this *plumbi natura*[249] which is to a certain extent in everyone not yet purified by the Holy Spirit, we may read *Dark Night of the Soul*, Bk. 1, ch. 6 (vol. 1, p. 364 ff.),[250] {which} brings

245. "regula *attinet ad doctrinam,* experientia *vero ad exercitationem operis,* magistra *autem et ad regulam et ad experientiam potest referri, i.e. regula magistra et experientia magistra sit*" ("rule pertains to teaching, and experience to putting into practice; teacher can be referred both to the rule and to experience—i.e. let the rule be a teacher and let experience be a teacher") (Hildemar, 79–80).

246. Hildemar, 80: "*plumbi enim natura gravis est et mollis.*"

247. Hildemar, 80: "*peccatores graves sunt malitia, molles sunt impatientia*" ("sinners are heavy because of malice, malleable because of lack of patience").

248. Hildemar, 80: "*sicut aurum purgatur in fornace, ita et justi probantur in praesentis temporis tribulatione*" ("as gold is purified in the furnace, so the just are tested in the tribulation of the present age").

249. "the nature of lead" (McCann, 14).

250. This chapter (Peers, 1.364–68), entitled "Of imperfections with respect to spiritual gluttony," discusses the desire of beginners for spiritual sweetness

out clearly the consequence of living by the "law of one's own desires," and the instability and weakness which follow from this. Note—the Lord always takes into account the inevitable frailty of man, but there is a culpable weakness that comes from neglecting the aids and graces by which God, in our regular life, seeks to make us strong.

4. It seems that in different degrees both the sarabaites and gyrovagues *seek to avoid* subjection. This is the gravest accusation against them. They prefer to be *sine pastore*[251] (it is implied). The gyrovagues quite obviously are not only running away from the regular life but are in full flight from all responsibility whatever. They are in a lamentable condition, escapists who cannot bear to face themselves or to face other men for any length of time, always hoping for something better just around the corner. It is clear that they are simply the *logical consequence* of sarabaitism pushed to its extreme. They are simply bums, and the implication is that they are often drunken bums as well—a very sad condition. {There can be} social explanations of this in certain ages—v.g. the Goliards—when to be a student one had to be a cleric, the immense number of clerics who really had no vocation to a consecrated life {points to a} failure to distinguish between an intellectual and secular life and the priestly or religious life. {This} led to decay of religion in the late Middle Ages. *Today*—obviously the sarabaite and the gyrovague exist only in spirit. St. Benedict's conclusion: *de horum omnium miserrima conversatione melius est silere quam loqui.*[252] There is no profit in talking at great length

---

that drives them to immoderate penances motivated by their own will and to frequent communion out of a craving for sensible consolation, and points out that failure to experience spiritual pleasure often leads to abandonment of ascetical practices; "These persons . . . are very weak and remiss in journeying upon the hard road of the Cross; for the soul that is given to sweetness naturally has its face set against all self-denial, which is devoid of sweetness" (n. 7; 368).

251. "without a shepherd" (McCann, 14).

252. "concerning the utterly wretched way of life of all these, it is better to be silent than to speak" (McCann, 16, which reads: "*de quorum omnium horum . . .*").

about the scandals that arise in religious life. We must indeed soberly inquire into causes and apply remedies when they are needed, but there is no need to dwell at great length and in great detail on the dark and negative side of the religious life—the tragedies which inevitably occur from time to time. St. Benedict takes a sober position. He does not idealize: he admits that these evils exist, takes them into account, shows why they occur, shows how they can be prevented, and then goes on to consider the *positive* and good side of the religious life, the way of faith and obedience which leads to God.

## The Abbot and His Monks

(chapters 2 and 64: The Abbot and his Election; chapters 3 and 63: Calling the Brethren to Counsel; The Order of the Community; chapter 65: The Prior; chapter 21; The Deans; chapters 31, 32: The Cellarer, and the Tools; chapter 57: The Craftsmen; chapter 53: Those who Deal with the Guests [cf. c. 66: The Porters]; chapters 60, 62: The Priests; Children: see chapters 30, 59).

{Note} the logical structure of the *Rule*—after an introductory chapter on different kinds of monks, there are two chapters on the abbot and the community, followed by two other large and important sections: a) the ascetic section—the spiritual heart of the *Rule* (cc. 4–7); b) the liturgical section—arrangement of the office; and after two chapters which seem to have been inserted—another long and important section on punishments. Then he goes into a discussion of the monks' daily life, observances, etc. He returns later to further chapters on the abbot, officers, etc. It will be more logical for us to take all that he says about the abbot and the officers and the constitution of the monastic community together here. A very detailed treatment is not required—what matters is to grasp clearly the importance of the *abbot* in St. Benedict's scheme of things. Chapter 2—*Qualis debeat abbas esse*.[253] This chapter is addressed to the abbot himself, and is for his meditation

253. "The Type of Person an Abbot Should Be" (McCann, 16).

and instruction. However it also has general bearing on monastic life as a whole. It is written in such a way that all can draw instruction from it—the subject can see, from what is said about the abbot's responsibilities, his own correlative obligations. The teachings also apply to others who represent the abbot and are deputed by him to form souls. *Note*: {the} key position of {the} abbot {is} due to {the} key role of *obedience* in monastic life. In {the} hermit life, {the} monk obeys God directly. In {the} cenobitic life, {the} monk obeys God through a man (this {is} necessary for *all* for at least a time). {The} basic {foundation is} to believe that God speaks through a fallible man. *Abbatem sibi praeesse desiderant*.[254] (Read from c. 5.[255]) Why? because they have chosen the "narrow way"[256] for the sake of life everlasting. Hence they do not live by their own will. They walk by another's judgement and orders.

I. The first thing that is evident is that St. Benedict makes the abbot shoulder a *tremendous responsibility*. He becomes in fact permanently responsible for the whole monastic family. Hence, he has to be first of all capable of assuming this responsibility—with the grace of God. He must be capable of being a "superior" —a "*major*."[257] This means not merely that he must have special natural qualities that mark him out above the other members of the community, but above all that he must be supernaturally picked out (n.b. {through} voting) as *another Christ*—i.e. {marked by} virtue, wisdom, spiritual *preeminence* in {the} community. He

254. "They desire an abbot to be over them" (McCann, 34).

255. This chapter (McCann, 32, 34) focuses on "obedience without delay" ("*obedientia sine mora*") as the first degree of humility, prompted by monastic commitment, fear of hell and hope of eternal life. It involves renunciation of self-will ("*voluntatem propriam*") through immediate compliance with the command of the superior, in imitation of Christ who said, "I came not to do my own will but the will of Him who sent me" (Jn. 6:38). Obedience given to superiors is to be understood as obedience to God, in accordance with Christ's words, "He who hears you hears me" (Lk. 10:16). Obedience should include both exterior and interior assent; obeying orders without good will and with internal complaint has no merit.

256. Mt. 7:14 (McCann, 32).

257. McCann, 16.

is to lead the monastic community as Christ led and formed and instructed the band of the Apostles. *Christi agere vices in monasterio creditur.*[258] He takes the place of Christ in the monastery. His leadership is the leadership not of a human organizer, but of Christ. His doctrine and formation are those of Christ. This does not follow automatically from the fact that one is chosen or appointed as abbot. The supernatural role of the abbot in the monastery depends on the *faith* both of the abbot himself and of the community. *Creditur. The abbot must see* his responsibility as another Christ, must strive in all things to conform himself to the model of Jesus as Head of the Monastic Church. *The community must also obey him as* Jesus Himself, accept his teaching as that of Jesus, etc. Hence the supernatural respect and veneration surrounding the person of the superior. This must be seen in {the} light of *faith,* not diplomacy. It is this *common faith of the abbot and the monks* that makes the whole institution live and function supernaturally. Without this foundation of faith, the abbotship is a meaningless and human thing, with little or no spiritual power. In such an event, the monks obey to the extent that they respect the abbot's natural talents or qualities, or to the extent that they appreciate his way of running the monastery, his "policy." And the abbot rules his subjects by expediency, attempting to win their respect for his qualities and to keep everybody happy and gain their support. The monastery tends to become a nest of politicians. The monks try to manipulate the abbot and the abbot manipulates the monks, and all play a political game—a very sad state of affairs, quite opposed to the mind of St. Benedict. On the other hand, St. Benedict does not rule out all natural feelings in the relationship between monk and abbot. The relationship is basically that between father and son. There should be respect, affection, trust, openness, unity, between the monk and his abbot. The abbot is not merely a "boss," he is a father. False supernaturalism {operates} as if relations could be supernatural only when

258. "He is believed to act in the place of Christ in the monastery" (McCann, 16).

completely frustrating and odious. True supernaturalism {is marked by} mutual trust and respect, in spite of deficiencies—{the} Holy Spirit will make up for the deficiencies on both sides. This relationship is by no means to be looked at in a sentimental light, but realistically and concretely: there should be *mutual confidence and understanding* between the abbot and the monk, {with a} confidence based on {the} presence and action of {the} Holy Spirit. The basis of this confidence and understanding once again is supernatural and spiritual. It is something that is brought into existence by grace, by the Holy Spirit. St. Benedict makes this clear by his quote from St. Paul (*Abba—Pater*[259]). The "spirit" that keeps the monastery united in peace and strength is the "spirit of adoption," the Holy Spirit Himself living and working in the hearts of the monks and of the abbot, establishing a relationship of charity, confidence, openness, understanding and affection, which expresses in some way the relationship between the Son and the Father in the Blessed Trinity. This of course is a high spiritual ideal—its realization is possible even where natural feelings and instincts may be *a*ffectively opposed to it. What is ruled out is *e*ffective opposition. *The strength of the monastic community* lies in the spiritual bond between the abbot and the monks and between the monks themselves, a supernatural charity based on faith and effected by the action of divine grace, the Spirit of Sonship, the Spirit of Christ.

II. *Consequences of this Fundamental Principle*

a) The abbot sees his position as a representative of Christ. The community accepts this situation in trusting faith. Consequently the abbot is obliged to base all his *teaching*, his *administration, his commands*, on the law of God. His teaching and his commands are to have a sanctifying, a "sacramental" character; they are to be a *"fermentum divinae justitiae"*[260]—having an active

259. "Abba—Father": Rom. 8:15 (McCann, 16).
260. "the leaven of divine justice" (McCann, 16).

and transforming part in the life of the monks. (Comment on the exact meaning of "*justitiae*" in this phrase!)

b) The abbot is responsible for *seeing that his commands are carried out*. He must not only teach abstract truths, and say what ought to be done, but get the monks to follow God's law and carry out God's will. The abbot is obliged, before God, to see that the monk does what appears to the abbot to be the will of God, not just to leave the decision always in the hands of the monk. The abbot is not just placed as an overseer who makes sure that what the monk does is all right, not scandalous, not openly wrong. He is there to see that the monk *fulfills God's will and this in matters of detail* (but *in foro externo*[261]). When he sees him not doing so, he is obliged to rebuke the monk and tell him, "You are going against the will of God." His responsibility is two-fold: *to the monk* and above all *to God Himself*. God places His signified will in the abbot's hands, to see that it is carried out, but the abbot must also be a man of discretion and not think his own will is always the will of God. The judgement is *his*—we must leave this to him—trusting that he is acting according to his conscience. However, *nemo ad impossibile tenetur*.[262] The abbot cannot compel the wills of unruly monks to act in the right way. If he has taken all the necessary steps to see that God's will is carried out, and the monks still refuse their cooperation, then they will be held accountable. The abbot's part is to *make very clear* what God wills, and to show the monk his obligation to fulfill that Holy Will. He is not obliged to do violence to the monk and force him to obey. (True obedience cannot be achieved by compulsion.)

c) An important part of the abbot's obligation is to show *by his example* what is to be done. In other words *he himself must be the first in fidelity to the will of God*. He must preach both by word and by example. Example has the special value of closing the mouth of potential critics and elements of resistance who look for every opportunity to evade their responsibilities. Even though

261. "in the external forum"; "in outward matters."

262. "no one is held to the impossible."

the abbot may have every reason to do certain things differently from the monks, he should reflect on the importance of his example, and on the fact that some might be totally unable to understand that his case is entirely different from theirs, and try to point to his different practices as precedent for changes in their own case. However, the abbot can never be in all things exactly like the monks. He is obliged by his charges and responsibilities to do some things differently and to take certain exceptional courses. It is pharisaism to demand critically that the abbot conform in *absolutely everything* with the common practice of the other monks. St. Benedict is here talking not just of an example of regularity, but of *sanctity*: *"omnia bona et sancta factis amplius quam verbis ostendat."*[263] All that is good and holy should be evident in the actions of the one who represents Christ in the community. (Yet at the same time, the community must be realistic, and remember that the abbot is human like everybody else, and has his faults and limitations. It would again be pharisaism to demand, on the basis of this chapter, that the abbot be absolutely perfect in all things, and to make this a prerequisite for obeying and respecting his authority! Some monks, alas, have this very blameworthy attitude.)

d) The community must *bear fruit for Christ* and the abbot is responsible for seeing that it does so. READ St. John 15:1-8.[264]

263. "let him show everything good and holy more in deeds than in words" (McCann, 18).

264. "I am the true vine, and my Father is the vine-dresser. Every branch in me that bears no fruit he will take away; and every branch that bears fruit he will cleanse, that it may bear more fruit. You are already clean because of the word that I have spoken to you. Abide in me and I in you. As the branch cannot bear fruit of itself unless it remain on the vine, so neither can you unless you abide in me. I am the vine, you are the branches. He who abides in me, and I in him, he bears much fruit; for without me you can do nothing. If anyone does not abide in me, he shall be cast outside as the branch and wither; and they shall gather them up and cast them into the fire, and they shall burn. If you abide in me, and if my words abide in you, ask whatever you will, and it shall be done to you. In this is my Father glorified, that you may bear very much fruit, and become my disciples."

Comment on this passage in the light of the abbot's position as *alter Christus*:[265]

1. *In this is the Father glorified*. The abbot, like Jesus Himself, must place before everything else the will and glory of the Father. He has come to do not his own will but the will of Him who "sent" him—his superiorship is a divine mission, committed to him by Holy Church in the name of God Himself.

2. *that you bring forth very much fruit*. This is very important. The community exists for the glory of God, *but God is not glorified unless the individual members of the community bring forth "very much" spiritual fruit*. It is of no use to have a community which does a lot of work, produces a lot of farm-goods, books, records, research scholarship, art works, or runs a lot of retreats, liturgical conferences, etc., *if the monks themselves do not grow* and thrive spiritually. Theoretically, in the active orders, if the active work of the order thrives that is already a great contribution to the Church, even though the members may not be bringing forth so much spiritual fruit—they are helping to bring forth fruit in others. (Actually, of course, where the members of an active order are not themselves sufficiently spiritual, the spiritual yield of their apostolate will be greatly diminished thereby.) But in our order, if the monks are not holy the monastery can be said to have produced *absolutely nothing*, because God does not need either cheese or chant. He wants the hearts of the monks. What is meant by fruitfulness? First of all, the monks must grow in natural and psychological maturity; they must broaden out; they must be wise and understanding men, capable of living a sane, mature human life, working well together, living in peace. If the monks remain mentally children, involved in trivialities and a prey to their impressions of the moment, they will not begin to bring forth fruit. Hence it is not enough merely to "keep them quiet" or to "keep them out of mischief." In some cases, unfortunately, that is the best that can be expected. But this is not spiritual growth—it merely protects the opportunities for spiritual growth

265. "another Christ."

in the other ones. But above all, what is meant is supernatural fruitfulness. What is this?

3. *He that abideth in me and I in him, the same beareth much fruit.* Spiritual growth is growth in discipleship of Christ, growth in understanding of His will, in union with His Sacred Heart by love and obedience—growth in the manner of our operation—more perfectly under the sway of the Divine Spirit. It means *abiding in Christ* more perfectly by love, intimacy, trust. The abbot must encourage this spiritual fruit by bringing souls to Christ their true Master, by opening their hearts to the Holy Spirit.

4. *Every one that beareth fruit He will purge it.* The Heavenly Father works directly on the soul of the monk, in spiritual purification. But He also uses the abbot as His instrument. The abbot is bound to see that good souls become better, and he is bound to remove obstacles to their progress. But in this, great care and spiritual enlightenment is necessary. It is not merely a matter of inflicting arbitrary and artificial trials and humiliations. He must be a *sapiens medicus*[266] having insight into the spiritual roots of our ills, and penetrating to these roots with kindness and wisdom. In purifying souls, the superior does not work merely from the outside. He must teach the soul to see itself and to understand itself and to work out its own problems for itself, not merely impose commands and directives from the outside, and getting them carried out without comprehension. "The abbot should realize that whatever the father of the family finds lacking in his sheep will be imputed to the fault of the shepherd."[267] However if the flock cannot be led, the abbot will be excused if he has made every effort to train them and bring them to the fold of the Lord. "*Veritatem tuam et salutare tuum dixi.*"[268]

e) The abbot cannot treat all souls alike. There are different classes of monks:

266. "a wise physician" (c. 28; McCann, 78).

267. McCann, 16.

268. "I have spoken your truth and your salvation" (Ps. 39[40]:11) (McCann, 18).

1. The *capaces discipuli*[269]—those who are open and receptive. These he needs only to teach and advise. A suggestion, a hint, are quite sufficient. They can do the rest themselves.

2. The *duri corde*[270]—these are prone to resist, stubborn, unreceptive. He does not necessarily impute to them serious ill will. They are slow to take advice from anyone. These must be commanded.

3. Among those who have to be commanded are the "somewhat stupid" (*simpliciores*[271]). It is a fact that often slowness of mind is one of the great obstacles to obedience. *Some people are just incapable of seeing another man's point of view, of looking at things the way he sees them.* This is important in obedience. A really obedient monk is one who enters into the views of the superior in order to do what he wants. Others are satisfied to do it somehow or other—but we should always ask: does the superior want this done in some special way, or does he just expect me to carry out the command according to my own lights? Note: the abbot makes clear to these God's will by explicitly showing them where it has been commanded—*divina praecepta*.[272] To all alike the abbot must back up his words by his example.

f) At the same time, he must avoid human favoritism. There should be no "respect of persons"[273] on a human basis—that is to say, the abbot must not let himself be impressed with human nobility or talents or other gifts of nature. Yet St. Benedict reasonably supposes that the abbot can recognize openly supernatural gifts and virtues. He will certainly have a tendency to "love more than others"[274] one who is truly humble and full of virtue. But this must be a spiritual love and one which does not imply any form of favoritism, or exclude others less gifted. The abbot will indeed have a very special care, in another way, for the

269. "capable disciples" (McCann, 18, which reads: "*capacibus discipulis*").

270. "hard of heart" (McCann, 18, which reads: "*duris corde*").

271. McCann, 18, which reads: "*simplicioribus*."

272. "the divine precepts" (McCann, 18).

273. Rom. 2:11 (McCann, 18).

274. McCann, 18.

sinners and the rebellious. In another place St. Benedict reminds the abbot not to be more impressed by rich travelers than by the poor (c. 53).[275] Here we see that he must take no account of the differences between those who were originally slaves and those who used to be noblemen—reason: for we are all one in Christ—a principle that is most important: *aequalis omnibus charitas*.[276] (But this does not mean that all receive exactly the same treatment—each one alike receives treatment according to *his needs*. Monks are not produced on an assembly line. All would receive the same *in the same circumstances*.) Charity will be shown in many different ways. It is charity to rebuke the sinner. It is charity to encourage the virtuous. It is charity to urge on the negligent. St. Benedict would have the abbot "cut off sins as soon as they appear."[277] But he would also have him be kind and discreet. Balance what is said in chapter 2 by what we find in chapter 64.

III. *What are the basic principles of spiritual direction which should be followed by the abbot in guiding souls*? Besides the basic theological principle that the abbot is the representative of Christ in the monastery and that his direction must be given and received in a spirit of faith and submission to the Gospel, there are other very important practical principles which govern the *manner* in which the abbot deals with the souls under him.

1. He must recognize the *difficulty of his task* and not take it too lightly or handle souls with rash confidence in his own judgement. *Sciatque* quam difficilem et arduam *rem suscepit, regere animas*[278] (c. 2).

2. The reason why his task is difficult is that he must know how to understand many different kinds of souls, and to *judge*

275. McCann, 120; Benedict actually says that the poor and pilgrims should be given particular attention, since the "*terror*" (!) the rich inspire will already gain them honor.

276. "equal love to all" (McCann, 20, which reads: "*caritas*" and includes additional words between "*aequalis*" and "*omnibus*").

277. McCann, 20.

278. "Let him know how difficult and arduous a task he has undertaken—to govern souls" (McCann, 20, which reads: "*suscipit*").

*rightly many different circumstances*. God alone knows what is in the heart of man. A man who, relying on his own knowledge and his quickness of mind, and other abilities, trusts too much in his own judgement, makes many serious mistakes, and does great harm to souls. He jumps to the wrong conclusion and treats souls unjustly. Yet perhaps he may be so attached to his own judgement that he heaps injustice upon injustice, being unable to admit that he could possibly be wrong.

3. The abbot must be *flexible and adaptable*, *MULTORUM SERVIRE MORIBUS*.[279] That is to say, he must not just manipulate persons by psychological means, but "serve" them in their various temperaments and characters, meaning he must lead them according to the best interests of their peculiar nature and circumstances, to union with God—not just for the sake of making them "fully developed persons" but *true and mature members of Christ*. St. Benedict emphasizes that {the} abbot must respect *individual differences*. {An} individual should not be expected to conform to type either in {the} *spiritual* or {the} *material* order, in punishments {or} in dispensations (cf. Hildemar: 444,[280] 447–448[281]).

4. He must always be, like Christ, the servant of the servants of God. "I am in the midst of you as one who serves."[282] *PRODESSE MAGIS QUAM PRAEESSE* (c. 64).[283] The abbot must be one

279. "to be of assistance to the characters of many different types of people" (McCann, 20).

280. "Therefore we cannot determine the measure of food for others more specifically, because all do not have the same characteristics; no mortal being can arrange satisfactorily that all receive equally in matters of food, drink, or clothing" (quoted in Sr. M. Alfred Schroll, OSB, *Benedictine Monasticism as Reflected in the Warnefrid-Hildemar Commentaries on the Rule* [New York: Columbia University Press, 1941], 140).

281. "Applying this principle, they [Hildemar and Warnefrid (364–65)] recommend that if the appointed measure of wine be insufficient for individuals, the allowance should be increased; if it be superfluous for some, it should be diminished" (Schroll, 140).

282. Lk. 22:27.

283. "to benefit more than to rule" (McCann, 146, who nicely reflects the play on the Latin infinitives by translating "rather to profit . . . than to preside").

who understands the right use of authority, and the purpose for which it has been given to him. This is difficult to fallen human nature. St. Bernard points out that it is much easier to live as a subject, with profit to one's own soul, than to profit oneself and others as a superior.[284] It would be folly for a monk, especially for a young monk, to entertain vain ambitions of superiorship! Those who desire to "be placed over" others are the ones least fit for the office of abbot.

5. The abbot's direction and rule of the community must be *at once kind and firm*. Firmness is stressed more in chapter 2; kindness is more in the foreground in chapter 64, the fruit of later years and of his most mature reflection. *Miscens terroribus blandimenta*[285] (c. 2); *durius arguere*[286] (c. 2); *increpet et corripiat*[287] (c. 2); *Neque dissimulet peccata . . . sed mox ut coeperint oriri radicitus ea . . . amputet*[288] (c. 2); *duros . . . verberum vel corporis castigatione*

284. See Thomas Merton, "Action and Contemplation in St. Bernard," in *Thomas Merton on St. Bernard*, Cistercian Studies [CS], vol. 9 (Kalamazoo, MI: Cistercian Publications, 1980), 68: "In comparing the purely contemplative life with the vocation to the care of souls, St Bernard tells us that the latter is more difficult, more dangerous, more meritorious, more necessary and more excellent. . . . *Non est ejusdem facilitatis devote quiescere et fructuose operari; humiliter subesse et utiliter praeesse*. Exposed to more numerous occasions of sin and imperfection, the Superior and guide of souls must be stronger than the monk called to the repose of Mary." The quotation is taken from *Sermones de Diversis*, 90.3 (*PL* 183, col. 709B, which reads: "*non esse* . . ."): "It does not take the same facility dutifully to be quiet and fruitfully to toil, humbly to be under, and usefully to be in authority" (100, n. 135); see also 66: "Sermon 18 *In Cantica* begins with the declaration that the Holy Spirit works in the souls of monks in two different ways. In one way, he produces virtues within our souls, for our own salvation. In another he works through us for the salvation of others." (The article originally appeared in *Collectanea Ordinis Cisterciensium Reformatorum* in three parts in 1953–54).

285. "mixing compliments with threats" (McCann, 20; text includes another phrase between "*miscens*" and "*terroribus*").

286. "to denounce more sternly" (McCann, 20).

287. "he should rebuke and reproach" (McCann, 20).

288. "Let him not ignore sins . . . but as soon as they begin to arise let him cut them off by the roots" (McCann, 20).

*in ipso initio peccati coerceat . . .*[289] (c. 2). If one were to take these phrases out of their context, St. Benedict would indeed be recommending great severity. {The} *wrong idea* {is} that the superior should punish *merely* to assert his authority, or revenge his outraged dignity—"I'll show them that *I* am the boss." In reality this belongs to *weak* characters. But the abbot must not be afraid to warn, to reprove, and to punish. However, St. Benedict is not advising indiscriminate or arbitrary severity, but only severity when it is really called for—in the case of those who are stubborn, who have ill will, who do not want to obey or follow advice, who show a kind of contempt for mere words and example. Remember that in his time there were rough and barbarous individuals in the monastery, quite frequently. St. Benedict does not suggest severity for its own sake, or as a matter of set policy. All who do not *really need* to be treated severely are to be treated with kindness, and even the most obdurate are to be treated with patience and understanding. One thing is definite: the abbot's approach to faults in the community must be *direct and uncompromising*. This directness is of great importance. St. Benedict would not encourage the superior to practice a vain and empty sympathy for the faults of his monks. It is one thing to understand that all men are weak, and to compassionate their weakness, treating them with patience and understanding. But it is quite another thing to "baby" a man who commits many faults, and merely try to "keep him happy" or "keep him quiet" by the wrong kind of condescension—permitting him to get away with things that are bad for him. A modern Catholic psychiatrist (Dr. Suzy Rousset) points out the harm done where a superior, out of "ill-inspired charity," tries to play up to the whims and faults of a more or less neurotic religious—the frustrated souls who always seek an inordinate amount of attention, either by scenes and exaggerated demands, or by constant gloom and sulking. To play up to such a one would result in greater harm: "the unfortunate person's

289. "Let him correct the recalcitrant at the very outset of their sinning by punishing the body with lashes" (McCann, 20).

state would be no better and would probably become incurable. To treat a regression by means of a similar regression is to make it worse" (see in *The Communal Life*, p. 262).[290] For such, St. Benedict says the superior must "*durius arguere*" not in the sense of being unkind (for one must always be kind, and one must not show resentment and anger of the wrong sort) but in the sense of being *firm* and uncompromising, and quite definite about opposing the fault committed. St. Benedict refers to Heli and his sons. (READ I Kings 2:12-17 and 3:11-18.[291]) The duty of every

290. Suzy Rousset, "Motives for Entering the Coenobitic Life," *Communal Life*, Religious Life, vol. 8, trans. Religious of the Sacred Heart, from *La Vie Commune* (Westminster, MD: Newman Press, 1957), 251–65; the passage reads: ". . . unfortunate woman's state . . . probably be worse and become . . ." and has single quotation marks around "To treat . . . worse" (which is not referenced).

291. "Now the sons of Heli were children of Belial, not knowing the Lord, nor the office of the priests to the people; but whosoever had offered a sacrifice, the servant of the priest came, while the flesh was in boiling with a fleshhook of three teeth in his hand, and thrust it into the kettle, or into the caldron, or into the pot, or into the pan; and all that the fleshhook brought up, the priest took to himself. Thus did they to all Israel that came to Silo. Also before they burnt the fat, the servant of the priest came, and said to the man that sacrificed: Give me flesh to boil for the priest, for I will not take of thee sodden flesh, but raw. And he that sacrificed said to him: Let the fat first be burnt today according to the custom, and then take as much as thy soul desireth. But he answered and said to him: Not so; but thou shalt give it me now, or else I will take it by force. Wherefore the sin of the young men was exceedingly great before the Lord, because they withdrew men from the sacrifice of the Lord" (1 K [i.e. 1 Sam.] 2:12-17). "And the Lord said to Samuel: Behold I do a thing in Israel, and whosoever shall hear it, both his ears shall tingle. In that day I will raise up against Heli all the things I have spoken concerning his house; I will begin, and I will make an end. For I have foretold unto him, that I will judge his house forever, for iniquity, because he knew that his sons did wickedly, and did not chastise them. Therefore have I sworn to the house of Heli, that the iniquity of his house shall not be expiated with victims nor offerings forever. And Samuel slept till morning and opened the doors of the house of the Lord. And Samuel feared to tell the vision to Heli. Then Heli called Samuel, and said: Samuel, my son. And he answered: Here am I. And he asked him: What is the word that the Lord hath spoken to thee? I beseech thee hide it not from me. May God do so and so to thee, and add so and so, if thou hide from me one word of all that were said to thee. So Samuel told

superior {is} to come out and take a definite stand against evil and injustice. This duty in a broader sense is incumbent upon every Christian. He who remains passive and uninterested in the presence of great evils that are done in the world, becomes responsible by cooperation. We should therefore never resent the fact that a superior corrects us clearly and firmly and points out our faults without hiding them. We should give him credit for good intentions and real charity, real concern for our welfare. The superior meanwhile has a difficult task—it is not easy to correct others and the temptation for many superiors is to evade the issue. If a superior corrects our faults, he may be making a difficult sacrifice in order to be of service to us, and we should appreciate it accordingly. On the other hand,

6. The Great Importance of Kindness and Discretion

a) Again, the main principle of chapter 64—*prodesse magis quam praeesse*.[292] One must realize that it is not to the advantage of souls merely to beat them down. One must try to sense when one is acting in such a way that the soul is merely repelled and antagonized. It is no use making a correction that merely antagonizes and upsets a soul. He will return to his fault inevitably.

b) *Superexaltet misericordiam judicio*.[293] While it is important, as we have seen, to stand up for the rights of justice and truth (stressed in c. 2), the superior who is obsessed with the objective fault to the point of forgetting the subjective weakness and excusing factors in the sinner, *will never really be able to profit souls*. To come out firmly and strongly for the rights of justice and of truth may be good in the sense that it is a testimony to the objective will of God. But God Himself is merciful, and He Himself has put mercy before justice. How has He treated our sins? In the Old Law, indeed, there were harsh punishments and stern, uncompromising

---

him all the words, and did not hide them from him. And he answered; It is the Lord. Let him do what is good in his sight" (1 K [i.e. 1 Sam.] 3:11-18).

292. See above, n. 283.

293. "Let him elevate mercy above judgement" (James 2:13) (McCann, 146).

testimonies to the objective truth of God's will. But in the New Law, God Himself shows the *deepest abysses of His Love in dying for sinners on the Cross*. To gain souls, one must first of all be merciful, and one's zeal for justice can be turned upon oneself—for we are all sinners. The superior, in the fear of God, will realize that "he himself must obtain mercy"[294] (c. 64) and that he himself is a sinner, and we are all sinners. Hence a totally new attitude {is present}. The superior should not merely say: "This is the Law of God—and you have sinned by violating it—now you must be punished, that God's honor may be vindicated . . ." This may be true, it may proceed from a sincere desire to honor God, but in the long run this is *the kind of thing that drives souls out of the monastery* and even out of the Church. He should rather take the approach: "Here is what God wills; here is His Law. We are trying to keep His Law, and do His will. We are all weak, we all fail, and now you have failed. I also have failed in many things. But come, we will help one another. In the charity of Christ, we will strive to see that God's will is done by us, and we will ask for His mercy together." This is the attitude that gains souls and leads them to courage and trust and sanctity.

c) Hence the next great principle: *ODERIT VITIA; DILIGAT FRATRES*.[295] True, the superior must hate evil, must detest every violation of the Law of God. But God seeks above all the salvation of souls. That is the purpose of God's Law—to bring souls to Him. God does not want the rights of His Law vindicated in such a way that souls are crushed in their weakness and made unable to come to Him in filial love. Hence the great principle is *the value of the human soul*, the value of the person, and not just the value of observance, and of "law" as if law were an end in itself. This gives us a clue to the real difference between "letter" and "spirit." The letter of the law is the cold, objective precept which is to be fulfilled. The spirit is the fulfillment of the precept *in such a way that its true end is attained*. "Love is the fulfillment of the law" (St.

294. McCann, 146.

295. "Let him hate the vices; let him love the brothers" (McCann, 146).

Paul).[296] Enforcement of the law *in its spirit* is enforcement of the law with love and discretion *so that souls are helped and saved* by its fulfillment. Enforcement of the letter of the Law is mere external enforcement, making sure that the precept is observed, without consideration of the effect on souls—without any real interest in their benefit or salvation. Example: the confessor who browbeats a sinner in the confessional in order that the confession may be sufficiently detailed, not considering that the penitent may be so repelled that he may leave the confessional never to return (one must naturally strive for integrity of confession, but with delicacy and charitable tact); or the confessor who becomes anxious over ill-understood principles of moral theology about "habitual sinners" and thinks it is his "duty" to refuse absolution to one who is in great trouble and may be broken by the refusal, whereas he could be helped by charity and understanding.

d) Hence St. Benedict's next important principle: *NE QUID NIMIS*[297]—avoid indiscreet zeal. Beware of this above all; give the benefit of doubt not to the letter of the Law, but to the spiritual peace and welfare of the offender, "lest being too zealous in removing the rust he break the vessel"[298] (c. 64). In administering correction, St. Benedict again warns the superior he must not think so much of the letter of the law as of HIS OWN FRAILTY. Would that severe souls would bear this in mind! They are as frail as the rest; their severity is a way of trying to allay their own anxiety about themselves, and they may unconsciously be punishing others in order to bolster up their own self-confidence. The superior must not break the bruised reed—*not that he must permit evils to grow,* but let him correct them PRUDENTLY AND WITH CHARITY considering circumstances, "in the way which may seem best in each case"[299] (c. 64).

296. Rom. 13:10.
297. "nothing in excess" (McCann, 146).
298. McCann, 146/147.
299. McCann, 146/147.

e) What are the weaknesses which the superior must watch out for in himself? (This applies to all in various degrees—minor superiors, confessors, even the ordinary religious when he goes about the duty of fraternal correction). Ask yourself: does my zeal proceed from restlessness and a spirit of violence (*turbulentus et anxius*[300]); does it proceed from a domineering and obstinate nature (*nimius et obstinatus*[301]); does it proceed from jealousy (*zelotypus*[302]); does it proceed from suspiciousness? Where such motives as these are present, there is lack of peace, lack of interior tranquility. But St. Benedict demands that the superior correct in a spirit of calm, tranquil, inner peace. He himself became a Father of souls only when the passions were calmed within him. There is no real helping of souls as long as we are moved too much by our own passions, fears, anxieties, etc.

f) Another fault that is more or less all-inclusive and leads to general hardness of heart and indifference to the real good of the brethren, *is an excessive care for temporal things*, a religious materialism and self-seeking which leads to all the faults mentioned in detail above and to many others. (N.B.—lack of {a} spirit of poverty means lack of trust in God and hence this is the root of innumerable sins, proceeding at once from greed and fear.) *ANTE OMNIA, NE DISSIMULANS AUT PARVIPENDENS SALUTEM ANIMARUM . . . . PLUS GERAT SOLLICITUDINEM DE REBUS TRANSITORIIS ET TERRENIS ATQUE CADUCIS . . .*[303] (c. 2). A wealth of instruction {is} contained here. When we are centered on material advance and prosperity (and our own reputation and self-satisfaction in so far as they are bound up with these things), we are basically self-seeking, do not seek the things of God, do not really seek souls, are deaf to their real needs and interests, refusing to see things as they are. Such a one may easily console himself with a spurious strictness and severity which pretends to be zeal

300. "upset and anxious" (McCann, 146).

301. "overbearing and stubborn" (McCann, 146).

302. "jealous" (McCann, 146).

303. "Before all, let him not have more concern for transitory, earthly, perishable things, overlooking or undervaluing the salvation of souls" (McCann, 22).

for the things of God, but is in reality simply a means of dominating and exploiting souls. Hence the need for all in the monastery, superiors and subjects alike, to have a great love for poverty and charity and to put aside all worldly cares in order truly to seek God with all their heart. This is the true office of the superior, to see that love is sought above all else in the monastery.

## The Monastic Community

We have seen that the abbot is the head and cornerstone of the monastic community. He represents Christ in the community. But the whole community represents Christ. Let us examine first of all the relations of faith and love which exist between the community and the abbot. It is obvious, first of all, that the abbot does not *do everything* in the community. He may be the head, but he is not the whole community in himself—he is not the only one who thinks and acts—the others remaining automatons. All think, act, work, praise God. All together form "one Christ" loving and praising the Father. For this to be true, the members of the community and the community itself must think, act, work, love. The abbot *leads* the others in all these things, points out the direction. The others follow his lead. But they do not follow merely passively and inertly. They have their *own contribution* to make. They collaborate with the abbot and with one another; they exercise a certain initiative, under the guidance of the abbot. They complete the abbot where he himself is limited. They are a *help* to the abbot and to one another, both materially and spiritually. We must get away from a conception of a community in which the abbot is and does everything and the monks simply hang around his neck or run after him tied to his apron strings. A community in which there is no collaboration is not a true community. Each should have his *contribution* to make—not merely an assignment to fulfill—under the guidance of the abbot, not making a fetish of {one's own} initiative, {with} detachment from {an} instinct of self-expression. {A} middle way always requires more virtue and strength of character.

1. *The Community Chooses the Abbot* (c. 64). First of all, the Holy Ghost, dwelling and acting in the community, guides them in their choice of an abbot. However, St. Benedict by no means equates a popular election with the decision of the Holy Ghost. The choice of the majority is, for St. Benedict, *only one* of the ways in which God shows His will in the choice of a Father for the monastery. (N.B.—see our present *Constitutions*, n. 64:[304] valid abbatial election demands an absolute majority of the votes.) St. Benedict also permitted that the abbot be elected by a smaller part of the community with better judgement (*saniore consilio*[305]). He even, more extraordinary still, permits that the abbot be chosen by the *local bishop*, by abbots of *neighboring monasteries*, or even by the *Christians of the region*. All this is merely a historical curiosity to us—it is no longer in force and has not been for centuries. The disadvantages these ways of electing an abbot involve are only too obvious to us, in retrospect. The point is, St. Benedict believes in the Holy Ghost acting in and speaking through the Church—not only through the community as such, but through any group of the faithful. He does not say precisely *how* one would recognize the Holy Ghost in a given minority. This would presuppose a charismatic gift—canon law does not take account of charisms.

2. *The Abbot Consults the Community in Important Matters* (c. 3). *Quotiens aliqua praecipua agenda sunt in monasterio . . .*[306] St. Benedict suggests that the abbot consult the community in *all* important matters in the monastery. What are these *praecipua*? Canon law states quite clearly those cases in which a vote *must* be taken (see our *Constitutions*, n. 46[307]). What was St. Benedict's

304. "For the validity of the election an absolute majority of the votes is required" (*Constitutions of the Order of the Strict Observance* [Dublin: M. H. Gill & Son, 1924], 20).

305. McCann, 144.

306. "As often as any significant matters are to be undertaken in the monastery . . ." (McCann, 24).

307. "Although, according to the Rule, the Abbot may, after hearing the opinion of the brethren, do what he considers to be most expedient, nevertheless

mind on the point? First, what do the commentators say? *Calmet*[308] includes among the *praecipua*, the important business which is of grave concern to all the community: the reception of novices, as well as their reception to profession; the expulsion of a rebellious or incorrigible monk (or excommunication of same); putting up new buildings (important projects); lawsuits, sale of monastery

---

—I.—The decision shall depend on the majority of the votes of the Conventual Chapter, and the approval of the General Chapter and of the Apostolic See shall be obtained, whenever there is a question of: (1) The alienation of precious objects. (2) The alienation of property, whether movable or immovable, the value of which exceeds 30,000 francs [N.B.—Normally, about £1,200.—Translator's Note.] (3) The contracting of debts and obligations exceeding the sum of 30,000 francs in a single year; or the making of any other contract above this sum, which would place the monastery in a worse condition. (4) The letting of property if the value of the lease exceeds 30,000 francs, and if the lease is for more than nine years. II.—The decision shall depend on the majority of the votes of the Conventual Chapter, and the approval of the General Chapter shall be obtained, whenever there is a question of: (1) The alienation of property the value of which exceeds 10,000 francs [N.B.—Normally, about £400.—Translator's Note.] (2) The contracting of debts and obligations amounting to 10,000 francs in a single year; or the making of any other contract to this amount, which would place the monastery in a worse condition. (3) The purchasing of real estate, the erection, demolition, or restoration of buildings, or the incurring of any other extraordinary and notable expenditure on real property to a sum exceeding 10,000 francs. (4) The letting of property, if the value of the lease exceeds 30,000 francs, and if the lease is not for more than nine years; or if the value of the lease exceeds 10,000 francs, and if the lease is for more than nine years. (5) The undertaking of an industrial enterprise. III.—The decision shall depend on the majority of the votes of the Conventual Chapter, whenever there is a question of: (1) The alienation of property the value of which exceeds 1,000 francs [N.B.—Normally, about £40.—Translator's Note.] (2) The letting of property if the value of the lease exceeds 1,000 francs, and if the lease is for more than nine years. (3) The incurring of any extraordinary expenditure on movable property, exceeding 10,000 francs. (4) The instituting of a lawsuit if there be question of an affair amounting to 10,000 francs. (5) The giving a power of attorney to anyone in an important matter. (6) The admission of a novice to profession, or of a religious from another monastery of our Order to stability in the community. IV.—Whenever there is a question of contracts, Canons 536, 1529, and 1543 of the Codex of Canon Law are to be observed, according as they apply in the circumstances of the case."

308. Calmet, 1.53.

property, long-term leases. In these he is simply summarizing the canonical legislation of his own time. It is close enough to our own present constitutions. *Martène*[309] is about the same; *Hildemar*[310] also, except that he goes into greater detail, says that the community can judge *how long* a brother is to be under penance, {and} adds that the brother is to be absent from these deliberations, and indicates that twenty jars of wine, depending on the local conditions, can be regarded as a "serious" matter, i.e. in a sale or business deal. He also says that the judgement of the community in the matter of an excommunication is *Dei judicium.*[311] So on the whole, in the most ancient commentator we find after all a somewhat democratic attitude, and the community does indeed have a certain amount to say. In fact it would seem that the community had more to say then than now! St. Benedict will say, further on in the chapter, that in *matters of lesser importance* the abbot should decide in consultation with his council. *Hildemar*, in explaining what are the matters of lesser importance (*si qua vero minora*[312]), says—the purchase by the cellarer of "*vasculis*" (barrels for the year's vintage); purchase by the tailor of cloth and clothing.[313] *Martène* says the *minora* are those things which do not necessarily affect the entire community but pertain to certain officers—the choice of the prior, or other officers; "*emere hoc aut illud ad ornandam ecclesiam*"[314] (cf. our building committee). He adds, anything which canon law does not prescribe as matter for a vote of {the} whole community can now be considered as *minor*.

3. *The Different Roles of the Abbot and the Community in these Meetings*:

309. *PL* 66, col. 237C.

310. Hildemar, 130–31.

311. "*necesse est super hoc, ut interrogetur omnis congregatio, ut quod non potest humanis rationibus discerni, Dei judicio discernatur*" ("on this matter it is necessary that the entire community be questioned, so that what cannot be discerned by human reasons may be discovered by the judgement of God") (Hildemar, 131).

312. "if any lesser matters" (McCann, 24).

313. Hildemar, 136–37.

314. *PL* 66, col. 237C: "to buy this or that for decorating the church."

a) The abbot is definitely the one who *decides the case*. The final decision rests with him alone, as does also the full responsibility (in the mind of St. Benedict). (N.B.—present legislation allows for certain cases in which the case is decided by the vote of the community.) St. Benedict says that the abbot *sets forth the matter; hears the advice of the brethren; takes counsel with himself; does what he judges to be most expedient*. He calls the brethren together, recognizing the fact that the Holy Spirit can easily reveal His designs to those who humanly speaking might seem less wise. Here the abbot must realize that the consultation of the community is not just a matter of form. As a truly humble man, he recognizes that he himself does not know everything, and cannot settle everything all by himself. Even though he holds the place of Christ in the monastery, he knows he is not omniscient, and is capable of making mistakes. He admits he might very well be wrong and someone else right, even someone who appears to be unwise. However, he is bound to take the final decision himself, after humbly and sincerely and objectively considering what has been suggested by others. Note that the members of the community may at times reveal the will of God for the community without quite realizing how they do so. The abbot can catch certain implications and nuances, and with the gift of counsel can detect something that the speakers themselves may not be clearly aware of. He can see the direction of the "common will"[315] which reflects the will of God. He does not just try to impose his own will on all the rest, but seeks the advantage of all. Is there no check on the judgement of the abbot? He must judge according to the virtues of *prudence* and *justice*. In so doing, he will above all *follow the Rule* himself. The abbot does not just interpret the *Rule* to suit his own pleasure and interest—he is guided by the *Rule* like the others; he *applies* the *Rule* with freedom and prudence. But his government follows the lines laid down by the

315. See St. Bernard, *In Tempore Resurrectionis, Sermo* 2.8: "*Porro communis voluntas charitas est*" ("Moreover the common will is charity") (*PL* 183, col. 286B); see also *In Tempore Resurrectionis, Sermo* 3.3 (col. 290A).

*Rule*. He does not "rashly depart from it."[316] Here too the abbot is expected to be a modest and humble man, endowed with circumspection and not trusting rashly in his own judgement. "The abbot himself should do all things in the fear of God and the observance of the *Rule*, knowing that he will certainly have to render an account of his judgements to God."[317]

b) The members of the Community should:

*give advice*[318]—they too should not regard the consultation as a mere formality. They should not just be "politicians" in the community and say only what they think the superior expects them to say, following the dictates of a kind of "party line" orthodoxy, like communist puppets. They are free men and sons of God and they should know how to speak out frankly and say what they really think, yet not take their opinions and ideas too seriously either.

*with all deference and humility*[319]—but they must also know how to combine frankness with reverence. This implies great humility on their own part. The monk who is always sure he is right and everyone else is wrong, will inevitably be brusque and rude in his manner of giving advice. He will unconsciously "lay down the law" even to his superiors, even when he thinks he is being very docile and polite. Reverence for authority and for the superior graces and lights of those placed in authority will restrain our impetuosity in giving advice. Incidentally even human good sense and courtesy should tell us that if we do not put forward our opinions in the proper manner, they will inevitably be ignored, or will antagonize and offend others.

*nor venture to defend their opinions obstinately*[320]—spiritual maturity implies detachment from one's self and one's own views. It is a sign of spiritual immaturity and imperfection when

316. McCann, 24/25.

317. McCann, 24/25, which reads: ". . . himself however should . . . and observance . . . of all his judgements . . ."

318. McCann, 24/25, which reads: "give them advice."

319. McCann, 24/25.

320. McCann, 24/25.

a monk cannot see anyone else's point of view but his own, and has to insist on his own opinion, as if to make everyone accept it by force. This implies a failure to realize that no one man sees the whole truth all by himself—that we get only partial views, which have to be completed by the contributions of others. Note: it is very often the superior who is humble and discreet and willing to accept the views of another, rather than the monks themselves who, when their own ideas are rejected or seem to be held of little account, pout and refuse to cooperate. Often those who no longer desire to contribute anything or make any suggestions are merely nursing injured pride which says: "They did not take my advice last time; I will withhold it from them in the future. They'll be sorry!"—as if depriving the rest of the community of a precious spiritual treasure!

*so that what the abbot has decided—all may obey*[321]—here again, detachment and humility crown the work of the disciple. He follows the decision of the superior with a truly supernatural spirit, and gives up the will of his own heart. This, again, is one of the tests of the true monk.

*Nullus in monasterio proprii sequatur cordis voluntatem*[322] (c. 3). This phrase sums up the wisdom of the whole chapter. Neither the abbot nor the community has come to the monastery to seek self. All alike seek the will of God, the abbot as a leader and Father, the community as sons and disciples. The disciple will refrain from arguing with the abbot, especially outside the monastery.

4. *The Order of the Community—Different Officers* etc.

{The} community {is} a body in which all members have their function—{they} supplement one another.

Chapter 63—The General Principle—all take their rank in the community according to *the time at which they entered*. St.

321. McCann, 24/25, which reads: "so that when he has decided what is the better course, all may obey."

322. "Let no one in the monastery follow the will of his own heart" (McCann, 24).

Benedict knows there must be *some* rank. He arranges things so that there will be order, and yet so that the rank of the brethren will be, as far as possible, *based on no human dignity* or *human preference*. To establish the rank of the brethren according to the time of their entrance into the monastery is to get as close as possible to a fair and non-committal disposition of ranks, and one which can be taken to be established by God Himself, the One Who called them to the monastery. {The} purpose {is} to avoid silly human jealousies and contentions about rank and priority {and} to emphasize the dignity that is imparted by God's choice—this leads to respect of one's *own* vocation. Exception: the abbot shall always have power to give a higher place to one of the monks, either because of his superior merit, or because he is a priest, deacon, etc. He shall also have power to *degrade* one of the monks as a punishment. To be the last in the community is regarded as a humiliation. But in all this the abbot must take care not to use his authority arbitrarily. *A further exception*: the young boys shall be in some sense subject to the control of all. This is the first time we see that there are *children* in the monastery, received in early childhood and being educated for the monastic life.

*Monastic Courtesy*

Besides simply legislating for the distinction of rank in the community, St. Benedict gives his real mind—the *order of charity* which underlies this exterior rank, and gives us its true spirit. The purpose of ranking the monks in order of seniority is:

a) the utilitarian purpose of seeing that they go in a certain order to communion, to choir, etc.; but above all:

b) to educate them in mutual respect and affection, in the pattern of a *hierarchical society*. Why is the senior considered in some sense superior to the junior? because he is a *channel of grace* for the junior. He has been in the monastery longer, he has suffered more, gained more experience, is closer to God, is wiser (we hope). His *example*, his *kindness*, his *advice*, his *warnings*, will help the younger monk along the way to God. In return, the younger monk will gain by *respecting* his seniors, and paying attention to them with supernatural docility—not just trying to please them by human courtesy, but revering them in a spirit of faith as members of Christ in whom, by rights at least, the Spirit of God should be dwelling more abundantly. Note that seniority is never a matter of *age*, only length of days in the monastery—a more supernatural attitude. *Hence, {there are} several basic principles of monastic courtesy—supernatural relations with one another* (cf. Confucius—recommend *Hsaio Ching*[323]).

a) *JUNIORES PRIORES SUOS HONORENT; PRIORES MINORES SUOS DILIGANT*[324] (c. 63). In order to preserve this atmosphere of supernatural respect and to educate the monks in it, there are special *appellations*: the younger ones call their seniors *nonnus*[325] (implying reverence and affection); the seniors call the younger ones "*frater*"[326] (brother). All revere the abbot, who is called *Dom'nus* (Dom) and *Abbas*[327]—not because of his own merits, but out of reverence for Christ Who dwells and acts in him. Hence it is not a contradiction of the Lord's command not to call anyone father but Him. READ Matthew 23:8-12,[328] which gives the true spirit of

323. *Hsaio Ching*, trans. Mary Leila Makra, ed. Paul K. T. Sih, Asian Insitute Translations (New York: St. John's University Press, 1961); in his essay "Love and Tao," in *Mystics and Zen Masters*, 69–80, Merton calls this "Classic of Filial Love" "a revelation of the deepest natural wisdom" that presents the "basically *personalistic*" ideal of Confucian ethics (78). This review essay was originally published as "Two Chinese Classics" in *Chinese Culture Quarterly* (June 1962) and in somewhat different form as "Christian Culture Needs Oriental Wisdom" in *The Catholic World* (May 1962); the latter version is found in *A Thomas Merton Reader*, ed. Thomas P. McDonnell (New York: Harcourt, Brace, 1962), 319–26; rev. ed. (Garden City, NY: Doubleday Image, 1974), 295–303.

324. "The junior monks should show honor to their seniors; the more experienced monks should love their newer brothers" (McCann, 142, which reads: ". . . *Juniores igitur* . . .").

325. McCann, 142, which reads: "*nonnos*."

326. McCann, 142, which reads: "*fratrum*."

327. McCann, 144.

328. "But do not you be called 'Rabbi'; for one is your Master, and all you are brothers. And call no one on earth your father; for one is your Father, who is in heaven. Neither be called masters; for one only is your Master, the Christ. He

this chapter of the *Rule*. It is a spirit of *simplicity* and fraternal union. The monk should never be pompous and in love with dignity. We can be glad that this spirit really exists in our monastery!!

b) Titles: *Nonnus* and *Frater*. The juniors should express their reverence for the seniors by using a special title—*Nonnus* (Father) (cf. the use of the appellation "Taita" in Inca communal life[329])—*quod intelligitur paterna reverentia*[330] ({n.b.} *"nonna"* = nun). The seniors in turn call the juniors *Frater*—out of affection and respect. The use of these titles should not be a mere outward formality. One should try to appreciate the inner spirit contained in them, and live accordingly. The junior *asks the senior's blessing (benedicite)*.[331] The "*benedicite*" which we use before speaking was part of the ancient salutation—the blessing that was asked by the junior when he met a senior. The custom is retained now only when we speak: the junior then says *benedicite*—asking a blessing, after which we can talk. Also {there is} the custom of standing when a senior comes to sit next to a junior. How {is this} observed today?—only among the professed. The spirit of these observances {is to accord} real respect for the seniors, especially for priests. It is sad in a monastery to see the young monks with a supercilious and disrespectful air towards others, seniors, even superiors. This is to their own great disadvantage, and is an obstacle to many graces in the monastic life—chiefly because it reflects an attitude that is largely devoid of faith and based more particularly on natural feelings and even on unmortified pas-

---

who is greatest among you shall be your servant. And whoever exalts himself shall be humbled, and whoever humbles himself shall be exalted."

329. "Taita" means "father" in Quechua, the language of the Inca, though it is apparently a loan word from early Spanish; see W. Bollaert, "Observations on the History of the Incas of Peru, on the Indians of South Peru, and on Some Indian Remains in the Province of Tarapaca," *Journal of the Ethnological Society of London (1848–1856)* 3 (1854), 157 n.

330. "which is understood as 'paternal reverence'" (McCann, 144).

331. McCann, 144, which reads: "*benedictionem*" ("*benedicite*" is the plural imperative; "*benedictio*" the noun).

sions, especially unmortified self-love. The practice of supernatural respect involves not only faith and charity, but also much patience, self-denial, prudence, discretion, mortification, and above all *humility*. In a monastery where all take a humble attitude towards one another, the Spirit of God clearly reigns. And where He reigns there is joy and peace. Otherwise there is bitterness, conflict, impatience, uncharitableness: and in the end the only criterion for treating others decently is whether they happen to suit the moods of the moment. Such a community is not living by the Spirit of Christ. At the same time, this observance does not imply that one closes his eyes to reality and makes a hypocritical pretense of viewing all things as "lovely and spiritual," when in fact they may not be so. *It is simply a question of taking things as they are, but with patience, humility and a spirit of faith*, and thus overcoming evil with good. Where there is no love, put in love and you will draw out love.[332] Those who complain that the community "lacks charity" are perhaps themselves the ones most at fault. Note that St. Benedict in several places takes into account the natural turbulence of the very young, the "kids" in his monasteries (children or adolescents). These were not yet trained in a supernatural monastic maturity, and consequently they could not be expected to understand this kind of thing right away. They would then have to be treated a little more firmly, and more or less by all (though not irresponsibly). There is no question of tolerating boyishness and spoiling the younger members by letting them do as they pleased. Overindulgence in this matter would also be harmful. St. Benedict with his usual discretion keeps a middle course ("supervision and discipline, until they come to age of discretion"[333]).

The Abbot is called Dom—*Dom'nus*—Lord. Explain: "For the *honor* and *love* of Christ"[334] (c. 63). How did all monks come

332. St. John of the Cross, Letter 22 (July 6, 1591), to M. María de la Encarnación (Peers, 3.296, which reads: ". . . put love . . . will find love").

333. McCann, 144/145.

334. McCann, 142, 144/143, 145.

to be "Doms" among the Black Benedictines: a reflection of medieval feudalism. They were all lords, in those days.

c) *Honore invicem praevenientes*[335] (c. 72). The whole chapter on Good Zeal is a kind of summary of the community spirit in the mind of St. Benedict. Above all there must be in the community an atmosphere of love and peace—*free from bitterness.* Here St. Benedict guards against *false and bitter zeal as the chief obstacle to a true community life*. This bitter zeal is not just something that spoils the peace of the community, but it even leads to hell and separates the monks from God—thus it goes against the very essence of the monastic life. Note that this bitter zeal is ZEAL—therefore it implies aggressiveness, energy, devotion to an apparent good. It masks as good—it seems to be fervor—it can wear the appearance of self-sacrifice and devotion to duty. Two scriptural texts: READ 1 Corinthians 3:1-15: St. Paul rebuking the evil zeal of the Corinthians.[336] Following their nature as Greeks,

335. "Anticipating one another in showing honor" (Rom. 12:10) (McCann, 160, which reads: "*honore se invicem praeveniant*").

336. "And I, brethren, could not speak to you as to spiritual men but only as carnal, as to little ones in Christ. I fed you with milk, not with solid food, for you were not yet ready for it. Nor are you now ready for it, for you are still carnal. For since there are jealousy and strife among you, are you not carnal, and walking as mere men? For whenever one says, 'I am of Paul,' but another, 'I am of Apollos,' are you not mere men? What then is Apollos? What indeed is Paul? They are the servants of him whom you have believed—servants according as God has given to each to serve. I have planted, Apollos watered, but God has given the growth. So then neither he who plants is anything, nor he who waters, but God who gives the growth. Now he who plants and he who waters are one, yet each will receive his own reward according to his labor. For we are God's helpers, you are God's tillage, God's building. According to the grace of God which has been given to me, as a wise builder, I laid the foundation, and another builds thereon. But let everyone take care how he builds thereon. For other foundation no one can lay, but that which has been laid, which is Christ Jesus. But if anyone builds upon this foundation, gold, silver, precious stones, wood, hay, straw—the work of each will be made manifest, for the day of the Lord will declare it, since the day is to be revealed in fire. The fire will assay the quality of everyone's work: if his work abides which he has built thereon, he will receive reward; if his work burns he will lose his reward, but himself will be saved, yet so as through fire."

loving argument and debate, apparently thirsting for truth, they were in fact dividing the Church by schisms. Paul had to warn them that their human zeal was harmful in the highest degree—it was not based on faith: "where there is envying and contention among you, are you not carnal?" Instead of wasting their energy and fervor in forming factions, they should realize that "neither Paul nor Apollos" is anything, but Christ alone is important. So too, sometimes in large communities, groups tend to form around certain directors or minor superiors with divergent attitudes and outlooks. One is of Paul, one of Cephas, one of Apollos. Zeal is wasted in the service of these divergent opinions; bitterness creeps in, uncharitableness, even political string-pulling. The supernatural unity of the community is thus easily destroyed and great harm can be done. Another text (READ): James 3: 13-18:[337] true and false wisdom. False wisdom is marked by envy and contention and this comes not from God but from the devil. Note the context: he is talking about the sins of the tongue, earlier in the chapter. Bitter zeal expresses itself first of all in indiscreet signs and in speech that savors of detraction. Where this exists, it is impossible for monks to supernaturally honor one another. They have an inordinate respect for some, which is human, and an inordinate contempt for others, which is diabolical. Where the Spirit of Christ reigns, then there is a supernatural respect for all. And note, once again, that this respect can be perfectly realistic, taking account of human failings and limitations, but *seeing beyond* all these. The natural attitude, which is that of bitter zeal,

337. "Who is wise and instructed among you? Let him by his good behavior show his work in the meekness of wisdom. But if you have bitter jealousy and contentions in your hearts, do not glory and be liars against the truth. This is not the wisdom that descends from above. It is earthly, sensual, devilish. For where there is envy and contentiousness, there is instability and every wicked deed. But the wisdom that is from above is first of all chaste, then peaceable, moderate, docile, in harmony with good things, full of mercy and good fruits, without judging, without dissimulation. The fruit of justice is sown in peace by those who make peace."

cannot see beyond the surface. It stops at the failings of the other and sees nothing else. It is blinded by them.

d) Mutual Obedience (c. 71). Obedience is due not only to the abbot—the monks owe it to one another "knowing that by this road of obedience they will go to God."[338] Juniors are to obey their seniors "with all love and diligence."[339] What is to be done to repair a fault by which a junior offends a superior or even a senior? What an expression of real humility St. Benedict demands! And note what great importance he attaches to it—note the expression: *obedientiae bonum*.[340]

e) *Ut nemo perturbetur neque contristetur in domo Dei*[341] (c. 31). It is not sufficient to "honor" one another in theory. We must also *in practice* respect the needs and the rights of others. The two go together. A merely "interior" respect for others, or one that shows itself in formal acts of politeness, but ignores their real convenience and welfare, is a pure illusion. In other words, honor of others must be based first of all on respect for their needs and their rights. We do not in fact honor a person unless we first take account of his rights as a person and as a member of the community. In point of fact, if we pretend to honor the "person" of another and in practice treat him badly or violate his rights, we are not honoring him but only honoring a projected idea of ourselves. Our "honoring" of others is then a pretense. The concrete and sincere expression for respect for our brethren is *considerateness* and *charity*. Basically, justice comes before charity and is included in it. We cannot love others and at the same time refuse them what is due to them. Note chapter 70 in which St. Benedict prohibits his monks from striking one another, or "excommunicating"[342] one another, not cutting others off, treating them

338. McCann, 158/159, which reads: ". . . will they go . . ."

339. McCann, 158/159.

340. "the good of obedience" (McCann, 158); the offender is to prostrate himself until he has been forgiven and blessed by the one offended.

341. "that no one may be troubled or saddened in the house of God" (McCann, 82).

342. McCann, 156.

as outcasts. This is the bare minimum; he gives a negative principle which is simply natural law: *QUOD TIBI NON VIS FIERI, ALIO NE FECERIS*.[343] In the chapter on the cellarer[344] St. Benedict prescribes that all should cooperate in seeing that things are done in the right way and at the right time, that the cellarer should receive sufficient help in his work, that the monks be considerate in asking for things, and that no one be put to any unnecessary inconvenience through the thoughtlessness of certain ones. This principle extends to all our relations with our brethren. We should not deliberately or needlessly hurt or sadden anyone in any way: by our attitude toward them, by rudeness, by lack of charity, by domineering, by being excessively critical and demanding, by being censorious, or just by neglect, carelessness, etc. We should be willing to meet others half-way in everything, and not make exorbitant demands on them, on their time, on their patience. We should always be willing to be *very positive* about sharing the burdens of others. Many think it is enough merely to *not offend* others. They avoid harming others, but they omit to do good to them, and to help them. There can be sins of omission in charity—and these may be more serious than certain sins of commission. In the parable of the Last Judgement,[345] Our Lord speaks principally of *sins of omission*. It is true that our silence isolates us and the *Rule* arranges things so that in fact there is very little opportunity to give spontaneous help to our brethren in general. We are not organized like nuns who run hospitals or teach school—*in view of* active charity. Our *Rule* tends to liberate us to a large degree from active works. But it would be a mistake to think that we never have opportunities to perform them. Such opportunities are innumerable—especially in the exercise of our jobs—at work, as servant of {the} refectory, in choir, etc., etc. We should be on the alert to make things easy and pleasant for our companions in

343. "What you do not want to be done to you, you should not do to another" (Tobit 4:16) (McCann, 156).

344. Chapter 31 (McCann, 80, 82).

345. Mt. 25:31-46.

community, in a discreet way. Our attitude and our relations with others should be such as to offer them constant encouragement and inspiration, not by a forced, artificial piety, but by humaneness, "naturalness," sympathy, understanding, charity, thoughtfulness, and a constant readiness to help if help is needed.

f) *ANTE OMNIA NE MURMURATIONIS MALUM PRO QUALICUMQUE CAUSA . . . APPAREAT*.[346] The basic requirement for a peaceful and charitable family life in the monastery is that each one should restrain the expression of his discontentment and refrain from "murmuring," even interiorly. THIS IS ONE OF THE STRICTEST POINTS IN THE *RULE* AND ONE TO WHICH ST. BENEDICT ATTACHES THE GREATEST IMPORTANCE. It is really fundamental to the whole Benedictine spirit, so that a monk who allows himself to complain and criticize, even if only interiorly, no matter how regular he may be in everything else, is not really a monk according to the mind of St. Benedict. St. Benedict makes this quite clear in the chapter on obedience (READ chapter 5—end[347]): even though the command of the superior is carried out, the one who obeys with protestations and complaints in his heart *is not regarded as truly obedient*. Why? because the virtue of obedience does not require merely that we carry out exteriorly the commands of another, but that we will what is willed by another. To will what is willed by the superior means to obey "*cum bono animo*"[348]—as a *hilaris dator*,[349] a cheerful giver. One who obeys thus, obeys gladly—even though he may disagree in theory with the ideas of the superior. *He wants to obey*. Theoretical disagreement is no obstacle to this desire, in

346. "Before all, do not let the evil of murmuring appear for any reason whatever" (c. 34; McCann, 86).

347. "For if a disciple obeys with a bad attitude, and if he murmurs, not just in speech but even in his heart, even though he carries out an order, it will nevertheless not be acceptable to God, who sees that his heart is murmuring, and for this act he obtains no grace; rather, he incurs the punishment due to murmurers, if he does not make up for it by reparation" (McCann, 34).

348. "with a good attitude" (McCann, 34).

349. 2 Cor. 9:7 (McCann, 34, which reads: "*hilarem datorem*").

a mature mind. But he who obeys *cum malo animo*,[350] does not want to obey. He "wills" it only in so far as he is impelled to do so by another. He does not really move himself to obey, he just lets himself be pushed by the superior to accomplish, unwillingly, what the superior wants done. He obeys "*cum responso* nolentis"[351] (at least interiorly). St. Benedict does not say that he violates his vow. To keep the minimum obligation of the vow, it is sufficient to comply with the command of the superior and carry it out exteriorly. But this is not the ideal of a good religious. An obedient monk, peacefully, and with freedom and gladness of heart, wants to obey and wills to obey. And for the rest his heart is free, not taken up with movements of resistance. The soul that is weak in love and freedom has to exhaust all its efforts in overcoming resistance to the superior's command, and often does not succeed. Immature souls are so weak in love that they are unable to overcome the interior resistance, and obey most unwillingly. They show this by their actions. (N.B. even souls who have progressed a great deal may be allowed to be tempted in this way, to realize their own weakness. They should *admit* their lack of love and strength and ask the Lord to help them, rather than get involved in complicated and bitter self-analysis and self-justification.) Obedience with complaints and unwillingness is *not accepted by God* in so far as it implies a refusal of His will. For in so far as it leads to a recognition of our own poverty and weakness, and prompts us to pray for help and forgiveness, the inner bitterness may be turned to good account. But it is self-love merely to cherish this negative attitude, this bitterness, and to nurse our injured feelings all the time. We should realize the necessity of rising above such things, and pray hard to do so. Otherwise we will incur what St. Benedict calls the "*poena murmurationis*."[352] The only way to avoid this is *cum satisfactione*

350. "with a bad attitude" (McCann, 34).

351. "with the response of someone unwilling" (McCann, 34).

352. "the punishment due to murmurers" (McCann, 34, which reads: "*poenam*").

*EMENDARE*[353]—a positive *reparation* (at least interior). Another principle—whenever the monks *have to do without* something that is strictly due to them, they must learn to do so without murmuring. For instance in chapter 40 (where they may have to do without wine!) they must learn to accept the sacrifice, to BLESS GOD AND NOT MURMUR (READ c. 40[354]). Here again St. Benedict stresses the positive side—not just abstain from murmuring but also and above all, to *bless God*. In the mind of St. Benedict, murmuring is against God, is related to blasphemy, is a dishonor to God, a vilification of His wisdom and love (cf. the Jews and Moses—READ Exodus {15:24-25; 16:2; 17:3}[355]). In order to avoid this "blasphemy" one must positively *bless God* in adversity, to thank Him and praise His wisdom in things that are not to our liking, realizing that they are for our good and manifest His love for us. {It is} *very important to cultivate this attitude*. Without it, the *Opus Dei* is really something of a mockery—our hearts must *live* the sentiments which we speak in choir. But in choir we *bless God* in all things, prosperity and adversity.

g) *SICUT REVERA CHRISTO*.[356] The picture of community relations in St. Benedict's *Rule* can be completed and summed up in this

353. "to make up for it by reparation" (McCann, 34).

354. In this chapter (McCann, 96, 98), Benedict somewhat reluctantly establishes the quantity of wine to be allotted daily to each monk, adding that those who abstain will be rewarded. He goes on to say that on hot summer days, or after particularly demanding work, more can be granted. He notes that it is said that wine is no drink for monks, but comments that in these times monks can't be persuaded to agree with this, so temperance rather than abstinence is the rule. However, he concludes, in times when less than the allotted portion is available, or even no wine at all, the monks should bless God and not "murmur"—he repeats, "*hoc ante omnia admonentes, ut absque murmurationibus sint*" ("making this warning above all—that they keep away from murmuring").

355. "As the people grumbled against Moses, saying, 'What are we to drink?' he appealed to the Lord . . ."; "Here in the desert the whole Israelite community grumbled against Moses and Aaron"; "Here, then, in their thirst for water, the people grumbled against Moses, saying, 'Why did you ever make us leave Egypt? Was it just to have us die here of thirst with our children and our livestock?'" (chapter and verse numbers left blank in typescript).

356. "indeed as Christ" (McCann, 90).

phrase taken from the chapter on the sick (c. 36): *De infirmis fratribus*.[357] The fact that the sick (c. 36) and all types of guests (c. 53) are to be looked on as Christ does not exclude the community itself. St. Benedict places special emphasis on seeing Christ in those with whom we might perhaps find difficulty in doing so at first. Naturally we will see Christ in the abbot and in our brethren more easily—because of their office, because of their virtuous actions, etc. The sick cannot measure up to all the demands of the *Rule*—they may not appear to be as sick as they are—we may not understand certain weaknesses which appear to us {to be} lack of virtue and religious perfection, etc. They are to be seen and served *as Christ*. (Read Matt. 25—on the Last Judgement, which St. Benedict calls to witness here.[358]) The chapter on the sick is important and interesting:

(a) the sick are to be served as Christ;

(b) the sick themselves should remember this fact, and it should make them humble and patient, and help them take a supernatural attitude toward their brethren and not be too demanding;

(c) the infirmarians should bear patiently with impatient patients—St. Benedict does not expect consummate perfection in anyone—he expects them to meet one another half-way and do the best they can in the situation;

(d) the abbot is held seriously responsible (*cura maxima sit abbati*[359]) for seeing that the sick are not neglected in *any way*;

(e) the sick have their own quarters;

(f) the infirmarian is called their *servant* (*servitor*[360]) and he must be distinguished by his supernatural spirit (*timens Deum*[361]) and by his diligence;

(g) the sick are allowed baths and meat (this would have been regarded by the Desert Fathers as a scandalous relaxation)—

357. "On Sick Brothers" (McCann, 90).

358. Benedict quotes the lines "I was sick and you visited me" (v. 36) and "Whatsoever you did to one of these least ones, you did to me" (v. 40).

359. "the abbot should take the greatest care" (McCann, 90).

360. McCann, 90.

361. "fearing God" (McCann, 90).

N.B. even today the Carthusians take a special vow not to eat meat ever, even when sick; however they get fish on their regular diet.

All this shows a spirit of discretion, mercy and human understanding in St. Benedict. He does not expect his monks to be made of iron, he expects infirmity and patience, and the infirmities of his monks, whether bodily or spiritual, are accounted for in his plan for the sanctification of all.

{In} chapter 53 (*De Hospitibus Suscipiendis*[362]), here again we learn many things about St. Benedict's conception of community life. ALL guests who happen to come along are to be received as Christ. Hospitality {is} an integral part of Benedictine monasticism. *Honor* {is} to be shown to the guests—his prescriptions seem exaggerated in our context. We must place ourselves in his position. Note that the superior will even break the monastic fast in order to join the guest at table, if necessary. This practice was approved by the Desert Fathers. Charity comes before austerity. The guestmaster, like the infirmarian, must have a supernatural outlook (*cujus animam timor Dei possideat*[363]) and he must take care of his domain wisely. This gives us another of St. Benedict's principles: *DOMUS DEI A SAPIENTIBUS ET SAPIENTER ADMINISTRETUR*.[364] Note the simplicity with which St. Benedict deals with the problem of keeping silence with the guests: the monk who does not speak with them simply tells them this and passes on, asking their blessing.

Having seen the principles on which community relations are based, let us now look at the officers of the community, who assist the abbot in his work and promote the smooth functioning of the community by serving their brethren and one another in a spirit of faith and love, "in the fear of the Lord."[365]

362. "On Receiving Guests" (McCann, 118, 120, 122).

363. "whose soul the fear of God controls" (McCann, 120, 122, which reads: "*possidet*").

364. "Let the house of God be administered wisely, and by wise men" (McCann, 122).

365. Both the cellarer (c. 31; McCann, 80) and the infirmarian (c. 36; McCann, 90) are described as "*timens Deum*" ("fearing God"); the actual phrase "fear of

Chapter 21: The Deans of the Monastery. What is a dean? {It is a} term from Roman military life: one in charge of ten soldiers—"*decanus*." In ancient monasteries, the dean was a monk placed over nine or ten others—either spiritually, or materially, or both. Read Exodus {18:13-26}: the "deans" chosen to help Moses in ruling the Chosen People.[366] {Here is the} scriptural basis for this chapter of St. Benedict. These deans were sometimes chosen by the abbot alone, sometimes by the abbot and the community, but not for life. Today, the institution of "deans" does not exist in the monastery. What is said of the deans applies to the officers in general.

---

the Lord" is found in the Prologue: "*timorem Domini docebo vos*" ("I will teach you the fear of the Lord," a quotation from Ps. 33[34]:12) (McCann, 8).

366. "The next day Moses sat in judgment for the people, who waited about him from morning until evening. When his father-in-law saw all that he was doing for the people, he inquired, 'What sort of thing is this that you are doing for the people? Why do you sit alone while all the people have to stand about you from morning till evening?' Moses answered his father-in-law, 'The people come to me to consult God. Whenever they have a disagreement, they come to me to have me settle the matter between them and make known to them God's decisions and regulations.' 'You are not acting wisely,' his father-in-law replied. 'You will surely wear yourself out, and not only yourself but also these people with you. The task is too heavy for you; you cannot do it alone. Now, listen to me, and I will give you some advice, that God may be with you. Act as the people's representative before God, bringing to him whatever they have to say. Enlighten them in regard to the decisions and regulations, showing them how they are to live and what they are to do. But you should also look among all the people for able and God-fearing men, trustworthy men who hate dishonest gain, and set them as officers over groups of thousands, of hundreds, of fifties, and of tens. Let these men render decisions for the people in all ordinary cases. More important cases they should refer to you, but all the lesser cases they can settle themselves. Thus, your burden will be lightened, since they will bear it with you. If you do this, when God gives you orders you will be able to stand the strain, and all these people will go home satisfied.' Moses followed the advice of his father-in-law and did all that he had suggested. He picked out able men from all Israel and put them in charge of the people as officers over groups of thousands, of hundreds, of fifties, and of tens. They rendered decisions for the people in all ordinary cases. The more difficult cases they referred to Moses, but all the lesser cases they settled themselves" (chapter and verse numbers left blank in typescript).

a) Qualifications: *fratres boni testimonii et sanctae conversationis.*[367] They live edifying lives. They are good monks: "*boni testimonii*" {means being} a "witness" {to} the Christ living in the monastery. *In quibus securus abbas partiatur onera sua:*[368] they are men who can be trusted. This means to say they are serious and mature—you can give them a job and be reasonably sure that it will be carried out. Monks must train themselves to grow in a sense of maturity and responsibility. Too often they do not carry out the job as it is given to them, but they waste time in something else, or accomplish nothing in spite of their efforts. A "*decanus*" must be someone who can be left on his own to carry out an assignment—not one who has to be constantly watched and told what to do next.

b) *Non eligantur per ordinem*[369]—it is not seniority that counts but *vitae meritum et sapientiae doctrinam.*[370] (What is meant by *sapientiae doctrina*?)

c) Finally, and above all, they must be *humble men*. Otherwise they are not fit for their post.

"THE SENIORS": note that though seniority is not in itself a requisite for a responsible post, and does not guarantee an appointment to one, the "seniors" in the monastery have a definite influence and function, not only by reason of example, but also because the seniority and prestige give them a certain responsibility with regard to the juniors. They are supposed to help keep order in the dormitory (c. 22). They are to be obeyed by the juniors. They are sent to comfort the excommunicated brethren and help them get back to regular life (c. 27). They are appointed as circators to see that the brethren read and do not waste time (c. 48). There must always be some seniors in the refectory to keep order in the absence of the abbot (c. 56). In all these cases

367. "brothers of good reputation and a holy way of life" (McCann, 68).

368. "with whom the abbot may share his burdens without worrying" (McCann, 68).

369. "let them not be chosen by rank" (McCann, 68, 70).

370. "by worthiness of life and teaching of wisdom" (McCann, 70).

the seniors may also be deans and probably are, but St. Benedict does not specify. The elder members of the community by reason of their seniority are responsible in some measure for discipline and good order everywhere.

Taking the chapters on the officers in the monastery in the order in which they come in the *Rule*, we find a group of chapters (30-38) in which the exterior and material side of the monastic life is regulated. In these chapters we learn about the CELLARER (c. 31) and those who work under the cellarer—those who keep the tools (c. 32), the weekly cooks (35), the infirmarian (36). Since the chapter on the reader comes here (38) we might as well consider him also, and then pass on to the chapter on work in general (48), the guest master (53), the craftsmen of the monastery (57), then the priests (62), the prior (65), and the gatekeeper (66). In all these chapters we get a detailed picture of the monastic community and of its members. The picture is very instructive.

THE CELLARER OF THE MONASTERY. First we must realize that for the purposes of our study, this chapter on the cellarer gives us something more than just an idea of the cellarer's job. It is rather a picture of *a completely mature monk,* according to the mind of St. Benedict. It gives us further insight into the qualifications of a monk to whom the abbot can entrust *responsibility.* The obvious conclusion is that this is a chapter not only for cellarers but for *all monks* to take seriously. Everyone in the monastery should strive to live up to this picture, in proportion to his job and situation. It is a very important chapter, showing not only St. Benedict's idea of a good serious monk, but also giving deep insight into his idea of the monastic life and of the monastic family. One who has not yet absorbed the teaching of this chapter does not yet fully appreciate the Benedictine spirit. Note that the cellarer can be a powerful force for good or evil in the monastery. Paul Warnefrid says in his commentary: "Through the cellarer many vices may be nourished or cut off in the monastery. It is well that St. Benedict stipulated what kind of man he ought to be, for he realized the great good that would follow if the cellarer of the monastery were wise, and the great danger that would threaten were he unwise."[371] {This is relevant to} relations of {the} monastery and "the world." Withdrawal {is} not an end in itself: it {allows for} getting a grip, a new perspective, returning undivided—not serving God and mammon: if the cellarer is undivided—OK.

1. *The virtues of the mature monk.* He is *sapiens*[372]—this does not mean that he overflows with infused wisdom, or is a mystic, but that he has a well-balanced mind and practical prudence. He is full of the *wisdom of life*—the kind of *sapientia* that is taught in the sapiential books of the Bible. This wisdom should not be regarded as something "merely natural"—it is a *wholesome blend of faith and common sense* which makes a man "supernaturally natural," and in the long run this combination is of much more value than an unbalanced, quasi-mystical combination of deep piety and no sense. *Maturus moribus*:[373] the word *maturus* contains the idea of *ripeness*, of something that has reached its full development, something that implies a long preparation, lack of haste. Hence, in his actions, this monk is not precipitous or impulsive, is not driven onward blindly by the impressions of the moment, but is in full control; is able to think and judge calmly, is not upset by every ripple on the surface of community life, or thrown into a dither by a chance remark of the superior, or a thoughtless act on the part of one of the brethren. {He is marked by} calm, peacefulness, good sense, control, discretion, patience: the ability to wait for things to come out in their own time, to attune oneself to the tempo of life, and not to try to force everything violently to take one's own tempo. Such are the ideas contained in *maturus moribus*. {This is} the character of a thoughtful and peaceful man. The adjectives that follow are developments of this idea:

371. Warnefrid, 310 (= Hildemar, 373), quoted in Schroll, 63, which reads: ". . . well that he stipulated . . ."

372. "wise" (McCann, 80).

373. "mature in behavior" (McCann, 80).

a) Sobriety—if he is calm and controlled, it is because he is temperate and restrained in everything, not carried away by any of his appetites. {He} does not eat much, is not proud and sensitive, touchy or bossy; is not a trouble-maker, sowing discord, upsetting people by his rough ways, insulting them, etc.; at the same time he is not slothful and slow, but prompt in his work and in his service of others (*non tardus*[374]); and finally he is not wasteful, not a thoughtless spender, an imprudent investor. It is worthwhile reflecting on the importance of all these things to St. Benedict. They do not constitute high sanctity, indeed, but they have a real part to play in monastic perfection.

b) Faith—"*timens Deum*":[375] all these possible vices are cut off at the root by the *fear of God*. To understand this better we must look at the degrees of humility (c. 7) but in any case the cellarer, the mature monk, is able to live constantly and quietly in the presence of God (see Ecclesiasticus 1:16-28[376]). Note that nowhere in this chapter does St. Benedict raise the issue of a possible conflict between action and contemplation. He presupposes that the cellarer, being a mature monk, is able to carry on his work in a spirit of prayer, and he also presupposes that the monastery being a house of prayer, and the life of the monastic family being run on supernatural lines, there will not be such an abundance of worldly business that the cellarer will be utterly distracted by it. The work and the material care of the monastery is of such a nature, in the mind of St. Benedict, that it is kept within rightful limits and does not lead to inordinate distractions. The normal distractions of an average day on the farm do not amount to anything in his eyes.

374. "not dilatory" (McCann, 80).

375. "fearing God" (McCann, 80).

376. These verses are part of the opening chapter in praise of personified wisdom, associated with the fear of the Lord; they recommend patience, prudence and humility, and counsel restraint in giving way to anger; they conclude by condemning duplicity and hypocrisy, and warn: "Exalt not yourself lest you fall and bring upon you dishonor; for then the Lord will reveal your secrets and publicly cast you down" (vv. 27-28).

c) KINDNESS—"*omni congregationi sit sicut Pater*":[377] {this is} a further commentary on the *juniores diligere*[378] (cf. c. 63 and c. 4). Those who have a job in the community which involves the care of others, should treat those in their care *as persons and not as objects*. This means having for them the care and affection of a father—understanding their needs and difficulties as a father understands those of his son. It means also excusing the weaknesses of others as a father understands and excuses the weaknesses of a child. It is important to note the tenderness and human sympathy implicit in this expression. The officers in a Benedictine monastery are *not mere functionaries or bureaucrats*. We must get as far away as possible from the mentality of the bureaucrat—the impersonal job-holder, the "civil servant" who deals not with persons, nor even with objects, but with "cases" and with red tape. Such a mentality would be the mentality of "the world" in its worst sense and is to be understood as one of the main things we must avoid, in our day, when, following St. Benedict, we try to "make ourselves strangers to the ways of the world" (*a saeculi actibus se facere alienum*[379]—c. 4).

d) HUMILITY—"*ante omnia*":[380] he must be *before all else* humble. {The} context is significant—he must not get angry *when he cannot provide* everything, not fear to be blamed or criticized—he must be above all that. He must be content with the poverty of the monastery and if he has nothing material to give he must give at least his charity. {He needs} understanding for irrational requests—patience: "*non spernendo eum contristet*";[381] "*sermo responsionis porrigater bonus*!"[382] This is a mark of a good and mature religious. From the fullness of the heart the mouth speaketh.[383]

377. "Let him be like a father to the whole community" (McCann, 80).
378. "to love the juniors" (McCann, 30; cf. 142).
379. McCann, 26.
380. "before all" (McCann, 82).
381. "he should not sadden him by scorning him" (McCann, 80).
382. "a good word should be offered in answer" (McCann, 82).
383. Mt. 12:34; Lk. 6:45.

2. *His responsibilities*. Discuss—exactly what is *responsibility*? the capacity to "answer for" a certain good entrusted to one's care; the ability to "take over" a charge and *develop* something that needs to be developed; the ability to account for harm that comes to a thing or person, and to make up for it. Basically, responsibility implies *love*—love for one's charge, for persons entrusted to one, for those to whom one is accountable—cf. {the} Parable of {the} Talents.[384] Love and responsibility in monastic life {mean} we are accountable *to God* for *His sons*: "*curam gerat de omnibus*"[385]—*all* the material side of the monastery is under his charge. He is really responsible; he is not just a figurehead—he does the work. But at the same time, he does his work *according to the desires of the abbot*. He is not an autonomous superior—he must consult his superior in everything and follow his instructions. It takes maturity and balance to be responsible and yet to exercise one's responsibilities according to the wishes of another. It takes a great deal of virtue to be at the same time an *effective* and a *dependable* subordinate. Many are so dependable that they are only yes men and one can depend on them for nothing. Others on the contrary are efficient but completely independent, and seek their own glory and the satisfaction of their own ambition in their work. They will do good work, but not in the way the superior wants it done. They are working for themselves.

3. *His dealings with the brethren*. "*Fratres non contristet*"[386]—he should always be considerate of their feelings even when they have been unreasonable with him. There will be requests made that cannot be fulfilled; they will indeed be stupid. But the cellarer must not just treat them as stupid. With all due respect for his brother, he must deny the request in a reasonable manner and not "*spernendo*"[387]—the word suggests replying with a kick, or a push—mental or otherwise.

384. Mt. 25:14-30; Lk. 19:12-27.

385. "let him take care of everything" (McCann, 80).

386. "he should not make the brothers upset" (McCann, 80).

387. "by scorning" (McCann, 80).

4. *His duty to his own soul.* He must use his job to save his soul—*animam suam custodiat.*[388] {This} does not mean just "keep recollected." {It involves} care and concern for all—especially the sick, the *poor* (note his obligation to others outside the monastery)—FOR ALL THESE HE WILL GIVE AN ACCOUNT TO GOD. The mature monk must be capable of taking responsibility for others.

*Lesser Responsibilities—Under the Cellarer*:

Chapter 32—the TOOL SHOP. Here again trustworthy brethren are placed in charge of the tools used on the farm and in the shops (*custodienda—recolligenda*[389]). {The} modern mentality {of} commercial society artificially promotes quick obsolescence—{this is a} falsification of perspective—{the} safety pin hasn't been[390] perfected since {the} bronze age—{cf. the} Shakers and {the} Cistercian mentality.[391] The abbot keeps the list of what is supposed to be there—and the brethren are accountable for losses, depreciation, breakage, etc. *All* must treat tools and other monastery property with great care. Punishment is imposed for any sloppy or negligent treatment (*sordide aut negligenter*[392]) of tools (c. {46}[393]). *All* should feel a certain responsibility in this regard. The *cellarer* above all must be as careful of tools etc. as if they were vessels of the altar (c. 31).

Chapter 46 shows what must be done to amend for carelessness in using tools etc. The one who breaks something must accuse himself and admit his fault. {The} application and meaning of this {is that it is} not just a formality—not a routine of showing broken shoelaces and bean plants one has hit by mistake

388. "let him guard his own soul" (McCann, 82).

389. "to be cared for—to be gathered together again" (McCann, 84).

390. Presumably Merton means "has been" here.

391. Merton relates Shaker and Cistercian craftsmanship in his discussion of *theoria physike* in *An Introduction to Christian Mysticism*, 133–34.

392. "sloppily or carelessly" (McCann, 84).

393. Text reads "36".

with the hoe. *Disciplinae regulari subjaceat?*[394]—the "seven steps."[395]

Chapter 35—The Weekly Cooks. All should take their turn cooking and serving in refectory. Why? St. Benedict sees the value of working for others and doing something to serve them and satisfy their needs. It is a source of merit and of natural good as well. *Exinde major merces et caritas acquiritur.*[396] Thus one grows in love and in perfection. We should see it in this light, not just as a "duty" which comes round and has to be done. (N.B. of course we no longer take turns in *cooking—Deo gratias.*[397]) (At Cluny, abbot, cellarer and deans cooked and served Christmas dinner!) Note again a principle that keeps coming up everywhere in the *Rule*: those who cannot handle the job alone should be given help, *ut non cum tristitia hoc faciant.*[398] Note also the significance of the prayers and ceremonies connected with the weekly service in the refectory.

a) The *mandatum*. {This is} to remind us of Jesus' own words—and of the fact that this is something *essential* in our life—this service of one another. Read St. John 13:1-17.[399]

394. "Let him undergo the discipline of the *Rule*" (c. 32; McCann, 84).

395. According to Warnefrid, 296 (quoted in Schroll, 91–92), the seven steps (drawn from *RB*, cc. 23, 24, 28, 30) are: (1) secret admonition; (2) public correction; (3) excommunication; (4) severe fasts; (5) corporal punishment; (6) prayer; (7) expulsion; see also Martène, cols. 870A (citing Hildemar and Bernard of Monte Cassino) and 872AC (citing Bernard of Monte Cassino, Boherius and Hildemar).

396. "From this a greater reward and more love is acquired" (McCann, 86).

397. "Thanks be to God."

398. "so that they may do this without sadness" (McCann, 86).

399. "Before the feast of the Passover, Jesus, knowing that the hour had come for him to pass out of this world to the Father, having loved his own who were in the world, loved them to the end. And during the supper, the devil having already put it into the heart of Judas Iscariot, the son of Simon, to betray him, Jesus, knowing that the Father had given all things into his hands, and that he had come forth from God and was going to God, rose from the supper and laid aside his garments, and taking a towel girded himself. Then he poured water into the basin and began to wash the feet of the disciples, and to dry them with the towel with which he was girded. He came, then, to Simon Peter. And Peter said to him, 'Lord, dost thou wash my feet?' Jesus answered and said to him,

Comment on some of the texts sung at our *mandatum*.[400]

b) *Munditias faciant*[401]—everything they have used during the week must be turned over clean and ready, to those of the following week.

---

'What I do thou knowest not now; but thou shalt know hereafter.' Peter said to him, 'Thou shalt never wash my feet!' Jesus answered him, 'If I do not wash thee, thou shalt have no part with me.' Simon Peter said to him, 'Lord, not my feet only, but also my hands and my head!' Jesus said to him, 'He who has bathed needs only to wash, and he is clean all over. And you are clean, but not all.' For he knew who it was that would betray him. This is why he said, 'You are not all clean.' Now after he had washed their feet and put on his garments, when he had reclined again, he said to them, 'Do you know what I have done to you? You call me Master and Lord, and you say well, for so I am. If, therefore, I the Lord and Master have washed your feet, you also ought to wash the feet of one another. For I have given you an example, that as I have done to you, so you also should do. Amen, amen, I say to you, no servant is greater than his master, nor is one who is sent greater than he who sent him. If you know these things, blessed shall you be if you do them. . . .'"

400. Cf. *Regulations of the Order of Cistercians of the Strict Observance* (Dublin: M. H. Gill, 1926), 185: "393. . . . Every Saturday of the year, before the lecture before Compline, the **Mandatum** takes place. This ceremony is performed by the servant of the refectory who has finished his week, and the religious appointed to succeed him on the following day. It is announced by five tolls of the great bell, some time before the lecture, earlier or later, according to the number of the religious. 394. All the community assist at it, although the feet of the choir religious only are washed. At the sound of the bell all repair to the cloister, and take their places in the same order as for the lecture before Compline. The Reverend Father Abbot uncovers his feet, as also do all the religious. Both feet are uncovered. . . . When the servants enter, the Abbot, or in his absence the Cantor, intones the antiphon **Postquam surrexit**, etc., without rising. The community continues the antiphon, which is repeated. The other antiphons are always intoned by the Cantor. Each religious, when his feet have been washed, makes a moderate bow to the servants. When the ceremony is nearly ended, the Cantor intones the antiphon **Benedicat nos Deus**. This antiphon, as also the first, should never be omitted. As soon as the **Mandatum** is finished, the lecture is begun, no bell being rung."

401. "Let them do the cleaning up" (McCann, 86, which reads: "*faciat*").

c) The prayers at the end of Matins, on Sunday—for the servant of {the} refectory. READ and explain them.[402]

Note {that} St. Benedict allows the mixt for the servants of {the} refectory—they and the reader were the only ones who got any "breakfast."[403] This is another indication of St. Benedict's spirit of discretion and charity, and of his desire that no one should be overburdened but that all might carry out their tasks peacefully and without excessive strain. His wish to temper all burdens and adjust them to the strength of the ones carrying them *amounts to a fundamental principle* in his *Rule*.

Chapter 38—The Weekly Reader. In this chapter we see St. Benedict's usual concern that everything in the monastery should be done with *order*, *humility* and *prayer*.

a) *Mensis fratrum lectio deesse non debet . . .*[404] The brethren must receive spiritual as well as bodily nourishment. Note that the reading helps to make meals a spiritual exercise like every

402. The outgoing server prays three times, "*Benedictus es Domine Deus, qui adjuvasti me et consolatus es me*" ("Blessed are you, Lord God, who have helped me and consoled me") (Dan. 3:26; Ps. 85[86]:17); then the incoming server prays, "*Deus in adjutorium meum intende, Domine ad adjuvandum me festina*" ("O God, come to my assistance; Lord, make haste to help me") (Ps. 69[70]:1), which is repeated three times by all the brothers (McCann, 88). See *Regulations of the Order of Cistercians*, c. 6 (215–16): "461. **The Prayers for the Servants**. On Sunday, towards the end of Lauds, the servant who has finished his week goes to the presbytery step, on the side where he is placed in choir, and salutes first the altar, and then the two choirs. After the verse **Fidelium**, he bows profoundly towards the altar and sings three times alternately with the choir, the verse **Benedictus es, Domine Deus, qui adjuvisti me et consolatus es me**. After the blessing, he salutes the altar and returns to his place. While he is receiving the blessing, his successor goes to the step on the opposite side. He acts in the same way as the other servant, but instead of the verse **Benedictus es**, he says the verse **Deus in adjutorium meum intende, Domine, ad adjuvandum me festina**; and when the blessing has been given, he withdraws into one of the first stalls of the lower choir. If the Office is not sung, both verses are said **in directum**."

403. McCann, 88.

404. "Reading should not be lacking at the meals of the brothers" (McCann, 92).

other. But even without the reading, a meal in the refectory is a spiritual as well as a corporal act, because the *community* ("Christ") is gathered together, the assembly and the food are blessed, the abbot presides taking the place of Christ, there is always at least some service offered by one to another. Even when there is not reading the meal can be a time of prayer and thought (mixt-collation). However the reading at meals is an important source of spiritual nourishment—and a source of grace. *Cassian* points out[405] that reading at meals did not originate in Egypt (where recollection was more perfect and there was greater silence at meals) but among the Cappadocian monks (cf. St. Basil[406]) who, says Cassian, were inclined to talk and quarrel at meals. Reading was instituted, according to him, to *promote peace* in the refectory. The reading is always taken in part from Scripture. In some monasteries today nothing but Scripture is read. In the old days Scripture was *sung*. The aim was to cover in the refectory all parts of the sacred books that were not read in choir. St. Benedict does not specify, just says let there be "reading." In modern monasteries there is usually a judicious mixture of reading from interesting and sometimes even topical books. The purpose of the reading {is} to help the monks. Reading does not help unless it is absorbed and understood. In trying to be "ultramonastic"—reading Scripture alone, and in a kind of monotone—one would risk putting many of the monks to sleep. We must remember that many of the busier brothers, at certain seasons, depend very much on public reading for their whole spiritual nourishment during these times of extra work.

405. *De Institutis Coenobiorum*, 4.17 (*PL* 49, cols. 174A–177A); see *Cassian and the Fathers*, 152.

406. Question 180 of the *Short Rules* asks: "With what mind and what attention should what is read to us as we are eating be heard?" Basil's response is: "With greater pleasure than that with which we eat and drink, so that the mind might be seen to be undistracted by the pleasures of the body, but rather to find greater enjoyment in the words of the Lord, just as he had been moved who said, 'they are sweeter than honey and the honeycomb' [Ps. 18[19]:11]" (J. P. Migne, ed., *Patrologiae Cursus Completus, Series Graeca*, 161 vols. [Paris: Garnier, 1857–1866], vol. 31, col. 1203).

The reader must therefore realize that his office is one of *fraternal charity and edification*. His efforts really mean something in the spiritual life of the ones listening. Often monks receive special lights and graces from the book in the refectory or chapter.

b) The reader is appointed for the whole week—reading is not done at random by the first one who feels like picking up the book.

c) {Note the} prayer at the High Mass (a solemn moment) that the reader may be protected against pride. But above all {he} prays for the grace of God to help him in his work. St. Benedict at every turn reminds the monk of his dependence on the divine mercy.

d) *summum fiat ibi silentium . . .*[407] {The} refectory {is} a place of special silence. Care {is taken} in not making useless or thoughtless noises. Signs {are} to be used in asking for what is lacking. (Note—the Black Benedictines are silent, as we are, in the refectory. But their service and their signs in general are more courteous and expressive than ours.) {The} reader {should foster an} atmosphere of peace and simplicity in {the} refectory, {marked by} silence, courtesy and concern, *humanitas*. (Comments?)

e) *No one should comment on the reading*—{this is} an important aside, {which} probably refers to Cassian and to the danger of arguments, differences of opinion arising.

f) The reader takes the mixt (cf. what was said about {the} servant of {the} refectory).

g) Not everyone should read in turn, "*sed qui aedificent audientes*"[408]—a common-sense observation, whose importance may sometimes be overlooked. The important thing is not that everyone should "do his duty" in the reader's pulpit, but that the community be edified. The emphasis {is} on the good of the community, not on the individual fulfillment of the task—"Everybody's got to do it!"

407. "there should be complete silence there" (McCann, 92, which omits "*ibi*").

408. "but those who might edify the listeners" (McCann, 94, which reads: "*aedificant*").

The Daily Manual Labor (c. 48). At this point we can consider the chapter on work and reading. Note that the two go together in St. Benedict's mind. Very often it is pointed out that the monk has three main obligations: choir, *lectio divina*, and manual labor—their importance graduated in this order. One might ask, is it not more truly the mind of St. Benedict to put it this way: the monk leads an overall life of prayer, in which two things are important (*ora et labora*[409]): (a) formal prayer whether public (divine office) or private; (b) useful activity:

1. *Lectio divina*, for the monk's own interior life and spiritual formation;

2. Manual labor, for the good of the community as well as for the monk himself.

All of this {is} to be carried on in an atmosphere of prayer and peace, sacrifice and self-dedication.

({For} *Oblati*—see Hildemar: 419,[410] 439,[411] 420,[412] 203,[413] 334,[414] 337,[415]

409. See above, n. 26.

410. "Thus all their needs are to be satisfied, so that, having been reared with plentiful nourishment, they will not require it when they are older" (quoted in Schroll, 142).

411. "Children ought to eat often but not so much [at a time]" (quoted in Schroll, 142).

412. "In summer, the children are not to anticipate the evening meal as they generally anticipate the midday meal, unless perhaps some are so small that such anticipation is necessary" (quoted in Schroll, 143).

413. See Schroll, 143: "In winter, when they enter the calefactory, their masters should be present to prevent their romping or playing about" (not a direct quotation).

414. See Schroll, 143: "In church they are to chant and pray, standing with their masters; this applies to the night Office as well as to the Hours of the day" (not a direct quotation).

415. See Schroll, 144: "In concluding the discussion, Hildemar insists that the recommendations he has just enunciated are based on the Rule; that he is not teaching new things, but rather, that he understands the commands of the Rule properly and has even seen them put into practice in the manner he has described."

578,[416] 190–191;[417] *Benedictine Monachism*: 323 f.[418])

*Otiositas inimica est animae.*[419] This basic principle sounds like a proverb—it certainly reflects much of the teaching of the Book of Proverbs (cf. Prov. 6:6-11—READ;[420] cf. Prov. 13:4—*vult et non vult piger*[421]). {Note} the importance of this in the life of prayer—cf. James 1:6-8: the hesitant man obtains nothing in prayer. Vacillation and inconstancy is of no use in the interior life. It ruins {the} life of the soul. {Note the} danger of daydreaming. A contemplative life that is all words and ideas and never takes effect in any kind of work is utterly useless. Work (intellectual or physical) integrates thought and life into a single unity. Without this integration, "contemplation" leads only to illusion and ruin. On the other hand, *busy and solicitous activity* or "activism" is

416. See Schroll, 144–45: "such as do not 'know discipline' ought never be permitted to rebuke or punish the children, because if these stupid and negligent ones were allowed to do this they would, through terror, make the children worse instead of better" (not a direct quotation).

417. Merton misreads Schroll's reference here: she is referring to pages not in Hildemar but later in her own book: after noting Hildemar's suggestion to encourage good behavior in boys by public praise and sharing food for guests with them (Hildemar, 419–20; Warnefrid, 347), Schroll notes, "He speaks elsewhere and forcibly of the highest spiritual motives" (146), and refers to pages 190–91, where the motives of fear of punishment, promises made at profession, love of heavenly inheritance, and love of God above all are enumerated (Hildemar, 188; Warnefrid, 124), and a passage on the traditional three-fold grouping of slaves, vassals (mercenaries) and sons (Hildemar, 188–89; Warnefrid, 124) is quoted.

418. Butler summarizes much the same material (taken from Warnefrid) as is found in Schroll, and refers also to the curriculum of the early monastic schools, focusing on the trivium of grammar, logic and rhetoric.

419. "Idleness is the enemy of the soul" (McCann, 110).

420. "Go to the ant, O sluggard, study her ways and learn wisdom; for though she has no chief, no commander or ruler, she procures her food in the summer, stores up her provisions in the harvest. How long, O sluggard, will you rest? When will you rise from your sleep? A little sleep, a little slumber, a little folding of the arms to rest—then will poverty come upon you like a highwayman, and want like an armed man."

421. "The sluggard wants and does not want."

equally ruinous for the monastic spirit. The monk must learn to strike the happy medium, in humble, peaceful and productive activity of mind and body. *Peacefulness and productivity* are regulated most of all by obedience—union with the will of God. Our work and thought are productive when they are in line with God's will, with God's plan, when they are in contact with reality and not just a spinning out of our own dreams. Hectic activism is usually devoted to projects which are not willed by God. The violence and tenseness with which this activism goes to work are signs that it is moved by self-love and self-seeking rather than by the will of God and the true desire for truth and for the good of the community as a whole. Activism is an attempt to *escape*, and even a very "active" person in this sense may be really lazy, and may evade responsibilities by running away from them into something else. "THE BRETHREN, THEREFORE, MUST BE OCCUPIED AT STATED HOURS IN MANUAL LABOR, AND AGAIN AT OTHER HOURS IN SACRED READING."[422] Taking the *Rule* as it stands, St. Benedict says *manual* labor. This does not mean intellectual work, although some such has to be done. But manual labor is an *integral part in the life of a monk*, and this cannot be passed over without harm and loss. To say that *any kind* of labor—clerical, apostolic, etc.—fills the bill is to distort the meaning of the *Rule*. It is true, some monks may have to do office work, and this is perfectly normal. But even they should not be altogether without manual labor at least from time to time. It would be a real deviation for *all* the monks to engage in non-manual work as a general rule. Such at least is the Cistercian interpretation of the *Rule* of St. Benedict. Such also is the evidence of common sense and monastic experience. St. Benedict himself says clearly: FOR THEN THEY ARE TRULY MONKS WHEN THEY LIVE BY THE LABOR OF THEIR HANDS LIKE OUR FATHERS AND THE APOSTLES.[423] This clearly means *manual labor* in the strict sense of the word:

422. McCann, 110/111, which reads: "labour."

423. McCann, 110/111, which reads: ". . . then are they truly . . . labour . . ."

a) because of the context—he is speaking of the harvest, in which all the monks would normally participate. (Some commentators seem to take this to mean that they only worked manually at certain seasons, like the harvest, and not even then if they could hire enough help. We do not understand it in that way. Such an understanding leads to a deviation from the real mind of St. Benedict.)

b) He refers to the Apostles, Paul who made tents, Peter who was a fisherman, etc. He refers also to the Desert Fathers ("our fathers") who lived by labor: some used to go and harvest for farmers in neighboring fertile regions; others, reproving this occasion of "dissipation," still worked in their own cells.

St. Benedict does not clearly say that all the monks should practice heavy outdoor work every day without fail. But apart from quibbling and hairsplitting we cannot avoid the evidence that he wanted them *to work with their hands and to earn their own living by that work*. Our work is a precious heritage, and it is a true safeguard of a genuine interior life. We should be thankful, and be very faithful to it. Note: it is not the "hardness" of the work that counts, but its *honest productiveness* and the fact that it is primarily *manual* labor.

*The time devoted to work and reading*:

a) {In the} summer season, work begins at prime—as early as five in the morning. In the heat of the day the brethren break off and read, take dinner, followed by siesta, and work again in the late afternoon. {The schedule therefore includes} work: 5 or 5:30 to about 10 (4½ or 5 hrs.); reading: 10 to 12 (2 hrs.); sext, dinner, siesta (12–2:30—reading permitted); work: 2:45 to 6 (3 hrs. plus)—total: 8 hours work; 2 hours (plus a little more before prime) perhaps 3 hours reading.

b) {In the} winter season: reading: 1 to 2 hours (plus) after vigils; after lauds—read until about 8 (total: 2 to 4 hours); work: 8–3 (6 hours) (with time out for tierce and sext); dinner (3:15); reading: one hour plus after dinner; total reading—over four hours; work: about six hours.

c) Lent: reading {is the} same as winter but prolonged one hour or more—to about 9 (5 hours plus); work: 9:15 to about 4 p.m. (about 7 hours); meal: after vespers.

*Lectio Divina*: {N.B.} its importance in our life: {it is} one of the three chief obligations of the monk. For a deeply interior life it is indispensable; without it the office is external only, and the work leads to activism and evasion. Public reading alone is not sufficient.

*Meaning of the term*: {it is} more than "spiritual reading." Spiritual reading {is} about virtues, life with God, {the} spiritual life: opening up a deeper level, interior silence, recollection and prayer. *Lectio divina* is more: {it is} reading not only *about* God but with God, in the sense of listening to God, hearing His word, and preparing to respond to His word with our whole being. Hence it is in *lectio* that we come to fully know God—not about Him, not just static knowledge of His attributes.

*Lectio divina*, {in the} Biblical and patristic context, {is concerned with the} recital of God's action in the world, his revelation of Himself in activity, {and with} man's response. {It focuses on} promise and fulfillment, especially centered in the Incarnate Word. *Lectio divina* {is} centered on Christ, on the mystery of Christ, the whole Christ, not just with our mind but our heart: {a} total response.

{The} *subject matter*: primarily and most important {is} the Bible, in {the} context of {the} liturgy; {then} the Fathers, especially the monastic Fathers, and the great Doctors of the Patristic Age: this means also books *about* the Bible and the Fathers (not *only* the Bible or early Fathers or the *Imitation* etc. except in *very special cases* and generally not in the novitiate); {the} Church: deals with revelation: theology (revealed truth and reason); truths of philosophy, science, culture, in so far as {they are} related to the Christian revelation. *Appetite* is usually a good indication, but with control; the problem of simplicity = a problem of *organic unity*. After that, {the rest is} less central: the "spiritual life," that is to say, all that affects liturgy, sacraments, prayer, meditation, asceticism, contemplation, *in the context of the above*. Saints and writers from {a} modern context {are} valuable to us in so far as they fit in with Biblical and traditional perspectives. All should devote themselves chiefly to {the} Bible, {the} Fathers, {the} spiritual masters. Some may also want to explore some of the following fields, at one time or other, or even more or less as a general thing: history, especially monastic—all have to know at least elements of this (Church history {is particularly} important); Biographies are a very fruitful source of knowledge in this field, and we will naturally read quite a few; philosophy: a little philosophical background to our reading is often helpful, whether scholastic, modern, or perhaps even classical (but within reasonable limits, especially in {the} novitiate); in a broad sense philosophical reflections like those of Pascal, {or} Max Picard, may be quite worth while for mature minds; essayists (v.g. Chesterton); poetry: for some, the great religious poets are a help (Dante, Claudel, Peguy).

{More} problematical: should we read magazines, should we read literature, even novels? {Concerning} magazines: in effect, some of the magazines in our library are virtually necessary for a real understanding of very important matters in our *lectio*: keeping up with Scripture, liturgy, theology—perhaps *not for all*; certainly a priest cannot entirely neglect the magazine rack. Novels, etc. are frowned on and not generally given out to the monks. Whether they are even remotely to be classified as *lectio divina* . . . In any event, {it is} better not {to read them} in the novitiate, unless there is some really extraordinary reason—not that literature is evil, but our time is limited and there are other more important things to be done.

Chapter 57—The Craftsmen of the Monastery. {This is} an important chapter, in regard to monastic work.

1. What is a craftsman, an *artifex*? (Read *Good Work*[424] and

424. *Good Work* was the quarterly publication of the Catholic Art Association (begun as the *Christian Social Art Quarterly* in December, 1937, renamed *Catholic Art Quarterly* in 1941, and *Good Work* in 1958); Merton's contributions to *Good Work* included "Conquistador, Tourist and Indian" (an abridged version of "Letter

Eric Gill.[425]) He is one who has "learned an art." In the ancient sense of the word, an art is a skill enabling one to make things—no clear distinction was made in early days between crafts and "fine arts." The man who made a table was an *artifex* as much as the man who made a statue, or vice versa. Both had their place. Both had an "art." They could do things with their hands; they could make things. Note: this *does not* apply directly to intellectual labor, to scholarship, research, writing books, etc.—printing, yes. A skill, an art, implies special apprenticeship, training. The mind of St. Benedict is that arts should be valued and reverenced, not for some false aesthetic reason, but because even humble skills are gifts of God and enable man to participate in some measure in the creative activity of God. In the exercise of his skills and arts, as well as in all other work, man acts as a child of His Father, the Creator. {We should recognize} the importance of arts and crafts, as well as of all labor, in our life of prayer. Work with the hands, the exercise of a skill, is truly a prayer. In this work, man is united with God His Father, in a simple and silent way. Work is very important in the spiritual life. But we must know how to work peacefully, silently, humbly, and for the glory of God. {Note the} problem of machines and technology. {It is} good to use machines {but we should} avoid using them merely to "get through work and get to prayer," avoid using machines to highlight {a} false opposition between work and prayer.

---

to Pablo Antonio Cuadra concerning Giants") (July, 1962), "Seven Qualities of the Sacred" (October, 1964), and "The Japanese Tea Ceremony" (April, 1969), as well as "Sincerity in Art and Life: From a Letter of Owen Merton" (April, 1967), which Thomas Merton edited and introduced; the poems "For My Brother: Reported Missing in Action, 1943," "The Vine" and "Death" had earlier appeared in *Catholic Art Quarterly*, the first two in April, 1945 and the third in June, 1945. *Good Work* ceased publication with volume 33 in 1970.

425. Eric Gill (1882–1940) was an influential British stonecarver, engraver and typography designer whose conversion to Catholicism in 1913 resulted in numerous religiously inspired works and in writings on the spiritual significance of craftsmanship; controversy about Gill has followed revelations about his dissolute personal life in Fiona MacCarthy's biography *Eric Gill: A Lover's Quest for Art and God* (New York: Dutton, 1989).

2. What is to be done to incorporate the craftsman into the spiritual life of the community? St. Benedict foresees only one problem: that those with special skills may try to exercise them for their own pleasure, or profit, or according to their own whims. This would be a desecration of God-given talent, turning it to the account of God's enemies. The talents of the monk are consecrated to God. He must use them in a consecrated way. For this, three things are necessary—*obedience, humility* and *reverence*:

a) First of all the command of the abbot: *si tamen jusserit Abbas*.[426] St. Benedict says "command" rather than permission. The initiative should be rather with the abbot than with the monk. This does not mean that we cannot make known our talents, or even ask for an opportunity to exercise them—but always in subjection to the abbot. We must not try to force our own desires on the abbot. We must make known the fact to him and then let him take the initiative. Note that in the exercise of a craft we come upon a great natural good and a deep, worthy human satisfaction. But from this, as from all other goods and satisfactions, the monk must be detached. {There is a} danger of getting so that one "has to have" a job that he likes or can do, {of} making life unbearable for {a} superior unless he gives us what we want. This is a danger to many monks, and greatly impedes growth in spiritual life, in fact makes true growth impossible. In any normal monastery there is plenty of demand for craftsmen and skilled workers: carpenters, tailors, cooks, shoemakers, and in modern times, dentists, mechanics, electricians, etc. If one has a skill, he need not fear that it will be left to moulder, provided one does not make it impossible or difficult for the superior to use it. Unfortunately it sometimes happens that there are in monasteries men *who could do* certain jobs and do them very well, but who have made it impossible for the superior to give them such work, because of the danger to themselves or to others. St. Benedict

426. "if the abbot has so commanded" (McCann, 128, which reads: "*si permiserit abbas*" ["if the abbot has permitted"]) as does *PL* 66, col. 801A—but the text Martène comments on reads "*si tamen jusserit abbas*" [*PL* 66, col. 801B]).

does not suggest that the abbot *deliberately frustrate* the talent of the monk without any special reason, merely to mortify him. The fact that one has a talent should not be a reason for *deliberately excluding* one from that kind of work. This is not {the} Benedictine spirit.

b) The monks must exercise their craft with *humility and reverence, cum omni humilitate et reverentia faciant ipsas artes*.[427] *Humility* {is used} in the sense of modesty, not being vain over one's work, not being ostentatious. It is natural for man to take pleasure in the work of his hands. This pleasure is good. Like all natural pleasure, it must be kept within bounds—a proper norm. There is no harm in *feeling* a little satisfaction; this is not pride. Where trouble comes is in *seeking inordinate satisfaction*—going out of one's way to seek praise, especially more praise than the work is worth—wanting to be praised and admired by everybody for a slight work; exploiting one's skill to demand extraordinary recognition and favors. Hence {the need for} humility—as opposed to real pride, *the conviction that one is better than others*, taking oneself seriously because of his skill. READ 1 Corinthians 4:7, in its context (vv. 3-7):[428] what distinguishes thee? What hast thou that thou hast not received? {This counters} the idea that the gifts we have received from God entitle us to *judge others*, implicitly placing ourselves above others. This is the heart of

427. "they should practice their crafts with all humility and reverence" (McCann, 128, which omits *"et reverentia"*).

428. "But with me it is a very small matter to be judged by you or by man's tribunal. Nay I do not even judge my own self. For I have nothing on my conscience, yet I am not thereby justified; but he who judges me is the Lord. Therefore, pass no judgment before the time, until the Lord comes, who will both bring to light the things hidden in darkness and make manifest the counsels of hearts; and then everyone will have his praise from God. Now, brethren, I have applied these things to myself and Apollos by way of illustration for your sakes, that in our case you may learn not to be puffed up one against the other over a third party, transgressing what is written. For who singles thee out? Or what hast thou that thou hast not received? And if you hast received it, why does thou boast as if thou hadst not received it?"

pharisaism—cf. the parable of pharisee and publican.[429] Our virtues do not entitle us to judge and condemn others, still less do arts and skills. *Reverence* {is used} in the sense of submission to authority, reverence for God in the superior, reverence for God's will, letting Him determine the use of the gift which He Himself has given—reverence in the sense of *respect for one's art*—respect for the gift itself. So many clever people, talented people, squander and ruin their talents. This is a great pity and a tragedy. {The} reasons for this {are that they are} seeking a *quick return*, emotionally, or otherwise. {It is} like using a precious and delicate article to pry open the lid of a can. These people have no respect for their skills and talents. One should have a wholesome respect for any gift he possesses, for this is due to God, the giver of the gift—cf. {the} Parable of {the} Talents.[430] Our talents are given to us that by them we may *give something* to God in return. Our productive work is the fruit He requires of our liberty and love. The penalty for those who are proud {is that} they are to be deprived of their work. St. Benedict does not demand a false humility. If by our work we help the community, or contribute something to the better functioning of the life, we are not supposed to pretend that we have contributed nothing. But the artisan should not boast or give himself airs, or act as if the community could not get along without him. This is an illusion, and the superior should not hesitate to show him the fact, by getting along without his work, even though it may involve difficulty for the community in some respects. The soul of the monk comes before the material good of the whole community.

3. What about the sale of the monk's work? St. Benedict wants to guard against *fraud* and *avarice*. Fraud {entails} that the individual monk or those who sell the products should not appropriate any of the income for themselves. What the monk makes belongs to the community. St. Benedict points out that one could sin mortally against monastic poverty by keeping back the

429. Lk. 18:9-14.
430. Mt. 25:14-30; Lk. 19:12-27.

fruits of one's labor. (See {the} reference to Ananias and Sapphira—note the implications—for St. Benedict the poverty of the monk is identical with the poverty of the first Christians. READ Acts 5.[431])

With regard to avarice, it would be difficult for us to exaggerate how much this was detested by the early monks. We cannot repeat too often that for a true monk poverty is not merely a matter of possessing things with permission. It is true that monks must have certain things given them for their use, and from these things they must be detached. The monastery owns property, and the community must be detached and "poor." But the *desire of gain* and especially *the desire to hoard up and accumulate money or goods* is absolutely alien to the monastic spirit and is disastrous to it—so much so that in a monastery where the love of money and possessions prevails, it is extremely difficult even for a detached monk individually to become a saint, except in some extraordinary way, for even though he may be extremely strict with himself, the situation in which he is placed may cause him to sin in many other ways, or to participate unconsciously in the sins of others. READ 1 Tim. {6}:6-12,[432] in which the Apostle warns

431. Acts 5:1-11 tells the story of Ananias and Sapphira, who were struck dead for pretending to give the community all their possessions, but it is the conclusion of chapter 4 (vv. 32-37) that tells of the Jerusalem community being "of one heart and one soul, and not one of them said that anything he possessed was his own but they had all things in common. . . . For those who owned lands or houses would sell them and bring the price of what they sold and lay it at the feet of the apostles, and distribution was made to each, according as any one had need."

432. "And godliness with contentment is indeed great gain. For we brought nothing into the world, and certainly we can take nothing out; but having food and sufficient clothing, with these let us be content. But those who seek to become rich fall into temptation and a snare and into many useless and harmful desires, which plunge men into destruction and damnation. For covetousness is the root of all evils, and some in their eagerness to get rich have strayed from the faith and have involved themselves in many troubles. But thou, O man of God, flee these things; but pursue justice, godliness, faith, charity, patience, mildness. Fight the good fight of the faith, lay hold on the life eternal, to which thou hast been

Timothy against the desire of gain: "Godliness with contentment is great gain" ({the} cornerstone of monastic simplicity). Realize that with a simple, poor, and fruitful life there is more true happiness than in the vanities and pomp of the world. This is in accordance with man's nature, as well as with divine grace which inspires us to detach ourselves even from necessities and share the indigence of the poor, for the love of Christ. The simple things of life are enough. To desire riches is to become a prey to the illusions of the devil and to lose one's soul in many vain desires. The desire of money *is the root of all evil*. And this desire leads to *loss of faith*. All this is to be taken seriously. The early monks took it very seriously. One can lose the faith in a monastery where worldliness prevails.

{There are various} aspects of "avarice"—the *avaritiae malum*[433] of which St. Benedict speaks has many aspects:

1. Formal avarice—miserliness. Out of love for money one becomes stingy and selfish and seeks only to hoard up pennies and gold pieces (or to have more and more in one's bank account); penny-pinching; hoarding. The monk can do this with possessions and not only with money. It is all right to be thrifty and to keep bits of string, paper, etc. which have a definite usefulness. But one can keep things just for the sake of keeping them. {The} danger comes rather in one's (work) department than in {the} private box.

2. Love of gain—here it is not a matter of loving money itself but rather the pleasure of acquiring it cleverly, the love of business for its own sake, as a kind of "sport." A monk in some official job may actually have no money in his hands, and yet lose himself in business dealings and in all the complicated contacts with business people that belong to that kind of life—the love of business competition, taking pleasure in outsmarting others, in putting through a smart deal. It may amount to nothing more than

---

called, and hast made the good confession before many witnesses" (text reads 1 Tim. 1:6-12).

433. "the evil of avarice" (McCann, 128).

the love of exercising one's natural cleverness in this kind of thing. But all this is alien to the mind of St. Benedict.

3. Exploitation—naturally, it goes without saying that *usury*, lending out money on interest, making money on money, is utterly foreign to the monastic life. In other words, business *speculation* is far more foreign to the true monastic spirit than mere selling and buying of goods for inordinate gain. {Note the} danger to {a} monastery when imprudent gambling on {the} stock market takes place with community funds! {This is the} reason why canon law keeps severe {a} check on business deals of the monastery.

*Remedy*—the monk should deliberately sell his products *cheaper* than the business man, to show that he is not interested in gain above all. He is entitled to an honest return for his work, but not to inordinate gain. This act of the monk is an act of faith in Divine Providence, an act of humility, an act of faith in the divine transcendence. Hence it is here that St. Benedict utters the famous words: *UT IN OMNIBUS GLORIFICETUR DEUS*.[434]

Now that the question of avarice has arisen, it is appropriate to consider some of St. Benedict's main ideas on *monastic poverty*. These are found principally in chapter 33: "Whether the monks should have anything of their own";[435] chapter 34: "Whether all should receive necessaries in like measure";[436] chapter 54: "Whether the monk should receive letters or anything else."[437]

*Chapter 33*—POVERTY. Here the question at issue is *proprium habere*.[438] The owning of property here is regarded as a vice. In a monk, it is a vice, though legitimate for seculars. The monastic community of course owns property—the buildings and land of the monastery belong to the community, as do all the articles and tools etc. for the work, study and prayer life of the monks. *Pro-*

434. "that in all things God might be glorified" (McCann, 128).

435. McCann, 84/85, which reads: "Whether monks . . ."

436. McCann, 86/87.

437. McCann, 122/123, which reads: "Whether a monk . . ."

438. "to have one's own possessions" (McCann, 84).

*prium habere* means the *exclusive possession* of property or objects. It means having things in such a way that others are prevented from having them, forbidden to have them. Obviously two people cannot wear the same cowl at the same time. When one is *using* the things assigned to him, this precludes their use, at the same time, by another. But no one in the monastery is supposed to have anything, to possess it in such a way that it is *completely and definitively withdrawn from use by others*. The "vice" of "*proprium habere*" is then the vice of withdrawing things from the common use and appropriating them to oneself in one way or another. This can be done: (a) by *keeping things back*, taking them out of circulation and keeping them out; (b) by *giving or lending* things, disposing of them on one's own initiative; (c) above all *by helping oneself* to things, simply taking them. Juridically speaking, permission based on a solid reason is sufficient to make any of the above acts legitimate. But St. Benedict is not talking merely from a juridical point of view. He is speaking of the virtue and the ascesis of poverty by which the monk shares in the poverty of Christ—*pauperes cum paupere Christo*.[439] Hence *even with permission* one may violate the *spirit* of poverty by taking things one does not need, accumulating things that are unnecessary and that others need, giving, selling, borrowing, lending in such a way that the rights of the community or of individuals are violated. But even where there is no question of a direct violation of justice and rights are intact, even when *nobody needs* the thing that I keep for myself, still if I am attached to the possession of these things, I have the "vice" of proprietorship, and I am *disposed to violate* the rights of others, and to withhold the depths of my own heart from God—my heart will be divided between God and possessions. I will be the slave of "things." {See} the story of St. Anthony and the man who wanted to enter the monastery keeping some of his money.[440] St. Anthony told him to go to the village and buy

439. "poor with the poor Christ" (*Exordium Cisterciense*, c. 15 [*PL* 166, col. 1507D], which reads: "*cum paupere Christo pauperes*").

440. *Apophthegmata* (*Antonius* 20) (*PG* 65, col. 82CD).

meat and apply it to his naked body and come with the meat all over his body along the road to the desert. He was torn and lacerated by dogs and birds of prey. St. Anthony showed him by this graphic lesson what happens to the soul of the man who wants to keep possessions in the monastery, and to keep things "for himself." The spirit of the *Rule* is to renounce all proprietorship, even spiritual—including attachment to everything that is distinctly "mine," even "my" spiritual life, "my" way of doing and seeing things, "my" contemplation. Naturally we retain our individuality and this is a distinct value, but we must not overvalue it and become attached to it for its own sake, not try to exploit it for self-love. St. Benedict is very strong on this question of ownership, proprietorship. It is not only a vice, but a dangerous one in his eyes, and it must be torn out by the roots. *RADICITUS AMPUTANDUM EST DE MONASTERIO*.[441] This vice especially—*praecipue*[442]—is to be rooted out, because poverty in union with Christ is absolutely essential to the monastic state. It is *not* something that can be dispensed {with} at will, or laid aside. To lay aside real monastic poverty is to cease to be a monk. *Radicitus*—Martène,[443] following Bernard of Monte Cassino, points out that this means *extirpating from the inmost heart of the monk* all attachment to possessions. "*Ut nec in* intentione *nec in* voluntate *remaneat aliquid de proprietate per quod possit ad actum aliquid pullulare*" (Bern. Cass.).[444] This means to say that it is not enough to try to restrain *acts* of proprietorship. This is only the bare minimum. One must get rid of the desires. "It will be useless for us not to have money if there remains in our heart the desire of having it," says Cassian.[445] And he goes on to point out that many have left great fortunes in the world and gone into solitude or entered a monastery, only to become attached to some small thing, a book, a pen, a cloak.

441. "It should be cut off by the root from the monastery" (McCann, 84).

442. "particularly" (McCann, 84).

443. *PL* 66, cols. 551D, 552D.

444. "Let there remain neither in intention nor in will any possessiveness through which anything can develop into action" (quoted in col. 551D).

445. *De Institutis Coenobiorum*, 7:21 (*PL* 49, col. 313B).

*Why is poverty so important?* {It means} dying with Christ—the bare Cross.

1. The monastic life reproduces the communal life of the first Christians. It is only in a monastic or religious community that absolute personal poverty and community of goods can be fully realized in fact—and this by the *charity of Christ*. Hence the duty of religious {is} to keep the precious heritage of poverty a *reality* in the Church.

2. We practice poverty not for its own sake, not just to make ourselves perfect in virtue, but because of our obligation as a community and as individuals to reproduce the *charity of the apostolic community gathered around Christ*.

3. One who injures monastic poverty injures charity, injures the community, and injures Christ. A religious community that is rich and powerful gives grave scandal and does very great harm to souls and to the Church.

*Nec dare nec accipere*.[446] No one is to *presume* to give or receive. No one is to take it upon himself, trust in his own initiative, his own ideas of what is right, even the most sincere. There exists of course such a thing as "presumed permission," but the way this sentence is worded in St. Benedict (i.e. outside {the} monastery) reminds us to take it with caution: not to give or receive anything. Here {it refers to an} exercise of control, of proprietorship, *sine jussione abbatis*.[447] *Jussio* implies more than permission. Certainly it is incompatible with an extorted permission. The will and judgement of the abbot is supreme in all matters relating to the allotment, disposal, etc. of material things in the monastery. The idea is that the abbot actively distributes and assigns the material things of the community as he sees fit. In a large community this is impossible, but the principle remains. One must learn to see things with the eyes of the superior and act according to his policy, and not ask for permissions which, though they may be

446. "neither to give nor to receive" (McCann, 84, which reads: "*dare aut accipere*").

447. "without the order of the abbot" (McCann, 84).

obtained, he would probably be *unwilling to give if he knew all the facts*. Indeed, one must be loyal in asking permissions—present the facts as they are and not conceal anything relevant. *Nec aliquid habere proprium*[448]—and St. Benedict gives examples, NULLAM OMNINO REM[449]—whether book, tablets or pen—these they may *receive and use* according to the mind of the superior, but the great principle is that they cannot possess anything since they do not even have full and free disposal of their own body and will! Note: {this refers to} ordinary things for {the} use of {the} monk of St. Benedict. The great principle behind this {is that} we cannot possess things since by our vows we have renounced our very selves. *Quippe quibus* NEC CORPORA SUA NEC VOLUNTATES LICET HABERE IN PROPRIA POTESTATE.[450] This is his strong interpretation of monastic obedience: at all times *our bodies and their actions, our time, our energies*, are to be ruled by obedience and not by our own whims. The *Rule*, or the superior, generally determines what we shall be doing at all times. Of course it must be remembered that no matter how strict obedience may be, there always remains an area which it never touches—in the interior of our soul—an area beyond obedience which is the territory of love and which, when we have obeyed in all things, still remains empty unless we fill it with love. The purpose of obedience is to clear the way so that we may travel freely in this region of love. Poverty has also the same function. Remember also that though we have renounced ourselves and our will, it does not mean that we no longer have a self or a will: it means that we freely keep our self and our will at the disposal of our superiors, so that when we act according to obedience we are acting freely and using our will, but not according to our own desires. This is in effect a higher freedom.

448. "not to have anything of one's own" (McCann, 84, which reads: "*neque* . . .").

449. "nothing whatsoever" (McCann, 84).

450. "Indeed it is permissible for these to have neither their own bodies nor their wills in their own power" (McCann, 84, which reads: ". . . *in propria voluntate*"—a reading that Merton had originally typed but then cancelled and replaced).

The second principle {involves} governing our practical conduct: *Omnia vero necessaria a patre sperare monasterii—nec cuiquam liceat habere, quod abbas non* dederit *aut* permiserit.[451] {The} important words {are} the *verbs*—as is usual in St. Benedict.

*Sperare—to hope for*:

a) Things are necessary, and we need them. The important matter is then not doing entirely without things, but "hoping to receive them" in the spirit in which a child hopes to receive all he needs from his father (*a* patre *monasterii*). {It involves} trusting that no need will be overlooked, asking confidently when necessary, and accepting refusal with the confidence that our request was needless and that all is well.

b) Hence the attitude of humility, patience, submission, trust, respect for the superior as {the} representative of God and instrument of Divine Providence.

c) Implicitly also, since the abbot is father of a family, our hopes are conditioned to some extent and limited by the common good and the needs of others. {The} poverty of the Benedictine monk is the poverty of a child rather than the poverty of a beggar (cf. {in contrast the} Franciscan ideal).

*Dederit aut permiserit*: the best thing in the eyes of St. Benedict is to be content with what the abbot gives of his own accord (cf. chapter 43 [end] where if the abbot offers a brother some food outside the time of meals and he refuses it, this is regarded as a fault for which amends must be made, therefore something of some note. Read—page 105: c. 43[452]). However, in a large community, the abbot cannot think of everything, and one may also

451. "to rely on the father of the monastery for all necessities—for it should not be allowed for him to have anything that the abbot has not given or permitted" (McCann, 84, which reads: ". . . *nec quidquam liceat* . . .").

452. "And let no one venture to take any food or drink before the appointed hour or afterwards. But if the superior offer a brother anything and he refuse it, then when he wants what he formerly refused or something else, let him receive nothing whatever, until he have made fitting amends."

have special needs. In this case one asks permission with simplicity and abides by the permission.

*Omnia omnibus communia*[453] sums up the poverty of the monk in the common life. No one should even call anything his own—hence the formula "our" cowl, etc. {This is a} very ancient practice. St. Benedict prescribes a sanction for those who indulge in this "most wicked vice";[454] hence it is definitely matter for sin and is considered highly important.

Chapter 34—*SI OMNES AEQUALITER DEBEANT NECESSARIA ACCIPERE.*[455] This is an absolutely necessary amplification of chapter 33. If we just had the previous chapter all by itself we would risk serious misinterpretation of St. Benedict. The heart of the previous chapter is the idea of *complete renunciation of all proprietorship* in order *to depend directly and completely on the abbot* (and through him on God) *for all one's needs.*

1. Here he makes clear that mathematical equality is not desirable. He gives the abbot a further principle to go on—again from Scripture—the practice of the early Church: *DIVIDEBATUR SINGULIS PROUT CUIQUE OPUS ERAT*[456] (read Acts 4:34-35[457]). This idea is correlative to the one of complete renunciation of property. The early Christians despoiled themselves of everything they owned. But they also gave it to the community and the proceeds were divided up among the faithful. These two elements are essential to the idea of monastic poverty. It is a poverty in which proprietorship is renounced *in favor of the community* (or of the whole Church). The monk becomes poor in order to share whatever earthly goods he may have had with the poor and with the community. He labors to share the poverty and labors of the poor. He shares the fruits of his labors with the poor. The fruits of the

453. "All have everything in common" (Acts 4:32) (McCann, 84, which reads: ". . . *omnibus sint communia*").

454. McCann, 86/87.

455. "If All Ought to Receive Necessities Equally" (McCann, 86).

456. "It was distributed to each according to each one's need" (Acts 4:35) (McCann, 86).

457. See above, n. 431.

monastic labor are then distributed by the abbot to the brethren *not according to their merit but according to their need.* "There should be no respect of persons but consideration of infirmities."[458] The monk who has worked hardest may find that he receives less than another. If he grumbles and complains about this, and begins comparing his merits with those of the weaker brother, he loses his sense of monastic poverty. We do not work for a material reward, in order to gain favors and privileges: but precisely this is an aspect of our poverty—we work in order to support others who are less well endowed with strength and skill. We bear one another's burdens. The reward of generosity is the merit of helping Christ in the weaker brother. Hence, in resumé, all should receive what they really need, irrespective of their merits, virtues, etc. The abbot remains the judge.

2. Now St. Benedict considers the proper dispositions of each monk. *"He that needeth less, let him thank God and not be discontented. . . ."*[459] {There should be a} supernatural realization that the ability to give and to do without is a greater gift and a greater benefit, if we use it rightly. *"He that needeth more, let him be humbled for his infirmity* and not made proud by the mercy showed to him. . . ."[460] Again the same principle {is given} for the weak as for the strong. The one who needs more material support should recognize that this makes him spiritually poorer as well as physically dependent. If he is puffed up and thinks himself better, because he receives more, he is showing great spiritual blindness and childishness. But if he is truly humbled by his infirmity, he can gain great merit while at the same time receiving special material consideration. This cannot be carried out in practice without a *deep spirit of faith.* *Ita omnia erunt in pace.*[461] St. Benedict's main idea is the peace of the monastery.

458. McCann, 86/87, which reads: "we do not mean that there should be respect of persons . . . but consideration for infirmities."

459. McCann, 86/87.

460. McCann, 86/87, which reads: ". . . mercy shown . . ."

461. "thus all will be in peace" (McCann, 86, which reads: ". . . *omnia membra* . . .").

3. He ends by another condemnation of all murmuring—and a threat of punishment for it. There is no spiritual loss in having an exception to the *Rule,* if one knows how to take it. But there is great spiritual loss in criticism and dissatisfaction. St. Benedict wants his monks to realize this very clearly. One can be a saint without fasting but one can never be a saint without charity and humility. We must be on our guard against petty jealousies and envies in the monastic life:

a) They are bad enough when they are about spiritual things.

b) They are ridiculous when they concern material things—little exceptions and differences. To be upset by these things is purely childish.

We might say that St. Benedict not only *tolerates* exceptions but that he gladly *accepts* them as reminding us of the common condition of mankind, and giving a lesson in realistic charity and broad-mindedness to the monks. The fact that there exist individual needs and differences is a *good thing* and not just a necessary evil. One must not exaggerate needs and take inordinate care of every little foible—one should not just cater to hypochondriacs. But the fact remains that there are individual needs and exceptions sometimes have to be made. The following points will be remembered—and practiced—by a mature monk:

a) All should desire to *follow the ordinary rule* and accept all its prescriptions with a spirit of generosity and simplicity.

b) Knowing our own weakness *we should fear exceptions* for ourselves and receive them from the superior when he manifestly desires us to have them: but we should hesitate to impose our will or extort exceptions in any way, even implicitly. We should *make known our needs with simplicity,* and then follow the superior's will.

c) We should *assume that others have an equal delicacy of conscience* on this point and that they are equally faithful in desiring to keep the whole *Rule.*

d) Hence when we see another getting an exception which *to us* would be useless, we will naturally understand that his case is different from ours. We will take it for granted that his need is a real one and we will *trust the superior's judgement* in the matter. To doubt this would be an act of uncharitableless and a rash judgement.

e) Even when there may be evidence that a monk is weak and exaggerates his own needs, we will *try to understand this weakness* and not condemn it. And again we will leave the judgement in the matter to the superior, who alone is responsible.

f) In a case where there are very numerous and extraordinary exceptions granted to a very large proportion of the members of the community—say over 30 or 40 percent, then it might be a matter of duty to take the matter up with the superiors or at the regular visitation.

One should be regular and zealous for the *Rule*, but avoid anything that savors of the bitter zeal which St. Benedict condemns (c. 72). This bitter zeal springs from murmuring, a spirit of criticism, envy, dissatisfaction and wounded self-love. It is highly censorious and meddlesome, and leads a person to imagine himself divinely appointed to reform the monastery. It is incapable of minding its own business, and pries into everything, secretly rejoicing in occasions for making trouble and raising a big fuss about something trivial. Such zeal does great harm to souls and to communities, and *even where there is a real abuse present* the use of this bitter zeal not only does not help to correct it but makes matters much worse.

Chapter 54—*SI MONACHUS DEBEAT LITTERAS VEL ALIQUID ACCIPERE.*[462] Here again—St. Benedict touches on the matter of poverty and detachment. This time he is concerned with *small matters* of no money value—letters, souvenirs, tokens of friendship, little gifts. But these things to a human heart *may have much greater significance* than something that is worth money. These are things which, because of the human friendships they represent, are something money cannot buy. The heart may derive much greater

462. "If a Monk Should Receive Letters or Anything Else" (McCann, 122, which reads: "*Si debeat monachus* . . .").

consolation from them than from a "possession." What are they? "*litteras*"—letters; "*eulogias*"—"devout tokens"[463]—blessed bread in St. Benedict's time; today, maybe a relic, a holy card; "*quaelibet munuscula*"[464]—any gifts—a book, a mass stipend. St. Benedict *does not condemn or forbid* these things. He knows they are not evil, and may indeed be a great good. But for the sake of detachment HE PLACES EVEN THESE PERSONAL TOKENS UNDER THE CONTROL OF OBEDIENCE. In the Benedictine life, even things with no money value can come under monastic poverty (*virtus*[465])—*ut non detur occasio diabolo*[466]—meaning what?

## THE DEGREES OF HUMILITY—Chapter 7

Everything that has been said so far in these conferences on the *Rule*, whether in the spiritual principles given in the Prologue, or in the notes on community life, or on work and poverty—all shows us one great theme which runs through everything. This theme is that *humility and obedience* are the heart of the Benedictine ascesis. The seventh chapter of the *Rule*, the longest of all, is also the most important, for while all the rest more or less stresses the exterior conduct and regulates how it must be carried out, mentioning certain interior dispositions at the same time, *here we have for St. Benedict the real interior life of the monk*. Hence this section of the *Rule* is of the greatest importance. Nothing is equal to it in the whole teaching of St. Benedict. This is, in a nutshell, the *whole* of the monastic life, if we remember that it is supposed, as St. Bernard says, to lead us to contemplation.[467] (St. Benedict himself

463. McCann, 122/123.

464. "any little gifts" (McCann, 122).

465. "virtue."

466. "so that no opportunity be given to the devil" (McCann, 122).

467. In the *De Gradibus Humilitatis et Superbiae* (*PL* 182, cols. 941-72), Bernard first presents the goal of the steps of humility as Truth, identified with Christ (c. 1; cols. 941B-942C); in chapter 2, this culmination of the ascent is equated with contemplation: "*Primus ergo cibus est humilitatis, purgatorius cum amaritudine; secondus charitatis, consolatorius cum dulcedine; tertius contemplationis, solidus cum*

implies this.[468]) To be more accurate—the degrees of humility are a summary of the whole *praxis* (active life) which prepares us for *theoria* (contemplation) which is hinted at as the chapter ends.

*A few points before we begin the study of this chapter*:

1. This chapter and the Prologue should be *known* most thoroughly by every novice—in fact its main points ought to be learned by heart. If this section is deeply rooted in the memory, then we will be able to reflect on it and practice it. There is little point in reading it over a few times and listening to it half-heartedly as it is read in chapter four times a year. This will not be enough.

2. This chapter should *be frequently meditated*—at some time or other, each one should use the seventh chapter of the *Rule* for meditative reading or meditation—in choir or out of it. No one can put into practice what he has not made a matter of conviction. We must be *convinced of the importance* of all these degrees in our interior life. For this, obviously we must understand their meaning.

3. To this chapter most of all we must apply the words of the Prologue—*admonitionem pii Patris* LIBENTER EXCIPE ET EFFICACITER COMPLE.[469] {There must be a} desire for humility—it is truth—pray for it.

*Libenter excipe*—gladly, eagerly receive this teaching about humility, which will in effect contain *the solution of many of our most difficult problems.* In fact most of our struggles and difficulties in the monastic life come from lack of humility, in its practical form of refusal to submit to God's will—*non serviam!*[470] But also,

---

*fortitudine*" ("For the first food is that of humility, cleansing with bitterness; the second, that of love, consoling with sweetness; the third that of contemplation, solid food that strengthens") (col. 944A).

468. See McCann, 48: "*Ergo his omnibus humilitatis gradibus ascensis, monachus mox ad caritatem Dei perveniet illam quae perfecta foris mittit timorem*" ("Therefore when all these steps of humility have been mounted, the monk will soon arrive at that love of God which, being perfect, casts out fear").

469. "freely receive and effectively fulfill the instruction of an affectionate father" (McCann, 6).

470. "I shall not serve!" (Jer. 2:20 [Vulg.]).

more accurately, our troubles are to be traced in large part *to false and deficient humility*, to a half-baked idea of humility that we have picked up—especially a humility that *is too exterior* and does not go down into the depths of the heart, and reach the real roots of our nature. This is so because we do not "gladly receive" the truth of genuine humility, but evade it and lull our conscience with false humility (consisting in large part of purely verbal expressions and exterior gestures, which reassure our minds and create the impression that we are humble, without making us really so).

*Efficaciter comple*—"faithfully fulfill"—we should apply ourselves with real fidelity and patient zeal to putting into practice, or trying to put into practice, *all* that is said here about humility. There are scores of monks who never seriously try to practice any degree of humility beyond the third. The rest is merely a matter of speculative interest, if that. How many are really interested in the sixth and seventh degrees of humility? or ever make the slightest effort to practice them? or even stop to think that they might have some practical point in their lives?

4. This chapter is one of those in which it is *vain to rely on commentaries*. Sometimes monks approach the question of humility as if it were difficult to understand, and put off practicing it until they understand it a little better ({due to the} habit of running to a book for everything). Perhaps they begin to "study" it in the wrong way. Humility cannot be learned from a book. No amount of commentaries can help us to understand St. Benedict's humility better if we do not *practice* it. There are few or no obscurities in most of the degrees of humility. The seventh degree may offer material for argument and misunderstanding, it is true. But here again, a commentary will never solve any problem that is raised by the seventh degree of humility—or by any other. Hence it is useless to raise *theoretical and intellectual* difficulties in connection with these degrees of humility, and try to *solve them in the abstract*. This is an evasion. Books are only of use to those who are earnestly convinced that these degrees of humility are *for them*, and who try to practice them. The real "difficulties" of

humility are *difficulties of practice*, not *difficulties of theory*. The books that will be of use are not so much direct commentaries, as books by the saints who have practiced this kind of humility, for instance St. Bernard, not only in the *De Gradibus Humilitatis* but in sermons where he speaks of humility;[471] also our other Cistercian Fathers, or St. Basil's Homily on Humility (see below[472]). For the moment we will stick to St. Benedict and regard it as a temptation and a delusion to go far afield seeking written "explanations" and clarifications of these simple degrees of humility. We know what they *say*. Let us try to put it into *practice*. Then only will we learn.

5. These Degrees of Humility are the very *heart of the vow of conversion of manners*. Not that the vow obliges us to ascend each degree, under pain of sin. But *the whole spirit of the vow of conversion of manners is centered in the degrees of humility of St. Benedict.* {The} vow of conversion of manners is {a} vow of humility {that will} apply to chastity and poverty {and} also to other vows. In practice, if we wish to effect the transformation to which the vow of conversion of manners demands that we tend, we must strive to practice these degrees of humility. This is especially clear in the first degree, which demands that we *renounce all self-will and sin* and determine to live our whole life in the presence of God. The second and third degree continue this course and give us special means of changing our life—*obedience to a superior* (third degree). The fourth degree *pushes the transformation into a crucial stage by demanding obedience* against serious difficulties and in time of trial. The following degrees show *how the transformation is* carried out, reaching down into the depths of the soul and then gradually taking possession of the monk's body and of his exterior actions, so that in the end he is humble through and through. If we wish to understand the proximate end of our vow of conversion of manners we must keep in mind the idea of a monk

471. See *De Diversis*, 20, 46, 47 (*PL* 183, cols. 592B–594A, 669B–670A, 670A–671A) and more generally the index for "*humilitas*" (cols. 1253–54).

472. See below, pages 161–65.

*completely mortified and humble* with all the characteristics implied by these degrees. A monk who lacks any desire or any tendency to acquire the principal qualities implied by these degrees (at least in a general way) is not fully living up to his vow of conversion of manners. This is not to say that one who fails to comprehend the sixth and seventh degrees is "sinning" in some way—far from it. But one should at least *desire* to enter wisely into the meaning and practice of even these degrees, for this is part of our *conversatio morum*. One should at least accept the idea sympathetically, once it is properly understood. One should at least want it to be "for us." One who arrogantly dismisses the fifth, sixth, and seventh degrees as absurd can never really acquire the true spirit of a Benedictine monk.

6. St. Bernard in his *De Gradibus Humilitatis* gives us the basic attitude a Cistercian should take towards these degrees of humility which are the heart of our monastic life.

a) We should emphasize *practice* (as has been said above)—*gradus . . . quod Beatus Benedictus* non numerandos, sed ascendendos proponit.[473] It is not sufficient to know what the degrees are—we must live them.

b) We should keep our eye on *the end to which they lead* because this will make the ascent easier. This is a very solid and helpful piece of advice. If we know where we are going, the way is easier and the journey more pleasant. If we do not have our objective in sight, we travel without courage or enthusiasm.

c) The end of the road? *Veritas*—not just abstract truth but Christ Himself, the Light of the World—the "light that illumines every man coming into the world."[474] In more abstract terms, then, the *fruit of humility is contemplation*. The active life of humility leads to the contemplative life of union with Christ by love. Pride is the one thing which more than any other makes the

473. *De Gradibus*, c. 1 (col. 941C, which reads: ". . . *de gradibus humilitatis, quos* . . ."): "steps which blessed Benedict presented not for listing but for climbing."

474. Jn. 1:9.

contemplative union of the soul with Christ impossible. Therefore, the way of humility is essential if we are to come to union with the humble Christ. However, St. Bernard is not proposing a pagan or Platonic ascent to contemplation by ascetic effort.

d) Christ is not only the end, *veritas*, but also the way, *via*, and the eternal life which crowns all, *vita*. *Ego sum via, veritas et vita.*[475] "*Ego sum via, quae ad veritatem duco; ego sum veritas quae vitam promitto; ego sum vita, quam do*"[476] (St. Bernard, *De Gradibus Humilitatis*, n. 1). It is by union with the humble Christ that we travel to union with Christ Who is Truth and Light. The way of humility is simply the way of the imitation of Christ. READ *Imitation of Christ*, Bk. iii, c. 56, esp. 1 and 2[477]—{it is} very similar to

475. "I am the way, the truth and the life" (Jn. 14:6).

476. "I am the way, which leads to truth; I am the truth which promises life; I am the life, which I give" (col. 942A).

477. This chapter, entitled "That We Ought to Forsake Ourselves and Follow Christ by Bearing His Cross," begins as Christ's own words: "My son, as much as you can abandon yourself and your own will, so much will you enter into Me. And as to desire nothing outwardly brings peace to a man's soul, so a man, by an inward forsaking of himself, joins himself to God. It is My will, therefore, that you learn to have a perfect abandonment of yourself and a full resignation of yourself into My hands, without contradicting or complaining, and follow Me, for I am the Way, I am the Truth, and I am the Life. Without a way, no man can go; without the truth, no man can know; and without life no man can live. I am the Way by which you ought to go, the Truth you ought to believe, and the Life you ought to hope to have. I am the Way that cannot be made foul, the Truth that cannot be deceived, and the Life that will never have an end. I am the Way most straight, the Truth most perfect and the Life most certain, a blessed Life and an uncreated Life that created all things. If you dwell and abide in My way, you will know the truth, and the truth will deliver you and you will come to everlasting life. If you would come to that life, keep My commandments; if you would know the truth, believe My teaching; if you would be perfect, sell all that you have. If you would be My disciple, forsake yourself; if you would possess the blessed life, despise this present life; if you would be exalted in heaven, humble yourself here on earth; and if you would reign with Me, bear the Cross with Me, for, truly, only the servants of the Cross will find the life of blessedness and of everlasting light." The remainder of the chapter consists of a dialogue between the reader, who asks for grace to bear the contempt of the world, and Christ, who in words adapted from John 14 promises to reveal himself to those who keep the commandments, to

this passage of St. Bernard {and is} to be meditated on deeply by anyone who wants to understand the reason for Benedictine Humility.

St. Bernard, *De Diversis* {26}, is on St. Benedict's {seventh} chapter:[478]

n. 1: *"Insipiens est enim et insanus . . .* [*qui non*] *in sola humilitate confidit."*[479] The Word is truth. [A]d humilitatis remedia tota mente confugere, *et quidquid in aliis minus habemus* de ea supplere.[480]

n. 2: *Totius humilitatis summa*[481] {is} subjection of our will to God's will. *Voluntaria subjectio*[482] {means} what He certainly wills we will; what He certainly does not will, we do not will; what is uncertain, *we leave uncertain,* and do not declare it is God's will: *neque velimus ex toto, neque penitus non velimus,*[483] *but remain in the open, ready to do anything that He makes known.* Here *humility* is necessary.

7. We have to realize that this chapter of St. Benedict has an even more *profoundly scriptural character* than any other part of the *Rule,* which nevertheless is filled with Holy Scripture. This is because St. Benedict believed that the way of humility was

---

which the reader responds with a promise to take up the cross, followed by an exhortation from the author to follow Christ on the way of the cross (Thomas à Kempis, *The Imitation of Christ,* trans. Harold C. Gardiner, SJ [Garden City, NY: Doubleday Image, 1955], 191–93).

478. Merton writes "De Diversis VII" and "12th chapter"; when he refers to this sermon (*PL* 183, cols. 609D–612A) in his conference to the novices he is unable to find it and realizes it is misnumbered—perhaps the chapter number was mistakenly transcribed as the sermon number; at some point Merton may also have misread "VII" as "XII" in preliminary notes and so refers to chapter 12 when it is clearly chapter 7 that Bernard is considering (see cols. 609D–610A).

479. Col. 610A: "For he is foolish and mad . . . [who does not] trust in humility alone."

480. Col. 610A: "to take refuge with one's whole mind in the remedy of humility, and from it to supplement whatever we are lacking in other things."

481. Col. 610B: "the height of all humility."

482. Col. 610B: "willing subordination."

483. Col. 610C: "let us neither will it totally nor reject it utterly."

essentially the way of the Gospel, and that it summed up in practice the whole ascesis of the Gospel. He makes this clear, as his basic principle, right at the beginning: CLAMAT NOBIS DIVINA *SCRIPTURA, FRATRES, DICENS: OMNIS QUI SE EXALTAT HUMILIABITUR, ET QUI SE HUMILIAT EXALTABITUR.*[484] These are the opening words of chapter 7. (The quote is from Luke 14:{11}—see context.[485]) {Note the} urgency. This line shows us at once that St. Benedict believes in the *supreme importance* of humility. Our salvation and sanctification as monks depend primarily, in his eyes, upon humility and obedience. In the beginning of the Prologue—i.e., as the foundation of the whole *Rule*—he says we are to go to heaven by the way of obedience. Here at the beginning of chapter 7, which is the heart of the *Rule,* he says we must go to heaven by the way of humility. Two quotes from Psalm 130[486] (learn—comment) indicate that by pride the soul becomes separated from God and is abandoned by Him. St. Benedict presents us his teaching on humility not just as a piece of good advice but *as a matter of faith.* It is a basic, revealed truth about the spiritual and Christian life. The Christian, and above all the monk, *must* be a humble man. (The ordinary Christian must have at least the first two degrees of humility. The monk for a minimum should have the first four. But he should strive for all.) Since this is a teaching of faith IT WILL SOMETIMES BE DIFFICULT AND EVEN INCOMPREHENSIBLE TO HUMAN NATURE. We must expect this doctrine to be sometimes

484. "The Holy Scripture cries out to us, brothers, saying: everyone who exalts himself will be humbled, and he who humbles himself will be exalted" (McCann, 36, which reads: ". . . *scriptura divina* . . .").

485. The verse is the conclusion of the parable about not choosing the highest seat at table but rather the lowest (text reads: 14:12).

486. *"Domine, non est exaltatum cor meum, neque elati sunt oculi mei; neque ambulavi in magnis, neque in mirabilis super me"* ("Lord, my heart is not exalted, nor are my eyes lifted up; I have not walked in great matters, nor in marvels that are beyond me"); *"Si non humiliter sentiebam, si exaltavi animam meam, sicut ablactatum super matrem suam, ita retribuis in anima mea"* ("If I did not have a humble attitude, if I lifted my soul on high, repay me in my soul like one who has been weaned from his mother") (Ps. 130[131]:1, 2) (McCann, 36).

hard. It is a matter of *faith*, not of human opinion. Hence this chapter is paradoxical and difficult, and it is the *supernatural* heart of the *Rule*. Once again we see the supreme importance of this chapter on humility. If we take the rest of the *Rule* and reject what is said about humility and obedience we will have a more or less human and comfortable view of the Benedictine life—a *reasonable* view, which is all right in itself, but which does *not go far enough*. If we leave out this supernatural cornerstone of the Benedictine life, we will not have a real monastic life at all—just a sensible country life, lived with simplicity and discretion. It is St. Benedict's *humility which gives full supernatural meaning to his discretion*. This elevates it to the fully Christian level, makes it prudence of the spirit rather than just prudence of the flesh. {Note} the link between humility and discretion—seen in the quote from Psalm 130: "I have not walked in great things nor in marvels that are beyond my reach." The monk sees inordinate spiritual ambition as a quasi-pagan form of self-exaltation and shies away from it, to be united with the interior humility of Christ. If we are discreet merely in order to spare ourselves unnecessary hardships and avoid disaster, we are naturally prudent. But if we avoid the lofty and showy things of the ascetic life in order to follow the simple humility of Christ *because we know the way of Christ is in reality more lofty* and more supernatural, then our humility makes our discretion truly Christian. N.B. {the} background of the Desert Fathers and Cassian—Cassian's story of the hermit who is wildly trying to break a huge rock with a hammer, and the devil is seen goading him on;[487] {and the} other story from Cassian of the hermit who was led by the devil to throw himself down a well out of presumption;[488] and the two hermits who went out into the desert to be fed by God alone, and were met by a hostile tribe who in an utterly extraordinary act offered them food—one took this humbly, the other who proudly insisted on receiving food

487. *Conference* 9.6 (*PL* 49, cols. 777A–778C).
488. *Conference* 2.5 (*PL* 49, cols. 529A–531A).

from God Himself, perished in the desert.[489] The danger of pride in the showy exploits of some Desert Fathers is behind St. Benedict's doctrine of humility.

8. St. Benedict's doctrine of humility is thus based not only on Scripture but also on *monastic tradition*. One of the best places to observe this fact is in St. Basil's *Twentieth Homily, on Humility*.[490] Note some of the main points of St. Basil's teaching:

1) The basic idea—man was created to have true glory in God. "Would that man had abided in the GLORY WHICH HE POSSESSED WITH GOD—he would have GENUINE INSTEAD OF FICTITIOUS dignity."[491] Here is the whole thing in a nutshell—St. Bernard takes this idea too. Man is *celsa creatura in capacitate majestatis*.[492] When the Fathers talk of humility, their starting point is the *real dignity* which man ought to have. They never try to take away from man anything real or good, but only to strip him of *false and illusory glory which he seeks by his own will*. Man's true dignity consists in being "ennobled by the power of God, illumined with divine wisdom, and made blessed with the possession of eternal life."[493]

2) This true glory was lost by pride. To recover it we must practice *humility* (cf. St. Benedict: *ut ad eum redeas* . . .[494]). "The surest salvation, the remedy of his ills, and the restoration of his original state is the practice of humility AND NOT PRETENDING THAT HE MAY LAY CLAIM TO ANY GLORY THROUGH HIS OWN EFFORTS

489. *Conference* 2.6 (*PL* 49, cols. 531A–534A).

490. St. Basil, *Ascetical Works*, trans. Sister M. Monica Wagner, CSC, Fathers of the Church, vol. 9 (Washington: Catholic University of America Press, 1950), 475–86.

491. St. Basil, *Ascetical Works*, 475 (emphasis added here and in subsequent quotations).

492. "an elevated creature with the capability for greatness" (*Sermones super Cantica*, 80.2; *PL* 183, col. 1167A, which reads: ". . . *quidem majestatis*").

493. St. Basil, *Ascetical Works*, 475, which reads: ". . . made joyful in the possession . . ."

494. "so that you may return to him" (Prol.) (McCann, 6, which reads: "*ad eum per obedientiae laborem redeas*" [". . . through the work of obedience . . ."]).

BUT SEEKING IT FROM GOD."[495] Explain "from God"—note the simple explanation: pride *consists not in seeking glory but in seeking it in and by and for* ourselves. Humility seeks glory where it is to be found, in and by and for God. In so seeking, we *have* this glory in ourselves. We truly possess it. The other way, we have nothing but illusion, and when the illusion is taken away, despair. {The} right way {recognizes that} all is gift, all {is} in dependence on God's will.

3) Humility is our only protection against the enemy of our souls who constantly tries to repeat and consolidate his work of destruction:

a) making us imagine that wealth brings glory; making us love luxury, pomp, power, possession of slaves, political honors, by which "men exalt themselves beyond what is due to their nature,"[496] lording it over others. READ St. Basil, *Ascetical Works*, p. 476:[497] pride in worldly things.

495. St. Basil, *Ascetical Works*, 475, which reads: ". . . salvation for him, . . . the means of restoration to his . . . is in practicing humility . . ."

496. St. Basil, *Ascetical Works*, 476, which reads: ". . . due their nature."

497. "But money is not by any means the only instigator of arrogance. Men do not take pride only in the costly food and clothing which money buys, nor in setting luxurious tables with unnecessary extravagance, wearing superfluous ornaments, building and furnishing immense piles for their homes and adorning them with all sorts of finery, and attaching to their person great throngs of slaves as attendants and innumerable hordes of flatterers. [Not only by reason of wealth,] but also because of political honors, do men exalt themselves beyond what is due their nature. If the populace confer upon them a distinction, if it honor them with some office of authority, if an exceptional mark of dignity be voted in their favor by the people, thereupon, as though they had risen above human nature, they look upon themselves as well-nigh seated on the very clouds and regard the men beneath them as their footstool. They lord it over those who raised them to such honor and exalt themselves over the very ones at whose hands they received their sham distinctions. The position they occupy is entirely out of keeping with reason, for they possess a glory more unsubstantial than a dream. They are surrounded with a splendor more unreal than the phantoms of the night, since it comes into being or is swept away at the nod of the populace."

b) Then there is the lure of moral and spiritual goods—*worldly wisdom*—its vanity—destroyed by the Cross of Christ, and defeated. "The profit of human wisdom is illusory for it is a meagre and lowly thing and not a great and pre-eminent good."[498]

4) *What is man's true glory*? "Let him that glorieth, glory, that he understandeth and knoweth that I am the Lord" (Jerem. 9:{24}).[499] St. Basil comments: "This constitutes the highest dignity of man, this is his glory and greatness: truly to know what is great and to cleave to it, and to seek after glory from the Lord of glory."[500] However, {this is} not {to take} pride in our knowledge of God. READ 1 Corinthians 1:30 ff.[501]—*Christ Himself is our glory*. {Note} the depth and sublimity of this teaching—what it means. READ St. Basil's explanation (p. 479):[502] mortifying ourselves in all things and placing all our hope in Christ, not in ourselves, we already possess, in hope, the foretaste of eternal glory. This gives us joy and peace even in this life, and is a sublime dignity *but it does not shine in the eyes of men*. This is as much as to say that we glory not in our own power and strength but rather in our infirmities, *and*

498. St. Basil, *Ascetical Works*, 478.

499. St. Basil, *Ascetical Works*, 478 (copy text reads: 9:12).

500. St. Basil, *Ascetical Works*, 478–79.

501. St. Basil, *Ascetical Works*, 479: "The Apostle tells us: 'He that glorieth may glory in the Lord,' saying: 'Christ was made for us wisdom of God, justice and sanctification and redemption; that, as it is written: He that glorieth may glory in the Lord'" (vv. 30-31; the quotation is from the verse of Jeremiah just cited).

502. "Now, this is the perfect and consummate glory in God: not to exult in one's own justice, but, recognizing oneself as lacking true justice, to be justified by faith in Christ alone. Paul gloried in despising his own justice and in seeking after the justice by faith which is of God through Christ, that he might know Him and the power of His resurrection and the fellowship of His sufferings, being made conformable to His death, so as to attain to the resurrection from the dead. Herewith topples the whole lofty pinnacle of arrogant pride. Naught, O man, remains for you to boast of, inasmuch as your glory and your hope consist in mortifying yourself in all things and in striving toward the life to come in Christ. The foretaste of this life we now enjoy, and we are already in possession of its goods, living as we do entirely by the grace and gift of God."

*in the mercy of God to us* (cf. St. Paul: 2 Corinthians[503]). This is true glory, and it is inseparable from humility and compunction and a peaceful realization of our own nothingness. Otherwise we might glory wrongly in the mercy that is given to us—lording it over others because we imagine we are great saints. St. Peter trusted too much in his own virtue—and was humbled. "He learned by discovering his own weakness to be merciful to the weak" (p. 481).[504] "NEVER PLACE YOURSELF ABOVE ANYONE, NOT EVEN GREAT SINNERS. Humility often saves a sinner who has committed many grievous transgressions."[505] Note the importance of this doctrine, which is to be taken seriously and literally.

5) The Incarnation {is} a school of humility. Here again, the doctrine of St. Bernard is anticipated.[506] "In everything which concerns the Lord we find lessons in humility."[507] READ St. Basil, p. 483—the examples he gives.[508] Christ shares His glory *with those who share His disgrace.*

503. Cf. "If I must boast, I will boast of the things that concern my weakness. . . . Gladly therefore I will glory in my infirmities, that the strength of Christ may dwell in me" (2 Cor. 11:30, 12:9).

504. Text reads: ". . . to be indulgent to the weak."

505. St. Basil, *Ascetical Works*, 481–82.

506. See *De Gradibus*, VII.21 (*PL* 182, col. 953BD): "*Ex qua prima conjunctione Verbi et rationis humilitas nascitur. . . . Digna certe, quae de schola humilitatis, in qua primum sub magistro Filio ad seipsam intrare didicit*" ("From this first union of the Word and reason humility is born. . . . She is indeed worthy who learns to enter into herself in the school of humility under the Son as teacher").

507. St. Basil, *Ascetical Works*, 483.

508. "In everything which concerns the Lord we find lessons in humility. As an infant, He was straightway laid in a cave, and not upon a couch but in a manger. In the house of a carpenter and of a mother who was poor, He was subject to His mother and her spouse. He was taught and He paid heed to what He needed not to be told. He asked questions, but even in the asking He won admiration for His wisdom. He submitted to John—the Lord received baptism at the hands of His servant. He did not make use of the marvelous power which he possessed to resist any of those who attacked Him, but, as if yielding to superior force, He allowed temporal authority to exercise the power proper to it. He was brought before the high priest as though a criminal and then led to the governor. He bore calumnies in silence and submitted to His sentence, although He could

6) *Humility in everything*: {this is} a beautiful passage which throws light on St. Benedict's degrees of *exterior* humility. READ p. 484 (bottom)[509]—{the} basis of monastic simplicity: avoiding *pretentiousness;* avoiding all show; gentleness to all, etc.

Conclusion (p. 486): "Love humility and it will glorify you. Thus you will travel to good purpose the road leading to that true glory which is to be found with the angels and with God. . . . *Christ will glorify you if you imitate His humility.*"[510] {This is} a beautiful text which gives us many indications of the inner meaning of St. Benedict's seventh chapter and St. Bernard's teaching on humility.

*The Degrees of Humility.* Let us now turn directly to St. Benedict himself. First he has an *Introduction*, in which he treats of humility and pride in general (lines 1–22):

---

have refuted the false witnesses. He was spat upon by slaves and the vilest menials. He delivered Himself up to death, the most shameful death known to men. Thus, from His birth to the end of His life, He experienced all the exigencies which befall mankind and, after displaying humility to such a degree, he manifested His glory, associating with Himself in glory those who had shared His disgrace" (483–84).

509. "But how shall we, casting off the deadly weight of pride, descend to saving humility? If such an aim governed our conduct under all circumstances, we should not overlook the least detail on the ground that we would suffer no harm therefrom. The soul comes to take on a resemblance to its preoccupations and it is stamped and molded to the form of its activities. Let your aspect, your garb, your manner of walking and sitting, your diet, bed, house and its furnishings reflect a customary thrift. Your manner of speaking and singing, your conversation with your neighbor, also, should aim at modesty rather than pretentiousness. Do not strive, I beg you, for artificial embellishment in speech, for cloying sweetness in song, or for a sonorous and high-flown style in conversation. In all your actions, be free from pomposity. Be obliging to your friends, gentle toward your slaves, forbearing with the forward, benign to the lowly, a source of comfort to the afflicted, a friend to the distressed, a condemner of no one. Be pleasant in your address, gentle in your response, courteous, accessible to all. Speak not in your own praise, nor contrive that others do so. Do not listen to indecent talk, and conceal insofar as you can your own superior gifts" (484–85).

510. Text reads: "Love it and it will . . . with God. Christ . . . will glorify . . ."

a) What is pride? He goes to the Scriptures, and for him pride becomes essentially EXALTATIO: *"omnem exaltationem genus esse superbiae."*[511] The psalms speak of *exaltatio cordis, exaltatio animae.*[512] What is this lifting up? Up from what? St. Augustine compares pride to smoke rising from a fire, and dissipating itself in the air, the further it gets from the fire, its source.[513] The fire {is} the reality of our nature; smoke—our estimation of ourselves—rising further and further above the reality, and vanishing into nothingness in proportion as it becomes more and more unreal. We are "exalted" in proportion as our estimate of ourselves is untrue and exaggerated. This is tested *by our measure of others.* We are "exalted" by the fact that we elevate ourselves above the common nature of man as it is found in others, *in practice.* All men are weak, sinners, limited, deficient in some way or other. We are not exalted if we simply accept this fact in ourselves and

511. "all exaltation is a kind of pride" (McCann, 36).

512. See Ps. 130[131]:1-2: *"Domine, non est exaltatum cor meum . . . . si exaltavi animam meam"* ("Lord, my heart is not lifted up . . . . if I exalted my soul"); both verses are quoted at the beginning of c. 7 (McCann, 36).

513. See *Enarratio in Ps. 36*, vs. 12 (*PL* 36, col. 370): *"Fumus a loco ignis erumpens in altum extollitur, et ipsa elatione in globum magnum intumescit: sed quanto fuerit globus ille grandior, tanto fit vanior; ab illa enim magnitudine non fundata et solidata, sed pendente et inflata, it in auras atque dilabitur, ut videas ipsam ei obfuisse magnitudinem. Quanto enim plus erectus est, quanto extentus, quanto diffusus undique in majorem ambitum, tanto fit exilior, et deficiens, et non apparens"* ("Smoke coming forth from the fire is lifted on high, and swells into a large sphere in this very rising: but the greater that sphere becomes, the emptier it is; for from that very size, not solid and substantial but flabby and puffed up, it goes into the air and is dispersed, so that you may see that its very size works against it. For the more lofty it is, the more extended, the more diffused in all sides into a larger circumference, the more it becomes distanced, and deficient, and not visible"); *Enarratio in Ps. 92*, vs. 3 (*PL* 37, col. 1184): *"Superbi quid? Quasi fumus: etsi alti sunt, evanescunt"* ("What are the proud? They are like smoke: though they are raised up, they vanish"); *Enarratio in Ps. 101*, vs. 4 (*PL* 37, cols. 1296-97): *"Quia defecerunt sicut fumus dies mei. Videte fumum superbiae similem, ascendentem, tumescentem, evanescentem: merito ergo deficientem, non utique permanentem"* ("My days vanish like smoke. Note that smoke is like pride—rising, swelling, disappearing: thus lacking in value, not at all something that lasts").

in others. We are exalted if, implicitly or explicitly or in any way whatever, we speak or act *as if we alone* were elevated above the common run of mankind, and belonged to a superior breed—"*non sum sicut caeteri homines.*"[514] READ the parable of the Pharisee and the Publican (Luke 18:9 ff.).[515] Read St. Bernard's comments on this—*De Gradibus Humilitatis* (Eng. Trans. Burch, p. 153).[516] The Pharisee "exults in himself exceedingly"; "deludes himself when he excludes only himself [from condemnation] and includes all others";[517] "gives thanks not that he is good but that he is *different*." Note that the Pharisee really did perform the acts of virtue which he described, but they became worthless by

514. "I am not like other men" (Lk. 18:11).

515. "But he spoke this parable also to some who trusted in themselves as being just and despised others. 'Two men went up to the temple to pray, the one a Pharisee and the other a publican. The Pharisee stood and began to pray thus within himself: "O God, I thank thee that I am not like the rest of men, robbers, dishonest, adulterers, or even like this publican. I fast twice a week; I pay tithes of all that I possess." But the publican, standing afar off, would not so much as lift up his eyes to heaven, but kept striking his breast, saying, "O God, be merciful to me the sinner!" I tell you, this man went back to his home justified rather than the other; for everyone who exalts himself shall be humbled, and he who humbles himself shall be exalted'" (Lk. 18:9-14).

516. "See how differently the proud Pharisee felt about himself. What did he exclaim in his passage? *God, I thank thee that I am not as other men are.* He exults in himself exceedingly; he insults all others arrogantly. David is otherwise. For he says, *All men are false.* He excludes none, and so deludes none, knowing that all have sinned and come short of the glory of God. The Pharisee deludes only himself when he excludes only himself and condemns all others. The prophet does not exclude himself from the common passion, lest he be excluded from the compassion; the Pharisee disdains mercy when he disclaims misery. The prophet maintains of all, as of himself, *All men are false*; the Pharisee complains of all, except himself, saying, *I am not as other men are.* And he gives thanks, not that he is good, but that he is different; not so much because of his own virtues as because of the vices which he sees in others. He has not yet cast out the beam out of his own eye, yet he points out the motes in his brothers' eyes. For he adds, *Unjust, extortioners*" (c. 5; n. 17) (Bernard, Abbot of Clairvaux, *The Steps of Humility*, ed. George Bosworth Burch [Cambridge, MA: Harvard University Press, 1942], 153, 155; this volume also includes the Latin text).

517. N.B. the translation reads: ". . . condemns all others."

reason of the fact that he exalted himself and separated himself from other men on their account. Summary—the Pharisee tries to take the mote out of his brother's eye when he does not see the beam in his own eye. The "mote" in this case {is the} real sin of the publican; the beam, the Pharisee's pride. *Conclusion*: the essence of pride lies in *exalting ourselves above others*, giving ourselves an exaggerated preference, imagining we are vastly greater than we actually are, or than others are. This means in effect placing ourselves practically in the position that belongs rightly to God alone. *Pride then is making of oneself one's own god*. Humility is only restoring the right order and truth. It begins essentially with *self-knowledge* (*verissima cognitione sui*[518]) and leads to a healthy depreciation of our own opinion of ourselves (*ipse sibi vilescit*[519]) (Latin phrases from St. Bernard's definition of humility, *De Gradibus Humilitatis*, p. 125—c. 1, n. 2[520]). St. Benedict quotes the laconic phrase of Christ—everyone that exalteth himself shall *be humbled*.[521] That is to say, a false idea of ourselves MUST NECESSARILY LEAD TO DELUSION AND EXPOSURE. This is the important point, practically speaking. One cannot get away with pride and falsity. It will make itself very evident, and will lead to ruin and confusion—the destruction of false hopes. PRIDE IS IRREVOCABLY FALSE. *The falsity of pride leads to frustration in vain hopes and fears and futile interior activity*. Everyone who is exalted will be humbled. By what force will he be humbled? Not by the power of a jealous God so much as by the fact that he exhausts himself in the service of his idol.

518. "truest knowledge of self" (*PL* 182, col. 942B, which reads: "*verissima sui agnitione*").

519. "he despises himself" (*PL* 182, col. 942B, which reads: "*sibi ipsi vilescit*").

520. The reference is to the Burch volume, in which the Latin text (which reads "*verissima sui cognitione*" and "*sibi ipse vilescit*") is actually on page 124; Burch's translation is on the facing page 125 ("Humility is that thorough self-examination which makes a man contemptible in his own sight").

521. McCann, 36/37.

a) *Vain hope*: pride, placing our hopes in our own illusory excellence and removing them from solid reality, inevitably makes our lives *insecure*.

b) This insecurity, this sense of the inherent falsity of our illusions, inevitably breeds *fear*—fear that the illusion will be shown up for what it is. The proud man is a vulnerable man. He is protecting an illusion. Note that some proud men are very aggressive about this defense of their illusions. They imagine that if they browbeat everybody else into accepting their false idea of themselves, they will thus make falsity into truth. Hence the energy wasted by one form of pride, in *dominating* others and beating them down into subjection, by fair means or foul. Another form of pride, less obvious, is more characteristically American: it is the belief that *popularity and love* are a justification and seal of approval upon our false idea of ourselves. Hence the "pride" of those who must at all costs feel themselves loved and approved of, and who fear rejection almost as much as death. Hence *servile conformity* can be a form of pride, even though it appears outwardly to be humility. Actually it is a fear of humiliation and rejection. It takes its revenge secretly in envies, jealousies, critical spirit of others and hidden attempts to reject others when they seem to reject us. This is the virulent form of pride that is hidden under the apparently sweet and humble, apparently self-deprecating exterior of so many of us in this country. It is a timid and masked form of self-exaltation, all the more harmful because it does not dare to take the open road of domination. A humble man is able to accept the fact that he may not be accepted and idolized by everybody. A proud man is disturbed and upset when even one person seems, by a mere expression of face, to reject him or disapprove of him.

c) Futile interior activity: the immense waste of energy that takes place in a proud and vulnerable soul—unlimited *distractions and anxieties* in which he labors to manipulate reality and make things come out in accord with his illusions about himself; endless *petty struggles* to compete with others, to outshine others, to gain approval; fits of discouragement and sulkiness when it is imagined that one has failed to attain the satisfactory degree of approbation; interior rebelliousness united with insecurity and fear and feelings of guilt, etc., etc. Most of the characteristic petty vices of monks spring from these roots. Little acts of uncharitableness, disobedience, self-will, interior murmuring, tepidity, discouragement—can almost always be traced to some such source as this. This being the case, *humility to face the facts like a man* brings relief and rest. It delivers us from a silly illusion, and from the tyranny of that illusion. We see *we don't have to* make ourselves popular, and there is no need for everybody to give open signs of approval every time we show our face. It is not that we have to accept rejection: this too is imaginary usually. What we have to do is be content with the ordinary acceptance and toleration that are due to a normal member of a normal society, and NOT DEMAND INORDINATE EXPRESSIONS OF APPROVAL which demands are the sign of an infantile emotionality. In this sense, he who humbles himself is exalted: he is relieved from the tyranny of his illusions about himself. He no longer has to struggle for vain feelings of security—he can have *real security* in acceptance of the truth. And he becomes *able to love*. It is the fruitful activity of loving others and forgetting ourselves that establishes us in true peace, and enables us to live productive lives—then we have the legitimate sense of satisfaction that comes from living as mature and spiritual men, and we also, incidentally, are more likely to fit in well with other people. Note—it would be a fatal error to imagine that "he who humbles himself will be exalted" means that one should gain approval by the practice of exterior humility. This is nothing but pride in disguise, and part of the error we are trying to get rid of.

*How does St. Benedict express this "exaltation" and "humiliation"?* By quotations from the Psalms: the exaltation of pride—"dwelling on high things and marvels beyond our reach."[522] But note that true humility implies courage to aim at difficult things that are not beyond our reach with the grace of God. Humility must not

522. Ps. 130[131]:1 (McCann, 36).

be taken as an excuse for evading all difficulties. The soul that is exalted by pride is like a weaned child. Explain: thirst, frustration, anger; cut off from God and from reality. *SI SUMMAE HUMILITATIS VOLUMUS CULMEN ATTINGERE . . .*[523] Here it is clear that St. Benedict demands a certain rightly understood ambition: not the ambition to excel everybody else and thus to glorify ourselves, but the desire to achieve peace in possession of the truth. But the goal is *EXALTATIO CAELESTIS*[524]—it is not something that can seen and enjoyed to the full in this present life—it is spiritual and hidden and does not belong to the temporal order of things. Note the fact that *faith in spiritual realities* is inseparable from true Christian humility. JACOB'S LADDER: Read GENESIS 28:10-19:[525] the original story {involves} Jacob's humiliation—his solitude and obedience—his reward comes from God. Humility expects all things from God, but with courage and confidence. It is not passive and defeatist, but full of faith. St. Benedict *applies* this to his own teaching. Our whole life is like the ladder—it is based on a "humble heart."[526]

523. "If we wish to reach the point of the highest humility" (McCann, 38).

524. "heavenly exaltation" (McCann, 38, which reads: "*exaltationem illam caelestem*").

525. "Meanwhile, Jacob left Bersabee and journeyed toward Haran. He came to a place where he spent the night because the sun had set. He took one of the stones of the place, put it under his head, and went to sleep there. He dreamed that a ladder was set up on the ground with its top reaching to heaven; angels of God were ascending and descending on it. The Lord stood beside him and said, 'I am the Lord, the God of Abraham your father, and the God of Isaac. I will give you and your descendents the land on which you lie. They shall be as the dust of the earth. You shall spread abroad to the west, to the east, to the north, and to the south; in you and in your descendents, all the nations of the earth shall be blessed. I will be with you and protect you wherever you go. I will bring you back to this land; indeed I will not forsake you till I fulfill my promise.' When Jacob woke from his sleep he said, 'Truly the Lord is in this place and I did not know it.' Reverently he continued, 'How awesome is this place! This is none other than the house of God; this is the gate of heaven.' Jacob arose in the morning, took the stone which he had placed under his head, set it up as a memorial pillar and poured oil over it. He called the place Bethel; formerly the name of the city was Lusa."

526. McCann, 38.

Without this basis of humility the ladder cannot rise up to God. The sides of the ladder {are} our body and soul—intimating that our life must be a unity, and that humility must gain possession of all our acts. The degrees of humility, to which we are called by God, depend on the integrated activity of body and soul together. St. Benedict is against {the} false humility of angelism. Compare St. Paul. Read Colossians 2:4-12:[527] false spirituality compared with true spirituality—which is founded in Christ—here humility and glory coincide—*qui gloriatur in Domino glorietur*[528] (1 Corinthians 1:31; cf. 3:31, 4:7. etc.).

The Degrees of Humility. It is important not only to *know* the degrees of humility as they are set forth by St. Benedict, but to understand the logic and the thought behind them—why for example the fifth degree is the fifth and not the first; and why the whole series culminates in the twelfth degree. These degrees represent *a progressive discipline and pacification of the whole man*, body and soul. They bring the whole person more and more under the control of grace until all one's actions, whether interior, in the heart, or exterior, of the body, are under the sway of divine grace. The degrees of humility begin with what is most essential—freedom from sin, and then progress to what is more a matter of accidental perfection, at last reaching the point where one's

527. "Now I say this so that no one may deceive you by persuasive words. For though I am absent in body, yet in spirit I am with you, rejoicing at the sight of your orderly array and the steadfastness of your faith in Christ. Therefore, as you have received Jesus Christ our Lord, so walk in him; be rooted in him and built up on him, and strengthened in the faith, as you also have learnt, rendering thanks abundantly. See to it that no one deceives you by philosophy and vain deceit, according to human traditions, according to the elements of the world and not according to Christ. For in him dwells all the fullness of the Godhead bodily, and in him who is the head of every Principality and Power you have received of that fullness. In him, too, you have been circumcised with a circumcision not wrought by hand, but through putting off the body of the flesh, a circumcision which is of Christ. For you were buried together with him in baptism, and in him also rise again through faith in the working of God who raised him from the dead."

528. "Let the one who boasts, boast in the Lord."

whole bearing is pervaded with humility and grace. They begin with the control of sinful desires, then go on to other desires, to our own will even in good things, to our speech, to our estimate of ourself, to laughter, to our bearing. Hence everything, the will, the thoughts, the sensibilities, the passions, the speech and other forms of self-expression, and all our conduct finally comes under the control of humility. This should be seen as *a real sacrifice of our whole being to God,* and it requires a spirit of self-oblation and self-forgetfulness which is heroic. But at the same time it is *not to be accomplished by strain, tension, "will-power," but more by obedience to grace* and submission to the will of God, the *Rule,* superiors, brethren, and to reality as it presents itself in our surroundings. The degrees of humility properly understood do not by any means imply an artificial and strained *perfectionism,* but rather a complete and integral adaptation to reality. The key to this is the seventh degree in which we have cast off any false image of self-perfection and forget self entirely, with no further thought of self-exaltation even in the sphere of virtue and the spirit. One who fails to understand this aspect of the degrees of humility will inevitably falsify them and turn them into a parade of sham virtues, culminating in a supremely artificial and self-conscious straining to carry out the twelfth degree, but this is a mockery of St. Benedict's true thought. Note that it is not really possible to apply oneself *directly* to the practice of humility and succeed at it. If we concentrate directly on humility, our humility will be false. If we concentrate on our relations with others, and with God, our humility will be true.

### I. *The First Degree*

The most important and longest of all, this is the foundation of the whole structure of humility as it is of the whole spiritual life. The first degree of humility means, in its essence, *the avoidance of all deliberate sin, especially mortal sin.* A great many ideas are contained in this degree. Some are concerned with the end in view, others are explanation of means to that end.

1) *Si timorem Dei sibi ante oculos semper ponens oblivionem omnino fugiat* etc.[529] The first and most important element in this flight from sin is the *awareness of what sin is,* and the consequent fear to offend God and incur His punishment. "The fear of the Lord is the beginning of wisdom."[530] This is the base—*constant* awareness of these ultimate moral values: attention, care, avoidance of all thoughtlessness. A careless and thoughtless monk cannot begin to be truly humble if his carelessness leads him into danger of sin. Humility then begins with the formation of *a tender conscience,* but not a scrupulous conscience. {It is a matter of} *judgement.* This conscience faithfully tells us what is displeasing to God—without exaggeration but without minimizing. Either extreme is useless and harmful to the spiritual life. The first degree also implies *a constant consciousness of the last things.* I must die. My actions must be judged by God—and they are judged at the moment when I perform them. This judgement will inevitably be made known at the moment of my death. If I die in a state of mortal sin I will be punished forever in hell. If I die in the friendship of God, the actions I have performed to please Him will be rewarded by union with Him forever in heaven. I cannot afford to be careless about my actions, or even my thoughts! A good monk will frequently think of these things, until the awareness of them becomes habitual and basic, and governs all his actions, keeping him from all sin—*animo suo semper evolvat*[531]—{this is} basic for understanding of Benedictine meditation. This is the *basis of truth,* which belongs to the very essence of humility. A man lives in the presence of *the most fundamental truth of Christian morality.* Humility is truth in the sense that it regulates man's whole life in accordance with the Truth.

529. "if one completely flees forgetfulness, keeping the fear of God before his eyes at all times" (McCann, 38).

530. Prov. 1:7.

531. "he is always considering in his mind" (McCann, 38).

2) CUSTODIENS SE OMNI HORA A PECCATIS ET VITIIS . . .[532] {The} result of the above attitude of "fear of the Lord" is SELF-CUSTODY, constant watchfulness and discipline to prevent every form of sin.

*peccatis et vitiis*—{we must} distinguish between the actual sin that is done with deliberation, and the vice which leads us to sin through habit, perhaps without deliberation. Note that if the habit is not combated, then these habitual actions are imputed as sins, though there may not be full deliberation.

*cogitationum*[533] {are} sins of thought, for instance angry thoughts, proud thoughts, unwholesome thoughts, resentments, jealousies, hostilities, vanities, ambition and rivalry, lack of faith, lack of hope: we must keep watch over our inmost thought. We take care *not to sin by deliberately musing on things which are sinful*—especially in the matter of uncharitableness, {and} realize the harmfulness of these thoughts, even though they do not proceed into action—they have effects!

*linguae*[534] {refers to} sins of {the} tongue or other forms of expression (signs): the danger of detraction, calumny, uncharitable talk, criticism, injustice, lying, exaggeration, boasting, distortion of the truth. It is not too difficult to sin with the tongue, even in a monastery. The monk must train himself to guard his tongue. Humility is impossible in one who lets his tongue go freely and says everything that comes into his head. Even when what is said may be true in itself—it may often be unjust or uncharitable or proud.

*manuum, pedum*[535]—{here one sins} by doing things, performing works, that should not be done—by going where one should not go, working far too much.

*vel voluntatis propriae*[536]—the great source of sin is self-will, disobedience. Once again, {note} the tremendous importance of

532. "guarding himself from sins and vices at all times" (McCann, 38).

533. "of thoughts" (McCann, 38).

534. "of the tongue" (McCann, 38).

535. "of the hands, of the feet" (McCann, 38).

536. "or of self-will" (McCann, 38).

thinking about this, of realizing the danger of self-will and guarding against it. Some monks never really form their conscience on this point; they never get the idea that *the pleasure felt by their own will* must not be interpreted *as a judgement of conscience that the act is good*. Immature souls do not know the difference between the judgement "this act is pleasing" and "this act is to be done."

*et desideria carnis*[537]—above all the desires of the flesh are sources of sin. We are usually aware of this. But do we fight them with sufficient resolution?

3) *AESTIMET SE HOMO A CAELIS A DEO RESPICI OMNI HORA . . .*[538] St. Benedict then gives us the great means for gaining control over all our thoughts and actions: the presence of God. This is the most fundamental thing in our life of prayer and contemplation. Atheists rebel against the thought of a "god" who can "intrude" into their inmost self and see what is going on there. But they do not realize that God is in no sense an intruder; rather He is the source and life of our whole being, and if He is absent, our life becomes empty, lifeless, sterile, stupid. Witness the dullness and stupidity of atheist-materialist society and culture: the culture of people with no inner life. The "presence" of God brings life, light, meaning, to our interior life. *To say that "God sees" what I do is to say that it has a meaning and a value quite apart from what I may be able to give to it myself.* He Who is infinitely real "sees" and judges my acts in proportion as they participate in His reality. Then some acts are better than others, some have meaning, others less so; some are good, some are bad. In the conscience of the materialist, nothing has meaning as a matter of conscience. The light of conscience goes out. With it goes all variety, life, sense, direction. One thing is as good as or as bad as another. Nothing has any special meaning except in so far as it may be *expedient* here and now—expedient for what? for my bodily life, for the state, for society. Such a man is *completely alienated* and lives as a slave to

537. "and the desires of the flesh" (McCann, 38).

538. "Let a person consider himself as being watched from heaven by God at all times" (McCann, 38, which reads: ". . . *de caelis* . . .").

things outside himself, without finding any sense or meaning in his own inner life.

St. Benedict does not mean that "God sees" merely in order to punish. We must not take it in this way. God also judges with mercy and sees our good motives and our weakness and the extenuating circumstances, and above all He *sees with love*: He sees our needs also and gives us grace and assistance. The thought that *Love* sees me is a deterrent from sin. Shall I hurt Him Who loves me infinitely? Shall I drive His love and light out of my soul by mortal sin? No one who realizes the meaning of the presence of God will do such a thing. At the same time, the thought that God sees me is a source of hope. He will give me grace; He is helping me, encouraging me, strengthening me in the struggle. God looks at us "from heaven." In the beginning of the spiritual life one can most easily take this objectivized view of God. Later one realizes that in a mysterious way God sees us from the depths of our own soul. But we must not strain ourselves trying to imagine this—or trying to imagine Him looking down from heaven either. The imagination is not much help in this. Faith is what counts.

St. Benedict takes some lines of the psalms to express his meaning: *scrutans corda et renes Deus*[539] is the best. And he goes on to emphasize the fact that all our thoughts are seen by God and known to Him. Remember that for St. Thomas, God's knowledge is His own being, and God knows all things in Himself, but also in themselves most perfectly, and more perfectly than they could ever know themselves: He knows them as participating in His own being and in His own perfections.[540] And He *shares* this knowledge of us with us by enabling us to judge, in the light of grace, all our thoughts as He Himself judges them. Thus the light of self-knowledge is a participation in the light by which God Himself knows us. Further, His knowledge of our thoughts becomes the cause of our own knowledge of our thoughts. Such are some of the implications of the "presence of God."

539. "God examines the hearts and inmost depths" (Ps. 7:10) (McCann, 38).
540. *Summa Theologiae*, 1a, q. 14, art. 4–6 (Gilby, 4.14/15–26/27).

4) *DOCEMUR ERGO MERITO NON FACERE NOSTRAM VOLUNTATEM . . .*[541] Having shown that God sees all our thoughts and gives us light to share in His vision of us, then St. Benedict goes on to the *will*. With our will, we have one great task: to turn aside from self-will (*a voluntatibus tuis avertere*[542])—to cooperate in the fulfillment of God's will in us. Self-will, as St. Bernard points out, is divisive—it is what is proper to ourselves alone, as opposed to all other wills.[543] It is not merely what pleases us or what gives us joy. It is what constitutes an act of *assertion of our own will against every other will* (*virtù*).[544] This is the essence of self-will, which is the deadly enemy of the will of God. God's will *is that which is most common*—it embraces not only our own private good but at the same time the good of others, the good of the universe, and the glory of God Himself. Hence if we learn to do the will of God we will have the highest joy and satisfaction and also at the same time exercise the highest freedom in our own wills. Why is this? because the removal of the barrier which we set up between our will and everything else, helps us to enter into the stream of reality. We do not have to *resist* reality and manipulate it for our own selfish ends: we are free to will without obstacle what is really

541. "therefore we are taught rightly not to do our own will" (McCann, 40, which reads: ". . . *nostram non facere* . . .").

542. "turn away from your own will" (Sirach 18:30) (McCann, 40).

543. See *In Tempore Resurrectionis, Sermo* 3.3 (*PL* 183, col. 289D): "*Voluntatem dico propriam, quae non est communis cum Deo et hominibus, sed nostra tantum: quando quod volumus, non ad honorem Dei, not ad utilitatem fratrum, sed propter nosmetipsos facimus, non intendentes placere Deo et prodesse fratribus, sed satisfacere propriis motibus animorum*" ("I call self-will that which is not held in common with God and other people, but is ours alone: it is when we do what we want, not for the honor of God or for the benefit of our brothers, but for ourselves alone, not looking to please God or to help our brothers, but to find satisfaction in the unique movements of our own minds").

544. In his recorded conference for September 7, 1962, Merton mentions a refectory reading on *virtù* as the Renaissance concept of power, exemplifying the deficiencies of a certain kind of Renaissance humanism that equates following nature with following the passions and spontaneous feelings, illustrating the ambiguities of the idea of "natural law."

good, what genuinely has value, what can bring us to true fulfillment. We are delivered from slavery to the illusion that fulfillment consists in self-assertion. On the contrary, fulfillment consists in *self-dedication*. The grain of wheat, falling into the ground, dies—it does not remain alone; it becomes a copious harvest. To protect us against self-will, St. Benedict says: *Sunt viae quae videntur hominibus rectae quarum finis in profundum inferni demergit.*[545] We cannot trust our own likes and dislikes and the fact that something appears to be good does not make it so in reality. We must therefore guard against self-assertion and learn from others. Especially *pleasure* is to be regarded as a source of *illusion and corruption.*

5) *Mors secus introitum {delectationis posita} est . . .*[546] St. Benedict emphasizes especially that we must be on our guard against being seduced by pleasure—by the desire to feel good, to enjoy ourselves, to taste an immediate satisfaction. This is one of the basic truths of the purgative way, and it is founded on the teaching of the Book of Proverbs, traditionally assigned to the purgative way. Read Proverbs c. 5:1-8:[547] the "harlot" {is the} embodiment of all temptation to pleasure. The desire for pleasure, even in spiritual things, can be the source of grave illusion and blindness. (Read St. John of the Cross, *Ascent* 1.6, pp. 34–35 [nn. 1, 3, 6].[548]) Hence we must realize the danger of following

545. "There are ways which seem to people to be right, the end of which sinks to the depth of hell" (Prov. 16:25) (McCann, 40).

546. "Death is placed close to the entranceway to delight" (McCann, 40) (copy text reads: ". . . *delecationis positum* . . .").

547. "My son, to my wisdom be attentive, to my knowledge incline your ear, that discretion may watch over you, and understanding may guard you. The lips of an adulteress drip with honey, and her mouth is smoother than oil; but in the end she is as bitter as wormwood, as sharp as a two-edged sword. Her feet go down to death, to the nether world her steps attain; lest you see before you the road to life, her paths will ramble, you know not where. So now, O children, listen to me, go not astray from the words of my mouth. Keep your way far from her, approach not the door of her house."

548. "1. In order that what we have said may be the more clearly and fully understood, it will be well here to set down and state how these desires are the

cause of two serious evils in the soul: the one is that they deprive it of the spirit of God, and the other is that the soul wherein they dwell is wearied, tormented, darkened, defiled and weakened, according to that which is said in Jeremiah, Chapter II: *Duo mala fecit Populus meus: dereliquerunt fontem aquae vitae, et foderunt sibi cisternas, dissipatas, quae continere non valent aquas*. Which signifies: They have forsaken Me, Who am the fountain of living water, and they have hewed them out broken cisterns, that can hold no water. Those two evils—namely, the privative and the positive—may be caused by any disordered act of the desire. And, first of all, speaking of the privative, it is clear from the very fact that the soul becomes affectioned to a thing which comes under the head of creature, that the more the desire for that thing fills the soul, the less capacity has the soul for God; inasmuch as two contraries, according to the philosophers, cannot coexist in one person; and further, since, as we said in the fourth chapter, affection for God and affection for creatures are contraries, and thus there cannot be contained within one will affection for creatures and affection for God. For what has the creature to do with the Creator? What has sensual to do with spiritual? Visible with invisible? Temporal with eternal? Food that is heavenly, spiritual and pure with food that is of sense alone and is purely sensual? Christlike detachment with attachment to aught soever? . . . 3. From this we are to learn that all creatures are crumbs that have fallen from the table of God. Wherefore he that feeds upon the creatures is rightly called a dog, and therefore the bread is taken from the children, because they desire not to rise from feeding upon the crumbs, which are the creatures, to the table of the uncreated spirit of their Father. Therefore, like dogs, they are ever hungering, and justly so, because the crumbs serve to whet their appetite rather than to satisfy their hunger. And thus David says of them: *Famen patientur ut canes, et circuibunt civitatem. Si vero non fuerint saturati, et murmurabunt*. Which signifies: They shall suffer hunger like dogs and shall go round about the city, and, when they see not themselves satisfied, they shall murmur. For this is the property of one that has desires, that he is ever discontented and dissatisfied, like one that suffers hunger; for what has the hunger which all the creatures suffer to do with the fullness which is caused by the spirit of God? Wherefore this fullness that is uncreated cannot enter the soul, if there be not first cast out that other created hunger which belongs to the desire of the soul; for, as we have said, two contraries cannot dwell in one person, the which contraries in this case are hunger and fullness. . . . 6. With regard to the first, it is clear that the desires weary and fatigue the soul; for they are like restless and discontented children, who are ever demanding this or that from their mother, and are never satisfied. And even as one that digs because he covets a treasure is wearied and fatigued, even so is the soul wearied and fatigued in order to attain that which its desires demand of it; and although in the end it may attain it, it is still weary, because it is never satisfied; for, after all, the cisterns which it is digging are broken, and cannot hold water to satisfy thirst. And thus, as Isaiah

our desires and living according to them, and realize that they can completely wreck our lives without our fully being aware of the fact. Thus to preserve ourselves from illusion and blindness and to retain our spiritual vision, we must *deny ourselves* and turn aside from our desires and try *to see things as God Himself sees them in us*. In its essence, this degree means fidelity in avoiding all occasions of sin, by virtue of constant attention to the living presence of God in our souls.

---

says: *Lassus adhuc sitit, et anima ejus vacua est*. Which signifies: His desire is empty. And the soul that has desires is wearied and fatigued; for it is like a man that is sick of a fever, who finds himself no better until the fever leaves him, and whose thirst increases with every moment. For, as is said in the Book of Job: *Cum satiatus fuerit, arctabitur, aestuabit, et omnis dolor irruet super eum*. Which signifies: When he has satisfied his desire, he will be the more oppressed and straitened; the heat of desire hath increased in his soul and thus all grief will fall upon him. The soul is wearied and fatigued by its desires, because it is wounded and moved and disturbed by them as is water by the winds; in just the same way they disturb it, allowing it not to rest in any place or in any thing soever. And of such a soul says Isaiah: *Cor impii quasi mare fervens*. The heart of the wicked man is like the sea when it rages. And he is a wicked man that subjects not his desires. The soul that would fain satisfy its desires grows wearied and fatigued; for it is like one that, being hungered, opens his mouth that he may sate himself with wind, when, instead of being satisfied, his craving becomes greater, for the wind is no food for him. To this purpose said Jeremiah: *In desiderio animae suae attraxit ventum amoris sui*. As though he were to say: In the desire of his will he snuffed up the wind of his affection. And later he tries to describe the aridity wherein such a soul remains, and warns it, saying: *Prohibe pedem tuum a nuditate, et guttur tuum a siti*. Which signifies: Withhold thy foot (that is, thy thought) from detachment and thy throat from thirst (that is to say, thy will from the indulgence of the desire which causes greater drought); and, even as the lover is wearied and fatigued upon the day of his hopes, when his attempt has proved to be vain, so the soul is wearied and fatigued by all its desires and by indulgence in them, since they all cause it greater emptiness and hunger; for, as they commonly say, desire is like the fire, which increases as wood is thrown upon it, and which, when it has consumed the wood, must needs burn away" (Peers, 1:35-38).

II. *The Second Degree*

*"Si propriam quis non amans voluntatem desideria sua non delectetur implere."*[549] Every word must be weighed here, if we are to see the difference between this and the first degree. In the first, there is question of avoiding what *must* be avoided—fully deliberate sin. In the second, there is question of avoiding what ought to be avoided—semi-deliberate sin, attachment to our own desires whether or not they are contrary to the will of God, {the} habitual tendency *to satisfy and gratify our own will*. When would one have the first degree of humility and not the second? When he would say: I want to do this, and since it is not a sin I can do it and will do it, even though it is just a matter of self-gratification. All that matters to me is that here is a case where I am permitted to gratify my own will; I can get away with it, therefore I will. It is possible that the second degree means, as Dom Anselme Le Bail thinks,[550] the avoidance of all deliberate venial sin. However, St. Benedict does not make the distinction thus implied. The first degree, according to St. Benedict's explicit words, is the avoidance of *sin*, the second the avoidance of habitual gratification of one's own will, understood *apart from sin*. The first degree {entails} avoidance of deliberate sin; the second degree, *avoidance of a basically selfish attitude*, which considers first of all the gratification of one's own desires, and seeks that rather than what is good in itself or good for others. The second degree of humility, then, puts us on our guard against *judging all things in terms of our own comfort and convenience*—our own private good.

Is the second degree important in the monastic life? Or does it apply rather to seculars? The second degree is a matter of great importance in the monastic life. In order to come to a monastery, it is true that we must normally have made an act of

549. "If someone does not love his own will and does not delight in fulfilling his own desires" (McCann, 42).

550. This connection is not made in Le Bail's discussion of the second degree in "The Spiritual Ideas Contained in the Rule of S. Benedict" (130–31: "2. The Humility which corresponds to Fear: The Second Degree of Humility").

self-renunciation which implies the second degree, the relinquishment of our own desires. But it quite often happens that one can fall back into self-gratification as soon as he has become accustomed to the new life. In point of fact many monks who are careless about their vocation and sloppy in their discipline, are men who have attained partially to the second and third degrees of humility: they obey their rules and the superiors to some extent, yet at the same time *they continue to gratify their own will in as many things as possible.* Examples: one who has this habitual tendency to self-gratification will do the following kind of thing:

a) He will *lack generosity in things which do not interest him*; he will only apply himself to work and tasks which he likes. Otherwise he will loaf or even by-pass the job altogether.

b) He will tend habitually to put his own comfort and desires before regular exercises, exact observance of the *Rule*, generous fulfillment of duties. He will in other words *cut many corners.*

c) He will tend to exploit others for his own interests—for instance, {he} will use them as a source of entertainment or consolation, to relieve boredom by signs, etc., not considering whether or not he may be harming them as well as himself.

d) He will expect everybody to cater to his likes and dislikes and will take it out on them in subtle ways if they do not.

e) As a consequence he will hardly be an obedient or charitable monk—he will tend to be hard to get along with, perhaps, and be a burden to others.

### III. *The Third Degree*

This is the shortest of all, except for the eighth and tenth—not even three lines. But very much is contained in it. The reason this is so short is that it treats of obedience, which is developed elsewhere in a whole chapter and is frequently brought up in all parts of the *Rule.* Hence this degree is crucial for a monk. It is what makes the monk, and with only the first two, one can not yet qualify as a good monk or as a monk at all. Actually the third degree is what makes a *monk*, a minimum requirement, and the fourth, fifth and sixth make a *good monk*. The seventh makes a *perfect monk*, a saint. The rest are trimmings and accidental perfections that embellish the monastic humility (whether or not the seventh degree is present). *UT QUIS PRO DEI AMORE OMNI OBEDIENTIA SE SUBDAT MAJORI, IMITANS DOMINUM*. . . .[551] In these few words is contained just as much matter as in any other single degree of humility.

1) *pro Dei amore*—The motive of LOVE is brought in here explicitly for the first time in the various degrees. The first two imply rather fear of God, prudence, justice, love of duty, the desire to obey Him as our Lord and Master. Now however the motive of love comes in to color the whole concept of humility. It is necessary at this point. It is for love of *God* that we embrace religious obedience—not for love of the religious superior, or for love of our own perfection. If one were to embrace religious obedience, but not out of love, it would still not really be the third degree of humility—it might come rather under the second degree—a way of abandoning our own will. But here the emphasis is placed on the service of love, on worship and filial self-dedication—our service of obedience is offered to God as a pleasing sacrifice, and the thought is *primarily to please Him*. Thus the third degree implies already *a deeper knowledge of God* and a love of Him for His own sake rather than merely for our own spiritual good. This is a very powerful interior motive, a great aid to true obedience.

2) *OMNI OBEDIENTIA*—not just obedience in a general or abstract way, but all obedience, obedience *in all things* (that accord with the *Rule* and the monastic state). To understand this we must refer back to the chapter on obedience—chapter 5. READ the second paragraph of chapter 5 (McCann, pp. 33–34[552]). And {note}

551. "that someone, out of love for God, submits himself to a superior in complete obedience, imitating the Lord" (McCann, 42).

552. "Such as these, therefore, immediately abandoning their own affairs and forsaking their own will, dropping the work they were engaged on and leaving it unfinished, with swift obedience follow up with their deeds the voice of him who commands them. And almost in the same moment of time that the

the innumerable places in the *Rule* where everything is in the hands of the superior and nothing is to be done without his blessing or command, even in matters concerning our own perfection—for instance Lenten penances.

3) IMITANS DOMINUM—This is another very important new idea—and one which again is essential to the monastic state: ours is a life of *imitation of Christ*, and not just of imitation of His virtues and life in general but above all imitation of *His Passion*. We will never really understand religious obedience if we fail to consider these two all-important elements: the love of God, which is our motive, and the *sequela Christi*[553] which gives it its form. Read Philippians 2:8.[554] Here we see the close connection between obedience and humility in the mind of St. Benedict. He is quoting St. Paul, Philippians 2:8, which speaks of Christ *emptying Himself* and becoming obedient unto death. Humility is the same thing for the monk. In imitation of Christ, the monk *empties himself of his worldly self* and renounces worldly liberty in order to become obedient even to the point of laying down his life if necessary. This shows that humility equals sacrifice in St. Benedict's mind. If we obey even unto death, it means there is nothing we will not give up for the sake of obedience. This is true humility and a true emptying of self. The third degree of humility clearly implies great perfection and self-denial.

---

master's order is issued, is the disciple's work completed, in the swiftness of the fear of the Lord; the two things being rapidly accomplished together by those who are impelled by the desire of attaining life everlasting. Therefore they choose the narrow way, according to the Lord's words: *Narrow is the way which leadeth unto life;* so that not living by their own will, and obeying their own desires and passions, but walking by another's judgement and orders, they dwell in monasteries, and desire to have an abbot over them. Assuredly such as these imitate that saying of the Lord wherein he saith: *I came not to do my own will, but the will of him who sent me*" (McCann, 33, 35).

553. "following of Christ."

554. "He humbled himself, becoming obedient to death, even to death on a cross" (see McCann, 42).

IV. *The Fourth Degree*

*In ipsa obedientia, duris et contrariis rebus vel etiam quibuslibet irrogatis injuriis tacita conscientia patientiam amplectatur . . .*[555] The fourth degree is the development of what was contained in the last part of the third. If we are to be obedient unto death, then it stands to reason that our obedience will not stop at the acceptance of hardship, difficulty, insult, opprobrium, and other highly unpleasant conditions. It is to be noted here that IN PRACTICE THIS FOURTH DEGREE IS THE CRUCIAL ONE IN THE STRUGGLE FOR MONASTIC PERFECTION. It is here that most monks stop; they never quite manage to get over this particular hurdle. They spend their lives trying, with more or less generosity, to take the difficulties implied here, and perhaps never quite succeeding. This is the *pons asinorum*[556] of monastic humility. Why? because *here we are really tested in self-renunciation*. We may be willing to renounce our will and to obey, but if we insist on being treated with special regard and reverence, and demand that our personality be respected, it is because we are still clinging to a "persona" in ourselves that is superficial. We are not willing to give up our superficial and outward self, and live in the depths where insults do not penetrate. But it is this superficial and worldly identity that must be renounced. And when this "person" is treated without respect, without consideration, then is our opportunity to really renounce it. Note—the human person is always worthy of respect and dignity and superiors should be careful always to observe this fact and act accordingly. But remember that the true person of a man, his inner spiritual self, is not affected by insults and lack of consideration; if he is strong and mature a man can

555. "In this very obedience, should hard and contrary things and even some injustices be imposed, let him embrace patience with a quiet mind" (McCann, 42).

556. "bridge of asses": a phrase associated in the Middle Ages with the fifth proposition of Euclid's *Elements of Geometry*, the first to require serious reasoning and hence a separation point between fools and those capable of complex reasoning.

grow in trial and humiliation and emerge with greater dignity as a result. But one who is weak and small-minded and not developed may be crushed by trial and humiliation, and it is not wise or right to assume that everybody "ought to be able to take it." But let us hope and assume that if God brings us into such trial it is because He has given us the grace to take it and to profit by it, and if we will correspond with this grace, by accepting the trial, we will certainly grow and become more perfect as spiritual men. {Note the} correlations {of this} paradox: {we must have} respect for our self—this is due to our deeper self; {but} we cling to the respect given to {the} exterior self. {We should} not cultivate an asceticism that implies contempt for others, yet {we must} be able to rise above {others'} deficiencies in this regard.

*What is the essence of the fourth degree?* In the first degree it was a question of refusing all sinful pleasures and resisting the attraction of every apparent good, in order to obey God and keep in His presence. In the fourth degree it is a question of *bearing evils* and not being deterred from doing good by any difficulty or hardship, and preserving, with love, an interior disposition of *silence, patience and perseverance*. It is a higher degree of humility, of fortitude, and of obedience. This degree highlights the fact that FORTITUDE is a constant element in all this ascent of humility. It is most strongly emphasized here, but it is implicit everywhere. St. Benedict proceeds to make himself clear and to show us the way to proceed by giving ample details as to the motives and aids which enable us to see and practice this degree of humility.

The heart of the fourth degree {is} *tacita conscientia patientiam amplectatur* (*conscientia*—{note the} depths implied): *with interior silence*—not fighting back or criticizing, not upset, not resisting—without resentment. One retains interior peace, but this does not exclude suffering, and perhaps a certain struggle to impose silence on our passions. Such silence is not possible without a full *acceptance* of the suffering and humiliation involved. Note—obviously this interior silence includes also exterior silence; one does not utter complaints, excuses, alibis, or try to avoid the humiliation. One will not succeed in this interior acceptance and silence until he has at least mastered to some extent the exterior compliance and obedience which are supposed by the second and third degrees. This interior and exterior acceptance, with peace and silence *and without resistance or attempts at self-justification*, is a *very great dynamic* force in the interior life. If we have the strength thus to embrace patience and to persevere in silence, it will have a great strengthening and purifying effect on our soul. The first step towards real interior humility is the *realization of this fact*. Many religious do not have any strength to practice this kind of humility because *they really do not believe it has any value*—they are still concerned more with getting things done their own way, and reaching a compromise between their own will and the will of the superior—making a deal. *They are not spiritual enough to see the value of giving in*—they think that if they do so, all will be lost. On the contrary all will be gained.

*sustinens non lassescat vel discedat*[557]—It is not merely a question of embracing gladly a momentary pain, a passing rebuff, but a long-drawn-out situation full of bitterness and humiliation and suffering—settling down with all one's heart to embrace this difficulty and bear with it and overcome it. This is the secret of the fourth degree—*giving up hope of the situation being otherwise than what it is*—renouncing our desire to make it pleasant or advantageous for ourselves by a successful resistance. Motives {come} from Scripture—"he that perseveres to the end shall be saved":[558]

a) "Let thy heart take courage and wait thou for the Lord":[559] the heroism of perseverance, of waiting, implies great *hope*.

b) Not only should we hope in the Lord, but it *is to be expected* that we must undergo suffering—"we are put to death all day long."[560]

557. "with endurance, let him neither grow weary nor withdraw" (McCann, 42).

558. Mt. 10:22 (McCann, 42).

559. Ps. 26[27]:14 (McCann, 42/43).

560. Rom. 8:36 (McCann, 42).

c) Our triumph is assured if we expect it from God and not from ourselves. "We overcome through Him that hath loved us."[561] Weigh these words!

d) We have to be tested as silver in the fire—this is a basic principle of the monastic life. And the chief form of our testing is by obedience to superiors.

e) Finally in bearing with all these things we are only carrying out the commands of Christ in the Sermon on the Mount—READ Matthew 5:38-48.[562]

It is necessary above all that the novice meditate frequently on this degree of humility and make up his mind firmly never to refuse Our Lord his cooperation when asked to practice it. We must be firmly persuaded of the absolute necessity of this if we are to be monks. We have absolutely no right to complain of hardships like this for we have engaged ourselves to bear them with a good heart and with peace of soul. But we cannot do this unless we resolve to accept the sufferings involved and go ahead with firm hope in the grace of Christ.

561. Rom. 8:37 (McCann, 42/43).

562. "You have heard that it was said, 'An eye for an eye,' and 'A tooth for a tooth.' But I say to you not to resist the evildoer; on the contrary, if someone strike thee on the right cheek, turn to him the other also; and if anyone should go to law with thee and take thy tunic, let him take thy cloak as well; and whoever forces thee to go for one mile, go with him two. To him who asks of thee, give; and from him who would borrow of thee, do not turn away. You have heard that it was said, 'Thou shalt love thy neighbor, and shalt hate thy enemy.' But I say to you, love your enemies, do good to those who hate you, and pray for those who persecute and calumniate you, so that you may be children of your Father in heaven, who makes his sun to rise on the good and the evil, and sends rain on the just and the unjust. For if you love those that love you, what reward shall you have? Do not even the publicans do that? And if you salute your brethren only, what are you doing more than others? Do not even the Gentiles do that? You therefore are to be perfect, even as your heavenly Father is perfect."

V. *The Fifth Degree*

*Si omnes cogitationes malas cordi suo advenientes . . . per humilem confessionem abbatem non celaverit.*[563] This is not going to be well understood without a little knowledge of the historical background. St. Benedict, who in all these degrees is simply following Cassian, is thinking of the typical situation of a neophyte among the Desert Fathers. One entered the tutelage of a monk or hermit, lived with him constantly, and learned of the spiritual life by imitating everything he did and manifesting to him every thought, good or bad, that came along, treating it according to the discernment of the spiritual father considered as a representative of God. The spiritual father in this case was not only in very close intimate contact with the neophyte, but also *had a special charismatic gift to "discern" the spirits* that moved him. He had indeed been chosen for this purpose. In the early days of Western monasticism, including Cistercian monasticism, the abbot was the confessor of all the monks, or of most of the monks. Nowadays this is forbidden by canon law and the abbot is also forbidden to induce any religious to make a manifestation of conscience to him unwillingly. Thus the situation has partly changed. We can therefore take this in a somewhat broader sense, as follows:

a) It refers at least to relations with one's spiritual director, novice master, master of students perhaps, and also to one's relations with the father abbot when they are sufficiently close to warrant such manifestations. It is in no way expected that a novice should make known the most intimate and subtle details of his interior to one who has only a general acquaintance with him as yet. But it is normal that this should come later, or indeed quite soon. Openness with the father abbot is to be encouraged as a source of grace.

563. "If through humble confession he does not conceal from the abbot any evil thoughts coming into his heart" (McCann, 44).

b) We should in general have a desire that our father abbot should know us thoroughly inside and out, and without starting immediately with the most intimate hidden thoughts and faults, we can at least start by giving him whatever information is necessary for him to have a good knowledge of our character and what kind of person we are.

c) This degree does *not* refer merely to completeness in the confessional. Integrity of confession is taken for granted and does not require a special "degree" of humility.

*In practice* what this degree means is: a complete, simple, perfectly open self-manifestation to one's spiritual father who is the one to whom the guidance of our soul has been entrusted. It means resolutely putting aside *all fear* of being known for what we are, of being known by another as we know ourselves, the good points and the bad points, without glossing things over, without ambiguities. It means complete sincerity with another about our interior life and inmost drives and thoughts, whether good or evil. *But it means at the same time a willingness to accept his judgement* on these things and to follow his advice at least in a general way. It would not yet be the fifth degree of humility if a monk were merely content to humble himself by manifesting thoughts and acts of which he is ashamed—*without any intention of abiding by the father's decision*. This would only be a form of pride. Though of course one is not absolutely bound to take all advice given, or to accept every interpretation, St. Benedict's fifth degree assumes that one is open to suggestions and to informed guidance. {The} *basis* {for this is} trust that God is using the spiritual father as His instrument, and that what he tells us is guided at least in a general way by the Holy Spirit. God will not fail to protect us in this way and give grace and light through direction, as a reward for our confidence in manifesting ourselves humbly and trustfully. THE FATHERS BELIEVED THAT THE MERE FACT THAT ONE INTENDED TO KEEP A THOUGHT SECRET FROM THE SPIRITUAL FATHER MIGHT BE A SIGN THAT IT CAME FROM THE DEVIL. Manifesting a temptation trustfully is often enough to overcome it completely. We will go into these matters further when we consider spiritual direction in the conferences on monastic observances.[564] Meanwhile a few hints will suffice:

*omnes cogitationes malas*—we should manifest all our important thoughts, good or bad, to our spiritual father. St. Benedict mentions only the bad ones, as being more obviously humiliating. It also takes humility to manifest good desires and aspirations with humility. *In practice* this does not mean that in our present situation it is necessary to manifest every passing trifle and phantasy. But one should make known *significant tendencies* (*cogitationes*!)—drives that are characteristic, that have a certain force for good or evil in our lives. Anything that really bothers or perplexes us, or is a potential problem, might well be mentioned. But do not create problems when there are none. This would be a form of pride. *Beware of trying to gain attention by being too interesting or important in the eyes of the director*. Just be yourself, *and desire to be known as you are, not as you would like to be.*

*mala a se absconse commissa*:[565]

a) Obviously, one should early gain the *habit of accusing himself of violations* of {the} *Rule* and other little faults. One can accuse himself to the father undermaster for purely external faults, breakages, etc. *But as soon as the fault is a breach of discipline, or a fortiori an interior fault, it should be manifested to* the father master, at least if it has any bearing on one's *novitiate formation and the question of vocation*. This is a matter of counsel however and not of precept. It is a very good practice.

b) *Doubts* and problems of conscience can and should normally and openly be discussed in spiritual direction, and one should not be held back from this by a false feeling of shame.

564. Merton includes a 20-page appendix (dated 1958), entitled "Spiritual Direction in the Monastic Setting" with the "Monastic Observances" conferences. See also Thomas Merton, *Spiritual Direction and Meditation* (Collegeville, MN: Liturgical Press, 1960), 3–42; *An Introduction to Christian Mysticism*, 251–332; Thomas Merson, "Spiritual Direction," *The Merton Seasonal*, 32.1 (Spring 2007), 3–17.

565. "hidden evils committed by himself" (McCann, 44).

c) *Past sins?* It is not absolutely necessary to make a general confession before receiving the habit or making profession, and in this one can rest with the decision of the confessor. In general it is not advisable. One can make known in a general way past failings in direction, in so far as the knowledge may cast light on present problems. But for the rest, it is better to let the past alone, and let sleeping dogs lie. There is no point in dragging out a lot of things that have been washed away in the Precious Blood of Our Lord Jesus Christ, and have been forgotten by Him.

d) The mere fact that one feels very ashamed of a certain thought is no reason for creating a big issue and worrying about whether or not one should manifest it. Manifestation of these things perhaps will bring peace by showing that it is not as terrible as one thinks. But if it is just a source of worry over nothing, it would be better to forget the whole thing. Some people think that the mere fact that a thought comes to them and makes them ashamed means that they have to manifest it. It may be merely a passing phantasy of no importance which is not really a thought because we have barely adverted to it. To take such a fantasy and start thinking and worrying about it would be to make a problem where no real problem existed, and would be a waste of time and energy. The scriptural principles which St. Benedict adduces to explain his meaning and prove his point emphasize the ideas of *mercy and remission of sin*. It is not a question of humiliation for its own sake, but of trustfully manifesting one's fault in the hope of grace, mercy and peace of soul. This should be the *fruit* of a truly humble manifestation. If this fruit is not forthcoming, perhaps we have not really understood St. Benedict's meaning, and are expecting something more complicated than he really intends. If we do not understand, it is a sign that we are not yet quite ripe for this practice.

VI. *The Sixth Degree*

*SI OMNI VILITATE ET EXTREMITATE CONTENTUS SIT MONACHUS*.[566] Here again we come face to face with the spirit of monastic poverty, so essential to a true monk and a true monastic community: *for what is said here applies not only to the monk but to the monastic community*. If everything in the community is always the best, and everyone is keeping a high standard of living, how will the individual monk be able to practice this sixth degree except in theory? *Vilitas*—the commentators refer this especially to matters of food, clothing, and shelter; one might add tools and work, liturgical vestments and vessels, etc., etc.

a) *Food, clothing*: in this as in other matters, the sixth degree of humility implies more than just the ordinary poverty to which every monk is obliged—that is to say to be content {with} *plain* things and to have them only in dependence on a superior. St. Benedict's idea for the ordinary monk is that they wear clothes of the quality and quantity of the people in the region. The ordinary monk is then bound to this level. The sixth degree of humility is for a monk to be *content and even grateful when he lacks what is normally good and necessary in his state of life*. That is to say, content with very poor clothes, perhaps very much worn and patched, or of very inferior quality to the others—garments barely sufficient for their purpose. Not that he should be in a state of penury, but he should be content when the clothing, bedding, etc. given him for his use is *not sufficiently good to enable him to live quite comfortably*, but *involves discomfort and sacrifice and even considerable difficulty*. This is not supposed to be the ordinary thing: the superior has an obligation to see that the monks are well clothed and suffer no serious needs, on the level of the average poor person: one is entitled to simple clothing, warmth and sleep. But if for some reason one is deprived in these matters, he should be content and even glad. The same applies to food: if the food is poorly prepared—or prepared in an unappetizing way—or consists of things

566. "Let a monk be content with everything poor in quality and of the lowest degree" (McCann, 44).

one does not like—or is not sufficient in quantity (*rarely* happens!)—if one misses a portion and it is not noticed: all these things should be accepted with peace and joy. It is no sin to feel it and to be disturbed at it, but one who takes these lacks seriously is deficient in Benedictine humility because he assumes that better things are *due* to him and tends to demand them, at least interiorly, and to resent their absence. True, they are due to him, but he has come to the monastery not to get his "due" because if everything that were due to him were given to him, he would have perhaps more temporal goods but might suffer many unexpected punishments in the spiritual order. For we are all sinners. {There are} three degrees {involved here}: (1) acceptance without protest—{this is} not {the} sixth degree; (2) without interior complaint; (3) with joy and *preference*. IT IS VERY IMPORTANT TO CULTIVATE A SPIRIT OF JOY IN SACRIFICE AND POVERTY, IN ORDER TO EXPIATE OUR SINS AND TO BECOME TRUE MONKS. If we do not cultivate this, but allow ourselves to become soft, complaining, and demanding creatures, we will lack one of the greatest joys of our monastic state, the consolation of being poor with Christ and knowing that we are really living up to our monastic vocation.

b) *Shelter*—The whole monastery is supposed to be simple and even poor. One should not complain when his monastery is not beautiful and supplied with every modern comfort—one should not be demanding that more and more new gadgets be installed. St. Jerome gives a general principle: "The Son of Man had nowhere to rest His head and shall you, a monk, desire spacious cloisters and lofty roofs?"[567] It was a common principle among the ancient monks to live in huts that they had thrown together in a couple of days. Benedictine and Cistercian monasteries are meant to be *solid and permanent* but not splendid and comfortable. There is always danger of grave scandal when the home of religious vowed to poverty is fine, even luxurious, and the poor are left with miserable broken-down houses and slum conditions.

567. *Letter* 14, to Heliodorus (*PL* 22, col. 550).

c) *The Church, Liturgical Ornaments*—a monk should not complain if his church is not splendid; indeed he should not have a taste for useless decorations. *Simplicity and beauty* go hand in hand, and the poverty of the early Cistercians resulted in great beauty and "splendor" of spiritual form in their monasteries, precisely because of the absence of superfluous ornaments. We should not grieve if our monasteries cannot afford fine works of art, splendid stained glass, fine vestments of the latest design, splendid chalices. The ideal of our Cistercian Fathers was, in this matter, to return to the plainest and humblest simplicity. Silk was banned, undecorated wool was used for chasubles, tunics and dalmatics were not used at first, silver chalices only, no statues or other decorations—only the crucifix—no such things as carpets, curtains, etc. This must be properly understood. (Read *Spirit of Simplicity*.[568]) *Ugliness is not poverty* and poverty should not imply a cult of ugliness. The sanctuary must have an atmosphere of simple beauty, in order to give glory to God. To tolerate hideous, misshapen, vulgar designs in a church edifice is an offence which is incompatible with the true monastic ideal. A true monk cannot be simply indifferent to ugliness and vulgarity if there is something that he can do about it. But in remedying matters, he should not seek what is expensive or showy. A monk with a sense of art as well as a religious sense, will know how to remodel an ugly place without show and without much expense, to render it worthy of divine worship. *In this matter poverty is simply not to be judged merely in terms of price.* Sometimes a low-priced chalice, chasuble, statue or picture may be in

568. The full title of this work is *The Spirit of Simplicity Characteristic of the Cistercian Order: An Official Report, demanded and approved by the General Chapter. Together with Texts from St. Bernard of Clairvaux on Interior Simplicity. Translation and Commentary by A Cistercian Monk of Our Lady of Gethsemani* (Trappist, KY: Abbey of Our Lady of Gethsemani, 1948). The Cistercian monk is Merton himself, who translated from the French and annotated an official report on simplicity in Cistercian life, approved by the general chapter of the order in 1925, and added a translation and discussion of selected texts on the topic of simplicity from the sermons and treatises of St. Bernard. This second section, "St. Bernard on Interior Simplicity," was reprinted as Part 2 of *Thomas Merton on St. Bernard*, 105–57.

fact full of the most vulgar showiness and striving for effect, an *imitation of luxury* which would be even worse and less monastic that luxury itself—for here we have the added note of *falsity, or pretense.* In a case where there would be a choice between a lower-priced chasuble that looked more showy and *pretended* to achieve the effect of luxury, and a higher-priced one that was simpler and more decent, a monk would be obliged, by his monastic spirit, to choose the better one—unless there were very grave reasons for not doing so, or unless he could get around it in some other way. This is not a class in liturgical art, so we will pass on. In any case, if one *has* artistic taste and through no fault of his own is obliged to wear hideous and vulgar ornaments, even expensive ones, and say Mass at an altar overlaid with stupid and incongruous decorations, he can practice the sixth degree of humility by accepting this in a spirit of contentment, peace and detachment. His opportunities may be more frequent than he imagines.

*The sixth degree of humility is certainly incompatible with liturgical or artistic snobbery.* The same things apply also to the chant. It is certainly a duty for monks to see to it that the chant in choir is in every way fitting and dignified and worthy as far as possible of the court of the King of Heaven. One could not simply say that it is monastic humility to be content with bad singing and let it go at that. However, if in a particular case the singing is bad and the individual monk can do nothing about it, he should certainly accept this with joy and indifference, and not get all upset about it. This too comes under his spirit of poverty.

To SUM UP—in all things the sixth degree of humility enables us to be *content with frustration* and willing to sacrifice our tastes, desires and legitimate wishes in all things, even the best of things. It is not that these tastes may not be in themselves very good and desirable and worthy to be encouraged, but it is always better to sacrifice them and be detached from them when God gives us the opportunity. The poor don't get what they want.

*Extremitas*—whereas the commentators refer *vilitas* more to material things, *extremitas* belongs rather to non-material benefits—such as honors, positions, offices and place in society.

a) *Honors*: the monk should not have any ambition for monastic or other dignities—for honors, for special jobs. St. Bernard complains in his Fourth Homily on the *Missus Est* that many "after they have contemned the pomp of the world and entered the school of humility, have learned pride therein, and have grown insolent under the kind wings of the Lord of Humility; they grow more impatient in the cloister than they did in the world. . . . For while, where everyone seeks honors, they were not able to merit any honor, now in the cloister where honors are contemned by all, they strive to appear honorable!"[569] This applies not only to exterior honors like jobs, offices, but also to one's reputation. *One should not desire to be esteemed a highly spiritual man, or highly regarded for virtue.* If one is content with *omni extremitate* he will not be grieved or surprised if nobody treats him especially as a saint or as someone worthy of great respect. He will be content and at peace if, instead of the respect due to every child of God he receives instead insult and bad treatment. Cf. St. Francis and Brother Leo.[570]

b) *Work*: it is part of the sixth degree of humility to be perfectly content with humble and menial jobs that are boring, and without special glamour—jobs in which the work is repugnant to the senses, perhaps, and in which nothing of any account is accomplished. St. Basil says: *Decet monachum viliora opera cum multa diligentia et animi promptitudine amplecti.*[571] This means not only not trying to get out of these works (for this comes under the second and third degrees) but above all *to embrace them gladly*

569. *PL* 183, col. 85AB.

570. This refers to the famous chapter (1.8) of the *Fioretti* entitled "How St. Francis Taught Brother Leo That Perfect Joy Is Only in the Cross," in which Francis tells Leo that perfect joy consists in being rejected even by one's own brethren as a way of sharing in the tribulations and afflictions of Christ crucified (see *The Little Flowers of St. Francis*, trans. Raphael Brown [Garden City, NY: Doubleday Image, 1958], 58–60).

571. *In Const. Monast.*, c. 24, quoted by Martène (col. 394D, which reads: "*Decet religiosum etiam viliora* . . ."): "It is proper for a monk [religious] to embrace more lowly tasks with great diligence and promptness of mind."

*and even to seek them by preference.* One should not try to do this without understanding what it really means—for those with immature minds who seem eager for these things, are perhaps in reality seeking honor in reverse—they are seeking "glory" in what is respected in the monastic milieu and are perhaps only trying to shine in the eyes of the brethren. Nevertheless, one should be encouraged to practice this kind of thing, not to please men, but in order to please God interiorly and in order to unite oneself with Christ in poverty and abjection. IT MUST ALWAYS BE REMEMBERED THAT ONE MUST NOT PRACTICE HUMILITY IN A SHOWY OR ECCENTRIC WAY FOR THIS IS ONLY THE PRACTICE OF PRIDE IN ANOTHER FORM.

c) Position in the monastery—or anywhere. One should be glad to be considered the last and the least. Bernard of Monte Cassino sums it up in the verse: *Spernere mundum, spernere nullum, spernere sese / Spernere se sperni, quattuor ista beant.*[572] It is not good poetry but it is good spirituality. If we want to be saints, or even perfect monks, it is absolutely necessary to make up our minds to embrace this kind of humility with all peace and joy, without desiring to recompense ourselves for the sacrifice by taking secret pleasure and self-gratification. If we really embrace all that is *vilis* and *extremus* we will not easily be able to contemplate what seems to us to be our own virtue, for we will lose sight even of that. Great peace and security belong to those who can fully accept this degree of humility—they will be able to forget themselves, and this is a priceless gift!

*Contentus sit monachus*—in listing all the things of which a monk may be deprived, we have still not quite come to the heart of the matter. The sixth degree of humility consists not in mere *deprivation* of the things which one might normally expect and seek in a monastery—it means *contentment and peace* in the sacrifice of the ordinary natural goods, or even in some way spiritual goods, of the monastic state. {The} emphasis {is} on contentment. We can choose to be content. IT SHOULD BE UNDERSTOOD THAT

572. Quoted by Martène (col. 395D): "To scorn the world, to scorn nothing, to scorn oneself, / to scorn being scorned oneself—these four bring blessing."

THIS IMPLIES A PEACEFUL AND EVEN GRATEFUL ACCEPTANCE OF FRUSTRATION AND DEPRIVATION EVEN IN THE BEST THINGS OF THE MONASTIC LIFE—including some of the normal aids to monastic perfection. A monk who has reached this degree of humility will not complain or even be surprised or distressed interiorly: if the community is not perfect, if there are many things lacking in it, if even the atmosphere of peace and regularity is somewhat lacking, provided it is not his own fault; if the liturgy is not perfect, if there is great poverty and tastelessness in the matter of chant, vestments, etc.; if the brethren are not always kind and charitable, and if brethren and superiors ignore him in his needs of health, work, etc.; if the work is unreasonable, unprofitable, stupid, or even in some sense not monastically "edifying"; if his health is very bad and he does not receive adequate care and attention; if he is forgotten by everybody or treated without consideration and respect; if it is a generally understood conviction in the community that he is a worthless religious, good for only the most menial and boring tasks, and not fit to be considered in any way for anything; if he is regarded with disapproval by the most fervent monks in the community as a disedifying and stupid person without religious spirit, intelligence or culture. *The basis of this* is not that the monk himself takes all this with secret complacency, knowing that "others are wrong," but that HE BELIEVES ALL THIS HIMSELF and does not consider that he has any right to any better treatment. The basis is Our Lord's statement in the Gospel—when you have done everything you should have done, still consider yourselves unprofitable servants: READ Luke 17:7-10.[573] The idea is not that the monk is a bad monk and remains passively unconcerned—he does all that he should do but

573. "But which of you is there, having a servant plowing or tending sheep, who will say to him on his return from the field, 'Come at once and recline at table!' But will he not say to him, 'Prepare my supper, and gird thyself and serve me till I have eaten and drunk; and afterwards thou thyself shalt eat and drink'? Does he thank that servant for doing what he commanded him? I do not think so. Even so you also, when you have done everything that was commanded you, say, 'We are unprofitable servants; we have done what it was our duty to do.'"

*realizes that this gives him no title* to be considered or treated in a special way, even no special title to be treated with ordinary kindness. *In other words, it is the humility of a man of virtue who has altogether ceased to attach any importance to his virtue,* and does not give himself any airs before God, knowing that his virtues are as nothing in God's sight. What matters is the will and the mercy of God. A special case would be that of the monk who *does not expect to have graces of prayer* or sentiments of fervor as a "reward" for virtue. So many monks are disconcerted because they have "made so many efforts" and still "don't get anywhere." Why do they think it so important to "get somewhere"? The important thing is to do the will of God, not to be rewarded for it in this life. Hence the quote *Ut jumentum factus sum . . .*[574] Understand this rightly. We remain in this life as dumb and useless beings, before God, and should be happy in this condition. It is a form of pride to be surprised and to get upset because we do not feel ourselves to be like saints. Who do we think we are?

VII. *The Seventh Degree*

It is the sixth and seventh degree that make the saints—especially the seventh. The seventh is simply a prolongation and logical conclusion of the sixth. In the sixth the man is content with lacking everything, even necessities, because he knows his good works do not give him any special title to good treatment, or to special graces. In the seventh he considers himself in the depths of his heart to be *nothing at all*. Humility {is} not morbid self-depreciation. {The} seventh degree {entails} *supernatural humility* as opposed to mere natural modesty—{it is a} gift of God. (What is an inferiority complex?) *Si se omnibus inferiorem et viliorem . . .*[575] This appears to us today as a scandalous statement. We are so unused to such things that it seems to be insincerity and a lie

574. "I am made like a beast of burden" (Ps. 72[73]: 22) (McCann, 44).

575. If [he declares] himself to be inferior and more insignificant than everyone else" (McCann, 44, which reads: "*si omnibus se . . .*").

to believe such things. First of all St. Benedict makes it clear that the monk *believes this in his heart* (*intimo cordis credat affectu*[576]) and not only pronounces it with his lips. It would certainly not be humility to say this with one's lips, not believing it. That indeed would be a lie, and it would not be right to encourage someone to try to learn this degree by "saying" he is the worst of all repeatedly, as if thus he would eventually come to believe it. This is not the result of a pious practice. This kind of humility is genuine only in so far as it is a *gift of God*. Here least of all can we afford to cultivate this kind of humility artificially—it will certainly be false then, and will appear flagrantly false to all who see it. But in order to understand this, let us go to the Fathers.

1) The Fathers agree that this is the summit of interior humility and all praise it. St. Bernard says: *Recta facere, et inutilem se reputare apud paucos invenitur* . . . ("It is a rare virtue to think oneself useless even when he does good works") and he adds especially: "This humility makes glorious monks more glorious and holy monks more holy. . . . In my opinion this virtue is something greater than prolonged fasts, watchings, and all bodily exercises, for this is true piety and is worth everything else."[577] We must understand it not as a morbid comparison of oneself with everyone else, always ending up with oneself on the bottom of the pile. Rather it is a question of accepting the fact, when one meets anyone else, that even though the other may be inferior in rank, age, virtue, or anything else, *he may be, and as far as you are concerned is, more worthy of honor and reward in the sight of God*. Hence in this degree one does not morbidly reproach himself as inferior, but he gladly recognizes a superiority in the other, and rejoices in this superiority with perfect selflessness, not groveling before it, but accepting it with joy and praise. It is a matter of complete self-forgetfulness in order to have one's eyes wide open to the wonderful qualities of others and to rejoice in these with childlike simplicity. Hence St. Basil: "*Humilitas est*

576. "let him believe in the inmost attitude of his heart" (McCann, 44).
577. *Epistola* 143, quoted by Martène (col. 397A).

OMNES SEIPSO SUPERIORES EXISTIMARE."[578] This is really laughably simple. What degradation is it for me if everyone else is better than I am? *The humble man does not regard himself as the last in a collection of criminals but the last in a community of saints.* This is the real key. Because he has so much love that he can see the wonders of goodness and grace in all, he is able to rejoice in the fact that he is one of this communion, even though the last—for just to be the last in such a body is itself an unbelievable and magnificent thing. (The question of who is first is of no interest to such a soul—just that all are good. And the affair of being last is again a matter of no concern. What does it matter?) Also we read in the *Verba Seniorum* (Desert Fathers): "That man hates evil who hates his own sins and looks upon every brother as a saint, and venerates him as a saint."[579] In substance, St. Thomas conforms to this view in explaining how it is possible for one to regard himself as the "worst of all"[580]—he sees in himself his sins which he knows, and does not see the sins of his brother, which he does not know. But he sees the divine likeness in his brother which he can apprehend by *faith. In a word, the seventh degree presupposes not only heroic humility and love but also great faith.* It is to be regarded as an expression of all the more important virtues of the Christian life, and not merely as an expression of humility. For this degree without love would be meaningless, and that is

578. *Regulae Brevius Tractatae*, 198, quoted by Martène (col. 396C): "Humility is to think all others better than oneself."

579. *Vitae Patrum*, III.132 (*PL* 73, col. 786AB); Merton translated this saying in almost identical language in *The Wisdom of the Desert: Sayings from the Desert Fathers of the Fourth Century* (New York: New Directions, 1960), 70–71 (#119) (also found in the earlier version of this collection, *What Ought I to Do? Sayings of the Desert Fathers* [Lexington, KY: Stamperia del Santuccio, 1959], 32 [#89]): "Once two brothers were sitting with Abbot Poemen and one praised the other brother saying: He is a good brother, he hates evil. The old man said: What do you mean, he hates evil? And the brother did not know what to reply. So he said: Tell me, Father, what it is to hate evil? The Father said: That man hates evil who hates his own sins, and looks upon every brother as a saint, and loves him as a saint."

580. *Summa Theologiae*, 2a 2ae, q. 161, a. 6, ad. 1, quoted by Martène (col. 397B).

why it is so often thought to be meaningless—by those who try to see it in the abstract, prescinding altogether from the love of God and of neighbor and from deep Christian faith.

*Intimo cordis credat affectu* . . . These words express what has just been said. The "faith" implied here is more than a human opinion; it is connected with theological faith. *Cordis affectu* implies a deep and sincere interior love, and also the peaceful *will* to be content and to rejoice in the last place.

1) This *will* to rejoice in the last place implies a very positive *love* of others and a rejoicing in their good.

2) The seventh degree looks more at the good of others than at our own sins, though it sees both clearly.

3) It implies sorrow for our sins, gratitude for the virtues of others and above all a *sense of communion* with others in their virtue. To interpret this degree as *isolating* us from others in our own sinfulness would be disastrous—and one could never really understand its meaning then. {An} emphasis on *communion* {provides the} right idea of {the} common life. It expresses *wholehearted acceptance.*

4) It implies also *union with Christ on the Cross*—and communion in His self-emptying. This is implied by the quotation from the messianic Psalm 21, clearly referring to the Passion: "*Ego autem sum vermis et non homo, opprobrium hominum et abjectio plebis.*"[581] This can only fruitfully be accepted in the context of *Christian faith and the belief that we can be united to Christ in His sufferings and thus share in His glory*—to try to practice this seventh degree without reference to the Cross of Christ and union with Him would be silly and morbid. Merely to consider oneself a worm and no man, as an isolated human individual lost in his own nothingness, without any access to God, would be almost hellish. One must be prepared to *feel* this extreme isolation, perhaps. But faith always shows us that the value of such a moral trial consists in our secret union with Christ, *and in the fact that*

581. "I am a worm and no man, a disgrace before others and an object of contempt to the people" (Ps. 21[22]:7) (McCann, 44).

*He suffers in us*—that consequently it is good to be humbled thus in the sight of men in order to be united to the sufferings of Christ, the key to all true glory.

*Summary of the Interior Degrees of Humility* (I-VII)—how are we to approach these degrees in practice?

1) We must cultivate a *deep understanding* for the spirit of humility contained in them, for this spirit is characteristic of our *Rule* and our life, and without this spirit we cannot fruitfully carry out our exterior observances.

2) We must *highly esteem these attitudes of soul* and if we cannot practice them immediately, we must at least *form our monastic ideal* in accordance with them. The fact that we cannot do these things all at once should not lead us to discouragement, or to forgetting all about them. We should think of these degrees frequently and meditate on them.

3) We should *desire and pray* to learn some day to practice even the sixth and seventh degrees, and should look for opportunities, even from the beginning, to practice them in some slight way—v.g. in matters of work, clothing, food, etc.

4) We should resolve firmly to be very *faithful to every opportunity to practice the fourth degree* (and *a fortiori* the first three) because this is so crucial to our monastic life, and so much depends on it.

5) We should be on our guard to resist those who try to belittle this ideal of humility, but at the same time we must not make this ideal something false and mawkish by our own lack of understanding.

### The Exterior Degrees (VIII–XII)

The degrees of exterior humility have no meaning, or very little meaning, when they are not founded on interior humility even up to the sixth degree, or at least up to the fourth. It is easy enough for a newcomer to the monastery to practice (outwardly) the eighth degree—simply to follow the established customs. It is easy enough for a person to practice exteriorly the tenth, eleventh and twelfth degrees without having first overcome his interior pride. Unfortunately if he does this, the exterior humility will only be an added defense of his interior pride and he will all the more likely become entrenched in it. We can take the exterior degrees in a more rapid survey, with less detail. For less detail is called for. Once it is understood that these follow from interior humility and express it outwardly, there are no more complications. *But for those who try to practice this exterior humility before the interior, the complications are almost infinite—the chief one being that they become acutely self-conscious and wonder what everybody is thinking about them*, etc., etc. This is useless.

VIII. *Si nihil agat monachus nisi quod communis monasterii regula vel majorum cohortantur exempla.*[582] Without interior humility, this would be *mere conformism* which would be a plague in the monastic life. The eighth degree applies to one who *could if he wished* practice very heroic austerities with a high degree of spiritual fruitfulness, but who sees that it is even better simply for him to keep the common rule in order that his efforts at high sanctity may be hidden and not remarked by anyone. St. Benedict himself gives us the example in this: in his early days he lived in the cave of Subiaco and rolled himself in thorns to overcome temptation. But in his later years he lived simply as a cenobite and did what the other monks did, reading peacefully and following the common rules without notable differences. It is better to avoid all suggestion of singularity, and therefore even to sacrifice the merit and the pleasure of doing extraordinary things, simply to keep the common practices in honor among the brethren of one's own community. Naturally, this excludes the restless itch to change everything and to make everything "better" by imposing one's own ideas on the community. It also includes the wish to give up even legitimate exceptions and mitigations, if superiors permit, in order to follow the common *Rule*. Accepting mitigations with simplicity, at the desire of the superior, can also come under this

582. "If a monk does nothing except what the common rule of the monastery and the example of the elders encourages" (McCann, 46).

eighth degree, however. St. Leo says: *Sacratius est quod publica lege celebratur quam quod privata institutione dependitur.*[583] Behind this {it is} important for there to be a sense of *love* and *community,* not just of law, but {a} realization of the presence of the Holy Spirit in the brotherhood. {It is important to} inform this with *charity* even more than obedience, {with} docility to {the} Spirit of love which lives in the brotherhood. "Love one another"—that is enough. This definition is then a further definition of *reality.* St. Peter Damian says:[584] when Christ came to earth He accepted the way of life He found there and lived like ordinary men—and allowed the people to carry out their ordinary customs in His regard, v.g. the anointing of His head and feet. He kept all the observances of the Old Law even though He had come to replace it with a far higher and nobler mode of life. He did this for love of us.

*Majorum exempla . . .* These *majores* can be either the ancient Fathers and monastic saints, or perhaps also even the seniors of the community, or the more virtuous monks, or those who have gone before in the monastery and have left behind an example of virtue.

### IX, X and XI—*The Ninth, Tenth and Eleventh Degrees*

These all refer to the monk's manner of speaking and his outward expression of what is in his soul. {They} should be {an} expression of inner *peace*—not severity. The inner soul of the monk is supposed to be *pacified* and brought into perfect order by the other degrees of humility. *Hence his silence is not mere mutism; his slowness to laugh is not mere insensibility or lack of humor.* His silence, his quiet, rare laughter, his modesty and temperance in speech—all these things are an eloquent expression of the interior peace and tranquility of a soul united to God. They do *not* simply manifest the straining of a sincere but misguided soul

583. *Sermo 3 de Jejunio Septimi Mensis,* quoted by Martène (col. 401B): "It is more blessed to celebrate something according to a common rule than to give up something according to a private custom."

584. *Opusculum* 47, quoted by Martène (col. 402B).

to practice external humility without having a sufficient interior basis for it. Nevertheless, it cannot be said either that one should wait until he has acquired the seventh degree before he even attempts to practice the exterior degrees of humility. Some would never begin at that rate. But one must:

a) remember that the interior humility is the most important, and so important that exterior humility without it is false and meaningless;

b) still, at the same time, *while we are trying to acquire interior humility we should also at the same time strive to acquire exterior humility* proportionate to our degree of the spiritual life.

Thus normally there will be a harmonious advance at the same time in exterior and interior humility, with the emphasis always on the latter. Examples of the relation between exterior and interior humility: the *third and fourth degrees* (obedience, especially under trying conditions) can very well be developed hand in hand with the *ninth and tenth degrees*—love of silence and refraining from laughter. It is quite normal that a monk who is trying to be obedient should keep his mouth shut and pay attention to others, and not be too anxious to air his own views or tell others how things should he done. The monk who is undergoing trial and striving to practice the fourth degree of humility will naturally be a *serious man*, and his seriousness will begin from the inside, naturally curbing useless and empty-headed laughter.

### *Degrees IX, X and XI*

a) Silence (IX)—*Si linguam ad loquendum prohibeat . . .*[585]—"holding" one's tongue {means} *swallowing the useless remark*, the opinion one is tempted to blurt out needlessly. This applies also to signs. *Keeping one's thoughts to oneself: this is essential* for silence. Don't say it. Silence is a farce if, *refraining from speaking, we express all our thoughts by* signs. *Cui bono*?[586] {It is}

585. "If he keep his tongue from speaking" (McCann, 46).
586. "for whose benefit?"

more honest just to speak! *In multiloquio non effugies peccatum*[587] —as usual, {the} motive {is taken} from Sacred Scripture: fear of sin. This shows there is a connection too between the ninth degree and the first also. Is it true that one can easily sin by much talking? READ St. James, chapter 3—*very important*. He who can control his tongue can probably control everything else too. {This reveals the} deep Christian implications of control of speech (vv. 8-18).[588] In chapter 6 of the *Rule* (on silence)—St. Benedict lays down the principle that we must refrain from speaking *even in good and edifying things* because of the great value of silence.[589]

b) Laughter—*NON SIT FACILIS VEL PROMPTUS IN RISU*.[590] He does not absolutely ban *all* laughter as such. He bans the laughter that bursts out easily and ends with a noisy guffaw. He bans all noisy laughter. The monk's laughter should be silent, gentle and restrained. It should be rather a smile than a laugh. But it should certainly extend to a smile, at least on occasion. It does not need to be a stupid grin! Let us not imagine that monastic cheerfulness should mean empty-headed laughter at anything and everything, whether it is funny or not. This is certainly out of place in a monastery and harms the

587. "in much speaking you will not flee sin" (Prov. 10:19) (McCann, 46, which reads: ". . . *effugitur* . . .").

588. "But the tongue no man can tame—a restless evil, full of deadly poison. With it we bless God the Father; and with it we curse men, who have been made after the likeness of God. Out of the same mouth proceed blessing and cursing. These things, my brethren, ought not to be so. Does the fountain send forth sweet and bitter water from the same opening? Can a fig tree, my brethren, bear olives, or a vine figs? So neither can salt water yield fresh water. Who is wise and instructed among you? Let him by his good behavior show his work in the meekness of wisdom. But if you have bitter jealousy and contentions in your hearts, do not glory and be liars against the truth. This is not the wisdom that descends from above. It is earthly, sensual, devilish. For where there is envy and contentiousness, there is instability and every wicked deed. But the wisdom that is from above is first of all chaste, then peaceable, moderate, docile, in harmony with good things, full of mercy and good fruits, without judging, without dissimulation. The fruit of justice is sown in peace by those who make peace."

589. McCann, 34, 36.

590. "Let him not be ready and quick in laughing" (McCann, 46, which reads: ". . . *facilis ac promptus* . . .").

formation of those who indulge in it. One should have a smiling face, indication of a cheerful heart, but not laugh stupidly when there is nothing to laugh at—just because it seems to be expected, or because a few others happen to be laughing.

In chapter 6 St. Benedict *bans frivolity and worldly jokes*. *SCURRILITATES VEL VERBA OTIOSA ET RISUM MOVENTIA . . . IN OMNIBUS LOCIS DAMNAMUS, ET AD TALIA ELOQUIA DISCIPULUM APERIRE OS NON PERMITTIMUS*.[591] This is very strong. However it is not a ban on *all humor*. A certain kind of wit and humor are necessary in the monastery as elsewhere, but of a different kind and degree. St. Bernard shows a humorous and witty turn of phrase in his sermons, though he is essentially serious. A certain spirit of play (*eutrapelia*) is found even in the sacred Scriptures—for instance in the book of Tobias. But this is never "funny" in the worldly sense of the word, and does not move to dissipated laughter. The humor and the wit are perceived more on a *spiritual* and *interior* level. {There is a} distinction between *amusement* (superficial, exterior, worldly) and *joy* (deep, interior, spiritual).

*Worldly laughter*—like all laughter, is a product of *surprise*. The surprising, unexpected contact of ideas that do not fit together produces *an explosion*, a release of emotion, *of passion*. The more crude the passions, the more worldly and sinful is the laughter. For instance, practical jokes produce crude surprises which release interior movements of *hostility and aggression*. These may be more or less harmless, but they are still an expression of undesirable passions. A monk should control these passions in some better way, not simply indulge them in a "harmless" form. The crudest level of practical joke is overtly and blatantly cruel—and laughter is produced by cruelty. This is proper to debased characters in the world. On a higher level, the surprise becomes more subtle, the expression more delicate, less crude, until the cruelty altogether disappears. But even then, it would be out of

591. "We condemn in all places jesting talk and words that are useless and prompting laughter, and we do not allow the disciple to open his mouth for such speech" (McCann, 36, which reads: "*Scurrilitates vero vel* . . .").

place in a monastery to exploit *personal characteristics* and idiosyncrasies as material for jokes. However, if this is done, and done without bad effect, or even with good effect, it is still a proof that those who need such things are still on a worldly level. *A fortiori* St. Benedict would ban humor and wit that exploit the baser passions—lust, greed, etc. All salacious double meanings and references to impurity, even though veiled in polite sophistication, should be kept out of the monastery; they are disastrous for the monastic spirit of simplicity and modesty and frank purity.

*Spiritual laughter*—here too there is surprise, but it is on a more spiritual level. Here too there is a release of human passions, aggression and love, but on a much higher level. The surprise is not produced so much by farce and slapstick or by worldly cleverness, but by delicate and subtle and simple references, plays on spiritual ideas. There is an essential humor in the *surprises* sometimes produced by divine action and grace in the world (again in Tobias—the spiritual "irony" and delight of the situation in which mortal men take their affairs so seriously, not knowing that all the while everything is in the hands of an angel sent from God). There is then an interior and spiritual joy that flows from the surprises of divine grace—cf. the laughter of Abraham (Gen. 17:17).[592] The laughter of the monk should then be childlike, spontaneous, gentle, silent. The monk should be in control of all impulses to laugh at base and worldly things and indeed should, if he is mature in the monastic life, *feel no temptation to laugh at such things*—they will simply leave him unmoved and cold. When you find yourself laughing, ask yourself sometimes what you are laughing at!

592. This laughter, like Sarah's in Gen. 18:12-15, actually seems to be rather incredulous: "And as Abraham fell prostrate, he laughed and said to himself, 'Shall a son be born to one who is a hundred years old? Shall Sarah who is ninety bear a child?'" Sarah's words when Isaac (whose name means "laughter") is actually born fit this description better: "Sarah said, 'God has given me cause for laughter, and whoever hears of it will laugh with me'" (Gen. 21:6).

c) How to speak (XI): *LENITER, SINE RISU, HUMILITER CUM GRAVITATE, PAUCA VERBA ET RATIONABILIA*.[593] When the monk *does* speak—then it is with all these characteristics: gentleness, seriousness, humility, *few words* and *with common sense*—NOT a turbulent flow of silly, useless, senseless verbiage. The monk should know what he is talking about, know how to say it, know when to stop, know the value of precise words, not waste words. The monk should have a high respect for language and use it better than other men, not worse.

XII. *THE TWELFTH DEGREE OF HUMILITY*—and the Conclusion

What is the twelfth degree? At first we are all tempted to say "going around with your eyes down." That is not the essence of this degree, just an *example* or *application* of what St. Benedict means by it. The true essence of this degree is that the monk's whole body and all his actions should be penetrated by humility and manifest it, just as his soul is penetrated and saturated with it. *SI NON SOLUM CORDE SED ETIAM CORPORE HUMILITATEM VIDENTIBUS SE SEMPER INDICET*.[594] A word to understand properly here, before we go any further, is *INDICET*. Does this mean that the monk *consciously* endeavors to cultivate a way of acting that manifests "his humility" to everyone? This does not make sense in view of the sixth and seventh degrees of humility—in which the interior humility of the monk implies complete self-forgetfulness. But it can mean that the monk by his attitude *expresses his consciousness of his own unimportance and his acceptance of the fact that he is worthless in himself*. But he does not "cultivate" anything here, nor does he attempt to convince others of anything about himself. This degree is not play-acting. If it is not sincere and spontaneous,

593. "gently, without laughter, humbly, with seriousness, with few and sensible words" (McCann, 46, which reads: "*leniter et sine . . . gravitate, vel pauca . . .*").

594. "If he always gives evidence of humility to those who see him not only with his heart but also with his body" (McCann, 46, which reads: ". . . *corde monachus, sed etiam ipso corpore . . .*").

even unconscious, it cannot really be called the twelfth degree. He does not intend to show others his humility; he just does so unconsciously. This implies that when we get to this degree, it is something which can only be observed by another, not by the monk himself. We never can really say or think, "I have reached the twelfth degree," but rather we are capable of saying, "*He* has reached it." Then the explanation—St. Benedict gives his portrait of an exteriorly humble monk. At all times, whether at prayer or at work or whatever else he does, he tends to have his head bowed and his eyes cast down thoughtfully, and with the spirit of compunction. Note again the importance of the idea that this is "everywhere." The twelfth degree implies that a man is everywhere just as quiet and collected as he is at prayer. He does *all things* in a spirit of peace, composure, attention, tranquility and compunction. Note however once again that this exterior attitude implies interior meditation and elevation of heart—indeed even interior joy. St. Basil {writes}: "*MONACHUM OPORTET OCULOS AD TERRAM HABERE DEJECTOS, ANIMUM AD COELUM ERECTUM*."[595] The twelfth degree, if it were merely a matter of looking at the ground, would be meaningless. The eyes are cast down because the mind is in heaven.

*Defixis in terram* . . .[596] Some authors believe that this can be meant in a symbolic sense such as thinking on the fact that we are dust or even, as one says, thinking of the Incarnation and of the fact that Christ came to this world and took on our "mortal clay" by assuming flesh from the Blessed Mother. {This is} a beautiful interpretation which should certainly enter into the spirit of the twelfth degree, though it was evidently not intended by St. Benedict directly. However all agree with the caution expressed by Dom Martène, that this must not develop into robot-like artificiality. "It is not the true spirit of a monk to stand stupidly like

595. *Sermo Asceticus*, quoted by Martène (*PL* 66, col. 407C) ("It is proper for a monk to have his eyes cast down toward the earth, his soul uplifted toward heaven").

596. "[eyes] fixed on the ground" (McCann, 46).

a statue or a brute beast, staring at the ground."[597] This would be pitiful. The twelfth degree implies anything but this kind of thing. The monk is humble but his humility is *vigilant, intelligent and attentive*. He is alert, though quiet. He is not in a stupor. As St. Dorotheus indicates, this "looking at the earth" means really "looking at what you are doing,"[598] paying attention to the work or task in hand—*age quod agis*.[599] This again is very important. St. Benedict drives his point home by an example from the Gospel—that of the Publican in the parable. This shows that anything savoring of pharisaism is very far from the true idea of exterior humility, in the twelfth degree or any other.

*Conclusion*:

Just as it is supremely important to realize that all the degrees of humility hang one upon the other and follow logically from one another, so too it is supremely important to realize that they all tend to one great end which is CHARITY. The degrees of humility have led the monk step by step, not to absolute perfection, nor even to the highest perfection possible in this present life, but only to the summit of the *bios praktikos* or active (ascetic) life. Here a new life begins, the life of charity and contemplation, the life of purity of heart. Charity is the important thing to note above all: *VIA AD CARITATEM HUMILITAS, VIA UTIQUE VERA ET SOLA* (Dom Martène).[600] But it is not just any charity, not just the "practice" of charity, but rather a certain fullness and maturity of love which gives one a whole new attitude toward life and *casts out fear*. This again is important. The degrees of humility begin with the fear of the Lord, taking root in the mind, so that the soul conceives the necessity of avoiding deliberate sin. It ends with the fear of the Lord in complete possession of both body and soul. But what

597. *PL* 66, col. 407D.

598. *Doctrina* 19, quoted by Martène (*PL* 66, col. 407C).

599. "do what you are doing."

600. *PL* 66, col. 408C, which reads: ". . . *charitatem humilitas. Via* . . ." ("Humility [is] the way to charity, indeed the true and only way").

then? The fruit of this is {to}[601] pass on to a charity *which casts out fear altogether*. This means in effect that *all the servility* is cast out of fear and that fear itself is transformed into love. Love then takes the place and assumes all the functions of fear. Love then becomes the guardian of faith and fidelity, the inspiration of all our good works, and performs this task much more effectively than fear. The effects of love enumerated by St. Benedict are especially:

a) *Spontaneity*: the good acts which before cost much effort and application are now done *without labor* and with interior and exterior joy. They are satisfying, rewarding, by reason of the love with which we do them. They bring us into direct contact with God, the source of our strength and of our joy.

b) *Union with Christ*: now it is no longer merely a matter of thinking of the Heavenly Father observing all our acts and judging them in secret, but of *union with the Incarnate Word*, implying the realization that all our works are His works and that all our faults have been assumed by Him: He gives us His love and His merits in the sight of the Father and takes upon Himself our faults and our sins so that we are no longer dominated by anxiety and fear but realize that by our confident love we enable Jesus to make good all our shortcomings and defects. This is accompanied by a *delight in virtue* (which does not exclude suffering and a certain difficulty) which attracts us to works that please the Lord and enables us to perform them with confidence and freedom.

c) *Purity of heart*: as a consequence of this union with Christ, though we still involuntarily commit faults and mistakes, they are immediately removed by the love of Christ in our hearts, for we are His "workman," indeed His instrument for good and for the glory of the Father. Hence we can be said to be pure of sin though we remain deeply conscious of our own sinfulness.

d) *The action of the Holy Spirit*: the soul is now submissive to the action of the Holy Spirit, and it is by this Divine Spirit that

601. Typescript reads "the."

Christ works in it and gives it love and all the qualities we have described.

UNDER THE GUIDANCE OF THE DIVINE SPIRIT THE HUMBLE MONK IS NOW READY FOR THE CONTEMPLATIVE LIFE for which St. Benedict refers us to other books, especially Cassian and the Fathers.

# {APPENDIX 1}

## {Additional Notes on the *Rule* of St. Benedict}

### {Note 1}[1]

*Cistercian Fathers on St Benedict—Pascit vita, pascit doctrina, pascit et intercessione.*[2] *St Bernard,* preaching on St. Benedict, {teaches that the} blessing of St. Benedict comes to {the} monks through him—if *they* listen. {He exclaims} (377), "*O abbas, et abbas!*"[3] {He speaks of} our obligation to imitate St. Benedict {and of} the "3 loaves": *reficiat vos sanctitas ejus*—in his *miracles,* {which} console us and confirm us in {our} vocation by intercessions; *justitia ejus*—in his *life* {which} leads us in peace; *pietas ejus*—in his *doctrine* {which} strengthens us.[4]

378 (#4): Benedict {is} a great tree growing in a well-watered valley (contrast {the} rhyme about {the} site of monasteries[5]); *vallem magis elige ad ambulandum;*[6] *in humility is stability*—not

1. Separate handwritten page inserted after page 2 of typescript (following "in the monastic tradition" [10]).

2. "*In Natali Sancti Benedicti Abbatis*" (*PL* 183, cols. 375D–382D): "He feeds by his life, he feeds by his teaching, and he feeds by his intercession" (#4; col. 380A).

3. The context is a comparison between himself and St. Benedict as abbots: "*Abbas fuit, et ego. O abbas, et abbas! Nomen unum, sed in altero sola magni nominis umbra*" ("He was an abbot, as am I. O abbot, and abbot! A single name, but in someone else there is only a shadow of the great name") (#2; col. 377A).

4. Col. 377B (#3): "May his holiness, his justice, his piety refresh us."

5. "*Bernardus valles, colles Benedictus amabat, / Franciscus vicos, magnas Dominicus urbes*" ("Bernard loved valleys, Benedict the hills, / Francis villages, Dominic great cities"). This anonymous couplet is quoted in Terryl N. Kinder, *Cistercian Europe: Architecture of Contemplation*, CS 191 (Kalamazoo, MI: Cistercian Publications, and Grand Rapids, MI: Eerdmans, 2002), 81.

6. Col. 378A (#4): "Choose rather a valley for walking."

desiring things too great for us. {Cf. the} tree: St. Bernard is taking branches from this tree to scatter before the *jumentum Christi*[7] which is the community: walk securely on these branches. A branch {is} St Benedict's hiding in Subiaco—not trying to bear fruit before {the proper} time. {He models} patience in temptation and generosity in penance.

(#9): {Here are} lessons from {the} Passion of Christ (this sermon {was preached} near Palm Sunday): like Christ we must empty ourselves (380): *exinanite vos, humiliate vos, seminate vos, perdite vos.*[8] *Bene seipsum perdit, qui nihil umquam pro se facit; sed omnis ejus intentio et omne desiderium tendit ad Dei placitum, et utilitatem fratrum suorum.*[9] Sow for man by good works, for angels by *occulta suspiria*[10]—i.e. intentions. How many have sowed before us—and we enter into their harvest—woe to us if we do not. {The} *atmosphere of* {the} *sermon* {is} *not complacent*—{there is a} sense of uncertainty and risk—{a} *need of fidelity*. {We} enter into {these} fruits only by *humilitas et labor*,[11] not by laziness and seeking honor.

### {Note 2}[12]

*Subiaco* {provided the} water supply for Rome—{there were} two aqueducts there {linked to the} Anio {River} ({cf. the name} Sublacqueum ?? {There were} two dams, built by Claudius? {The} village {was} "under the lake" below.) *Nero's* villa {was located there.} {According to} Pliny the Elder {there were} *3* beautiful

7. Col. 378A (#4): "Christ's donkey."

8. "Empty yourselves; humble yourselves; sow yourselves; lose yourselves."

9. Col. 380C (#9) (which reads ". . . *unquam* . . ."): "He truly loses himself who never does anything for his own sake, but whose every intention and every desire is directed toward pleasing God and toward the benefit of his brothers."

10. Col. 380D (#10): "hidden sighs."

11. Cols 381B–382A (#11) (which reads "*per humilitatem et laborem*"): "humility and work."

12. Separate handwritten page inserted after page 7 of typescript (following "friends, relatives, etc." [22]).

lakes;[13] St. Gregory speaks of only one. {The} dam burst in {the} Middle Ages—no more lake. {The} villa—near where St. Scholastica's Abbey now is—was probably still standing in St. Benedict's time. {The} aqueduct was still serving Rome at that time. St. Benedict may have settled later with monks in a part of Nero's villa. (Trajan also had a villa in this region.) *Monasticism* in {the} Anio region {was} brought in by Oriental monks who took refuge there in {the} time of Julian the Apostate (?). {The} Monastery of Farfa *antedated* St Benedict. {It} is {the} monastery on the Monte Taleo above the cliff where {Benedict's} cave was; another {was located} at Vicovaro—dedicated to Sts. Cosmas and Damian. {Here were} the twelve monasteries of St. Benedict (+ 1?—no). ({There is a} debate between S. Speco[14] and Sta. Scholastica over who gets {the} title of Protocenobium—St. Benedict probably had no *monastery* at S. Speco. {The} S. Speco monastery {was} built in {the} eleventh to fourteenth centuries. Before that {it was} a sanctuary. In {the} eleventh century a hermit—Palumbus—gets permission to live there [1090].) {The} first monastery {was} by a *lake*—probably in part of Nero's villa (??) {dedicated} in honor of St. Clement or {the} Blessed Virgin Mary.

**{Note 3}**[15]

*Rule of St. Benedict* (Strafcodex[16]): *Faults and their punishment* according to early commentators:

13. See Pliny, *Natural History*, trans. H. Rackham and W. H. S. Jones, Loeb Classical Library, 10 vols. (Cambridge, MA: Harvard University Press, 1938–1962), 2:80/81: "*at ex alia parte Anio in monte Trebanorum ortus lacus tris amoenitate nobilis qui nomen dedere Sublaqueo defert in Tiberim*" ("In another direction the Teverone rising in Mount Trevi drains into the Tiber three lakes famous for their beauty, from which Subiaco takes its name").

14. I.e., Sacro Speco, the "sacred cave" in which Benedict lived as a hermit at the outset of his monastic life.

15. Separate handwritten page inserted after page 33 of typescript (following "blameworthy attitude" [84]).

16. I.e. "Strafkodex" ("punishment code")—chapters 23–30 of the *Rule*, that focus on faults and penalties (see McCann, ix).

C. 24—Minor Excommunications: *in levioribus culpis*:[17] Warnefrid etc. refers to these as more *interior*, less externally scandalous (cf. interior murmuring and pride, not very manifest disobedience etc.).[18] Penance {would include} not intoning in choir; eating later; *not saying Mass if a priest* (Hildemar).[19]

C. 25—*De Gravioribus Culpis*[20] (theft, adultery, intoxication—external and scandalous): {these would entail} full excommunication.

*Breaches of regular discipline* (c. 42-46): talking after compline—*gravi vindictae subjaceat*;[21] lateness in office or meals—{a} special form of penance {was} prescribed; {in the case of} lateness for meals {one would} eat later, without wine; mistakes in {the} oratory; breaking, losing things etc.: {there would be a} greater penance if they do not accuse themselves spontaneously.

*Disciplina Regularis*[22]—formed Passion ({these were for} "lighter faults" only—{cf.} earlier references). {This} means precisely what? {There were} seven stages:

(1) secret admonition (given more than once);
(2) public correction (i.e. before {the} whole community as such);
(3) excommunication (held in custody);
(4) severe fasts (even eating only every two or three days; or bread and water);
(5) corporal punishment (not useful for all—{the} abbot must be discreet);
(6) prayer of {the} community for him;
(7) expulsion (but he can be received back [c. 29]); re expulsion:

17. McCann, 72 ("in lighter faults").

18. Warnefrid, 276–77, 279–80, cited in Schroll, 90.

19. Hildemar, 348, cited in Schroll, 93.

20. McCann, 74 ("Concerning More Serious Faults"—title of c. 25).

21. McCann, 100 ("let him be subject to serious punishment").

22. "the discipline of the rule" (cc. 3, 32, 54, 60, 62, 65, 70; McCann, 24, 84, 122, 136, 140, 150, 156).

1. {there is an} interpolation in {the} *textus receptus*—"one who leaves by his own fault or *is expelled*";[23]

2. {a} distinction {is} made by commentators: for some grave faults—{one is} not received back;[24]

3. commentators say {the} abbot should receive him back up to three times—but *may* go beyond this in mercy (i.e. {he is} not limited to three).[25]

{For} *graver faults* {the punishment is} immediate excommunication, and then expulsion.

**{Note 4}**[26]

*Regula Magistri*:[27] {this} appeared in {the} *Concordia Regularum* of St. Benedict of Aniane,[28] who gave it this title (alius *Regula Macarii* or *Patrum*—sc. of Egypt: Serapion, Macarius, Paphnutius[29]). {It} has been known all along—but regarded as secondary—as a paraphrase of {the} *Rule* of St. Benedict, of {a} later date.

23. Quoted in Schroll, 103–104, which reads: "a brother who has left through his own fault or has been expelled" (though the Latin is in the present tense); see also McCann, n. 50 (183–84).

24. See Schroll, 104.

25. See Schroll, 105 (citing Hildemar, 367–68).

26. Separate handwritten page inserted after page 42 of typescript (following "outside the monastery" [103]).

27. *PL* 88, cols. 943-1052; for a translation, see *The Rule of the Master*, translated by Luke Eberle with an Introduction by Adalbert de Vogüé, CS 6 (Kalamazoo, MI: Cistercian Publications, 1977). For Merton's interest in the *Regula Magistri*, see Thomas Merton, *Pre-Benedictine Monasticism: Initiation into the Monastic Tradition 2*, ed. Patrick F. O'Connell, MW 9 (Kalamazoo, MI: Cistercian Publications, 2006), xvii–xx.

28. *PL* 103, cols. 713–1380; while Benedict does use the *Regula Magistri* in *Concordia Regularum*, his "commentary" on the *Rule* of Benedict using parallel excerpts from other monastic rules, Merton may be thinking of the *Codex Regularum*, Benedict's vast collection of these rules, of which the *Regula Magistri* is the fourteenth in Part II, "*Regulae SS. Patrum Occidentalium ad Monachos*."

29. For these variant titles see *La Règle de Maître*, I, ed. Adalbert de Vogüé, Sources Chrétiennes, vol. 105 (Paris: Éditions du Cerf, 1964), 145–51.

*Dom Genestout* (*RAM* 21 [1940], p. 51[30]) finds it is earlier than {the} Benedictine *Rule*. {In} 1953 the edition diplomatique {was published} of two sixth-century mss. of {the} *Rule* which are very much different: mss. from Saint Germain des Près in {the} Bibliothèque Nationale, Paris (originally from Corbie).[31]

**{Note 5}**[32]

Festugière: {The} Monk and Study[33]—{this chapter has a} polemical tone. Background—{is the} monastic vocation charismatic ({as} opposed to {an} *institutional* emphasis)? But exaggerations {are} possible—{there are} pros and cons (the old argument). Festugière {is} against {the} anti-intellectualism of ancient monks ({cf. the} story from {the} *Life of Pachomius* [p. 80][34]). Study {is seen} as pacifying {and} purifying. {The} objections to study {are} that it brings pride {and} distraction; {but this} applies to half-baked youths; {with regard to} serious and sustained intellectual work, no. {Note the} references to the Origenist conflict in {the} sixth century, {and the} Nestorian conflict, in which monks, without theology, believing their holiness guarantees truth, defy authority, justice, charity.[35]

30. Augustin Genestout, OSB, "La Règle de Maître et la Règle de S. Benoît," *Revue d'Ascetique et de Mystique*, 21 (1940), 51–112.

31. *La Règle du Maître: Édition Diplomatique des Manuscrits Latins 12205 et 12634 de Paris*, ed. Hubert Vanderhoven and François Masai (Brussels: Éditions Erasme, 1953).

32. Separate handwritten page inserted after page 55a of typescript (following "things to be done" [135]).

33. A. J. Festugière, OP, *Les Moines d'Orient I: Culture ou Sainteté: Introduction au Monachisme Oriental* (Paris: Éditions du Cerf, 1961), c. 4: "Le Moine et Étude," 75–91.

34. In this story a young monk puts his hand into the fire as evidence of spiritual achievement; he is able to do it by the power of demons, which later throw him bodily into a fire, burning him to death. (A variant of this incident is found in the Latin *Vita* [*PL* 73, cols. 234–35] and is referred to by Merton in *Pre-Benedictine Monasticism*, 108).

35. See Festugière, 83–91.

**{Note 6}**[36]

*Lectio Divina*:

1. *How to Read the Bible*—what to look for: cf. G. E. Wright: *God Who Acts*.[37] {He focuses on} *Heilsgeschichte*:[38] "Man's involvement in a God-directed history; God's activity relative to man's need."[39] {He emphasizes the} crucial importance of {the} Old Testament in its relation to the New Testament: both throw light on each other. {The} New Testament without {the} Old tends to become an ethic, based on {the} imitation of Christ as {a} model; {the} Old Testament alone {tends to become} a law. Together {they have a} dynamism, {creating a} *Theology of Recital* (cf. midrash). {This is a} reading of God in history—entering into {the} historical recital in order to situate ourselves in God's plan now:[40]

1. *Kerygma*[41] of the Gospel: *salvation {is} proclaimed in Jesus Christ*. {This} must be seen as {the} culmination of {the} Old Testament kerygma—*God's demand for participation*:

a) *Choice* of the *qahal*[42]—*through whom He effects His plan in history*;

b) {The} Covenant—God as King and Lord, showing *misericordia* (*chesed*) {and} *veritas* (*emeth*)[43] ({which are} united in Jesus: John 1:14). {This is a} preparation for {the} Kingship of Christ (Col. {1:13}).

c) Man's resistance: sin and atonement—{this involves} man's subjection to {the} power of Satan, {his} resistance to God's

36. Separate handwritten page inserted after Note 5.

37. G. Ernest Wright, *God Who Acts: Biblical Theology as Recital* (London: SCM Press, 1952).

38. "salvation history."

39. Wright, 116, which reads: "Biblical theology . . . is rather a reflective discipline which seeks to portray the peculiar Biblical concern with man's involvement in a God-directed history and with God's activity relative to man's historical problem, need and hope."

40. See Wright, 112–13.

41. "proclamation".

42. "congregation, assembly" (i.e. the People of Israel).

43. "mercy (steadfast love)"; "truth (fidelity)."

action in history by {a} resort to his own plans for security; {then the} redemptive acts of Christ, especially *the Cross*, {the} center of {the} Bible ({cf. the} cross and sacraments {as represented in} typology); {also required is} man's cooperation ({cf.} Acts, Epistles).

d) The fulfillment: eschatology—the life of the world to come, the resurrection of the body, eternity as the redemption of time.

2. {The} Bible—history or myth? See George E. Wright (p. 126–127): "The Bible, while dealing with the facts of history in its own particular way, *continually pushes beyond what is factually known*."[44]

**{Note 7}**[45]

*Lectio Divina* in the Patristic tradition: Cassian and {the} desert tradition seem to insist that {the} cenobite is active and ascetic; {the} hermit is contemplative and mystic. St. Benedict provides for contemplation in his *lectio divina*. In {the} early Church, *lectio divina* is {the} foundation of *both theology* and *spirituality*: i.e. reading Scripture under {the} guidance of {the} Holy Ghost who inspired Scripture. N.B. St. Benedict bases contemplation on humility, obedience and charity. *Jean de Fécamp*, {a} Benedictine born about 990 {at} Ravenna {develops a} *spirituality of lectio divina* ({in} works ascribed to Anselm and Augustine): GS[46] 26–27—{the} *Confessio Theologica* {is a} collection of texts woven together in a continuous prayer (*read* quote—bottom of p. 27:[47] personal,

44. Wright, 127 (emphasis added).

45. Separate handwritten page inserted after Note 6.

46. Gerard Sitwell, OSB, *Spiritual Writers of the Middle Ages*, Twentieth Century Encyclopedia of Catholicism, vol. 40 (New York: Hawthorn Books, 1961).

47. Sitwell, 27–28: "There are many kinds of contemplation in which the soul devoted to Thee, O Christ, takes its delight, but in none of these do I so rejoice as in that which, ignoring all things, directs a simple glance of the untroubled spirit to Thee alone, O God. What peace and rest and joy does the soul find in Thee then. For while my mind yearns for divine contemplation, and meditates,

simple, direct, quiet, *dulcedo*,[48] *Verbo Dei vacare*,[49] *otium quietis*[50]). Peter of Celle {wrote a} *Treatise on Mortification and Reading* {which emphasizes} *saporabilis lectio*;[51] meditation sentence by sentence, to digest what is read; {the} classical progress: *lectio—meditatio—contemplatio*, but based on good works (read p. {41}[52]). St. Bernard *In Cantica* = sharing in *his lectio divina*. Summary—{*lectio* involves} experience of the presence of God as manifested in Scriptural terms.

---

and expresses Thy glory to the best of its ability, the burden of the flesh weighs less heavily upon it; the tumult of thoughts dies down; the weight of mortality and misery no longer exerts its accustomed pressure; all is silent and tranquil. The heart burns within, the spirit rejoices, the memory grows fresh, the intellect clear, and the whole spirit, on fire with longing for the vision of Thy beauty, sees itself carried away to the love of those things which are invisible. And so it is not from any presumptuous boldness, but from a great longing to feel a desire for Thee that I have made this little posy, so that I might always be able to carry about with me a short manual of the word of God, from the reading of which I might rekindle the flame of my love." This passage is part of the conclusion of the third and final part of the *Confessio Theologica*.

48. "sweetness."

49. "to make room for the Word of God" (quoted in Sitwell, 29).

50. "the leisure of quiet."

51. "reading as tasting" (quoted in Sitwell, 39).

52. "The service of the brethren and the daily manual labour, performed in the cloister or the fields as time and necessity demand, form the root of good works. Beyond this, giving alms, visiting the sick, consoling the afflicted, helping widows, receiving the poor and pilgrims, the defence of the oppressed, and such things, are the branches of this tree, not of death but of life, which is called good works" (*Of Conscience*). Sitwell comments, "It is entirely in keeping with this view of the contemplative life, which we have seen is characteristic of John and Peter, that he says three things concur to bring about this state, good works, protracted prayer, and an ardent desire for God. It is only the first of these that he treats with any clearness . . . . It is a perfectly unequivocal account of the active life, but he takes it for granted that this goes hand-in-hand with the contemplative" (text reads: "p. 40").

**{Note 8}**[53]

St. Benedict "the Roman":[54] Modernism tended to exaggerate the Roman character of the *Rule*. {There was a} distortion of perspectives, due to one-sided suppositions:

1) overemphasis on the genius of St. Benedict as organizer—as if he were in this unique, and as if he thus contrasted sharply with other writers of monastic rules—St. Pachomius, a Copt, was perhaps an even greater and more original "organizer." It is true that St. Benedict is practical and that among the Orientals he follows the more practical Basil. He considers the practical needs of his contemporaries in Western Europe.

2) overemphasis on {the} monastic community in the "*familia Romana*";[55] {it is} not {the case that the} *paterfamilias*[56] {is the} abbot: *Abbas* = Christ; {the abbot} is not the only father[57]—cf. {the} cellarer;[58] monks are *fratres* rather than *filii*;[59] {the} community {is} not called "family" but *domus Dei*[60] (cf. c. 64—transfer of Luke

53. Separate handwritten page inserted after Note 7.

54. See Ildefons Herwegen, OSB, *St. Benedict, A Character Study*, trans. P. Nugent (St. Louis: Herder, 1924), 67: "It was reserved for St Benedict the Roman to erect the whole structure of his monastic community clearly and distinctly on the principle of paternity." Merton also discusses this issue in the Prologue to his conferences on *Pre-Benedictine Monasticism* (3–6).

55. "the Roman family/household" (not a term used in the *Rule*).

56. The term is used in c. 2 to refer not to the abbot but to God (McCann, 16).

57. The abbot is referred to as a father in the Prologue and in cc. 2 and 33 (McCann, 6, 20, 84).

58. In c. 31 the cellarer is said to be one "*qui omni congregationi sit sicut pater*" ("who should be like a father for the entire community") (McCann, 80).

59. The monk is addressed as "*fili*" ("son") in the opening line of the Prologue (McCann, 6) and the quotation from Proverbs 23:14 in c. 2 refers to striking "your son" ("*filium tuum*") with a rod (McCann, 20), but otherwise the term is only used in relation to God.

60. "*domui Dei dignum constituant dispensatorem*" ("Let them choose a worthy steward for the house of God") (McCann, 146); the phrase is also found in cc. 31 and 53 (McCann, 82, 122).

12:42: {he} changes *familia* to *domus*).[61]

3) the monastery and the Roman legion:

a) {cf. the} traditional idea that the monk is {a} soldier of Christ (cf. St. Paul[62])—this is in {the} *Rule*;[63]

b) It is true that the term *conversatio morum* occurs in a version of {the} Roman military oath of allegiance;

c) However {the} abbot {is} not a general, {the} monks {are} not just a regiment, *a fighting unit*—the "*militari*"[64] traditionally refers to personal ascetic effort (however cf. {the} Clairvaux Dedication—{it is} compared to {an} armed castle by St. Bernard[65]).

4) {the} formula of profession and Roman law: {there has been an} overemphasis on {the} juridical clarity and wisdom of Benedict's "Roman mind" as if he were a lawyer![66] (Some even assert he studied law). {The} source of {the} formula of profession {is} in {the} Coptic tradition (Schenuti).[67]

5) even the "Latinity" of the *Rule* is bad by Roman sixth-century standards, due to its reliance on liturgy and contemporary monastic tradition.[68]

{Should one go to the} opposite extreme? St. Benedict the "Pneumatic," the charismatic? {This entails an} overemphasis on the idea of {the} monastic vocation as a charismatic grace—{it is} arbitrary and does not accord with Benedictine tradition.

61. "Who, dost thou think, is the faithful and prudent steward whom the master will set over his household . . . [*familia* in Latin]."

62. See Eph. 6:10-17, 1 Thes. 5:8, 1 Tim. 1:18, 6:12, 2 Tim. 2:3-4.

63. See the Prologue: "*Domino Christo vero Regi militaturus, obedientiae fortissima atque praeclara arma sumis*" ("fighting for Christ the Lord, the true King, may you take up the very strong and outstanding weapons of obedience") (McCann, 6); Merton refers to this imagery in the *Rule* in connection with similar phrases in the *Historia Monachorum* in *Pre-Benedictine Monasticism* (31).

64. See cc. 1, 58, 61 (McCann, 14, 130, 138).

65. *In Dedicatione Ecclesiae*, *Sermo* 3 (*PL* 183, cols. 523D–526B).

66. See Herwegen, 22.

67. For Merton's discussion of Shenoute (Schenuti), including the formula of profession, see *Pre-Benedictine Monasticism*, 120–23.

68. See above, pages 42–46.

St. Benedict desires for his monks the *gift of grace,*[69] the *gift of fraternal love, love of Christ, love of abbot.*[70] It can be said that a kind of "special grace" is diffused through the community, a general atmosphere of intense and simple love. But {it is} not miraculous—simply {the} ordinary Christian life in its purity.

**{Note 9}**[71]

"Personalism" in the *Rule*: without making a "fetish" of the "person" we can say that the *Rule* is a document of sane Christian personalism. The person = {the} fully developed Christian who takes responsibility for his life before God: {he} is *compos sui.*[72] Note {the use of} direct address: *Ausculta* is first word of {the} *Rule;*[73] *pervenies* is the last.[74]

a) *Honestas morum,*[75] *maturitas morum*[76] = full development in {the} common life, in interrelation with others, traveling to heaven in {the} common life.

b) Education of the individual according to individual needs—in {the} chapter on {the} abbot: *multorum servire moribus;*[77] *secundum {uniuscujusque} qualitatem vel intelligentiam ita se aptet . . .*[78]

69. See the Prologue: "*quod minus habet in nobis natura possible, rogemus Dominum ut gratiae suae jubeat nobis adjutorium ministrare*" ("let us ask the Lord to direct that what is not possible for us to have by nature may be made available to us by the aid of his grace") (McCann, 10, 12).

70. See c. 72 (McCann, 158, 160).

71. Separate handwritten page inserted after Note 8.

72. "self-possessed" (the term is not found in the *Rule*).

73. "Listen" (McCann, 6).

74. "you will arrive at" (McCann, 162).

75. See c. 73: "*aliquatenus vel honestatem morum . . . nos demonstremus habere*" ("May we show that we have integrity of conduct to some degree") (McCann, 160).

76. In c. 31, the cellarer is described as one who should be "*maturus moribus*" ("mature in his conduct") (McCann, 80).

77. "to be of service to many different character types" (c. 2; McCann, 20).

78. "let him thus adapt himself according to the character and intelligence of each one" (c. 2; McCann, 22, which reads: ". . . *se omnibus conformet et aptet*"

c) c. 72 {stresses} equilibrium—{the} balance of all man's capacities, nature and grace—in sonship; among {the} brethren. How {is it} attained: *infirmitates tolerent;*[79] *honore se praeveniant;*[80] *obedientiam . . . sibi impendant;*[81] *caritatem fraternitatis casto amore;*[82] *abbatem diligant;*[83] *Deum timeant;*[84] *Christi nihil praeponant.*[85]

**{Note 10}**[86]

Degrees of Humility—{it is a} question of perspective:

1. The archetypal image of the ladder—we are *viatores:*[87] {cf. the} *Scala Paradisi* of John Climacus:[88] 30 chapters = 30 degrees = 30 years of Christ's life; the dream of St. Perpetua;[89] St. Jerome:

---

["let him conform and adapt himself to all"]; copy text reads "*secundum uniusquisque . . .*").

79. McCann, 160, which reads: "*Infirmitates suas sive corporum sive morum patientissime tolerant*" ("Let them bear very patiently their weaknesses, whether of body or of behavior").

80. McCann, 160, which reads: "*honore se invicem praeveniant*" ("Let them anticipate one another in showing honor"), a quotation from Romans 12:10.

81. McCann, 160, which reads: "*obedientiam sibi certatim impendant*" ("Let them compete in being obedient to one another").

82. McCann, 160, which reads: "*caritatem fraternitatis casto impendant amore*" ("Let them compete in showing brotherly affection with pure love").

83. McCann, 160, which reads: "*abbatem suum sincera et humili caritate diligent*" ("Let them love their abbot with genuine and humble love").

84. "Let them fear God" (McCann, 160).

85. McCann, 160, which reads: "*Christo omnino nihil praeponant*" ("Let them prefer nothing at all to Christ").

86. Separate handwritten page inserted after page 63 of typescript (following "meaning what?" [152]).

87. "wayfarers" (the term is not found in the *Rule*).

88. St. John Climacus, *The Ladder of Divine Ascent*, trans. Archimandrite Lazarus Moore (New York: Harper & Brothers, 1959).

89. "I saw a golden ladder of marvelous height, reaching up even to heaven, and very narrow, so that persons could only ascend it one by one; and on the sides of the ladder was fixed every kind of iron weapon. There were there swords, lances, hooks, daggers; so that if any one went up carelessly, or not looking upwards, he would be torn to pieces, and his flesh would cleave to the iron weapons. And under the ladder itself was crouching a dragon of wonderful size, who lay

15 degrees (*Com. on Ps. 119*);[90] "naked following the naked cross, you will ascend the ladder of Jacob free and light";[91] visions of early saints; v.g. St. Stephen Harding.[92] Origen says ({in the} *Contra Celsum*): "So great is the doctrine of humility that we have no

---

in wait for those who ascended, and frightened them from the ascent. And Saturus went up first, who had subsequently delivered himself up freely on our account, not having been present at the time that we were taken prisoners. And he attained the top of the ladder, and turned towards me, and said to me, 'Perpetua, I am waiting for you; but be careful that the dragon do not bite you.' And I said, 'In the name of the Lord Jesus Christ, he shall not hurt me.' And from under the ladder itself, as if in fear of me, he slowly lifted up his head; and as I trod upon the first step, I trod upon his head. And I went up, and I saw an immense extent of garden, and in the midst of the garden a white-haired man sitting in the dress of a shepherd, of a large stature, milking sheep; and standing around were many thousand white-robed ones. And he raised his head, and looked upon me, and said to me, 'Thou art welcome, daughter.' And he called me, and from the cheese as he was milking he gave me as it were a little cake, and I received it with folded hands; and I ate it, and all who stood around said Amen. And at the sound of their voices I was awakened, still tasting a sweetness which I cannot describe" ("The Passion of the Holy Martyrs Perpetua and Felicitas," trans. R. E. Wallis, *Ante-Nicene Fathers*, ed. Alexander Roberts and James Donaldson, rev. A. Cleveland Coxe, 10 vols. [New York: Scribner's, 1885, 1926; rpt. Grand Rapids, MI: Eerdmans, 1973], 3.700).

90. *PL* 26, col. 1278A: the reference is to the fifteen "gradual psalms" ("songs of ascents" or "psalms of the steps": Pss. 119[120]-133[134]) that lead to the heights of holiness.

91. *Ep*. 58.2 (to Paulinus) (*PL* 22, col. 580).

92. See *Exordium Magnum Cisterciense, Distributio Prima*, c. 23 (*PL* 185, col. 1019AB): "*Hoc ergo perfecte humilitatis scuto, quae in ore sonabat et in corde vigebat, munitus, hominem exuit, et omnia nequissimi adversarii tela, quamvis ignea, quamvis sulphurea, potenter repellens, aereas potestates securus pertransiit, et ad portas paradisi coronandus ascendit*" ("Fortified perfectly by this shield of humility, which sounded in his mouth and ruled in his heart, he left behind his mortal humanity and powerfully repelled all the arrows, whether fiery or sulfurous, of the wicked enemy; he safely passed by the powers of the air and arose to the gates of paradise to be crowned"). (This chapter corresponds to c. 31 of the critical edition: see Conrad d'Eberbach, *Le Grand Exorde de Cîteaux, ou Récit des Débuts de l'Ordre Cistercien*, trans. Anthelmette Piébourg, *Studia et Documenta*, vol. 7 (Brepols: Turnhout; Cîteaux: Commentarii Cistercienses, 1998), 54.

common teacher to instruct us in it but it is our great Saviour Himself who says to us, 'Learn of me . . .'"[93]

2. "to ascend by descending": Luke 14:11: "Everyone who exalts himself will be humbled" (read {the} whole pericope—Luke 14:6-14[94]).

3. Kenotic humility:

a) {entails} the absolute necessity of self-emptying, littleness, not asserting the self by virtues and asceticism, considered as possessions.

b) The true way of the Cross—true imitation of Christ crucified (n.b. in the principal degrees . . .); "*Tota paradisi clavis tuus sanguis est*" (Tertullian);[95] "*Crux Christi clavis paradisi est*" (St. Jerome).[96]

c) But {it must} not {be} violent {but rather} gentle and gradual. The monastery a mother, in which we are quietly and gradually

93. Origen, *Contra Celsum*, trans. Henry Chadwick, 6.15 (Cambridge: Cambridge University Press, 1953), 329.

94. "But he also spoke a parable to those invited, observing how they were choosing the first places at table, and he said to them, 'When thou art invited to a wedding feast, do not recline in the first place, lest perhaps one more distinguished than thou have been invited by him, and he who invited thee and him come and say to thee, "Make room for this man"; and then thou begin with shame to take the last place. But when thou art invited, go and recline in the last place; that when he who invited thee comes in, he may say to thee, "Friend, go up higher!" Then thou wilt be honored in the presence of all who are at table with thee. For everyone who exalts himself shall be humbled, and he who humbles himself shall be exalted.' But he also said to him who had invited him, 'When thou givest a dinner or a supper, do not invite thy friends, or thy brethren, or thy relatives, or thy rich neighbors, lest perhaps they also invite thee in return, and a recompense be made to thee. But when thou givest a feast, invite the poor, the crippled, the lame, the blind; and blessed shalt thou be, because they have nothing to repay thee with; for thou shalt be repaid at the resurrection of the just.'" (The passage actually begins with v. 7.)

95. "Your blood is the only key to paradise" (*De Anima*, c. 55 [*PL* 2, col. 745A]).

96. "The cross of Christ is the key to paradise" (*Ep*. 129.2 [to Dardanus] [*PL* 22, col. 1101, which reads: "*Sanguis Christi* . . ." ("The blood of Christ . . .")]).

formed in the likeness of Christ (Peter of Celle[97]). {The} monastery {is likened to} Mary ({n.b. the} significance {of this}).

4. Summary: St. Basil: *Deinde ut indesinenter et absque ulla cessatione in omnibus actibus, et in omni negotio humiliores caeteris inveniri studeamus, et in hoc exercitium nostrum ponamus*[98] (but, {n.b. the} danger of the comparative, relative attitude).

97. In his letter to Theobald, abbot-elect of Cluny (*Ep.* 145; *PL* 202, col. 589D), Peter adapts the words of Jesus from the cross to Mary, "Woman behold thy son" (Jn. 19:26) to a monastic context: the Abbey of Cluny is the mother providing nourishment for the novices in her charge, and Theobald himself is identified with the son of the quotation, taking special responsibility for his mother.

98. "Let us be eager, then, unceasingly and without any pause, in all acts and in all business, to be found more humble than others, and let us place our effort in this" (*Regula, Interrogatio* 62 [*PL* 103, col. 517B]).

# {APPENDIX 2}

## *Life of St. Benedict* by St. Gregory the Great Selected Texts[99]

### Praefatio[100]

Fuit vir vitae venerabilis *gratia Dei Benedictus et nomine, ab ipso pueritiae suae tempore* cor gerens senile. Aetatem quippe moribus transiens nulli animum voluptati dedit. *Sed dum in hac terra*

99. The text of these passages does not correspond either to that in the *Patrologia Latina* or to that in the *Acta Sanctorum*, March III (21), 277–88. Variants are not recorded, but a phrase from chapter 35 inadvertently omitted by the typist due to eye-skip has been restored in braces, and a few other minor errata are silently corrected. Bracketed additions are Merton's handwritten marginalia on the typescript.

100. Preface—There was a man whose life was worthy of deepest respect, blessed by the grace of God, called Benedict; from the time of his youth he possessed a mature heart. Surpassing his age by his habits, he gave his mind to no pleasure. But while he was still on this earth, he despised the flourishing world, which he could have freely used for a time, as though it were already barren. He came from a highly placed family of the province of Nursia, and had been sent to Rome for a liberal education in literature. But when he realized that many engaged in these studies were going to the extremes of vice, he pulled back from the step that he had taken in the way of the world, lest he himself, touched by this sort of knowledge, might also afterwards go completely into this yawning chasm. And so, having set literary studies at nought and left behind his ancestral home and possessions, desiring to please God alone, he sought the habit of a holy way of life. Therefore, knowingly ignorant and wisely uninstructed, he withdrew. I have not learned of all his deeds, but the few which I am telling I heard through the reports of four of his disciples—Constantine, that most highly respected man, who succeeded him in the direction of his monastery; also Valentinian, who for many years has led the Lateran monastery; Simplicius, who governed his community as the third after him; and Honoratus, who even now is in charge of the cloister in which he had first taken up religious life.

*adhuc esset, quod temporaliter libere uti potuisset,* despexit jam quasi aridum mundum cum flore. *Qui liberiori genere ex provincia Nursiae exortus, Romae liberalibus literarum studiis traditus fuerat. Sed* cum in his multos ire per abrupta vitiorum cerneret, *eum, quem quasi in ingressu mundi posuerat, retraxit pedem, ne si quid de scientia ejus attingeret, ipse quoque postmodum in immane praecipitium totus iret.* Despectis itaque literarum studiis, relicta domo rebusque patris, soli Deo placere desiderens sanctae conversationis habitum quaesivit. *Recessit igitur scienter nescius et sapienter indoctus. Hujus ego omnia gesta non didici, sed pauca, quae narro, quattuor discipulis illius referentibus agnovi,* Constantino *scilicet reverendissimo valde viro, qui ei in monasterii regimine successit;* Valentiniano *quoque, qui annis multis Lateranensi monasterio praefuit;* Simplicio, *quo Congregationem illius post eum tertius rexit;* Honorato *etiam, qui nunc adhuc cellae ejus, in qua prius conversatus fuerat, praeest.*

## Caput 1[101]

{. . .} *Sed Benedictus* plus appetens mala mundi hujus perpeti, quam laudes, pro Deo laboribus fatigari, quam vitae hujus

101. Chapter 1—. . . But Benedict, preferring to endure the hostility of this world more than to receive its praises, and to be worn out by work for God more than to be elevated by the favors of this life, secretly fled from his nurse and sought the solitude of a deserted place, nearly forty miles away from the city of Rome, the name of which is Subiaco, which pours forth cold and clear waters. There the abundant waters are first gathered in a broad lake and from there it flows on in its course. As he was proceeding there in his flight, a certain monk named Romanus encountered him as he went and asked where he was headed. When he had learned of his desire, he both kept his secret and gave him assistance; he provided the habit of a holy way of life and was of service to him to the extent he was able. When the man of God arrived at that place he stayed for three years in a very narrow cave, remaining unknown to anyone except the monk Romanus—this Romanus lived in a monastery not far away under the rule of his abbot Deodatus. But he piously escaped the notice of this same abbot at times, and on certain days brought Benedict bread which he had been able to put aside from what was to be eaten by himself. There was no pathway from Romanus' cell to this cave, which had above it a tall cliff; but from this same cliff Romanus

favoribus extolli, *nutricem suam occulte fugiens* deserti loci secessum petiit, *cui Sublacus vocabulum est, qui a Romana urbe quadraginta fere millibus distans frigidas atque perspicuas emanat aquas. Quae illic videlicet aquarum abundantia in extenso prius lacu colligitur, ad postremum vero in amne derivatur. Quo dum fugiens pergeret, monachus quidam Romanus nomine hunc euntem repperit, quo tenderet inquisivit. Hujus cum desiderium cognovisset, et secretum tenuit et adjutorium impendit* eique sanctae conversationis habitum tradidit et in quantum licuit ministravit. *Vir autem Dei ad eundem locum perveniens* arctissimo specu se tradidit tribus annis, *excepto Romano monacho hominibus incognitus mansit: qui videlicet Romanus non longe in monasterio sub Deodati Patris regula degebat. Sed pie ejusdem patris sui oculis furabatur horas, et quem sibi ad manducandum subripere poterat, diebus certis Benedicto panem ferebat. Ad eundem vero specum a Romani cella iter non erat, qui excelsa desuper rupis eminebat; sed ex eadem rupe in longissimo fune religatum Romanus deponere panem consueverat in qua etiam resti parvum tintinnabulum inseruit, ut ad sonum tintinnabuli vir Dei cognosceret, quando sibi Romanus panem praeberet, quem exiens acciperet. Sed antiquus hostis unius caritati invidens, alterius refectioni, cum quadam die submitti panem conspiceret, jactavit lapidem et tintinnabulum fregit. Romanus tamen horis congruentibus ministrare non desiit.* {. . .}

## Caput 2[102]

*Quadam vero die* dum solus esset, tentator affuit. *Nam nigra parvaque avis quae vulgo merula vocatur, circa ejus faciem volitare*

---

used to let down the bread tied to a very long rope; on this rope he also attached a small bell, so that at the sound of the bell the man of God would know when Romanus was bringing him bread, which he would go out and retrieve. But the ancient enemy, envying the charity of the one and the meal of the other, on a certain day when he saw the bread being sent down, threw a stone and broke the bell. Nonetheless, Romanus did not stop being of service at suitable times. . . .

102. Chapter 2—One day, while he was alone, the tempter appeared. For a little black bird, which is called a "*merula*" by the common people, began to

*coepit ejusque vultui importune insistere, ita ut capi manu posset, si hanc vir sanctus tenere voluisset: sed signo crucis edito recessit avis. Tanta autem carnis tentatio ave eadem recedente secuta est, quantam vir sanctus nunquam fuerat expertus. Quandam namque aliquando feminam viderat, quam malignus spiritus ante ejus mentis oculos reduxit, tantoque igne servi Dei animum in specie illius accendit, ut se in ejus pectore amoris flamma vix caperet, et jam pene deserere eremum voluptate victus deliberaret, dum* subito superna gratia respectus ad semetipsum reversus est atque urticarum et veprium juxta densa succrescere fruteta conspiciens, exutus indumento nudum se in illis spinarum aculeis et urticarum incendiis projecit, *ibique diu volutatus toto ex eis corpore vulneratus exiit, et per cutis vulnera eduxit a corpore vulnus mentis, quia voluptatem traxit in dolorem. Cumque pene poenaliter arderet foris, extinxit quod illicite ardebat*

---

flutter around his face and to keep right in front of it in an annoying way, so that if the holy man had wanted to grab it he could have taken it in his hand; but when he had made the sign of the cross the bird withdrew. However after the bird had disappeared there followed such a temptation of the flesh as the holy man had never experienced. He had once seen a certain woman, whom the evil spirit now brought before the eyes of his mind: the imagination of the servant of God burned with such fire at this appearance that the flame of love scarcely kept itself within his breast. Almost overcome by desire, he was considering abandoning his place of solitude; then suddenly, protected by grace from above, he returned to himself, and seeing a thick patch of nettles and briars growing nearby, he cast away his clothing and threw himself naked amid the stings of the thorns and the burning of the nettles; for a considerable time he rolled around there, leaving only when his entire body was covered with wounds from them: through the wounds in his skin, the wound to his soul was expelled from his body, for pleasure was transformed into grief. When he was almost on fire externally with this penance, he extinguished what had been burning within unlawfully. Thus he overcame sin by exchanging fires. And from that very time, as he himself later told his disciples, the temptation of pleasure had been overcome in him so that he did not in the least feel any such movement in himself again. After this, many began to abandon the world and hasten to heed his instruction. Free from the defect of temptation, he rightly became the teacher of virtues. So is it taught by Moses during the exodus that Levites should enter service when twenty-five years old and above, and become guardians of the sacred vessels from their fiftieth year.

*intus.* Vicit itaque peccatum, qui mutavit incendium. *Ex quo videlicet tempore, sicut post discipulis ipse perhibebat, ita in illo est tentatio voluptatis edomita, ut tale in se aliquid minime sentiret.* [*apatheia?*] *Coeperunt postmodum multi jam mundum relinquere atque ad ejus magisterium festinare. Liber quippe a tentationis vitio, jure jam factus est virtutum magister. Unde et per Moysen in Exodo praecipitur, ut Levitae a viginti quinque annis et supra ministrare debeant, ab anno vero quinquagesimo custodes vasorum fiant.*

## Caput 10[103] [at Monte Cassino]

*Tunc in conspectu viri Dei placuit, ut in loco eodem terram foderent, quam dum fodiendo altius penetrarent, aereum illic idolum fratres envenerunt. Quo ad horam casu in coquinam projecto, exire ignis repente visus est, atque in cunctorum monachorum oculis, quia omne ejusdem coquinae aedificium consumeretur, ostendit. Cumque jaciendo aquam et ignem quasi extinguentes perstreperent, pulsatus eodem tumultu vir Domini advenit. Qui eundem ignem in oculis fratrum esse, in suis vero non esse considerans caput protinus in orationem flexit et eos, quos phantasmatico repperit igne deludi, vocavit fratres ad oculos suos, ut et sanum illud coquinae aedificium cernerent adsistere et flammas, quas antiquus hostis finxerat, non viderent.*

103. Chapter 10—Then it seemed good in the sight of the man of God to dig up the ground in that same place. While they were delving deeper in their digging, the brothers came upon a brass idol there. When for the time being they tossed it by chance into the kitchen, suddenly a fire seemed to burst forth, and it appeared to the eyes of all the monks that the whole building containing the kitchen was being consumed. When they were making a lot of noise throwing water and trying to put out the fire, the man of the Lord arrived, drawn by that commotion. Realizing that the fire was visible to the eyes of the brothers but not to his own, he bowed his head in prayer and called the brothers whom he found to be deluded by the imaginary fire, to see as he did, so that they realized that the kitchen building stood undamaged, and they did not see the flames that the ancient enemy had fabricated.

## Caput 18[104] [Spirituality of St. Benedict—monastic formation etc.]

*Quodam quoque tempore Exhilaratus noster, quem ipse conversum nosti, transmissus a domino suo fuerat, ut Dei viro in monasterium vino plena duo lignea vascula, quae vulgo flascones vocantur, deferret: qui unum detulit, alterum vero pergens in itinere abscondit. Vir autem Domini, quem facta absentia latere non poterant, unum cum gratiarum actione suscepit et descendentem puerum monuit dicens: Vide, fili, de illo flascone, quem abscondisti, jam non bibas, sed inclina illum caute et invenies, quid intus habet.* [obedience] *Qui confusus valde a Dei homine exivit. Et reversus volens adhuc probare, quod audierat, cum flasconem inclinasset, de eo protinus serpens egressus est. Tunc praedictus puer Exhilaratus per hoc, quod in vino repperit, expavit malum, quod fecit.*

## Caput 20[105] [humility; not murmuring; peace and silence of heart]

*Quadam quoque die dum venerabilis Benedictus Pater vespertina jam hora corporis alimenta perciperet, ejus monachus, cujusdam Defensoris filius, fuerat qui ei ante mensam lucernam tenebat. Cumque vir Dei ederet, ipse autem cum lucernae ministerio adstaret, coepit per superbiae spiritum in mente sua tacitus volvere et per cogitationem dicere: Quis est hic, cui ego manducanti adsisto, lucernam teneo, servitium impendo? Qui sum ego, ut isti serviam? Ad quem vir Dei statim*

104. Chapter 18—At one time our Exhilaratus, whom you know entered religious life himself, had been sent by his master to bring to the man of God at the monastery two wooden vessels full of wine, called flasks by the common people. He brought one, but the other he took for himself and hid along the way. The man of the Lord, from whom even deeds done in his absence could not be hidden, received the one flask with an expression of gratitude, and then warned the boy as he was departing, saying: "Be careful, son, not to drink from the flask you stole, but tip it carefully and you will discover what is inside it." Much abashed, he departed from the man of God. On his return he wanted to check out what he had heard, and when he had tipped the flask, a serpent came out of it. Then the boy Exhilaratus, having been forewarned, was terrified, because of what he found in the wine, by the evil he had done.

105. Chapter 20—On a certain day while the venerable Father Benedict was taking bodily nourishment at the evening hour, one of his monks, son of a certain high official, was holding a lamp for him in front of the table. While the man of

*conversus vehementer eum coepit increpare dicens: Signa cor tuum, frater, quid est, quod loqueris? signa cor tuum. Vocatisque fratribus statim praecepit, ei lucernam de manibus tolli, ipsum vero jussit a ministerio recedere et sibi hora eadem quietum sedere. Qui requisitus a fratribus, quid habuerit in corde, per ordinem narravit, quanto superbiae spiritu intumuerat et quae contra virum Dei verba per cogitationem tacitus dicebat. Tunc liquido omnibus patuit, quod venerabilem Benedictum latere nil posset, in cujus aure etiam cogitationis verba sonuissent.*

## Caput 25[106]

*Gregorius. Quidam ejus monachus mobilitati mentem dederat et permanere in monasterio nolebat. Cumque eum vir Dei assidue corriperet et frequenter ammoneret, ipse vero nullo modo consentiret in congregatione persistere atque importunis precibus, ut relaxaretur, immineret:*

---

God was eating, the other was standing there doing lamp duty; in a spirit of pride be began silently to turn things over in his mind, and to think to himself: "Who is this for whom I am standing here holding the lamp while he eats, acting like a servant? Who am I that I should wait on him?" Suddenly the man of God turned to him and began to scold him strongly, saying, "Make the sign of the cross on your heart, brother—what is it that you are saying? Make the sign of the cross on your heart." Summoning the brothers, he immediately ordered that the lamp be taken from his hands and commanded him to withdraw from service and sit quietly by himself at that very hour. When asked by his brothers what had been in his heart, in response he related with how great a spirit of pride he had been filled, and what he was silently saying in his mind against the man of God. Then it was clear to all that nothing could be hidden from the venerable Benedict, in whose ear the very words of one's thoughts had rung.

106. Chapter 25—Gregory: One of his monks had given up his soul to restlessness, and was unwilling to remain in the monastery. While the man of God continually reproached him and often warned him, in no way would he agree to remain in the community, and with constant pleading longed to be released, until one day the venerable Father, worn down with weariness by his excessive begging, angrily ordered him to leave. As soon as he left the monastery, he came upon a dragon standing with wide open mouth facing him on the road. When this dragon which had appeared wanted to devour him, he began to tremble and shake and to cry out with a loud voice, saying, "Run, run, for there

*quadam die isdem venerabilis Pater nimietatis ejus taedio affectus iratus jussit, ut discederet. Qui mox ut monasterium exiit, contra se adsistere aperto ore draconem in itinere invenit. Cumque eum isdem draco, qui apparuerat, devorare vellet, coepit ipse tremens et palpitans magnis vocibus clamare dicens: currite, currite, quia draco iste me devorare vult. Currentes autem fratres draconem minime viderunt, sed trementem atque palpitantem monachum ad monasterium reduxerunt. Qui statim promisit, nunquam se esse jam a monasterio recessurum, atque ex hora eadem in sua promissione permansit, quippe qui sancti viri orationibus contra se assistere draconem viderat, quem prius non videndo sequebatur.*

## Caput 35[107]

*Alio quoque tempore* Servandus, *diaconus atque abbas ejus monasterii, quod in Campaniae partibus a Liberio quondam patricio fuerat constructum, ad eum visitationis gratia ex more convenerat. Ejus quippe monasterium frequentabat, ut, qui isdem quoque vir doctrina gratiae coelestis influebat, dulcia sibi invicem vitae verba transfunderent et suavem cibum coelestis patriae, quia adhuc perfecte gaudendo non poterant, saltem suspirando gustarent. Cum vero hora jam quietis exigeret, in cujus turris superioribus se venerabilis Benedictus, in ejus quoque inferioribus sese Servandus diaconus collocavit, quo videlicet*

---

is a dragon that wants to devour me!" The brothers came running but saw no dragon at all; they brought the trembling and shaking monk back to the monastery. Immediately he promised that he would never leave the monastery, and from that hour he remained faithful to his promise. It was of course through the prayers of the holy man that he had seen the dragon arrayed against him, whom he was previously following without seeing it.

107. Chapter 35—At another time Servandus, a deacon and the abbot of his monastery, which had been built by the nobleman Patricius in the territory of Campania, had come to him on a visit as he was accustomed to do. He was a regular visitor to Benedict's monastery; he also was a man pervaded with the teaching of heavenly grace, and they poured out to one another the sweet words of life and they tasted at least by their sighs the delightful food of their heavenly fatherland which they could not as yet fully enjoy. When the hour of quiet arrived, the venerable Benedict ascended to his room in the upper story of the tower, and Servandus the deacon went into the room just below, from which a stairway was

*in loco inferiora superioribus pervius continuabat ascensus.* [Contemplation] *Ante eandem vero turrim largius erat habitaculum, in quo utriusque discipuli quiescebant. Cumque vir Domini Benedictus adhuc quiescentibus fratribus, instans vigiliis, nocturnae orationis tempora praevenisset,* ad fenestram stans et omnipotentem Dominum deprecans, subito intempesta noctis hora respiciens vidit fusam lucem desuper cunctas noctis tenebras exfugasse tantoque splendore clarescere, ut diem vinceret lux illa, *quae inter tenebras radiasset. Mira autem {res valde in hac speculatione secuta est: quia, sicut post} ipse narrabat,* omnis etiam mundus velut sub uno solis radio collectus ante oculos ejus adductus est. *Qui venerabilis Pater, dum*

---

accessible that continued up to the upper story. In front of this tower there was a larger building in which the disciples of each man were taking their rest. While his brothers were already at rest, Benedict, the man of the Lord, had anticipated the time of the night office by standing in vigil at a window and praying to the almighty Lord. Looking out in the darkest hour of night, he suddenly saw that a beam of light from above had dispersed all the shades of night and shone with such splendor that it had spread out in the darkness and was brighter than day. A very wondrous occurrence followed upon this vision; for afterward, as he himself related, the entire world was as if gathered in a single ray of the sun and brought before his eyes. While the venerable Father focused his sharp sight on the splendor of this glittering light, he saw the soul of Germanus the bishop of Capua carried into heaven by angels in a fiery sphere. Wanting to have another witness to such a great miracle, he called the deacon Servandus by name over and over, a second and a third time, with a loud cry. When he had been brusquely awakened by the noise, he went up and looked out, and saw the final fading of the light. The man of God told him, as he stood struck with wonder, of such an awesome miracle and the events that had happened. Right afterward he ordered the devout man Theoprobus to go into the town of Cassino and to send someone that very night to the city of Capua to find out and report what had happened to Bishop Germanus. This was done, and the one who had been sent reported that the most holy bishop Germanus had just died, and asking carefully found out that his death had taken place at the very moment when the man of the Lord had witnessed his ascent. . . .

Hold fast, Peter, to what I am saying—to the soul who sees the Creator every created thing is narrow. Once he has perceived a little in the light of the Creator, everything created becomes insignificant to him, because by the very light of this interior vision, the constrictions of the mind are loosened and expanded in God, so that he is raised above the world. The soul of one who sees

*intentam oculorum aciem in hoc splendore coruscae lucis infigeret, vidit Germani, Capuani episcopi, animam in sphaera ignea ab angelis in coelum ferri.* [Contemplation not of world only—but of divine art—mercy of God—salvation of Germanus] *Tunc tanti sibi testem volens adhibere miraculi, Servandum diaconum iterato bis terque ejus nomine cum clamoris magnitudine vocavit. Cumque ille fuisset insolito tanti viri clamore turbatus, ascendit, respexit partemque jam lucis exiguam vidit. Cui tantum hoc obstupescenti miraculum vir Dei per ordinem, quae fuerant gesta, narravit statimque in Casinum castrum religioso viro Theopropo mandavit, ut ad Capuanam urbem sub eadem nocte transmitteret, et quid de Germano episcopo ageretur, agnosceret et indicaret. Factumque est, et reverentissimum virum Germanum episcopum is, qui missus fuerat, jam defunctum repperit et requirens subtiliter agnovit, eodem momento fuisse illius obitum, quo vir Domini ejus cognovit ascensum.* {. . .}

*Fixum tene, Petre, quod loquor,* quia animae videnti creatorem angusta est omnis creatura. *Quamlibet etenim parum de luce creatoris aspexerit, breve ei fit omne, quod creatum est, quia ipsa luce visionis intimae, mentis laxatur sinus tantumque expanditur in Deo, ut superior existat mundo. Fit vero ipsa videntis anima etiam super semetipsam;* cumque in Dei lumine rapitur super se, in interioribus ampliatur, et dum sub se conspicit, exaltata comprehendit, quam breve sit, quod comprehendere humiliata non poterat. *Vir ergo, qui intueri globum igneum, angelos quoque ad coelum redeuntes videbat, haec*

---

this even becomes above itself; when it is carried beyond itself in the light of God it is enlarged within itself, and while it is raised up and looks beneath itself, it understands how small everything is that it could not comprehend in its lowly state. Thus the man who saw the fiery globe and the angels returning to heaven undoubtedly could not have perceived such things except in the light of God. What is surprising, then, if he who had been raised beyond the world in the light of the spirit saw the whole world gathered up before him? To say that the world was gathered up before his eyes means not that heaven and earth were made small but that the soul of the one seeing was expanded: carried away in God, he could see everything that is less than God without difficulty. In that light, then, which shone before his exterior eyes, there was a light for his interior self that carried away the soul of the visionary to a higher state, and showed how narrow all lesser things were. . . .

*procul dubio cernere non nisi in Dei lumine poterat. Quid itaque mirum, si mundum ante se collectum vidit, qui sublevatus in mentis lumine extra mundum fuit? Quod autem collectus mundus ante ejus oculos dicitur, non coelum et terra contracta est, sed videntis animus dilatus, qui in Deo raptus videre sine difficultate potuit omne, quod infra Deum est. In illa ergo luce, quae exterioribus oculis fulsit, lux in interiori mente fuit, quae videntis animum, quia ad superiora rapuit, ei quam angusta essent omnia inferiora monstravit.* {. . .}

## Caput 36[108]

*Gregorius. Libet, Petre, adhuc de hoc venerabili Patre multa narrare; sed quaedam ejus studiose praetereo, quia ad aliorum gesta volvenda festino. Hoc autem nolo ut te lateat, quod vir Dei inter tot miracula, quibus in mundo claruit, doctrinae quoque verbo non mediocriter fulsit. Nam scripsit monachorum regulam, discretione praecipuam, sermone luculentam, cujus si quis velit subtilius mores vitamque cognoscere, potest in eadem institutione regulae omnis magisterii actus invenire, qui sanctus vir nullo modo potuit aliter docere, quam vixit.*

108. Chapter 36—Gregory: It is pleasant, Peter, to be telling so many stories thus far about this venerable Father, but I am purposely passing over certain things because I am in a hurry to take a look at the deeds of others. However I don't want to have you miss the fact that in the midst of so many miraculous deeds through which he became celebrated throughout the world, the man of God was also illustrious in his teaching. For he wrote a rule for monks that is outstanding in its discretion and excellent in its expression. If anyone wants to learn more deeply of his life and character, he can discover in the provisions of this rule how he acted as a leader, for the holy man could in no way teach differently than he lived.

## Caput 37[109]

*Eodem vero anno, quo de hac vita erat exiturus quibusdam discipulis secum conversantibus, quibusdam longe manentibus, sanctissimi sui obitus denuntiavit diem, praesentibus indicens, ut audita per silentium tegerent, absentibus indicans, quod vel quale eis signum fieret, quando ejus anima de corpore exiret. Ante sextum vero sui exitus diem aperiri sibi sepulturam jubet. Qui mox correptus febribus acri coepit ardore fatigari: cumque per singulos dies languor ingravesceret, sexto die portari se in oratorium a discipulis fecit ibique exitum suum Dominici corporis et sanguinis perceptione munivit atque inter discipulorum manus imbecillia membra sustentans erectis in coelum manibus stetit et ultimum spiritum inter verba orationis efflavit. Qua scilicet die duobus de eo fratribus, uni in cella commoranti, alteri autem longius posito, revelatio unius atque indissimilis visionis apparuit. Viderunt namque, qui strata palliis atque innumeris corusca lampadibus via recto*

109. Chapter 37—The same year in which he was to leave this life, while certain disciples were conversing with him and others were far distant, he announced the day of his most sacred passing, indicating to those present that they should conceal in silence what they had heard, and to those absent what sort of sign would appear to them when his soul departed from his body. On the sixth day preceding his departure he ordered his tomb to be opened. Soon he began to be attacked by a fever and worn out by its severe heat. As his weakness increased daily, on the sixth day he had himself carried into the oratory by his disciples, and there received strength for his journey by receiving the body and blood of the Lord; supporting his weakened body by the hands of his disciples, he stood with his own hands lifted toward heaven, and poured forth his final breath in words of prayer. On that day the revelation of an identical vision of him appeared to two of the brothers, one remaining present in the monastery, the other located far away. For they saw a pathway covered with cloaks and glittering with innumerable lamps making a straight way in the East from his cell all the way into heaven. A man shining in brilliant clothing who was present above asked each of them whose passageway they were looking at. But they admitted that they didn't know. He said to them, "This is the path by which Benedict, the beloved of the Lord, ascended into heaven." And so, as his disciples who were present witnessed the departure of the holy man, so those who were absent knew of it through the sign that he had foretold to them. He was buried in the oratory of blessed John the Baptist, which he himself had built where the altar of Apollo had been thrown down. . . .

*Orientis tramite ab ejus cella in coelum usque tendebatur. Cui venerando habitu vir desuper clarus assistens, cujus esset via, quam cernerent, inquisivit. Illi autem se nescire professi sunt. Quibus ipse ait: Haec est via, qua delectus Domini coelum Benedictus ascendit. Tunc itaque sancti viri obitum, sicut praesentes discipuli viderunt, ita absentes ex signo, quod eis praedictum fuerat, agnoverunt. Sepultus vero est in oratorio beati Joannis Baptistae, quod destructa ara Apollinis ipse construxit.* {. . .}

# APPENDIX A

## Textual Notes

### Readings Adopted from Ditto

| | |
|---|---|
| 1 | CONFERENCES ON] *omitted* |
| | 1960] 1957 |
| 3–4 | TABLE OF CONTENTS . . . the subject.] *omitted* |
| 5 | NOTES ON] *preceded by* (to go in beginning of all the notes) *added in upper margin* |
| 17 | born] *preceded by* 480 *added in left margin* |
| | Perhaps] *preceded by* 495 *added in left margin* |
| | About] *preceded by* 500 *added in left margin* |
| 18 | "cells"] *preceded by* 503 *added in left margin* |
| | Monte Cassino around] *preceded by* 529 *added in left margin* |
| | The *Rule* was] *preceded by* 534 *added in left margin* |
| | Benedict died] *preceded by* 547 *added in left margin* |
| 36–37 | The physiognomy . . . existence.] (Typist—please copy these pages, beginning bottom of p. 50 "The physiognomy of St Benedict . . . . to end of chapter on top of p. 52) |
| 38 | Eucharist.] *followed by Texts from St Gregory go here in the complete set of notes* |
| 41 | Gospels] Luke 14:8-11 *added in left margin* |
| 104 | *hierarchical*] *preceded in left margin by* mutual respect |
| 134 | *Lectio Divina* . . . our life:] *preceded on opposite preceding page by* Lectio Divina. Importance of intellectual work Special kind of reading—Lectio Divina: partly study partly prayer Need variety in Lectio Divina *Basic* A The *Scriptures* This |

requires study of Scriptures use of the new material coming out The *Fathers* + the liturgy + monastic traditions The *Spiritual Writers* B. Theologians Historians Biographies Poets—Arts. What is excluded?

135 to be done.] *followed in lower margin by* (follows—*manner*)

143 Juridically] *preceded in left margin by* jurid.
But St.] *preceded in left margin by* ascetical
Hence *even*] *preceded in left margin by* spirit
But even] *preceded in left margin by* attachment

144 The spirit of] *preceded in left margin by* [ ] of spirit.
This means] *preceded in left margin by* important

147 b) Hence] *preceded in left margin by* Providence

151 *SI . . . ACCIPERE*.] Si . . . accipere *followed by* Capitals

159 Two quotes] *preceded in left margin by Ps 130*

**Additions and Alterations Included in Ditto**

5 *is like*] *preceded by x'd out was like*
go into] *preceded by x'd out* treat in

7 Popes] *followed on new line by cancelled* St Benedict and the Eastern Church.

8 He worked] He *typed over* It
For this, . . . through St. Benedict.] *added on line*
bring its values] *preceded by x'd out* be seen
We must see] *preceded by x'd out* without

9 roots,] *preceded by x'd out* context

10 obstruct the] the *altered from* their
This tradition] *preceded by x'd out* But
*pure*] *preceded by x'd out* springs

11 witness] *preceded by x'd out* guarantee of
strengthen and nourish] *altered from* strengthens and nourishes
we . . . monks] *typed interlined and marked for insertion*
letter which] *preceded by x'd out* law which

12 has the] *preceded by x'd out* is as or
13 *adapt*] *followed by x'd out* and
14 contribute] *altered from* contributes
16 Book II] *preceded by x'd out* the
17 The best . . . charm.] *added on line*
(496?)] *interlined with a caret*
18 temple] *preceded by x'd out* former
19 obsessed] *preceded by x'd out* dictated the
A dominant] *preceded by x'd out* It is a dmoni [*sic*]
frown] *preceded by x'd out* drown out all spontaneity with frowns.
and that . . . *choice.*] *added on line*
20 who prudently] *preceded by x'd out* prudently
Schuster . . . *educated.*] *added on line*
21 He realized] He *added in left margin*
22 stony] *preceded by x'd out* arid gorge
23 yet] *added in left margin and marked for insertion*
*St. Benedict overcomes*] *St. added in left margin*
24 zeal] *typed in left margin before x'd out* love
will overcome us.] *added on line*
means] *preceded by x'd out* steps
27 Dom Augustine] *preceded by x'd out* Dom Cuthber [*sic*]
28 At Subiaco,] At *altered from* at *preceded by cancelled* At this time,
c. 4] 4 *typed over* 6
to deliver] to *interlined and marked with arrow for insertion*
30 sternness –] *followed by x'd out* matter
lady.] *preceded by x'd out* dame
31 issue] *preceded by x'd out* fault
5. He is . . . *thoughts.*] *added on line*
31–32 We conclude . . . to St. Benedict's spirit] *opposite page*
32 unyielding] *preceded by x'd out* unbending
penance;] *followed by x'd out* Zeal for the common
33 with her] *preceded by x'd out* staying with her
principle] *followed by x'd out* on this occasion.

35 Interior . . . for prayer.] *added on line*

36 6] *added in left margin*

37 This is the key . . . *is Christ.*] *added on line*

38 The beautiful . . . Eucharist.] *opposite page*

42 in classical] in *altered from* on

*psalmorum*] *preceded by x'd out lectionum*

42–43 completed . . . Schmidt] *interlined above cancelled* followed along

43 single] *preceded by x'd out* signal

44 a qualification] *preceded by x'd out* that one m

Nevertheless, . . . follow it.] *added on line*

45 such texts] *preceded by x'd out* this kind

It is also] *preceded by x'd out* There

cut and dried] *preceded by x'd out* and

46 for centuries] *followed by x'd out* have pre

47 (Paul Warnefrid] *interlined with a caret*

wrote . . . France.] *interlined with a caret*

a unique . . . Aniane.] *opposite page*

Note here . . . Migne.] *added on line*

useful] *preceded by cancelled* We [ ] it *and followed by cancelled* if [ ] available

is lacking] is *added on line following cancelled* was

a good . . . *omnium"*] *added on line*

50 *Dom C. . . . Monachism*] *added on line*

all should . . . study of St. Benedict.] *opposite page*

best in modern] best *interlined above cancelled* justest

*Dom Symphorien* . . . definitor.] *added in lower margin*

having gained] having *interlined above cancelled* and

should be consulted.] *interlined above cancelled* are available.

51 our lawgiver.] our *interlined below cancelled* the

is made up] *preceded by x'd out* in a nutshell

52 are all summed] *preceded by x'd out* call

However, . . . cause.] *added on line*

deep] *preceded by x'd out* great

54 a *negation,*] *preceded by x'd out* denial

aimlessness,] *preceded by x'd out* lack of direction
56 desires] *preceded by x'd out* lusts
57 a most] a *altered from* an
58 our spirit] our *interlined below cancelled* the
all-important,] *followed by x'd out* to
realize its] its *interlined above cancelled* the
urgency] *followed by cancelled* of it
59 "*hodie*] *preceded by x'd out* if y
occur] *preceded by x'd out* are
merely] *followed by x'd out* God's
60 three] *interlined above cancelled* two
AUDITE] *interlined and marked with arrow for insertion*
*listen* to me] *interlined and marked with arrow for insertion*
Love calls . . . of St. Benedict.] *opposite page*
61 This means . . . later on.] *opposite page*
as St. Benedict] St. Benedict *interlined below cancelled* he
63 vocation] *interlined above cancelled* life
64 love] *preceded by x'd out* life
67 at every moment;] *preceded by x'd out* also
(St. Bernard).] *followed by x'd out* Hence
This is . . . faith.] *added on line*
69 never] *interlined and marked with arrow for insertion*
But as Dom . . . labor.] *opposite page*
71 In this . . . road!] *added in lower margin*
72 Old Testament] Testament *altered from* Testaments
blamed,] *followed by x'd out* but we must not deduce
were not destined] *preceded by x'd out* did not
Note: all . . . of God] *interlined*
notion of] *followed by x'd out* cenobites,
73 at all times] *interlined with a caret*
outside] *preceded by x'd out* beyond
sense).] *followed by x'd out* N.B. in our modern psychology perhaps we could call the vitia carnis
74 consolation] *followed by x'd out* of
He is . . . war."] *added on line*

or through the angels] *interlined and marked with arrow for insertion*
knowing . . . *to Him*] *added on line*
condemning] *followed by x'd out* the
75 lack of self-renunciation.] *added on line*
Here St. Benedict . . .harm.] *opposite page*
76 substantially] *preceded by x'd out* read
77 *Dark Night*] *preceded by x'd out* Ascent to Mou
78 hoping] *preceded by x'd out* putting
religious life.] *followed by x'd out* Hence many abu
79 A very . . . of things] *added in lower margin*
80 The teachings . . . souls.] *added on line*
81 led] *preceded by x'd out* lead an
82 (*Abba—Pater*)] *added on line*
action] *preceded by x'd out* mystical acts
83 Comment . . . phrase!] *interlined*
not just . . . monk.] *added on line*
but the abbot . . . of God] *added on line*
(True . . . compulsion.)] *added on line*
87 3] *added in left margin*
*simpliciores*] *altered from simplicior*
lights?] *altered from* lights.
gifted.] *followed by x'd out* In another place
88 (c. 53)] *added on line*
All . . . *circumstances*.)] *added on line*
would] *interlined below and marked with arrow for insertion*
89 to union . . . *Christ*.] *added on line*
91 But] *added in left margin*
to punish.] *followed by x'd out* His approach must
vain] *followed by x'd out* complacency
93 cooperation.] *preceded by x'd out* participation.
temptation] *preceded by x'd out* usual
a testimony] *preceded by x'd out* an obj
94 This is the Law] This *typed above x'd out* There
precept] *preceded by x'd out* act is

95 confession may] *followed by x'd out* fulfil the requirements
considering] *followed by x'd out* what
96 a domineering] *preceded by x'd out* jealousy
99 as well as] *interlined with a caret*
100 summarizing] *preceded by x'd out* refer
i.e. . . . deal] *added on line*
In fact . . . now!] *interlined*
101 decided] *preceded by cancelled de facto*
counsel can] *preceded by x'd out* council can
102 yet not . . . either.] *added on line*
103 get only] only get *marked for transposition*
SEQUATUR CORDIS] CORDIS SEQUATUR *marked for transposition*
(c. 3)] *added on line*
104 closer to God] *followed by cancelled* (perhaps)
106 to see] *preceded by x'd out* where there
106–107 unmortified passions] *preceded by x'd out* vice
107 uncharitableness:] *preceded by x'd out* conflict
"supervision . . . discretion"] *added on line*
"For . . . (c. 63).] *added on line*
108 chapter] *followed by x'd out* of
109 sometimes] *preceded by cancelled* in the monastery
They] *altered from* they *and preceded by x'd out* For either
110 It stops . . . by them.] *added on line*
note the . . . *bonum.*] *added in lower margin*
due to them] *followed by x'd out* in strict
110–11 Note chapter . . . FECERIS.] *opposite page*
111 charity—] *followed by x'd out* fail
*omission.*] *followed by x'd out* I was hungry and you gave me not to eat, etc, Matthew 25. (READ IT).
112 restrain] *followed by x'd out* his
113 involved] *preceded by x'd out* engaged in a
For] *interlined with a caret*
leads] *preceded by x'd out* implies
115 with whom] with *typed interlined*

116 now look] now *altered from* not
118 on his own] *followed by x'd out* and
responsible post] *typed above x'd out* job
119 prior] *followed by x'd out* and (66)
It gives] *preceded by x'd out* A monk
showing] *preceded by x'd out* for the indivian
121 life] *preceded by x'd out* thin
122 a job] *preceded by x'd out* charge
d) HUMILITY . . . charity.] *opposite page*
123 Discuss . . . *sons*] *opposite page*
*dependable*] *preceded by x'd out* faithful
124 The mature . . . others.] *added on line*
129 fulfillment] *preceded by x'd out* effort and
"Everybody's got to do it!"] *added on line*
132 passed over] *preceded by x'd out* dispense
133 one to two . . . vigils] *typed above x'd out* about 1 hour after vigils or even more
139 could not] *preceded by x'd out* should n
140 use,] *followed by x'd out* but
141 share] *followed by x'd out* our surplus with others for the love of Christ.
(work)] *interlined and marked for insertion*
kind of life] *followed by x'd out* This
142 POVERTY] *added on line*
though . . . seculars.] *interlined with a caret*
145 dying . . . Cross.] *added on line*
the bare] *preceded by cancelled* with
Hence . . . Church.] *added on line*
A religious . . . Church.] *added on line*
147 c. 43] *added on line*
148 whole Church).] *followed by x'd out* We have at once the
149 dependent.] *followed by x'd out* But
This . . . *faith.*] *added in left margin and marked for insertion*
150 differences.] *followed by x'd out* This
from the superior] *preceded by x'd out* when

151 we will *trust*] *preceded by x'd out* that
take] *preceded by x'd out* make
152 the longest] *preceded by x'd out* one of
154 trying to] *followed by x'd out* do
155 sermons] *preceded by x'd out* other
or St. Basil's . . . below).] *added on line*
transformation] *followed by x'd out* demanded
The second] *preceded by x'd out* It gives
156 any desire] *followed by x'd out* to tend towards
159 separated] *followed by x'd out* and
160 tribe who] *followed by x'd out* out of
162 Explain "from God"] *added on line*
163 b) Then] *preceded by x'd out*—the lure of
However, . . . of God.] *added on line*
165 484] *preceded by x'd out* 485
166 dissipating itself] *followed by x'd out* further and far
unreal.] *followed by x'd out* Exlatatio [*sic*]
167 Luke 18:9 ff.] *added on line*
170 petty vices] *preceded by x'd out* vices
demands] *preceded by x'd out* are
172 Compare] *interlined above cancelled* cf
begin] *preceded by cancelled* then
173 our bearing.] our *interlined below cancelled* one's
our conduct] our *interlined below cancelled* one's
Note that . . .true.] *interlined*
174 a scrupulous] *preceded by cancelled* of
I cannot . . . thoughts!] *interlined*
basic . . . meditation.] *added on line*
175 realize . . . action] *added on line*
176 never get] *followed by cancelled* over
Atheists] *preceded by x'd out* It
178 essence] *preceded by cancelled* one
179 says] *added on line following cancelled* again quotes Scripture:
182 II.] *interlined above* 2 *added interlined and cancelled*
fully] *preceded by x'd out* sin.

183 *The Third Degree*] *preceded by x'd out* The Third Degree

184 monastic humility] *preceded by x'd out* perfection of

This is a . . . obedience.] *interlined*

185 Read Philippians 2:8.] *added in left margin*

The third . . . self-denial.] *added in lower margin*

187 One will not succeed in this] *added in left margin following cancelled* It is very important not to try to cultivate this

188 are supposed] are *interlined below cancelled* is

force] *preceded by x'd out* power

189 Matthew] *followed by x'd out* 10

190 treating] *preceded by x'd out* and

He had] He *interlined with a caret above cancelled* and

should make] *followed by x'd out* himse make

Openness . . . grace.] *added on line*

191 person we are.] *followed by x'd out* This applies a fortiori to relations with the Novice Master

Integrity of confession] *interlined above cancelled* This

and does . . . humility] *added on line following cancelled* before hand.

evil] *followed by cancelled* and

192 *interior fault*] *followed by x'd out* or perhaps a sin

at least] *preceded by x'd out* unless it is pu

193 Some people] *preceded by x'd out* Work it out in di

practice.] *followed by x'd out* We su

194 *clothing*] *followed by cancelled* and shelter

suffer no] *followed by x'd out* ordinary wants

195 are left] are *interlined below cancelled* and

196 showy.] *followed by x'd out* He shoul

*In this matter*] *preceded by x'd out* Chalices

197 obliged,] *followed by x'd out* ceteris par

one *has*] *preceded by x'd out* some

possible of] *followed by x'd out* divine worship

gives us the opportunity.] *added on line after cancelled* indicates His desire of the Sacrifice.

society.] *added on line after cancelled* life.
198 *highly regarded*] *preceded by x'd out* regarded regard
199 not to please men] *interlined and marked with arrow for insertion*
Great . . . gift!] *added in lower margin*
200 and charitable,] and *typed above x'd out* of
brethren] *preceded by x'd out* they ig
forgotten] *preceded by x'd out* ignored and
intelligence or culture.] *added on line*
201 even] *preceded by cancelled* or
Who . . . are?] *added in lower margin*
This appears] *preceded by cancelled* First of all
202 this virtue] *followed by x'd out* if preferable
204 1) This . . . then] *opposite page*
and communion . . . self-emptying] *added on line*
This can . . . accepted in] *typed above x'd out* To accept this out of
205 not make] *preceded by x'd out* try
(outwardly)] *interlined with a caret*
customs.] *followed by x'd out* The eight
206 and mitigations] *typed interlined*
207 *his silence*] *preceded by x'd out* is
209 gentle] *preceded by cancelled* and
at least . . . grin!] *added on line*
Let us] *preceded by cancelled* However
210 or because . . . laughing] *interlined*
because] *followed by cancelled* every
This is proper . . . world.] *added on line*
211 worldly] *preceded by cancelled* very
lust,] *preceded by x'd out* Spiritual
When you . . . at!] *interlined*
When] *followed by cancelled* everyone
213 exterior attitude] *preceded by x'd out* in

**Additions and Alterations Not Included in Ditto**

7 *Rule* {is to be understood} as . . . of God.] *added on line*

12 proves . . . Church.] *interlined and marked for insertion*
13 *Read* #13, 14] *added in left margin*
14 N.B.. . . wisdom?] *opposite page*
#16] *added in left margin*
#19] *added in left margin*
English translation . . . emphasis] *opposite page*
15 (Read #29-30.)] *added on line*
17 see . . . Prologue] *added in left margin*
26 St. Gregory's explanation . . . helped] *opposite page*
27 *not* . . . psychological sense.] *added on line*
emphasis . . . truth.] *added on line*
40 see his edition] *interlined and marked with arrow for insertion*
45 (Note . . . office)] *added on line*
54 St. Benedict's asceticism: . . . own.] *opposite page*
55 Cf. *bonum* . . . means] *added on line*
64 ({we} need . . . on this)] *added on line*
N.B.. . . application.] *added on line*
66 Cf. St. Bernard: . . . you.] *interlined*
read] *added in left margin*
67 detachment from results] *added on line*
68 N.B. the *ecstatic* . . . this.] *added on line*
70 But he did . . . murmuring.] *interlined*
3. Conservation of charity:] *added in left margin*
it is not . . . mortification.] *interlined*
71 meaning of . . . please] *opposite page*
unspeakable . . . mature] *opposite page*
80 *Note*: . . . orders.] *opposite page*
I.] *added in left margin before cancelled* 1
n.b. {through} voting] *added in left margin*
i.e.. . . community.] *added on line*
81 Hence . . . diplomacy.] *opposite page*
81–82 False . . . sides.] *opposite page*
82 confidence . . . Spirit] *added on line*
II.] *added in left margin before cancelled* 2
83 but *in foro externo*] *added on line*

The judgement . . . conscience.] *opposite page*

88 III] *interlined above cancelled* 3

89 St. Benedict emphasizes . . . 448).] *opposite page*

91 *wrong idea* . . . characters.] *opposite page*

97 A community . . . character.] *opposite page*

100 (cf. our building committee)] *added on line*

103 community {is} . . . one another.] *opposite page*

104 to emphasize . . . vocation] *interlined*

but above all] *added on line*

105 Note that . . . attitude.] *opposite page*

cf. Confucius . . . *Ching*] *added on line*

106 It is . . . monastery!!] *added in lower margin*

cf. the use . . . life] *opposite page*

"*nonna*" = nun] *opposite page*

107 especially . . . self-love.] *added on line*

109 READ] *added in left margin*

111 or just . . . etc.] *added on line*

112 READ . . . end] *added on line*

114 READ c. 40] *added in left margin*

118 What . . . *doctrina*?] *added on line*

c)] *added in left margin*

119–20 Note that . . . OK.] *opposite page*

121 see Ecclesiasticus 1:16-28] *added on line*

122 understanding . . . speaketh.] *opposite page*

124 *custodienda—recolligenda*] *added on line*

modern . . . mentality.] *opposite page*

*All* should . . . regard.] *added on line*

125 *Disciplinae* . . . steps."] *interlined*

129 {The} reader . . . (Comments?)] *opposite page*

130 *ora et labora*] *added in left margin*

130–31 *Oblati* . . . 323 f.] *opposite page*

131 danger of daydreaming] *added on line*

133 Note: . . . labor.] *interlined*

or 5:30] *interlined*

4½ or] *interlined*

reading permitted] *added on line*

2 to 4 hours] *followed by cancelled* plus

over four] four *interlined above cancelled* five

134–35 *Lectio Divina*: . . . to be done.] *inserted typed page*

134 not *only* . . . *unity*] *opposite page*

central.] *followed by x'd out* The above apply

135 event,] *followed by x'd out* Only specia

135–36 Read . . . Gill.] *interlined*

136 Note: . . . yes.] *interlined*

But we . . . God.] *added on line*

problem . . . prayer.] *opposite page*

137 *obedience, . . . reverence*] *added on line*

143 (a)] *added in left margin*

(b)] *added in left margin*

(c)] *added in left margin*

145 1.] *added in left margin*

2.] *added in left margin*

3.] *added in left margin*

i.e. . . . monastery] *added in left margin*

146 Note: . . . Benedict.] *added in lower margin*

POTESTATE] *interlined above cancelled* VOLUNTATE

152 In the Benedictine . . . what?] *added in lower margin*

153 desire . . . for it.] *interlined*

154 (habit . . . everything)] *interlined*

155 vow of conversion . . . vows.] *added on line*

158 St. Bernard *De Diversis* . . . necessary.] *opposite page*

159 urgency] *added in left margin*

(learn—comment)] *interlined*

162 right way . . . will.] *added in lower margin*

164 cf. St. Paul: 2 Corinthians] *added in left margin*

174 *judgement*] *added on line*

175 unwholesome thoughts] *added in left margin*

they have effects!] *added on line*

working far too much] *added in left margin*

178 *virtù*] *added in left margin*

182 our own private good.] *added on line*

187 correlations . . . regard.] *opposite page*

*conscientia*—. . . implied] *added in left margin*
188 making a deal] *added in left margin*
191 informed] *added in left margin*
192 *cogitationes*!] *added in left margin*
195 three degrees . . . *preference*.] *opposite page*
196 Read *Spirit of Simplicity*] *added on line*
197 The poor . . . want.] *added in lower margin*
199 emphasis . . . content] *added on line*
201 Humility . . . gift of God.] *opposite page*
What . . . complex?] *interlined*
204 emphasis . . . common life.] *opposite page*
207 Behind . . . *reality*.] *opposite page*
He did . . . of us.] *added on line*
should be . . . severity.] *interlined*
230–31 Origen says . . . me . . .'"] *opposite page*
237 *apatheia*?] *added in left margin*
at Monte Cassino] *added on line*
238 Spirituality . . . formation etc.] *added in left margin*
obedience.] *added in left margin*
humility; . . . heart] *added in left margin*
241 Contemplation] *added in left margin*
242 Contemplation not . . . Germanus] *added in lower margin*

# APPENDIX B

## Table of Correspondences:

### *The Rule of St. Benedict*—Lectures and Taped Conferences

| Date | Page # | Opening Words | TMC CD # | Published Tape Title & # |
|---|---|---|---|---|
| 7/11/62 | 153/ 229 | its main points / 1. The archetypal image | 11-3 | The Holy Rule: On Humility (AA2105) |
| 7/20/62 | 231 | b) The true way | 12-3 | The Holy Rule (AA2105) |
| 7/–/62 | 154 | 4. This chapter is one | 13-3 | |
| 7/25/62 | 158 | St. Bernard, *De Diversis* | 14-2 | Conversion (AA2106) |
| 8/28/62 | 173 | I. *The First Degree* | 20-2 | Conversion (AA2106) |
| 9/7/62 | 176 | 3) *Aestimet se homo* | 21-4 | Formation of Conscience (AA2107) |
| 9/19/62 | 155 | This is especially | 22-4 | |
| 9/26/62 | 186 | IV. *The Fourth Degree* | 25-4 | |
| 10/3/62 | 187 | Such silence | 26-3 | The 4th Degree of Humility (AA2108) |
| 10/–/62 | 190 | V. *The Fifth Degree* | 27-3 | The 4th Degree of Humility (AA2108) |
| 10/24/62 | 194 | VI. *The Sixth Degree* | 29-3 | The Vow of Poverty (AA2102) |

| Date | Page # | Opening Words | TMC CD # | Published Tape Title & # |
|---|---|---|---|---|
| 11/7/62 | 199 | Bernard of Monte Cassino | 31-2 | |
| 11/–/62 | 200 | *The basis of this* | 32-1 | |
| 11/–/62 | 201 | VII. *The Seventh Degree* | 34-1 | |
| 12/–/62 | 205 | The Exterior Degrees | 37-4 | |
| 12/19/62 | 207 | IX, X and XI | 35-2 | |

The published tapes are those produced by Credence Communications (Kansas City, MO: 1987– ).

# APPENDIX C
## For Further Reading

### A. Other Writings by Merton on Topics Treated in *The Rule of St. Benedict*


*Basic Principles of Monastic Spirituality*. Trappist, KY: Abbey of Gethsemani, 1957.

*Contemplation in a World of Action*. Garden City, NY: Doubleday, 1971.

"Monastic Courtesy," ed. Patrick Hart OCSO. *The Merton Annual*, 12 (1999), 13–21.

*The Monastic Journey*, ed. Brother Patrick Hart. Kansas City: Sheed, Andrews & McMeel, 1977.

*Monastic Peace*. Trappist, KY: Abbey of Gethsemani, 1958.

*The Silent Life*. New York: Farrar, Straus & Cudahy, 1957.


### B. Significant Writings by Other Authors on Topics Treated in *The Rule of St. Benedict*

#### *The Life of St. Benedict*


St. Gregory the Great. *Dialogues*, trans. Odo J. Zimmerman. Fathers of the Church, vol. 39. New York: Fathers of the Church, 1959.

———. *The Life of St. Benedict*, trans. Hillary Costello and Eoin de Bhaldraithe, commentary by Adalbert de Vogüé. Petersham, MA: St. Bede's Publications, 1993.

* * * * *

Clark, Francis. *The Pseudo-Gregorian Dialogues*, 2 vols. Leiden: Brill, 1987.

———. *The 'Gregorian' Dialogues and the Origins of Benedictine Monasticism*. Leiden: Brill, 2002.

Cusack, Pearse. *An Interpretation of the Second Dialogue of Gregory the Great: Hagiography and St. Benedict*. Lewiston, NY: Edwin Mellen Press, 1993.

Peterson, Joan, M. *The "Dialogues" of Gregory the Great in Their Late Antique Cultural Background*. Studies & Texts, vol. 69. Toronto: Pontifical Institute of Medieval Studies, 1984.

**The *Rule* of St. Benedict**

*RB 1980: The Rule of Saint Benedict in Latin and English with Notes*, ed. Timothy Fry, OSB. Collegeville, MN: Liturgical Press, 1981.

Kardong, Terrence. *Benedict's Rule: A Translation and Commentary*. Collegeville, MN: Liturgical Press, 1996.

*****

Böckmann, Aquinata. *Perspectives on the Rule of St. Benedict: Expanding Our Hearts in Christ*, ed. Marianne Burkhard, trans. Marianne Burkhard & Matilda Handl. Collegeville, MN: Liturgical Press, 2005.

Chittister, Joan. *The Rule of Benedict: Insights for the Ages*. New York: Crossroad, 1992.

———. *Wisdom Distilled from the Daily: Living the Rule of St. Benedict Today*. San Francisco: Harper & Row, 1990.

De Waal, Esther. *A Life-Giving Way: A Commentary on the Rule of St. Benedict*. Collegeville, MN: Liturgical Press, 1995.

———. *Living with Contradiction: Reflections on the Rule of St. Benedict*. San Francisco: Harper & Row, 1989.

Dreuille, Mayeul de. *The Rule of Saint Benedict: A Commentary in Light of World Ascetic Traditions*, trans. Mark Hargreaves. New York: Newman Press, 2002.

Elder, E. Rozanne, ed. *Benedictus: Studies in Honor of St. Benedict of Nursia*. Cistercian Studies [CS], vol. 67. Kalamazoo, MI: Cistercian Publications, 1981.

Henry, Patrick, ed. *Benedict's Dharma: Buddhists Reflect on the Rule of Saint Benedict*. New York: Riverhead Books, 2001.

Stewart, Columba. *Prayer and Community: The Benedictine Tradition*. Maryknoll, NY: Orbis Books, 1998.

Swan, Laura. *Engaging Benedict: What the Rule Can Teach Us Today*. Notre Dame, IN: Christian Classics, 2005.

Vogüé, Adalbert de. *Community and Abbot in the Rule of St. Benedict*, trans. Charles Philippi. CS 5 (2 vols.). Kalamazoo, MI: Cistercian Publications, 1978.

———. *Reading Saint Benedict: Reflections on the Rule*, trans. Colette Friedlander. CS 151. Kalamazoo, MI: Cistercian Publications, 1994.

———. *The Rule of Saint Benedict: A Doctrinal and Spiritual Commentary*, trans. John Baptist Hasbrouck. CS 54. Kalamazoo, MI: Cistercian Publications, 1983.

# INDEX

Aaron: 114
abandonment: 157
*abba*: 54, 82, 105
abbot: xx, xxii–xxiv, xxviii, 5, 44–46, 48, 56, 73, 79–98, 100–105, 110, 115–19, 124–26, 137–38, 148–49, 185, 190–91, 217, 220–21, 226, 228–29, 234, 240; administration of: 82; as *Dom'nus*: 107–108; as father: 14, 81, 98, 103, 147; as instrument: 86; as leader: 103; as representative of Christ: xxiii–xxiv, 5, 80–82, 85, 88, 97, 101, 128; as servant: 89; authority of: 84, 104; commands of: 82–83; decisions of: xxiv, 101–103; desires of: 123; direction of: 90; doctrine of: 81; election of: 79, 98; example of: xxiii, 83–84, 87; faith of: 81; faults of: 84; formation of: 81; guidance of: 97; judgement of: 83, 145, 149; leadership of: 81; limitations of: 84; mission of: 85; obligations of: 80; office of: 90; order(s) of: 56, 145; permission of: 145; responsibilities of: 5, 80; role of: 100–102; rule of: 90; subjection to: 137; supernatural role of: 81; tasks of: 5; teaching of: xxiii, 80, 82; will of: 83, 145
Abbott, Walter, SJ: liv
abjection: 21, 199
Abraham: 171, 211
absolution: 95
abstinence: 114
abuse(s): 72, 151
acceptance: 170, 195, 204
action(s): xii, xxviii, xxx, xxxiii, 31, 51–52, 84, 90, 113, 115, 121, 144, 146, 165, 172, 174–76, 212, 215, 224; divine: l, 51, 65, 134, 211, 215, 223–24; exterior: 155, 172; interior: 172; outward: xxxiii, 51; supernatural: 9
activism: xxvi, 131–32, 134
activity: xxvi, 13, 33, 63, 130–32, 134, 165, 170, 172, 224; creative: xxvii, 136; divine: 223; interior: 168–69
admonition: 125, 220
adultery: 220
adversity: 114
advice: 87, 101–104, 191
Aeneas: 21
affection(s): xxv–xxvi, 21, 27, 81–82, 104–106, 122, 180–81, 229
afflicted: 225
afflictions: 198
*aggiornamento*: liv
aggressiveness: 108, 210–11
Agnes, St.: xxxvii
Ailred (Aelred), St.: 11
aimlessness: xx, 54
Alberic, St.: xxxvii
alertness: 214
Allodi, L.: 48
alms: 225
altar: 29, 124, 127, 197

ambition(s): 90, 123, 160, 171, 175, 198
amusement: 22, 37, 210
Ananias: 140
anchorite(s): xxii, 13, 73–74
angel(s): ix, xxii, 74, 165, 171, 211, 218, 241–42
angelism: 172
anger: 24, 34, 92, 121–22, 171, 175
Anio River: 218–19
Anselm, St.: 224
Anthony, St.: xv, xxxvii, 9, 21–22, 40, 143–44
anxiety: 95–96, 169, 215
*apatheia*: xlix, 24–26, 237
Apennines: 22
Apollo: 18, 244
Apollos: 108–109, 138
*Apophthegmata*: 40
apostle(s): xxiii, 81, 132, 140
apostolate: 13, 21, 85
appetite(s): 121, 134
approbation: 170
architecture: vii
ardor: 64
argument(s): 109, 129, 154
arrogance: 162
art(s): vii, xxvii, 14, 136, 139, 196; fine: 136; liberal: 15; liturgical: 197
*artifex*: 135–36
artisan: 139
artists: 19
Asbury Seminary: xl
ascent: heavenly: 241; pagan: 157; Platonic: 157; spiritual: xlii, 58, 152, 156, 187, 230–31
ascetes: 17, 20–21
asceticism: xvi, xx, xxix, 5–6, 13, 26, 32, 69, 73, 75, 78, 134, 143, 159, 187, 224, 227, 231; Benedictine: xxviii, 152; monastic: xlvi, xlviii
ascetics: 36
aspiration(s): xxxi, 192
assembly: 223
assent: exterior: 80; interior: 80
assistance, divine: 68, 177
Athanasius, St.: xxxvi
atheist(s): 54, 176
atonement: 223
attachment(s): xxvii, 32, 36, 55–56, 144, 180, 182
attention: 51–52, 54, 91, 128, 174, 200, 208, 213–14
Augustine, St.: 36–37, 40, 166, 224
austerity: xviii, 13, 17, 69, 116, 206
authoritarianism: 69
authority: 13, 90–91, 102, 104, 139, 162, 164, 222
autonomy: li
avarice: 73, 139–42; formal: 141

Baker, Augustine: 27
balance: xxvi, 14, 25, 88, 123, 229
Bamberger, John Eudes, OCSO: lxi
baptism: 164, 172
Bartholemew, St.: xxxix, lviii
Basil, St.: xv, xxix, 9, 40, 57, 128, 155, 161–65, 198, 202, 213, 226, 232; WORKS: *Homily 20*: xxix, 155, 161–65; *Long Rules*: 232; *Short Rules*: 128, 202
beauty: 58, 66, 196, 225
behavior: 229
Bellarmine University: xii, xl, lvi, lxi, 6
Benedict of Aniane, St.: 47, 221
Benedict of Nursia, St.: ix–xviii, xxi–xxiii, xxviii–xxxi, xxxiv, xliii, xlvii, xlix–liii, lv, 5–7, 10, 12–39, 41, 43, 45–46, 50, 54–56, 59–62, 64, 68–75, 78–82, 84, 87–89, 91–92, 95–96, 98, 100, 103–104, 107, 110, 112–17, 119, 121–22, 125, 127–29, 132, 137, 139, 141, 143–52, 154–56, 158–61, 165, 168, 170–72, 176–79, 182, 187,

190–94, 202, 206, 209–19, 224, 228, 233–45; as abbot: 26, 217; as ascete: xvii, 18, 20; as author of *Rule*: xii, 243; as beloved of the Lord: 244; as cenobite: xvii, 18, 206; as doctor: 57; as father: 9, 11, 15, 34, 52, 57, 60; as Father of Europe: 16; as father of souls: 26, 96; as Father of Western Monasticism: 9, 25; as guide: xiii, xv, 9–10; as hermit: xvii, 18, 21–26, 219, 234–36; as instrument of God: 11, 57; as lawgiver: 9, 11, 15, 51; as layperson: x; as leader: 12, 243; as master: 52; as miracle worker: 18, 21, 28; as model: xlvii, 5; as model of prayer: xviii; as organizer: 226; as "pneumatic": 227; as quasi–sacrament: xvi, 10; as teacher: 12; as teacher of virtues: 236; as witness: 11, 57; asceticism of: 54, 75; blessing of: 30, 217; body of: 236, 244; calm of: 34; character of: xvi, 5, 28, 36, 243; charismatic acts of: 11; charismatic gifts of: 38; charity of: 127; confidence in: 11; contemplation of: 36, 38, 241; conversion of: 18; death of: 18, 38, 244; detachment of: 19; disciples of: 13, 17–18, 24, 26, 28–29, 233, 236, 241, 244; discretion of: 30, 32, 107, 127; doctrine of: xx, 10–12, 51, 161, 217; education of: 20, 233; example of: 11, 15; experience of: 18, 20; family of: 17, 233; fatherhood of: 7; Feast of: 11; Feast of Translation of: xl, 11–12, 18; fidelity to: 10; generosity of: xvii, 24; genius of: 13, 36; gentleness of: 28; gravity of: 19; heart of: 19, 62; heroism of: 23; holiness of: 217; imitation of: 217; instruction of: 236; intercession of: 11, 217; interior life of: 33–34; intervention of: 9; justice of: 217; kindness of: 28, 36; knowledge of: 9; life of: xvi, xviii, 5, 11, 16–38, 217, 233–45; love of: xv, 9; maturity of: 18–19, 233; mediation of: 9; mind of: xix, xxv–xxvi, 9, 44–46, 81, 98–99, 101, 104, 108, 112, 114, 119, 121, 130, 133, 136, 142, 185; miracles of: 11, 21, 28–29, 217; miraculous deeds of: 243; miraculous knowledge of: 30; mission of: 9, 11, 16, 25; moral qualities of: 36; mortification of: 70; nurse of: xvi, 21–22, 234; ordinary life of: 70; physiognomy of: 36; piety of: 217; practice of: 5, 37; prayer of: 33, 35, 37–38; principle(s) of: 15, 30–33, 35, 95, 116, 127, 193, 209; prophetic power of: 31; respect for: 9; revelation of: 244; sanctity of: 8, 16, 18, 70; seriousness of: 19; severity of: 30, 33; simplicity of: li; sons of: xvii, xix, 8–9, 15, 31, 50; soul of: 9, 36–38, 236, 244; spirit of: xvii–xviii, 8, 11–12, 18, 24, 31–32, 35, 127; spirituality of: 12, 21, 238; sternness of: 30; strength of: 12; teaching of: xviii, xxi, xxviii, xliii, 10–11, 40, 57, 69, 152, 159, 171, 217, 243; temptations of: 234–36; "the Roman": 226–27; thought of: 173; tomb of: 244; trust in: 9; understanding of: 10; union with: 9; virtues of: 11, 15; vision of: xvii, 29, 38, 241–42, 244; vocation of: 22; wisdom of: xxiv, 12, 20; wounds of: 236; youth of: 18–19, 34

Benedictines: viii, x–xi, xv, xix, xlvi–xlvii, 8, 14–15, 18, 50, 108, 129; primitive: lv

benefit(s): 149, 178, 218

benevolence: 13

benignity: 13

Berlin Crisis: xxxix

Bernard of Clairvaux, St.: xi, xvi, xxxvi, xlii, xliv, 10–11, 27, 58, 66–68, 71, 90, 101, 152–53, 155–58, 161, 164–65, 167–68, 178, 196, 198, 202, 210, 217–18, 225, 227; WORKS: *De Conversione*: 58; *De Diligendo Deo*: 66; *De Diversis*: 71, 90, 155, 158; *De Gradibus Humilitatis*: 27, 152–53, 155–57, 164, 167–68; *De Gratia et Libero Arbitrio*: 67; *In Dedicatione Ecclesiae*: 227; *In Natali Sancti Benedicti*: 11, 217–18; *In Tempore Resurrectionis*: 101, 178; *Super Cantica*: 90, 161, 225; *Super Missus Est*: 198
Bernard of Monte Cassino: 48, 125, 144, 199
Bernigaud, Symphorien, ocso: 50
Bersabee (Beersheba): 171
Bethel: 171
Bible: 120, 134–35, 223–24
biography: 135
*bios praktikos*: xxxiv, 214
bishops: 98; Benedictine: 15
bitterness: xxv, 107–109, 113, 153, 188
blasphemy: 114
blessedness: 157, 231
blessing: 29, 106, 110, 114, 116, 127–28, 185, 199, 209, 217
blindness, spiritual: xxx, 149, 179, 181
boasting: 175
Bochen, Christine: lv
body: xxvi, xxxiii, 32, 68, 91, 128, 132, 144, 146, 155, 172, 212, 214, 224, 229
Boherius: 48, 125
boldness: 225
Bollaert, W.: 106
bomb, atomic: xliii
boredom: xx, 54, 183
breviary: Benedictine: 12; Cistercian: 40
brotherhood: 207
Bruno de Jésus-Marie, OCD: 37
Buddhism: xliii
Burch, George B.: 167–68
Butler, Cuthbert, OSB: xix, 18, 40–45, 47–50, 131

Caieta: 21
calm: 36, 96, 120–21
Calmet, Augustin: 49, 99
calumny: 164, 175
Camaldolese: x, xlvi–xlvii, lv
Camillus, St.: xxxviii, lviii
Campania: 240
cantor: 126
Capua: 38, 241
Cardenal, Ernesto: xxxv
care(s): xxii, xxvi, 35, 54, 68, 72, 86–87, 97, 115, 122–24, 129, 174, 200; of souls: 90
carelessness: 32, 111, 124, 174
Carmelites: xv, xxxvi, 8
carpenters: 137
Carthusians: xlvi, 116
Cassian, John: xxxiv, 10, 25, 40, 48, 57, 73, 128–29, 144, 160, 190, 216, 224
Cassino: 241
Catholic Art Association: 135
cellarer: xxv–xxvi, lii, 79, 100, 111, 116, 119–25, 226, 228
cenobite(s): xi, xxii, 51, 72–74, 224
cenobium: xxii, xlvii, 73
ceremonies: 125–26
Cesarius of Arles, St.: 18, 39–40
Ceylon: xxxviii
chalice: 29, 196
change: vii, ix–x
chant: 85, 197, 200
chapter: 129, 153; conventual: 99; general: 99, 196
character: 97, 191, 228
charism(s): liv, 98

charity: xxvii, xxxiv, xlvii–xlix, 7, 13–15, 33, 52, 56, 59–60, 70, 82, 88, 91, 93–95, 97, 101, 107, 110–12, 116, 122, 127, 140, 145, 150, 183, 200, 207, 214–15, 222, 224, 235; fraternal: 13, 15, 129; to neighbor: 15
Charlemagne: 43
chastity: l, 155, 209
chasuble: 196–97
cheerfulness: 209
*chesed*: 223
Chesterton, G. K.: 135
childhood: 19; spiritual: xliii
childishness: 149–50
children: 79, 104, 107, 130–31
China: xxxvi
Chittister, Joan, OSB: lxi
choir: xxvi, 28, 30, 37, 104, 111, 114, 127–28, 130, 153, 197, 220
Christ: xv, xxi–xxii, xxviii, xlv, 7, 9, 13–14, 27, 33, 63, 76, 108–109, 216, 230; abiding in: 86; as carpenter: 15; as exemplar: xxi, 65; as Father: 226; as glory: 163; as Incarnate Word: xxxiv, 134, 215; as King of Peace: xlix; as Life: xxviii, 157; as Light: xxviii, 156–57; as Light of the World: 61, 156; as Lord: 75, 126; as Lord of humility: 198; as Master: 86, 105, 126; as model: 223; as only-begotten Son: 22; as Savior: xlix, 231; as Son of God: xlix; as True King: 75; as Truth: xxviii, 152, 156–57; as vine: xxi, 66, 84; as Way: xxviii, 157; birth of: 165; blood of: 193, 231, 244; body of: 244; charity of: xlix, 94, 145; commands of: 189; contemplation of: xlvi; cross of: xxi, xxvii, xxxii, xlv–xlvi, 71, 145, 163, 204, 224, 231–32; crucified: 198; death of: l, 163, 165; discipleship of: 86; dying with: xxvii, xlviii, 145; following of: xlv, 157–58, 185; fools for: 72; glory of: 165, 204; guests as: xxv, 15, 35, 115–16; heart of: li, 86; humble: xxix, xxxii, 157; humility of: xxii, 76, 160, 165; imitation of: xxviii, xxx, xlvii, l, 80, 157, 165, 185, 223, 231; Incarnation of: xviii, xlviii, 29, 164, 213; *kenosis* of: xxxi; Kingship of: 223; life of: xxiv, 164–65; likeness of: xxi, xlviii, 8, 65, 232; love for: xviii, l, 15, 37; love of: xviii, xxx, 37, 60, 107, 141, 215, 228; members of: xlv, 7, 89, 105; mercy of: 71; mystery of: 76, 134; obedience of: xxiii, xxx, xlvii, l, 76, 185; other people as: xxv; passion of: xxii, xxx, xlv, xlvii–xlviii, 54, 61, 71, 76, 185, 204, 218; poor as: 15, 33; poverty of: 143, 195; redemptive work of: xlvi, 224; resurrection of: xlviii, 61, 163, 172; reverence for: 105; risen: xlviii–xlix; rising with: xlviii; salvation in: xx; self–emptying of: xxxii, xlv, 185, 204, 218; separation from: xlv; sick as: xxv, 15, 33, 114–15; Spirit of: xlviii, 82, 107, 109; strength of: 164; study of: xlvi; sufferings of: xxxiii, l, 163, 204–205; teaching of: 157; union with: xi, xxi–xxii, xxviii–xxxiv, xlviii–l, 71, 76, 86, 144, 156–57, 199, 204, 215; unity in: 88; victory of: 61; virtues of: xxx, 185; voice of: 57; warning of: 21; way of: 157, 160; will of: 86, 157; words of: 125; works of: xxxiv, 215
Church: xxii, xxvii, xliii–xliv, xlviii, 8, 12, 15, 56–57, 59, 61, 74, 85, 94, 98, 109, 134, 145, 148; early: 148, 224; monastic: 81
circator: 118
circumcision: 172
Circumcision, Feast of: xxxvii

circumspection: 102
Cistercians: viii–xi, xv, xix, xxvi, xlvi, lv, 8, 10, 124, 126, 132, 156, 196
Cîteaux, Abbey of: xi–xii, lvi, 10
Civate: 47
civilization: vii
Clairvaux, Abbey of: 227
Clark, Francis: xvi
classic(s): vii–viii, x
Claudel, Paul: 135
Claudius, Emperor: 218
clemency: 13
Clement, St.: 219
cleric(s): x, 34, 78
cleverness: 142, 211
cloister: lvi, 8, 71, 126, 195, 198, 225, 233
clothing: xvii, 89, 100, 140, 162, 194, 205
Cluny, Abbey of: 125, 232
collaboration: 97
collation: 128
Columbia: xxxvi
comfort: 182–83, 195
commandments: 54, 60, 68, 71, 157
commitment: 80
communion: xxxii, 9, 203–204; holy: 78, 104, 244; of saints: 74
Communism: 75, 102
community: x, 16, 207; apostolic: xxvii, 145; Jerusalem: xxvii, 140; lay: x; monastic: xviii, xx, xxii–xxv, xxvii–xxviii, xxxii, xlix–l, 7, 37, 56, 74, 80–82, 84–85, 90–91, 97–152, 194, 200, 206, 218, 220, 226, 228, 233, 239; of goods: 145; of saints: 203; order of: 103–104; religious: 145; representing Christ: 97
compassion: xviii, 167
complacency: 200
complaint(s): 28, 45–46, 80, 112–13, 187, 195
compline: 126, 220
composure: 213
compromise: 31–33, 35, 56
compulsion: 75, 83
compunction: 22, 35, 58, 164, 213
concern: 52, 129
concupiscence: 24
condemnation: 150, 167
conduct: 147, 152, 173, 228
confession: 95, 141, 190–91; general: 193
confessor: 95–96, 190, 193
confidence: xxi, 33–34, 60, 64, 82, 88, 147, 171, 191, 215
conflicts: l, 22, 107
conformism: xxxiii, 169, 206
Confucius: 105
confusion: 56, 168
congregation: 223
Conrad of Eberbach: 230
conscience: xi, xliii, 51, 83, 150, 154, 174, 176, 190, 192, 225; manifestation of: xxxi, xliii, 193
consciousness: 174, 212
consecration, monastic: xvii, 23
considerateness: 110
consideration: xxxi, 186, 200
consolation(s): xxxii, xliv, 22, 32, 66, 70, 74, 78, 152, 183
constancy: 35
Constantine (monk): 17, 233
Constitutions, Cistercian: 98–100
contemplation: xxvi–xxviii, xxx, xxxiv, xlix, 13, 26, 38, 90, 121, 131, 134, 144, 152–53, 156–57, 176, 214, 224, 241
contempt: 91, 109, 157, 187
contention: 109, 209
contentiousness: 109
contentment: xxxi–xxxii, xlv, 140–41, 197–99
control: 104, 120–21, 134, 145, 173, 176
convenience: 28, 110, 182

*conversatio morum*: xii, 23, 46, 156, 227
conversion: xxi, 21, 46, 55, 58; of life: x, 46; of manners: xii, xxviii, l, 23, 46, 155–56
cook(s): xxvi, 119, 125, 137
cooperation: 189, 224
Corinthians: 108
Corn Islands: lv
Corpus Christi, Feast of: xxxviii
correction(s): 95–96, 125, 220
corruption: 19, 179
Cosmas, St.: 219
council(s), Church: xvi
counsel(s): xliii, 20, 77, 79, 101, 138, 192
courage: vii, 55, 94, 156, 170–71, 188
courtesy: li–lii, 102, 129; human: 105; monastic: li–lii, 104–16
Cousins, Norman: liv
covenant: 223
covetousness: 140
cowardice: 56
cowl: 29, 42, 143, 148
Coxe, A. Cleveland: 230
crafts: 14, 136–38
craftsmanship: xxvii, xl, 124, 136
craftsmen: 79, 119, 135–37
creation: xviii, 30, 38
creature(s): 27, 38, 54, 180
Cressy, Serenus: 27
criticism: xxix, 150–51, 175
cross: xxi, xxvii, xxxii, xlv–xlvi, li, 68, 71, 78, 94, 145, 157–58, 185, 198, 204, 224, 230–31; sign of: 25, 236, 239
crucifix: 196
cruelty: 210
Cuban Missile Crisis: xliv
Cuernavaca: lv
culture: vii–viii, xiv, 16, 134, 176, 200
Cunningham, Lawrence S.: xxxvi
*curiositas*: 27
cursing: 209
*custodia cordis*: xvii–xviii, 26–27
custody: 220
customs: l, 30, 106, 205, 207
Cyrilla: xvi, 21–22, 234

Daggy, Robert E.: lxi
dalmatics: 196
Damian, St.: 219
damnation: 140
Dante: 135
Dark Ages: 14–15
darkness: 11, 38, 56, 58, 60–61, 138, 241
David, King: 167, 180
deacon: 104, 240
dean(s): 79, 117–19, 125
death: xliii, 7, 29, 53, 60–61, 63–64, 71, 76, 169, 174, 179, 185–86, 188, 225; to self: xlv
deceit: 62, 172
deception: 21, 62
deference: 102
degradation: 203
Delatte, Paul, OSB: 50, 69
deliberation: 175
delight: 179, 211, 215
delusion: 155, 168, 237
demon(s): 26, 222
dentists: 137
Deodatus, Abbot: 234
dependence: 129, 149, 194; on God: xliv, l, 162
deprivation: xxxi, 200
desert: 22, 72, 74, 114, 144, 160–61, 234
desire(s): xxi, xxiv, xxix–xxxii, li, 13, 20, 22, 24–25, 28, 32, 55–56, 60, 71, 75, 78, 94, 112, 127, 132, 137, 140–41, 144, 156–57, 171, 173, 176, 179–85, 188, 191–92, 197, 205, 218, 234, 236; for God: 22, 225; of gain: 140–41; of God: 51; sinful: 173

despair: 162
destruction: 140, 162
detachment: xxiv–xxv, xxvii–xxviii, xxxi, 15, 32, 45, 67, 97, 102–103, 137, 140–41, 151–52, 180–81, 197
detraction: 109, 175
devil: xviii, 23, 29–30, 64, 73, 109, 125, 141, 152, 160, 191, 235–37
devotion: 108
diabolism: 30, 70
Dickey, Terrell: xxxvi
difficulty: 186
dignity: 15, 41, 91, 104, 106, 161–63, 186–87, 198
diligence: 110, 115, 198
direction, spiritual: 88, 191–93
director, spiritual: xxxi, xliv, 190, 192
disagreement: 112
discernment: xxiii, 190
disciple(s): xxiv, 64, 67, 84, 87, 103, 112, 125, 157, 185, 210
discipleship: xlv, 86
discipline(s): xx, xxii, xlviii, 7, 13–14, 39, 51, 53, 69–70, 73, 75, 107, 119, 125, 131, 172, 175, 183, 192, 220, 223
discomfort: xxxi, 194
discontentment: xxv, 112
discouragement: 169–70, 205
discretion: xxiii, xxv, 12, 45, 83, 93, 95, 107, 116, 120, 127, 160, 179, 243
dishonor: 121
disobedience: xx–xxi, 30, 51, 54, 170, 175, 220
dispensations: 89
disposition(s): 149, 152
Disraeli, Benjamin: vii
dissatisfaction: 150–51
dissension: 56
dissimulation: 109, 209
dissipation: 37
distraction(s): 28, 36, 121, 169, 222
docility: 105, 207, 209
doctors of the Church: 134
doctrine: 53, 58, 77
Dominic, St.: 217
Donaldson, James: 230
Dorotheus of Gaza, St.: 214
doubt: 192
Douzy, Council of: 12
dragon: 229–30, 239–40
drama: vii
duty: xxx, 13, 36, 39, 49, 92–93, 95–96, 108, 125, 129, 145, 151, 183–84, 197

Earll, Mary Beth: lxi
earth: 157
Easter: 61
ecstasy: 68
Ecuador: lv
edification: xvi, 129
education: 7, 228; liberal: 233
effort: 55, 69–70, 75, 118, 161, 215; ascetic: xxxii, 157, 201, 227; human: xlvi
ego: xliv; empirical: xxxi
Egypt: 11, 72, 114, 128
electricians: 137
*emeth*: 223
emotion(s): 210
emotionality: 170
emptiness: 55, 181
enclosure: liii, 10
encouragement: 112
endurance: 22, 188
energy: 24, 108–109, 146, 169
Enfide: 17, 20–21
enlightenment: 86
entertainment: 183
enthusiasm: 156
envy: 109, 150–51, 169, 209, 235
equality: 148
equanimity: xxv
equilibrium: 229

eschatology: 224
essence, divine: 38
eternity: 224
eucharist: 38, 42
Euclid: 186
*eulogias*: 152
Europe: 13, 16
*eutrapelia*: 210
evil(s): xxii, xxv, 56, 61–62, 77, 79, 93–95, 107, 119, 140, 150, 180, 187, 192, 203, 209, 238
exaggeration: 6, 175
exaltation: 166–68, 170–71
excommunication: 6, 99–100, 110, 118, 125, 220–21
exercise(s): 27, 33, 37, 183; bodily: 202; spiritual: 127
Exhilaratus: xvi, 31, 238
*Exordium Parvum*: xi
experience: xliv, 39, 63, 76, 104; human: 20; monastic: 132; spiritual: xxii, 76
expiation: 16
exploitation: 142
expulsion: 125, 220–21
*Exsultent Hodie*: 16

failings: 109–10, 193
fairness: 70
faith: vii, xiv, xxiii, xxv–xxvi, xxxiii, l, 6–7, 9, 11, 14, 21, 33, 52, 55, 58–59, 63–64, 67, 79, 81–82, 88, 97, 105–107, 109, 116, 120–21, 140–42, 149, 159–60, 163, 172, 175, 177, 203–204, 215; bad: 31; theological: 204
faithful: 98, 148
faithfulness: 31, 205, 240
falsehood: xxix
falsity: 168–69, 197
family: Benedictine: 9; monastic: 10, 14, 80, 112, 119, 121
fancies: 75
Farfa, Monastery of: 219
fasting: ix, 31, 45, 116, 125, 150, 202, 220
father(s): xxxiv, 9, 41, 57, 132, 134–35, 161, 191, 202, 207, 216; cellarer as: 122; Church: 49, 57; Cistercian: xi, xv, 7, 10, 155, 196, 217; desert: xlvii, 8, 17, 28, 32, 54, 115–16, 133, 160–61, 190, 203; Egyptian: 40; Greek: 25; monastic: 134; spiritual: 25, 27, 77, 190–92
fault(s): xxxii, xxxiv, xli, 19, 34, 55, 77, 91–93, 96, 110, 124, 147, 191–93, 200, 215, 219–21
fear(s): xxi, xxx–xxxi, xxxiv, xlvii, 13, 34, 51, 55, 80, 96, 131, 168–70, 174, 191, 209, 214–15; holy: 58; of the Lord: xxvi, xxxiv, 21, 60, 67, 94, 102, 115–17, 121, 174–75, 184–85, 214, 229; servile: 60
feasts, liturgical: lviii
feelings: 81, 113, 123, 170, 178; natural: 14, 106
fervor: 70, 108–109, 201
Festugière, A. J., OP: xli, 222
feudalism: 108
fidelity: xi, xviii, 31–32, 35, 70, 83, 154, 181, 215, 218, 223
firmness: xxiii–xxiv, 13, 90
flesh: 24–25, 74, 160, 172, 176, 213, 225, 229, 236
Fleury, Abbey of: 18
flexibility: x
Florentius: xvi, 18, 29
Florentius the Deacon: 29
food: 23, 32, 89, 128, 131, 140, 147, 153, 160, 162, 180, 194, 205; spiritual: 240
foresters: xxxviii
forgetfulness: 174
forgiveness: xxv, 110, 113
formation: monastic: xiii, xx, 7, 51, 77, 192, 238; spiritual: 130

fortitude: 187
Fox, Peggy: lx
frailty: 95; human: xviii, 34, 78
France: 42, 47
Francis of Assisi, St.: 198, 217
Franciscans: 72, 147
frankness: 102
*frater*: 105–106, 226
fraud: 139
freedom: xxiv, l–li, 13, 69, 101, 113, 146, 172, 178, 215
frivolity: 210
fruitfulness: 85–86, 206
frustration: 168, 171, 197, 200
Fry, Timothy, OSB: 47
fulfillment: 129, 134, 179, 224
*Fulgens Radiatur*: xvi, 12, 14–15
futility: xx, 54, 56

gain: xxvii, 140–42
Gardner, W. H.: 69
gatekeeper: 119
*Gaudium et Spes*: liv
generosity: 21, 68, 70–71, 149–50, 183, 186, 218
Genestout, Augustin, OSB: 222
gentleness: 28, 34, 165, 211–12
Germanus of Capua: 38, 241
Gethsemani, Abbey of: ix, xii–xiii, xvi, xxxviii, xli, li, lv–lvii, lxi, 5, 50
gift(s): 87, 149, 151–52, 162, 165, 199, 228; charismatic: xviii, 30, 98, 190; of God: xxvii, 52, 63–65, 68, 136, 138–39, 163, 201–202
Gilby, Thomas, OP: 25, 38, 177
Gill, Eric: xl–xli, 136
Gilson, Étienne: 27, 68
Ginn, Romanus, OCSO: xxxvi
gladness: 113
glory: xxix, xxxiii, 61, 65, 85, 123, 161–64, 172, 196, 199, 205, 209; eternal: 163; false: 161; illusory: 161; of God: 136, 167, 178, 215, 225; true: 161, 163–64
gluttony: 56, 73, 77
God: as almighty Lord: 241; as Creator: xxvii, 136, 180, 241; as Father: xx, xxvii, xlv, 15, 20, 34, 52–53, 61, 66–67, 71, 85–86, 97, 105, 125, 136, 189, 209, 215; as King: 223; as King of Heaven: 197; as Lord: 184, 223; as Love: xxx, 177; as Master: 184; as Person: xvii, 20; as Savior: 52; as source of being: 176; being of: 177; call of: 58; face of: xviii, 35; friendship of: 174; greatness of: 19; image of: xxix, xliv, 7; intimacy with: 22; likeness of: 58, 209; majesty of: 15; mouth of: 63; omnipresence of: 41; omniscience of: 41; plan of: 132; presence of: ix, xxx, 121, 155, 176–77, 181, 187, 225; return to: 55, 57; service of: 6; sons of: xxi, 20, 52, 54, 58, 60, 66, 68, 102, 123; transcendence of: 72; voice of: xxi, 58–60, 62
godliness: 140–41
Goliards: 78
good: xxv, xxxiv, 55, 61–62, 64, 67, 77, 107, 111, 114, 119, 123, 137, 152, 163; apparent: 108, 187; common: 147; material: 139; natural: 125, 137; of community: l, 129–30, 132; of obedience: 54, 110; of others: 178, 204; private: 178, 182; spiritual: 52, 184
*Good Work*: xl–xli, 135–36
goodness: xlv, 55, 62, 203
goods: xxvii, xxxi, 36, 140, 142; earthly: xxviii, 148; heavenly: 16; moral: 163; natural: xxxii, 199; spiritual: xxxii, 163, 199; temporal: 195
Gospel(s): xviii, xxix, 8–9, 12–13, 33, 37, 41, 53, 60, 63, 88, 159, 200, 214, 223
Goth(s): xvi, 28–29, 34

governance, abbatial: xxiv, 45
government: vii
grace(s): xxi–xxii, xxv, xxx, xlv, l, 9, 11, 24–25, 51–53, 55, 58, 61, 63–69, 71, 74, 76, 78, 80, 82, 102, 104, 106, 108, 112, 128–29, 141, 157, 163, 170, 172–73, 177, 187, 189–91, 193, 201, 203, 211, 227–29, 233, 236, 240
grammar: 131
Granada: 37
gratitude: 64, 200, 204, 238
greatness: 163
greed: l, 96, 211
Greeks: 108
Gregory the Great, St.: xii–xiii, xvi, xviii, xxxviii, xlvii, lviii–lix, 14, 16–20, 22, 24, 26, 29, 36, 219, 233, 239, 243; WORKS: *Dialogues*: xii, xvi–xviii, xxxviii, xlvii, lviii–lix, 14, 16–26, 28–31, 33–35, 38, 233–45; authorship of: xvi; credibility of: 16–17; historicity of: xvi, 16–17; spirituality of: 17, 26–27
grief: 181, 236
growth: vii; spiritual: 85–86, 137
Guerric of Igny, Bl.: 11–12
guestmaster: 116, 119
guests: xxv, liii, 15, 35–36, 79, 115–16, 131
guidance: 63, 191
guilt: 170
gyrovagues: xxii–xxiii, 56, 72, 76, 78

habit(s): 175, 233; bad: 70; good: 70
habit, monastic: xvii, 23, 193, 233–34
Haeften, Benedict van, OSB: 48
Hanekamp, Herman: xxxvii
happiness: 16, 69, 141
Haran: 171
hardship(s): 70, 186–87, 189
harmony: 37, 109
Hart, Patrick, OCSO: xxxv, li, lxi, 46, 49
health: 200
heart: xvii, xxiv, xxviii, xlviii, 6, 9, 15, 20, 26–27, 31–32, 35, 52–54, 56, 58–59, 61, 66, 68, 82, 85–87, 89, 97, 103, 109, 112–13, 122, 125, 134, 138, 140, 143–44, 151, 153–54, 159, 166, 171–72, 177, 181, 188–90, 201–202, 209–10, 212–13, 215, 225, 230, 233, 238–39; hardness of: 87, 96; of God: x
heaven: 11, 16, 38, 67, 71, 131, 157, 159, 171, 174, 176–77, 189, 213, 228–29, 241–42, 244
*Heilsgeschichte*: 223
Heli (Eli): 92
hell: 56, 80, 108, 174, 179
hermit(s): 21–22, 36, 50, 73–74, 80, 160–61, 190, 224
Herwegen, Ildefons, OSB: 226–27
hierarchy: x
Hildemar: xli, liii, 44, 47, 77, 89, 100, 120, 125, 130–31, 220–21
history: xiv, 14, 135, 223–24; Church: 135; monastic: 45, 135; salvation: 223; scholarly: 17
holiness: liv, 7, 21, 56, 217, 222, 230, 233–34; of God: 35
Holy Cross, Feast of: xxxix, lviii
Holy Spirit: xx, xxiii, xxxiv, xliii, xlviii–li, liii, 8–9, 11–12, 18–19, 21, 37, 51, 57, 59–61, 72, 77, 82, 86, 90, 98, 101, 105, 107, 180, 191, 207, 215–16, 224
homage: 54
honesty: xxxi
honor(s): lii, 15, 88, 94, 107–10, 116, 162, 178, 197–99, 202, 218, 229
Honoratus: 17, 233
hope: xxx, 54–56, 61, 67, 80, 147, 163, 168–69, 175, 177, 181, 188–89, 193, 223
hopelessness: xxi, 55
Hopkins, G. M.: 69

hospitality: x, 35, 116
hostility: 21, 175, 210, 234
*Humanae Salutis*: liv
humaneness: 112
humanism: 178
*humanitas*: 129
humanities: 14
humanity: xxix, 230
humiliation(s): li, 86, 104, 169–71, 187–88, 192–93
humility: x, xiv, xx–xxii, xxiv–xxvi, xxviii–xxxiv, xl, xliii–xlviii, 5–7, 13–14, 22, 32, 35, 37, 45, 55–57, 64, 69, 76, 80, 87, 101–103, 106–107, 110, 115, 118, 121–22, 127, 132, 136–38, 142, 147, 149–50, 152–218, 224, 230–32, 238; Benedictine: 158, 195; degrees of: xxviii, xxx–xxxiv, xlii–xlv, xlvii–xlviii, 5, 26–27, 41, 121, 152–56, 159, 165–216, 229–32; exterior: 165, 170, 205–208, 214; false: 139, 154; ideal of: 205; interior: xxxiii, 202, 205–206, 208, 212; kenotic: 231; ladder of: xxxiv, 229; spirit of: 205; supernatural: xlvi, 201; way of: 157
humor: xlii, 207, 210–11
Hus, John: xliii
hypocrisy: 56, 62, 121

ideal(s): Benedictine: 10; false: xlvi; monastic: 43, 196, 205
identity: xxxi, xlv, 186
idleness: 13, 131
idol(s): 168, 237
illusion(s): xxii, xxvi, xxix–xxxi, xliv, liv, 19, 75, 110, 131, 139, 141, 162–63, 169–70, 179, 181
imagination: 177
*Imitation of Christ*: 134, 157–58
immaturity: 102
impatience: 107, 198
imperfection(s): 77, 90, 102
imprudence: 20
impurity: 73, 211
Incarnation: xviii, xlviii, 29, 164, 213
Incas: 106
inconstancy: 131
indifference: 96, 197
indigence: 141
individuality: 144
inertia: xx, 54, 56
infirmarian: 115–16, 119
infirmity: 116, 149, 163–64
initiative: xxv
injustice: l, 89, 93, 175, 186
Innocent, St.: xxxix
insecurity: xxix, 169–70
insensibility: 207
insincerity: 201
inspiration: 18, 112, 215
instability: 78, 109, 209
insult(s): xxxi, 186, 198
integration: xxvi
integrity: 228
intellect: 225
intelligence: 58, 200, 228
intention(s): 62, 144, 218
intimacy: 86
intoxication: 220
introspection: xviii, 27
introversion: 27
irony: 211
Isaac: 171, 211
Isaias (Isaiah): 60–61, 180–81
isolation: xxxiii, 204
Israel: 92, 117, 223
Italy: xvii, 13, 21

Jackson, Augustine, ocso: lxi
Jacob: 171
James, Bruno Scott: xxxvi
James, St.: 209
Jansenism: 49

Jaramillo, Guillermo: xxxvi
jealousy: xxix, 96, 104, 108–109, 150, 169, 175, 209
Jean de Fécamp: 224–25
Jeremiah: 163, 180–81
Jerome, St.: 48, 195, 229–31
Jews: 61, 114
Joan of Arc, St.: xliii
John Climacus, St.: 229
John of the Cross, St.: xv, 8, 25, 37–38, 77–78, 107, 179–81
John the Baptist, St.: 164, 244
John the Evangelist, St.: xlvii, 60–61, 66, 84
John XXIII, Pope: liv
jokes: 210–11
joy(s): xxi, xxxiv, xlix, 15, 22, 53–54, 65, 71, 107, 163, 178, 195, 197, 199, 202, 210–11, 213, 215, 224; perfect: 198
Judas Iscariot: 125–26
Jude, St.: xxxix, lviii
judgement: xliii, 60, 80, 88–89, 93, 98, 100, 102, 117, 138–39, 145, 151, 174, 176–77, 185, 191
Julian the Apostate, Emperor: 219
junior(s): xxv, 104–106, 110, 118, 122
Jupiter: 18
just: 11, 77
justice: xxiv, 24, 36, 82–83, 93–94, 101, 109–10, 140, 143, 163, 184, 209, 217, 222
justification: 138, 163

Kandy, Ceylon: xxxviii
Kardong, Terrence, OSB: xvi
*kenosis*: xxxi
*kerygma*: 223
Kinder, Terryl N.: 217
kindness: xxiii–xxiv, xxvi, 28, 86, 90–91, 93, 104, 122, 201
Kingdom of God: xxi, l, 54, 71
knowledge: 89, 135, 177, 191, 233; God's: 177, 179; of God: 134, 163, 184; spiritual: xxii, 20, 76; worldly: 20
Kramer, Victor A.: xvi
Krushchev, Nikita: xxxviii

labor(s): xxviii, 16, 22, 35, 63, 108, 133, 136, 140, 148, 215; apostolic: 132; ascetic: xxi, 69; clerical: 132; dignity of: 15; intellectual: 136; manual: xxvi, xlviii, 10, 14, 37, 130, 132–33, 225; monastic: 149
ladder: golden: 229–30; Jacob's: 41, 171–72, 230
last things: 174
Lateran Monastery: 233
Latin America: lv
lauds: 11, 127, 133
laughter: xxxiii, 173, 207–12; spiritual: 211; worldly: 210
law: 60, 75, 78, 95, 102, 207; Benedictine: 11, 13; canon: 98–100, 142, 190; letter of: 94–95; monastic: 13; natural: 111, 178; New: 94; of God: 24, 69, 82–83, 94; Old: 93, 207; Roman: 227; spirit of: 94–95
laziness: 56, 218
learning: 14–15, 20, 48
Le Bail, Anselme, OCSO: 50, 182
Leclercq, Jean, OSB: xvi, 49
*lectio divina*: xxvi, xli, xlviii, lviii, 63, 130, 134–35, 223–25
leisure: xxi, 69, 225
Lemercier, Gregorio, OSB: lv
Lent: 40, 134, 185
Leo, Brother: 198
Leo the Great, St.: 40–41, 207
Levites: 236
levity: 32
liberty: xxxi, l, lii, 69, 139, 185

life: vii, xxvi, 61, 85, 131, 225; active: xviii, xxxiv, xlix, 8, 24, 153, 156, 214, 225; anchoritic: xlvii; apostolic: 8; ascetic: xxxiv, xlix, 160, 214; Benedictine: xiv, xviii, xlvii, lii, liv, 8, 14, 16, 24, 152, 160; bodily: 176; cenobitic: xlvi, 13, 80, 92; Christian: xiv, xlviii, 14, 159, 203, 228; Cistercian: 196; common: xi, xviii, 32, 148, 204, 228; communal: xxxv, 106, 145; community: l–li, 13, 108, 116, 120, 152; consecrated: 78; contemplative: xi, xxi, xxvi, 38, 71, 90, 131, 156, 216, 225; eremitic: 13; eternal: 80, 140, 157, 161; everlasting: 61, 80, 157, 185; family: 14; hermit: xlvi, 80; hidden: 22; humble: 22; inner: 176–77; intellectual: 78; interior: xxvi, xxviii, liv, 37, 51, 63, 130–31, 133–34, 152–53, 176, 188, 191; monastic: xii, xiv–xv, xvii–xix, xxii, xxv–xxviii, xxxiii, xliv, xlvi–xlviii, liii–liv, lvi, 5, 8, 10–11, 13–14, 18, 37, 46, 49–51, 64, 69–72, 80, 104, 106, 108, 119, 123, 142, 145, 152–53, 156, 160, 182, 189, 200, 205–206, 211, 219; of prayer: xxxvi, 28, 130–31, 136, 142; of unreality: xxi; ordinary: ix, xxxiii, 15, 65, 70; present: xxxiv, 171, 214; priestly: 78; regular: xxiii, 78, 118; religious: 71, 78–79, 233, 238; secular: 78; solitary: 13; spiritual: xiv, xix, xxvii, xxxii, 6, 28, 35, 46, 51, 58, 63, 72, 76–77, 129, 134, 136–37, 144, 159, 173–74, 177, 190, 208; with God: 134; worldly: 13

light: 38, 60–61, 176–78, 191, 241; deifying: 53, 58, 65; divine: 58; inner: 53; of God: 11, 25, 242; of life: 53, 60; of love: xxi, 65

likeness, divine: 203

limitations: 109

literature: vii, 15, 135, 233

littleness: 231

liturgy: xvi, xlviii, 11, 41, 59, 79, 134–35, 200, 227; of the hours: xii, 130

logic: 131, 172

longanimity: 34

Louis XIV, King: 49

Louisville, KY: xii, xxxiv, xxxvi, lxi, 6

love: xi, xiv, xxi, xxiv, xxix–xxx, xliv, l, 6–7, 9, 13–14, 16, 21, 24–25, 35, 52, 54, 60, 65, 67, 69, 71, 86–88, 95, 97, 107–108, 110, 113–14, 116, 123, 125, 139, 146, 153, 156, 169–70, 184, 187, 189, 203, 207, 211, 214–16, 225; divine: xx, 51; ecstatic: 68; filial: 94, 105; for Christ: xviii, l, 15, 37; fraternal: 228; God's: xvi, xxx, 10, 20, 22, 53–54, 62–64, 94, 114, 177, 189; humble: 229; inordinate: 27; interior: 204; mutual: 7; of abbot: 228–29; of brothers: 37; of Christ: xviii, xxx, 37, 60, 107, 141, 215, 228; of enemies: 189; of God: xiv, xvii, xxiv, l, 6, 13, 15, 20–22, 37, 55, 60, 73, 131, 153, 184–85, 204; of Holy Spirit: 60; of monastic tradition: xv; of neighbor: 37, 189, 204; of others: xxiv, 204; of poor: xviii, 37; of *Rule*: xiv–xv, 6; of St. Benedict: xv, 9; prevenient: 66; pure: 229; spiritual: 87; steadfast: 223; supernatural: 68

Luke, St.: 41

lust: 211

luxury: 162, 197

lying: 175, 201–202, 209

Mabillon, Jean: 14

Macarius, St.: 40, 221

MacCarthy, Fiona: 136

magisterium: 12

magnanimity: 55

malice: 77

Maloney, Bp. Charles G.: xxxvi

man, fallen: 51, 54–56
*mandatum*: 125–26
María de la Encarnación: 107
Maritain, Jacques, 25
marriage: vii, 8; mystical: xi
Martène, Edmond: xix, 7, 44, 47, 49, 100, 125, 137, 144, 198–99, 202–203, 207, 213–14
Mary, Blessed Virgin: xxxvi, xxxix, 68, 213, 219, 232
Mary of Bethany, St.: 90
Masai, François: 222
Mason, Herbert: xxxix
Mass: 197, 220; high: 129
Massignon, Louis: xxxix
master of novices: xxxi, 190, 192
master of students: 190
masters, spiritual: 135
materialism: 176; religious: 96
matins: 127
maturity: xxv, 85, 107, 118, 123, 214, 228, 233
Maur, St.: 28–29
Maurists: 49
McCann, Justin, OSB: lx, 6, 8, 15, 23, 26–27, 29, 31–33, 37, 39, 42, 44–46, 51–71, 73–82, 84, 86–91, 93–96, 98, 100, 102–103, 105–108, 110–118, 120–27, 129, 131–32, 137–38, 141–42, 144–49, 151–53, 159, 161, 166, 168, 170–71, 174–79, 182, 184–86, 188–90, 192, 194, 201–202, 204, 206, 208–10, 212–13, 219–21, 226–29
McCormick, Anne: lx
McDonnell, Thomas P.: 105
Meade, Mark: lxi
meals: 45, 127–28, 130, 147, 220, 235
meaning: 176–77
mechanics: 137
meditation: xxviii, 8, 13, 47, 51, 69, 79, 134, 153, 189, 205, 213, 224–25; Benedictine: 174; Buddhist: xliii
meekness: 34, 62, 109, 209
Meeuws, M. D.: 16
Mège, Antoine: 49
memory: 9, 153, 225
mercenaries: 131
mercy: xviii, xxx, li, 14, 62, 93–94, 109, 116, 149, 164, 167, 177, 193, 209, 221, 223; of God: xxi, 19, 63–64, 66–67, 71, 164, 201
merits: 29, 67, 104, 125, 149, 206, 215
Merton, Thomas: viii–xi, 131, 158; as master of students: li, 5; as novice master: xii, xxxiv, xlvi, li; as translator: 14, 65; dissatisfaction of: lv; Fourth and Walnut experience of: liv; hermitage of: xliii, lvi; humor of: xlii–xliii; journals of: xxxv; monastic aspirations of: xlvii; monastic commitment of: liv; monastic vision of: liii, lvi; monastic vocation of: liv; restlessness of: lv; sensitivity of: xliv; turn to the world of: liv; vocation crisis of: lv–lvi; WORKS: *Basic Principles of Monastic Spirituality*: xlviii–xlix; *Cassian and the Fathers*: xiii, xlii, 73, 128; *Cistercian Contemplatives*: xi; *Conjectures of a Guilty Bystander*: liii–liv; "Conquistador, Tourist and Indian": 135; *Contemplation in a World of Action*: lvi; "Death": 136; "For My Brother: Reported Missing in Action, 1943": 136; *Introduction to Christian Mysticism*: xv, 26, 124, 192; "Japanese Tea Ceremony": 136; "Letter to Pablo Antonio Cuadra Concerning Giants": 135–36; "Life of the Vows": xii–xiii, 5, 46; "Monastic Courtesy": li–lii; *Monastic Journey*: xlviii–li, 46; "Monastic Observances": xii–xiii, 6, 192; *Monastic Peace*: xlix–li; *Mystics and Zen Masters*: 27, 105; *Nativ-*

ity Kerygma: xxxvii; *Pre–Benedictine Monasticism*: xiii, xlii, 221–22, 226–27; *School of Charity*: xxxv, xlvi, xlviii–xlix, lv, 49; *Search for Solitude*: xxxvi–xxxix, xlix, liii–lv; "Seven Qualities of the Sacred": 136; *Silent Life*: xi, xlvi–xlvii; "Sincerity in Art and Life": 136; *Spirit of Simplicity*: 196; "Spiritual Direction": 192; *Spiritual Direction and Meditation*: 192; *Survival or Prophecy?*: 49; *Thomas Merton on Saint Bernard*: 90, 196; *Thomas Merton Reader*: 105; *Turning Toward the World*: xvi, xxxviii–xli, lv, lvii; "Vine, The": 136; *Waters of Siloe*: xi; *What Ought I to Do?*: 203; *Wisdom of the Desert*: 203; *Witness to Freedom*: xxxix, lv
Middle Ages: 44, 78, 186, 219
midrash: 223
Migne, J.–P.: 7, 47, 49, 128
Milan: 47
mildness: 13, 140
mind: viii, xxiii, xxvi, 13–16, 19, 26, 52, 61, 76, 87, 89, 95, 120, 128, 132, 134–35, 146, 154, 158, 174, 178, 186, 198–99, 213–14, 224, 239, 241; mature: 113; Roman: 227
miracle(s): 63, 241
miserliness: 141
misery: 167, 225
mixt: 127–29
moderation: x, xviii, 209
modesty: 138, 165, 201, 207, 211
Molesme, Abbey of: xi, lv
monastery: viii–ix, xi, xiv, xx, xxiii–xxv, xxvii–xxviii, xxxiii, xxxv, xlviii, li–lii, 5–6, 13, 23, 28, 30–33, 39, 42, 44, 48–49, 51, 70–71, 80, 82, 85, 88, 91, 94, 97–99, 101, 103–106, 112, 117–24, 127–28, 135, 137, 140–45, 147, 149, 151, 175, 182, 185, 195–96, 199, 205–207, 209–11, 217, 219, 227, 232–34, 238–40, 244; as ghetto: lii–liv; as house of God: 71; as mother: 231–32; as school of charity: li; as school of freedom: li; as school of God: 71; as school of obedience: 52; as school of the Lord's service: xxi, li, 52, 69, 71, 76; Benedictine: viii, xi, xxvi, 122, 195; Cistercian: viii, 195
monastic(s): x
monasticism: xlix, liv, 9, 72; Benedictine: xli, 9, 116; Cistercian: 190; in Italy: xvii, 219; oriental: xxii, 8, 13, 72; pagan: 72; Western: 9, 190
money: xxvii, 140–44, 151–52, 162
monk(s): viii–ix, xi–xii, xv–xvi, xviii, xx, xxiv–xxviii, xxx, xxxii–xxxiv, xlvi–liii, lvi, 5–14, 18, 20, 23, 28, 30–35, 42, 44, 46–48, 51, 56–57, 62, 69–70, 72–73, 75–77, 79–85, 88, 90–91, 99, 102–106, 108–14, 116–20, 129–30, 132–35, 138–42, 144, 146, 148, 150–55, 159–60, 170, 174–76, 183, 185–86, 189–91, 194–202, 206–14, 216–17, 219, 222, 237–40; ancient: 195, 222; as peacemaker: xlix; as soldier of Christ: xviii, 29, 227; bad: 77, 200; Benedictine: 147, 156; Cappadocian: 128; cenobitic: xx; classes of: 86–87; early: 141; glorious: 202; holy: 202; mature: xxv, lii, 119–21, 124, 150; oriental: 219; perfect: 199; types of: xx, xxii–xxiii, 71–79; wandering: xxii, 72
Monte Cassino: viii, xvi–xvii, 17–18, 29–30, 36, 39, 43–48, 237
Monte Taleo: 219
morality, Christian: 174
More, Gertrude: 27
mortality: 225
mortification: xxv, 10, 24, 27, 70, 107, 138, 156, 163, 225

Moses: 11, 114, 117, 236
Mount Trevi: 219
murmuring: xxv, 45–46, 56, 70, 112–14, 150–51, 170, 220, 238
Muslims: xxxix
mutism: 62, 207
mystery: 65, 76, 134; of Incarnation: xlviii; of union: xlix; paschal: xxi, xlvi
mystic(s): x, 120, 224
mysticism: 38; Benedictine: 27
myth: 224

Nanayakkara, Bp.: xxxviii
Naples: 18
naturalness: 112
nature: 30, 32, 68, 89, 178, 228–29; domineering: 96; fallen: 90; gifts of: 87; human: xxviii, xlix, 14, 32, 90, 141, 154, 159, 162, 166; obstinate: 96; sensible: l; sinful: 32
needs: xlix, 75, 88, 96, 110, 125, 130, 147–51, 177, 223, 226, 228
neglect: 111
negligence: 28
Nero, Emperor: 17, 218–19
Nestorianism: 222
New Testament: 41, 57, 223
Nicaragua: xxxv
*nonnus*: 105–106
nothingness: xxxii, xliv, 19, 22, 164, 166, 204
nourishment: 130; bodily: 127; spiritual: xvi, 127–28, 232
novice(s): ix–x, xv, xvii–xviii, xxv, xxviii, xxxiv–xxxv, xxxvii, xlii–xlv, li, lvi, 23, 51, 54, 70, 99, 153, 158, 189–90, 232
novitiate: xiii, 44, 48–50, 134–35, 192
nuns: viii, 18, 106, 111
Nursia: 17, 233

obedience: x, xii, xviii, xxi–xxiii, xxx–xxxi, xliii, xlvi–xlviii, l–li, lvi, 4–9, 13–14, 16, 29, 31–33, 37, 52, 54, 56, 59, 61, 68–70, 73, 76, 79–80, 83, 86–87, 103, 110, 112–13, 132, 137, 146, 152, 155, 159–61, 171, 173, 183–89, 207–208, 224, 229, 238; mutual: lii, 110
oblate(s): viii, xxxv, 130–31
obligation(s): 5, 23, 83, 113, 124, 134, 145, 217
observance(s): 207; exterior: 205; monastic: xi, l, 10, 39, 46, 67, 70, 79, 94, 102, 106–107, 183
O'Callaghan, Tommie: lx
O'Connell, Patrick F.: x, xiii, xv, lv, 26, 73, 221
office: divine: xii, xxvi, 6, 8, 39, 42, 45, 59, 63, 79, 130, 134, 220; monastic: 115, 129, 197–98; night: 40, 45, 130, 241
officers, monastic: xxv–xxvi, 5, 39, 79, 100, 103, 116–19, 122
Old Testament: 41, 57, 72, 223
openness: xxxi, lvi, 81–82
oppressed: 225
opprobrium: 186
*opus Dei*: xii, xxvi, 6, 14, 114
oratory: 220, 244
order: 35–36, 127, 207; good: 35, 51, 119; material: 89; of charity: 104; of community: 79, 104; right: xxix, 168; spiritual: 89, 195; temporal: 171
order(s): active: 85; mendicant: xxii, 72; monastic: 48, 85
ordinances: 13
Origen: 230–31
Origenism: 222
ornaments, liturgical: 196–97

Pachomius, St.: xvii, 18, 40, 222, 226
pacification: 172

paganism: 30
pain: 53, 188
painting: vii
Palumbus: 219
Paphnutius, Abbot: 221
paradise: 71, 230–31
Pascal, Blaise: 135
passion(s): xlix–l, 20, 24–25, 73, 96, 106–107, 167, 173, 178, 185, 187, 210–11
passivity: xliv, 56
Pasternak, Boris: xxxix
paternity: 226
patience: xxv, 34, 53–54, 64, 71, 77, 91, 107, 111, 115–16, 120–22, 140, 147, 186–88, 218
Patricius: 240
Paul, St.: xlv, 68, 82, 94–95, 108–109, 133, 140, 163–64, 172, 185, 227
*Pax Bulletin*: xxxix
Pax Movement: xxxix–xl
peace: xxxii–xxxiii, xxxvi, xlix, 11, 13–16, 26, 36, 53, 62, 69, 82, 85, 95–96, 107–109, 128–30, 149, 157, 163, 170–71, 187–89, 193, 195, 197–200, 207, 209, 213, 217, 224, 238; interior: xlv, 37, 62; monastic: xlvi, l; with brethren: 62
peacefulness: xxvi, 120, 132, 136
Pearson, Paul M.: lxi
Peers, E. Allison: 25, 77, 107, 181
Peguy, Charles: 135
Peifer, Claude, OSB: 47
penalties: xli, 219
penance: xviii, 6–8, 13, 21–22, 24, 32, 68, 70, 78, 100, 185, 218, 220, 236
penitent(s): 71, 95
Perez, Antonio: 48
*Perfectae Caritatis*: liv
perfection: xxxiv, 13, 57, 73, 115, 121, 125, 172, 177, 184–86, 189, 200, 214
perfectionism: xxx, 173
permission(s): 30, 32, 145–46, 148
Perpetua, St.: 229–30
perseverance: xxiii, 32, 77, 187–88
*persona*: xxxi, 186
personalism: 105, 228–29
personality: xxxi, 186
personhood: xxxi, 59, 89, 94, 110, 122, 172, 186, 191, 228
Peru: 106
Peter (deacon): 241, 243
Peter, St.: 109, 125–26, 133, 164
Peter Damian, St.: 207
Peter of Celle: 225, 232
pharisaism: 84, 139, 167–68, 214
philosophy: 134–35, 172; classical: 135; modern: 135; scholastic: 135
Picard, Max: 135
piety: xxxiii, 6, 8–9, 112, 120, 202, 217, 234
pilgrim(s): liii, 36, 88, 225
Pius XII, Pope: xvi, 12–16
Placid, St.: 28–29
play: 210
pleasure: 75, 78, 101, 128, 137–38, 141, 176, 179, 187, 199, 206, 233, 236
Pliny the Elder: 218–19
Poemen, Abbot: 203
poets, religious: 135
politeness: 110
pomp: 162
poor: xviii, xxviii, xxxi, l, 15, 37, 88, 124, 141, 148, 195, 197, 225, 231; in spirit: 28
pope(s): vii, 7; Benedictine: 15
popularity: 169
Porter, Thomas Aquinas, OCSO: xlviii
porters: 79
positions: 197, 199
possessions: xxvii, 32, 140–44, 152, 231, 233
possessiveness: 144
postulant(s): xxxv–xxxvi, lvii

poverty: xviii, xx, xxv, xxvii–xxviii, xl, xliv, l, 5, 10, 22, 30–33, 96–97, 113, 122, 131, 140, 146, 148, 152, 155, 194–97, 199–200; monastic: 139, 142–52, 194; spiritual: li
power: l, 13, 15, 36, 60, 68, 81, 104, 162–64, 168, 178; of God: 19, 55, 64, 161; of Satan: 223
practice(s): vii, xxviii, xlv, 5, 13–14, 70, 77–78, 84, 110, 153–56, 192, 199, 202, 205–206, 214
praise: 14, 21–22, 37, 63, 65, 67, 114, 131, 138, 165, 202, 234
*praxis*: xiii, xxviii, 25, 153
prayer: ix, xviii, xxi, xxv–xxvii, xxxii, xxxiv, 6, 8–9, 11–14, 16, 21–22, 28–29, 32–37, 40, 42, 52, 55, 57–58, 62, 64, 66, 68–70, 74, 113, 121, 125, 127–28, 130, 134, 136, 142, 153, 176, 201, 205, 213, 224–25, 237, 240, 244; communal: li; formal: xxvi, 130; interior: xviii, 35; liturgical: xlviii; mental: 28, 30, 33; of petition: 38; of supplication: 38; personal: li; private: xxvi, 35, 130; public: xxvi, 130
presumption: 160
pretense: 197
pretentiousness: 165
pride: xxix, xxxi–xxxii, xlii, xlv, 27, 56, 73, 103, 129, 138, 156, 159–63, 165–66, 168–71, 175, 191–92, 198–99, 201, 206, 220, 222, 239
priest(s): 18, 26, 34, 79, 104, 106, 119, 135, 220
prime: 133
printing: 136
prior: 44, 56, 79, 100, 119
productivity: 132–33
profession, monastic: xii, 11, 75, 99, 131, 193, 227
progress, spiritual: xxxii, 86, 172
promise(s): xii, 63, 131, 134, 158, 240
property: xxvii, 99–100, 140, 142–43, 148
prophecy: l
prophets: 41, 61, 63, 72, 167
proprietorship: xxvii, 143–45, 148
prosperity: 96, 114
providence, divine: l, 13, 142, 147
prudence: xxiv–xxv, xxx, 13–14, 70, 101, 107, 120–21, 160, 184
psalms: 41–42, 166, 170, 177; gradual: 230; invitatory: 59; messianic: 204
psychology, religious; 73
publican: 139, 167, 189, 214
punishment(s): 6, 29, 39, 79, 89, 93, 104, 112, 124, 131, 150, 174, 177, 195, 219–21; corporal: 28, 56, 91, 125, 220
purification: xlvi, 86; ascetic: xlix
Purification, Feast of: xxxvi
purity: xi, xlix, 10, 21, 211, 228; of conscience: 27; of heart: xviii, xxxiv, 30, 73, 214–15

qahal: 223
Quechua: 106
Quemoy: xxxvi
quiet: 27, 36, 69, 214, 225, 240
Qur'an: xxxix

Rancé, Armand de: 49
rank, monastic: x, 103–104, 118, 202
Ravenna: 224
reader: 119, 127–29
reading: xxvi, 14, 39, 127–30, 133, 153, 206, 224–25; public: 128, 134; sacred: 132; spiritual: xx, xxvi, 63, 134
realism: 45
reality: xxix–xxx, xlvi, 6, 22, 35, 55, 75, 107, 132, 166, 169, 171, 173, 176, 178, 207

reason: 58, 134, 162; natural: 58; right: 70
rebelliousness: 56, 170
recollection: 62, 124, 128, 134
redemption: xlviii, 163, 224
refectory: xxvi, xlii–xliii, lii, 111, 118, 125–29, 178
reflectiveness: xxvi, xxviii
reform, monastic: xv, liii–liv, 10
regression: 92
regularity: xxii, xxxii, 48, 73, 84, 200
rejection: 54, 169–70
relationships: 173
relaxation: 32
religious: 96, 113, 126, 145, 188, 190, 195, 198; choir: 126; mature: 122; neurotic: 91; worthless: 200
Renaissance: 48, 178
renewal: liii, lvi
renunciation: l, liv, 148; of self: xvii, 24, 32, 80
reparation: 112, 114
repose: 16
reputation: 21, 96, 118, 198
research: 136
resentment(s): xxxi, 92, 175, 187
resignation: xlv, 157
resistance: 26, 35, 56, 83, 113, 188, 223
respect: xxxii, 19, 45, 54, 81, 104–107, 109–10, 123, 139, 147, 186–87, 198–200; mutual: xxv, 82, 104; of persons: 87, 149; supernatural: 109
responsibility: xxiii, xxv–xxvi, l, 78, 80, 83–84, 101, 118–19, 123–24, 132, 228
rest: xxix, 170, 224
restlessness: 96, 239
resurrection: 163, 224, 231
retirement: 21
revelation: 105, 134
reverence: 68, 102, 105–106, 137–39, 186
reward(s): 108, 125, 149, 171, 174, 191, 201–202, 215
rhetoric: 131
rich: 88
Richardson, Nelson: lvii
riches: 141
righteousness: 24, 67
rights: 13, 16, 93, 110, 143
rigidity: 46
rigorism: 48–49
ripeness: 120
risk: 218
rivalry: 175
Roberts, Alexander: 230
Romanus: 23, 234–35
Rome: xxxvi, 17–19, 22, 218–19, 233–34
Rosweyd, Heribert: 40
Rousset, Suzy: 91–92
rudeness: 111
Rufinus: 40
rule(s): xxii–xxiii, 30, 40, 57, 73, 75–77, 150, 183, 226, 234; common: xxxiii, 206–207
*Rule* of St. Benedict: viii–xiv, xviii, xl, xlix, li–lii, lv–lvi, 5, 12–13, 16, 18, 24, 26, 56, 98, 101–102, 111–12, 114, 125, 130, 132, 146, 150–52, 158, 160, 173, 183–85, 205, 219, 227, 229; and legal code: xx, 51; and *Rule of the Master*: 221–22; as guide: x, xiii, 51; as spiritual not legal document: ix–x, 51, 77; authority of: 12; commentators on: x, xix, xxviii, xli, lii–liii, 7, 46–50, 99–100, 133, 154–55, 194, 197, 219–21; date of: xviii, 18, 39; discipline of: xx, 51, 125, 220; essence of: xlvii; exceptions to: 206; flexibility of: ix; foundation of: 159; guidance of: xxxiv; heart of: xx, 5, 79, 159–60; horarium of: 39; integrity of: xii; interpretation of: 44–46; language of: 42; letter of: ix, xi–xii, liii; literal

application of: xi; love of: xiv–xv, 6, 8; mitigations of: 206; moderation of: ix; obedience to: xxiii; personalism in: 228–29; principles of: xx, xxiv, 5, 50–51, 88–97, 125, 127; purity of: xii; purpose of: xlviii–xlix, 6; realism of: xxv; Roman character of: 226; sources of: xviii, xxxiv, 40–42, 216; spirit of: ix, xii, xxvii, liii, 6, 50, 144; spiritual ideas of: xx, 50; structure of: 27, 79; study of: xiv–xv, 7–9, 51; teaching of: 9, 50–51, 153; text of: xix, 42–46; themes of: xx–xxi; theology of: xx–xxi; theories of: xvi; values of: ix–x; violations of: 192, 219–21; Prologue: xx–xxi, 5–6, 8, 18, 26, 40, 51–71, 74–76, 117, 152–53, 159, 161, 226–28; c. 1: xx, xxii–xxiii, 71–79, 227; c. 2: xxiii–xxiv, 56, 79–93, 96, 226, 228; c. 3: 31, 44, 79, 98–103, 220; cc. 4–7: 79; c. 4: 15, 27, 37, 40, 70, 122; c. 5: 56, 70, 80, 112–13, 184–85; c. 6: 44, 209; c. 7: xx, xxviii–xxxiv, xlii–xlvii, 6–7, 41, 48, 57, 60, 76, 121, 152–61, 165–216; cc. 8–20: xii; c. 9: 45; c. 17: 42; c. 21: 23, 79, 117–18; c. 22: 6, 118; cc. 23–30: 219; c. 23: 70, 125; c. 24: 125, 220; c. 25: 220; c. 27: 118; c. 28: 86, 125; c. 29: 220; cc. 30–38: 119; c. 30: 79, 125; c. 31: lii, 29, 79, 110–11, 116, 119–24, 226, 228; c. 32: 79, 119, 124–25, 220; c. 33: 32, 40, 142–48, 226; c. 34: 70, 112, 142, 148–51; c. 35: 40, 70, 119, 125–26; c. 36: 33, 115–16, 119; c. 38: 119, 127–29; c. 40: 40, 70, 114; c. 41: 45, 70; cc. 42–46: 220; c. 43: 6, 40, 147; c. 44: 6; c. 46: 124–25; c. 47: 6; c. 48: 40, 63, 118–19, 130–33; c. 49: 40; c. 50: 6; c. 52: 6, 40; c. 53: liii, 70, 79, 88, 115–16, 119, 226; c. 54: 40, 142, 151–52, 220; c. 55: 42; c. 56: 118; c. 57: 79, 119, 135–42; c. 58: xii, 6, 18, 23, 40, 46, 227; c. 59: 79; c. 60: 79, 220; c. 61: 75, 227; c. 62: 79, 119, 220; c. 63: 79, 103–107, 122; c. 64: xxiv, 40, 79, 88–90, 93–98, 226–27; c. 65: 56, 79, 119, 220; c. 66: 39, 79, 119; c. 67: 6; c. 69: 56; c. 70: 56, 110, 220; c. 71: lii, 54, 110; c. 72: lii, 37, 39, 56, 108–10, 151, 228–29; c. 73: 57, 228

*Rule of the Master*: 221–22

Rust, Eric: xli

Ryelandt, Idesbald, OSB: 36

sacraments: 134, 224

sacrifice: xxxii, li, 28, 70–71, 75, 92–93, 114, 130, 173, 184–85, 194–95, 197, 199

Sacro Speco: 219

sadness: 125

saint(s): xviii, xxvii, xxxii, 13, 30, 35, 67, 70, 134, 140, 150, 155, 164, 184, 198–99, 201, 203, 207

St. Mihiel, Abbey of: 47

St. Paul, MN: xlix

St. Scholastica, Abbey of: 219

St. Vannes, Congregation of: 49

salvation: xx, xlv, 12, 27, 51–52, 60, 67, 86, 90, 94–96, 159, 161–62, 223

Samuel: 92

sanctification: 9, 116, 159, 163

sanctity: xxii, l, 7–8, 13, 15, 72–73, 75, 84, 94, 121, 206

sanctuary: 196

sanity: lii, 25

Sapphira: 140

sarabaites: xxii–xxiii, 56, 75–76, 78

Sarah: 211

Satan: 223

satisfaction: 24, 123, 137–38, 170, 178–79, 215

Saturus: 230

scandal: 195

Schenouti (Shenoute), St.: 227
schism: 109
Schmidt, Edmund, osb: 42–43
Schmitz, Philibert, osb: 39, 44
scholarship: xix, 46, 85, 136
Scholastica, St.: xvi–xvii, 33
scholastics: 49
schools, monastic: 131
Schroll, M. Alfred, osb: xli, 89, 120, 125, 130–31, 220–21
Schuster, Ildefonso, osb: 17, 20–21
science(s): 134; profane: 13; sacred: 13
scripture(s): x, xviii, xxi, xxix, 12, 41–42, 52, 57–59, 62–64, 117, 128, 135, 148, 158–59, 161, 166, 188, 209–10, 224–25
scrupulosity: xxxi
Sczygielski, S., osb: 48
seculars: 142, 182
security: xxix, 170, 199, 224
self: xlviii, 102–103, 146, 185, 231; deeper: xliv, 187; exterior: 187; inmost: 176; interior: 242; outward: xxxi, 186; real: xliv; spiritual: xxxi, 186; superficial: xxxi, xliv–xlv, 186; true: 26; worldly: xxxi, 185
self-analysis: 113
self-assertion: 179
self-concern: xlv
self-confidence: 95
self-consciousness: 206
self-custody: xviii, 27, 175
self-dedication: 130, 179, 184
self-denial: xviii, xxv, 29, 32, 68, 70, 78, 107, 185
self-denigration: xlv
self-depreciation: xxxii, 201
self-emptying: xxxii, 185, 204, 231
self-esteem: xlv
self-exaltation: 160, 169, 173
self-examination: 168
self-expression: 97, 173
self-forgetfulness: xxxii, xlviii, 173, 202, 212
self-gratification: 182–83, 199
self-isolation: liv
self-justification: 113, 188
self-knowledge: 27, 168, 177
self-love: xiv, xlv, li, 6, 32, 107, 113, 132, 144, 151
self-manifestation: 191
self-oblation: 173
self-perfection: 173
self-pity: xliv
self-renunciation: 75, 183, 186
self-sacrifice: 108
self-satisfaction: xxxi, 96
self-seeking: 37, 96, 132
self-surrender: l
self-will: xlvii, 80, 155, 170, 175–76, 178–79
selflessness: 202
senior(s): xxv, 104–106, 110, 118–19, 207
sense(s): 120, 180, 198; common: xxvi, 120, 129, 132, 212; good: 102, 120; religious: 196; spiritual: 65
sensibilities: 173
sentimentality: 60
Serapion: 221
seriousness: 208, 212
Servandus: 240–41
servant(s): 21, 106, 108, 115, 126, 200, 239; of God: 13, 89, 236; of refectory: 111, 126–27, 129
service: xxvi, 16, 93, 121, 125, 128–29, 184, 225, 228, 234–35, 239; of God: xiv, 53, 65
servility: 215
Seven Sleepers of Ephesus: xxxix
severity: xviii, 13, 34, 91, 95–96, 207
sext: 133
Shakers: xl, 124
shame: 41, 192–93, 231

Shannon, William H.: xxxix, lv
shelter: 194–95
shoemakers: 137
sick: xxv, 15, 115–16, 124, 225
Sidon: 64
signs: 109, 129, 175, 183, 208
Sih, Paul K. T.: 105
silence: xxi, xxxiii, xlviii, 8, 10, 13–14, 20, 34, 37, 62, 71, 111, 116, 128–29, 136, 164, 187–88, 207–209, 211, 225, 238, 244; exterior: 187; interior: 134, 187
Silo (Shiloh): 92
simplicity: xi, xviii, xxxii, 6–7, 13–14, 27, 34–36, 67, 106, 116, 129, 134, 141, 148, 150, 160, 165, 196–97, 202, 206, 211; Benedictine: 17
Simplicius: 17, 233
sin(s): xlv, 13, 30, 32, 69, 88, 90–93, 96, 109, 140, 148, 155–56, 168, 172, 174–77, 181–82, 193, 195, 203–204, 209, 215, 223, 236; deliberate: xxx, 173, 175, 182, 214; mortal: 31, 139, 173–74, 177; of commission: 111; of omission: 111; semi–deliberate: 182; venial: 182
sincerity: 27, 191, 212
sinfulness: xx, xlv, 204, 215
singing: 197
singularity: xlv, 206
sinner(s): 53, 63–64, 70, 88, 93–95, 164, 166–67, 195; habitual: 95
Sitwell, Gerard, OSB: xli, 224–25
skill(s): xxvii, 136–39, 149
slave(s): 75, 88, 131, 162, 165
slavery: 15, 34, 179
sloth: xx–xxi, 13, 28, 32, 51, 54–55, 58, 73, 121
Smaragdus of St. Mihiel: liii, 47
Smith, Adam: xliii
snobbery: 197
sobriety: xxvi, 41, 121
society, hierarchical: 104
solidity: 34, 63
solitude: xi, xxii, xlvii–xlviii, 20–22, 26, 171, 234, 236
son, prodigal: 26
sonship: 229
*Sophia*: 38
sorrow(s): xlix, 22, 35, 53, 204
Sortais, Gabriel, OCSO: xxxv, xxxix, xlvi, xlviii–xlix, lv
soul(s): viii, x–xi, xxi, xxv, xxx, xxxiii, xlix, 8, 13, 16, 22, 24–27, 29, 36, 45, 51, 53, 58, 63, 65, 67, 69–71, 80, 86, 88–97, 113, 116, 124, 131, 139–41, 144–45, 151, 155, 157, 159, 162, 166, 169, 171–72, 176–77, 180–81, 188–89, 191, 193, 203, 205, 207, 212, 214, 224, 236, 239, 241–42, 244
speech: xxxiii, 20, 23, 27, 43, 109, 112, 165, 173, 207, 209–10
spirit(s): xlix, li, 10, 22, 41, 51, 58, 67–69, 73, 104, 147, 160, 172–73, 190, 213, 224–25, 242; ancient: 47; Benedictine: xxv, 14, 17, 112, 119, 138; carnal: 73; community: 108; critical: 32, 169, 224; evil: 28, 236; family: 14, 32; humble: xxxiii, 205; inner: 106; monastic: xviii, xxvi–xxvii, 37, 48, 132, 140, 142, 197; of adoption: 82; of faith: xxv, 14, 105, 107, 149; of generosity: 150; of play: 210; of poverty: 143; of prayer: 121; of simplicity: 150; of sonship: 82; of the Church: 59; of vows: 155; rational: 25; religious: 200; supernatural: xxiv, 32, 103, 115
spirituality: viii, x, xv, 8, 17, 26, 48, 199, 224; Benedictine: 8; Carmelite: xv, 8; Cistercian: 8; false: 172; monastic: 47; true: 172
spontaneity: lii, 19, 212, 215
stability: xii, xxiii, l, 8, 14, 63, 77, 217
state: 161; monastic: xxxii, 56, 144, 184–85, 195, 199

statuary: vii, 196
Stephen Harding, St.: xi–xii, 230
stewardship: x
Stoics: 26
*Strafcodex*: 219
stranger: liii
strength: xliv, 22, 41, 55, 82, 113, 149, 163, 188, 215, 244; of character: 97
strictness: xxi, liii, 69–70, 96
strife: 108
strong: 13, 149
struggle(s): xliv, 22, 26, 30, 74, 153, 169–70, 177, 186–87
study: xxi, 14–16, 18, 39, 69, 142, 154, 222, 233
stylitism: 72
Subiaco: 17–18, 21–22, 28, 34, 36, 39, 206, 218–19, 234
subject(s): 81, 90, 97
subjection: xxii, 76, 78, 169, 223
submission: l, 13, 45, 52, 54, 88, 139, 147, 173
suffering: xlv, 22, 61, 71, 77, 187–89, 204, 215
sulkiness: 19, 169
superior(s): xxiii–xxiv, xliii, 13, 28, 32, 56, 76, 80–81, 86–87, 90–97, 102–103, 106, 109–10, 112–13, 116, 120, 123, 137, 139, 145–47, 150–51, 155, 173, 183–86, 188–89, 194, 200, 206; as guide: 90; office of: xxiv
supernaturalism: false: 81; true: 82
support: 74
surprise: 210–11
suspiciousness: 96
Sweeney, James: 27
sweetness: 53, 71, 77–78, 153, 165, 225
sympathy: 91, 112, 122
synergy: 51

tact: 95
tailors: 100, 137
*taita*: 106
talent(s): 137–39
Tarapaca: 106
taste, artistic: 197
tastelessness: 200
tears: 35
technology: xxvii, 136
temperament(s): 71, 89
temperance: 114, 207
temptation(s): xvii, xxx, 21, 23–24, 26, 73–74, 93, 140, 155, 179, 191, 206, 211, 218, 236
tempter: 235
tenderness: xviii, xxi, 34, 60, 122
tenseness: 132
tepidity: 170
Teresa of Avila, St.: xv, 8
Terracina: 35
Tertullian: 231
thanksgiving: 63
theft: 220
Theobald of Cluny, Abbot: 232
theology: 51–52, 69, 74, 134–35, 222, 224; biblical: xli, 223; moral: 95; of recital: 223
Theoprobus: 241
*theoria*: xxviii, 25, 153; *physike*: 124
theory: 155; ethical: 20
Thérèse of Lisieux, St.: xliii–xliv
Thomas à Kempis: 158
Thomas Aquinas, St.: 14, 25, 38, 177, 203
Thomas Merton Center: xii, xxxiv, xl, lvi, lxi, 6
thought(s): xxi, xxvi, 69, 73, 128, 131–32, 172–78, 181, 190–93, 208, 225, 239; evil: xxxi, 27, 190–92; good: 191–92; proud: 31
thoughtfulness: 112
thoughtlessness: 111, 174
Tiber River: 219
tierce: 133

time: vii, 53, 64, 68, 133–35, 146, 184, 224
Timothy, St.: 141
Tivoli: 17
Tobias: 210–11
toleration: 170
tools: 79, 119, 124, 142, 194
Tortola: lv
tradition: 45, 57; abstract: 10; authentic: xlviii, liii; Benedictine: viii, xix, lvi, 9, 50, 227; Cistercian: 10; contemplative: xv; desert: 224; human: 172; monastic: xiii, xv–xvi, xxix, xxxiv, 9–10, 18, 161, 227; Pachomian: 28; patristic: xxix, xli, 224; spiritual: 8; theological: 24–25
training: 74, 77
Trajan, Emperor: 219
tranquility: xxxiii, xlv, 16, 36, 96, 207, 213, 225
transcendence, divine: 142
transformation: xxi, xxviii, 155; inner: xxxiii
Trappists: xv, 10
Traube, Ludwig: 42–43
Trent, Council of: 48
trial(s): xxxiii, 22, 71, 86, 155, 187, 204, 208
tribulation(s): 77, 198
Trinity: 82
Trithemius: 48
triumph: 189
*trivium*: 131
trust: xxi, xliv, 9, 55, 61, 63, 81–82, 86, 89, 94, 96, 147, 191
truth: xxviii–xxix, xliv, 8, 27, 36, 62–63, 68, 83, 86, 93–94, 103, 109, 132, 134, 152–54, 156–59, 168–71, 174–75, 179, 209, 222–23; dogmatic: 51
tunics: 42, 196
typology: 224
Tyre: 64
ugliness: 196
uncharitableness: 107, 109, 151, 170, 175
undermaster of novices: 192
understanding: xxvi, 9, 72, 82, 86, 91, 95, 112, 116, 179, 205
union: fraternal: 106; with Christ: xi, xxi–xxii, xxviii–xxxiv, xlviii–l, 71, 76, 86, 144, 156–57, 199, 204, 215; with God: xiv, xviii, xx–xxi, xxxiii, l, 6, 25, 35–37, 53, 62, 89, 132, 136, 174, 207
unity: xxvi, xlix, 16, 81, 109, 131, 172; organic: 134
unwillingness: 113
urgency: xxi, 58, 60
usury: 142

Valentinian: 17, 233
value(s): xxxiii, xlviii, 20, 22, 43, 66, 94, 144, 174, 176, 179, 188, 204, 209; worldly: 19
Vanderhoven, Hubert: 222
vanity: xxix, 20–21, 73, 141, 163, 175
Vatican City: vii
Vatican Council, Second: liv
veneration: 81
Verdun: 47
vespers: 11–12, 134
vessels, liturgical: 29, 124, 194, 236
vestments: 194, 196, 200
vice(s): xxiv, 19, 25, 60, 73, 94, 119, 121, 142–44, 148, 167, 170, 175, 233
Vicovaro: 26, 219
vigil(s): 35, 59, 133, 241
violence: 34, 58, 83, 96, 132
*virtù*: xlii, 178
virtue(s): xvii, xxiv, xxx, xxxii, xlv–xlvi, xlix, 11, 13–15, 25, 27–28, 33, 37, 60, 75, 80, 87, 90, 97, 101, 112, 115, 120, 123, 134, 143, 145, 149, 164, 167, 173, 185, 198, 200–204, 207, 215, 231, 236

vision: interior: 241; of divine essence: 38; of God: 38; spiritual: viii, xxx, 22, 181, 244
visitation: 151
vocation, monastic: xi, xviii, 63, 68, 73, 78, 90, 104, 183, 192, 195, 217, 222, 227
Vogüé, Adalbert de, OCSO: xvi, 221
vow(s): xi–xii, xvii, 5–7; monastic: xxviii, xlviii, l, liv, 14, 23, 46, 113, 146, 155–56, 195
vulgarity: 43, 196–97

Waddell, Chrysogonus, OCSO: lxi
Warnefrid, Paul: xli, liii, 47, 89, 119–20, 125, 131, 220
warnings: 104
watchfulness: 175
watching: 202
way: narrow: 68, 80, 185; of Christ: 157, 160; of life: 8, 14, 18, 23, 53, 57, 62, 78, 118, 233–34; of salvation: xx, 51, 60; of the cross: 231; of the world: 233; purgative: 179
weak: 13, 149
weakness(es): xxiii, xxv, 14, 32, 55, 78, 91, 93–94, 96, 113, 115, 122, 150–51, 164, 177, 229, 244
wealth: 162
welfare: 93, 95, 110
Wetten Abbey: 42
will: xxiv, xxx–xxxi, xliii, 9, 31–32, 41, 55–56, 58, 71, 75, 78, 80, 83, 101, 103, 112, 144–46, 150, 157–58, 161, 173, 176, 178, 180–86, 188, 204; common: 101; free: 51, 67; good: 80; ill: 87, 91; of Christ: 86, 157; of God: xvi, xviii, xxiii, xxxii, xliv, l, 10, 15, 20, 22, 24, 27, 51–52, 54–55, 58, 61–63, 83, 85, 93–94, 98, 101, 103, 113, 132, 139, 153, 158, 162, 173, 178, 182, 201; of superior: 32, 56, 150; rational: 25
wisdom: xiii, xxiv, xxvi, 19, 80, 86, 103, 109, 118–21, 131, 164, 174, 179, 209, 227; Christian: 14; false: 109; human: 163; natural: 105; of God: 19, 38, 114, 161, 163; Roman: 13–14; true: 109; worldly: 163
wit: 210–11
withdrawal: 120
witness(es): 72, 118, 141
Wolter, Maurus, OSB: 16
word of God: xi, xxi, xxvi, 52, 56–64, 66, 134, 225
work(s): xxvi–xxvii, xxxiv, 5–6, 13–14, 16, 30, 35–36, 54–55, 61, 85, 108–109, 111, 114, 119, 121, 123, 125, 128–34, 136–39, 141–42, 152, 161, 175, 183–84, 194, 198–200, 205, 213–15, 218; active: 111; for God: 234; good: xviii, xxi, 32, 52, 64, 66–67, 69, 77, 123, 201–202, 215, 218, 225; intellectual: xxvi, 16, 131–32, 222; monastic: xx, 39, 45, 135; of Christ: xxxiv, 215; of God: xviii, 6, 35; of grace: 68; physical: xxvi, 131; productive: 139
world: xvii–xviii, xliv, liii, 11, 19–22, 30, 36, 38, 61, 75, 93, 120, 122, 134, 140–41, 156–57, 172, 198–99, 210–11, 213, 233–34, 236, 241–42; changing: xlviii; contemporary: liv; higher: 29; monastic: xiv; non–monastic: xiv; secular: xxvi; separation from: liv
worldliness: 141
worship: 184, 196
Wright, G. Ernest: xli, 223–24
writers: 135

Zalla: xvi, 34
zeal: xxi, 24, 51–52, 55, 60, 94, 96, 109, 154; bitter: 108–109, 151; evil: 56; good: 108; human: 109; indiscreet: 95
Zen: xliv